PREVENTING AND RESOLVING CONFLICTS OF JURISDICTION IN EU CRIMINAL LAW

PREVENTING AND RESOLVING CONFLICTS OF JURISDICTION IN EU CRIMINAL LAW

A EUROPEAN LAW INSTITUTE INSTRUMENT

Katalin Ligeti | John Vervaele | André Klip

ELI REPORTERS

WITH ARTICLES EDITED BY

Katalin Ligeti | Gavin Robinson

OXFORD
UNIVERSITY PRESS

OXFORD
UNIVERSITY PRESS

Great Clarendon Street, Oxford, OX2 6DP,
United Kingdom

Oxford University Press is a department of the University of Oxford.
It furthers the University's objective of excellence in research, scholarship,
and education by publishing worldwide. Oxford is a registered trade mark of
Oxford University Press in the UK and in certain other countries

Publication based on a research project funded by the Luxembourg
National Research Fund (FNR): Project OPEN O13-5651210

First Edition published in 2018

Published in the United States of America by Oxford University Press
198 Madison Avenue, New York, NY 10016, United States of America

British Library Cataloguing in Publication Data
Data available

Library of Congress Control Number: 2018942491

ISBN 978-0-19-882911-9

Fonds National de la
Recherche Luxembourg

FOREWORD

Founded in 2011 and partly modelled on the famous American Law Institute (ALI), the European Law Institute (ELI) is an independent non-profit organisation established to initiate, conduct, and facilitate research, make recommendations, and provide practical guidance in the field of European legal development. The ELI is a membership-based organisation, counting excellent judges, legal professionals, academics, and other jurists from over fifty jurisdictions as well as EU institutions, international organisations, European stakeholder organisations, national supreme courts, and many other important players among its ranks. At the heart of the ELI's work are projects, which are conducted not only by an appointed small team but involve the whole ELI membership, not least through the establishment of a Members Consultative Committee, as well as through critical input at the ELI's Annual Conference and ultimately approval or rejection by, normally, a General Assembly vote. It is the active involvement of an extremely broad and diverse constituency, the need to convince this constituency of the quality and merits of project results, and the repeated improvements and revisions after feedback has been received that make ELI projects what they are and is precisely why they deserve to be influential.

The 'Draft Legislative Proposals for the Prevention and Resolution of Conflicts of Jurisdiction in Criminal Matters in the European Union' are the core results of an ELI project on the 'Prevention and Settlement of Conflicts of Exercise of Jurisdiction in Criminal Law', which commenced in 2013 and was finally approved, by an overwhelming majority of both the ELI Council and the ELI General Assembly, in 2017.

The outcome is both timely and important. Among the challenges of our era is the growth in cross-border crime. Criminal justice systems have thus increasingly been confronted with situations in which multiple Member States have legitimate jurisdiction over the same case, at times resulting in both positive and negative conflicts of jurisdiction. If manifold prosecutions of the same crime, possibly resulting in a rush for a quick judgment, or failures to prosecute in any single jurisdiction are to be avoided, the pressing need for international and European criminal law to identify the most appropriate jurisdiction in criminal cases becomes apparent.

The Working Group has elaborated no less than three alternative legal frameworks for the European legislator to choose from and draw upon as sources of inspiration. For this and the convivial cooperation, the ELI is most grateful. A special acknowledgement is owed to the Reporters, Professors Katalin Ligeti, André Klip, and John Vervaele, to the other members of the Working Group, and to the many members of the Advisory Committee and Members Consultative Committee, for producing opportune and workable solutions capable of transforming the current legal landscape.

The ELI would also like to thank the various observers from European institutions and stakeholder representatives for having enriched the work with their insights, views, and expertise.

With this volume, the ELI responds to repeated requests that ELI project results be published in print, and not only electronically, and that they be accompanied by background materials which are made available and published by one or several of the Reporters themselves. The ELI would like to thank Oxford University Press for supporting this initiative, which will make sure the ELI's work reaches a still wider audience and will therefore enhance the ELI's quest for contributing to the formation of a more vigorous European legal community.

Christiane Wendehorst
President, European Law Institute
April 2018

ACKNOWLEDGEMENTS (PART I)

Working Group Reporters:

Professor Katalin Ligeti (University of Luxembourg)
Professor John Vervaele (University of Utrecht)
Professor André Klip (University of Maastricht)

Working Group Members:

Mr. Miguel Carmona Ruano (Spanish Liaison Magistrate to the UK)
Professor Gilles Cuniberti (University of Luxembourg)
Mr. Hans-Holger Herrnfeld (former German national member of Eurojust—Criminal Law Department of the German Federal Ministry of Justice)
Professor Burkhard Hess (Max Planck Institute—Luxembourg)
Ms. Andrea Kenez (Judge at the Metropolitan Court of Budapest)
Professor Michiel Luchtman (University of Utrecht)
Dr. Angelo Marletta (University of Luxembourg)
Professor Dr. Holger Matt (Chair of the European Criminal Bar Association)
Mr. Jeannot Nies (Council of State; Office of the General Public Prosecutor—Luxembourg)
Dr. Pietro Ortolani (Radboud University, Nijmegen)
Dr. Gavin Robinson (University of Luxembourg)
Dr. Michele Simonato (University of Utrecht)
Dr. Martin Wasmeier (European Commission—Legal Service)

Advisory Committee:

Professor Petter Asp (Stockholm University), Sweden
Professor Dr. Martin Böse (Rheinische Friederich-Wilhelms University), Germany
Judge Margherita Cassano (President of the Court of Appeal of Florence), Italy
Professor Dr. Aukje van Hoek (University of Amsterdam), Netherlands
Professor Maria Kaiafa-Gbandi (Aristotle University of Thessaloniki), Greece
Judge Gabor Molnar (Head of Panel at the Criminal Department of the Curia of Hungary), Hungary
Tim O'Sullivan (Senior Crown Prosecutor at Crown Prosecution Service), UK
Jean-Philippe Rivaud (Deputy Prosecutor General), France
Professor Dr. Helmut Satzger (Ludwig-Maximilians University), Germany
Professor Anne Weyembergh (Université Libre de Bruxelles), Belgium

Representatives of Eurojust:

Ms. Catherine Deboyser (Eurojust Administration)
Mr. José Guerra (Deputy National Member for Portugal)
Ms. Maria Poza Cisneros (Deputy National Member for Spain)
Mr. Pietro Suchan (Assistant to the Italian desk)

Representatives of the European Commission:

Ms. Anna Hodgson (DG Justice)
Ms. Tania Schröter (DG Justice)

Representatives of the European Parliament:

Mr. Massimiliano Mini (Assistant to MEP Caterina Chinnici)

The views set out in this Instrument should not be taken as representing the views of those bodies, on whose behalf individual members of the working party and advisory group were also acting.

LIST OF CONTRIBUTORS (PART II)

Paulo Pinto de Albuquerque is a judge at the European Court of Human Rights.

Miguel Carmona Ruano is a judge, currently retired, and was Spanish Liaison Magistrate to the United Kingdom until his recent retirement.

Hans-Holger Herrnfeld is head of unit in the Criminal Law Department of the German Federal Ministry of Justice and Consumer Protection.

Aukje van Hoek is professor of private international law and civil procedure at the University of Amsterdam.

Katalin Ligeti is professor of European and international criminal law at the University of Luxembourg.

Michiel Luchtman is professor of transnational law enforcement and fundamental rights at Utrecht University.

Angelo Marletta is a postdoctoral researcher in European criminal law at the University of Luxembourg.

Frank Meyer is professor at the Department of Criminal Law and Criminal Procedural Law, including International Criminal Law, at the University of Zürich.

Pietro Ortolani is assistant professor at University, Docent, Radboud University, Nijmegen.

Gavin Robinson is a postdoctoral researcher in criminal law and IT law at the University of Luxembourg.

Michele Simonato is a postdoctoral researcher at the Utrecht Centre for Regulation and Enforcement in Europe, Utrecht University.

Martin Wasmeier is a staff member of the Legal Service of the European Commission.

Christiane Wendehorst is professor at the Institute for Civil Law of the University of Vienna, and President of the European Law Institute.

CONTENTS

TABLE OF CASES

EUROPEAN UNION

EUROPEAN COURT OF HUMAN RIGHTS AND EUROPEAN COMMISSION OF HUMAN RIGHTS

DOMESTIC CASES

Germany

Netherlands

Spain

United States

TABLE OF LEGISLATION

INTERNATIONAL INSTRUMENTS

EU SECONDARY LEGISLATION

Regulations

Directives

Decisions

DOMESTIC LEGISLATION

France

Germany

Italy

Malta

Spain

United Kingdom

PART I

INSTRUMENT OF THE EUROPEAN LAW INSTITUTE

Draft Legislative Proposals for the Prevention and Resolution of Conflicts of Jurisdiction in Criminal Matters in the European Union

PREFACE TO PART I

FRANK MEYER

I. SETTING THE SCENE

At the heart of the problems that this book addresses lies the question of overlapping jurisdictions. Overlapping criminal jurisdictions are an important, but still neglected aspect of law enforcement reality. There is no monocausal explanation for this social phenomenon. It is not enough to point the finger at the growing number of multilateral or supranational crime control instruments that deliberately oblige European Union (EU) Member States to cast an ever-wider jurisdictional net. A general disregard of national legislatures for jurisdictional matters is equally or, perhaps, even more important. National legislators are either entirely oblivious to the rules governing the applicability of their respective national codes or they labour under the perception that an extension of jurisdiction is always an extension of power and as such a good thing that comes at no cost to the national budget or criminal justice system.

Both impressions are wrong. Overly broad scopes of jurisdiction increase administrative costs. They have profound procedural ramifications. Almost all Member States have special provisions for extraterritorial cases at their disposal designed (ironically) to get rid of them. Hence, different procedural regimes for territorial and extraterritorial cases coexist clandestinely in almost every Member State. The general indifference towards jurisdictional questions may also distort the function of punishment and the coherence of punishment concepts within national systems.[1]

As regards the individuals that find themselves in the cross hairs of unreflected extensions of criminal jurisdiction, other studies have identified several human rights-based objections against such net-widening effects.[2] This European Law Institute (ELI) project appears to be most concerned with freedom of movement and legality but there may be other rights at stake as well; in particular

1 *Böse/Meyer*, ZIS 2011, 336 (338); *Pawlik*, in: Hoyer/Müller/Pawlik/Wolter (eds), Festschrift für Friedrich-Christian Schroeder zum 70. Geburtstag, 2006, 382 ff.

2 *Böse/Meyer/Schneider*, Conflicts of Jurisdiction in Criminal Matters, Nomos 2014; *Eisele*, Jurisdiktionskonflikte in der Europäischen Union: Vom nationalen Strafanwendungsrecht zum Europäischen Kollisionsrecht, Zeitschrift für die gesamte Strafrechtswissenschaft 125 (2013), 27; *Luchtman* (ed.), Choice of Forum in Cooperation against EU Financial Crime, Eleven International 2013; *Zimmermann*, Strafgewaltkonflikte in der Europäischen Union, Baden-Baden: Nomos, 2015; also in Part II of this volume *Michiel Luchtman*, Choice of forum, European citizenship and fundamental rights: the position of the defendant.

non-discrimination, the requirement of individual blameworthiness (guilt principle), and the right to respect for privacy and family life.[3]

Despite these severe consequences both at the systemic and the individual level, nothing happens, nothing changes. Quite the contrary, the situation is further exacerbated by the international omnipresence of a non-reflective attitude among policy-makers. In reaction to international organised crime and cross-border crimes in general, they invariably vote in favour of more and tighter overlaps of jurisdictions. These overlaps do not give rise to a conflict of laws comparable to the situation in international private law; rather, the web is perceived as a menu of enforcement options. And it therefore should not come as a surprise that the very few existing international selection mechanisms are predominantly concerned with facilitating the effective use of law enforcement resources and successful prosecutions. The proposals for a new Eurojust regulation and the regulation for the establishment of a European Public Prosecutor's Office (EPPO)[4] will only add to this lopsidedness.[5] Nothing in the new criminal law instruments for the Area of Freedom, Security, and Justice (AFSJ) addresses any of the above-mentioned problems in any satisfying and comprehensive way. As a consequence, a legislative gap is yawning at the centre of the EU cooperation architecture. Bearing in mind its far-reaching implications it is high time to act. The ELI project therefore came at the perfect time. Its project leaders, contributors, and advisers have succeeded in drafting not only one, but three comprehensive legislative proposals within a very short period of time. All instruments have been included in the final instrument that was endorsed by the ELI Council in March 2017. Each legislative proposal would deserve a separate chapter. Within the narrow framework of a preface, however, a few comments must suffice. Some general observations leading over to the specific instruments will help make them easier to decipher and digest conceptually.

II. GENERAL OBSERVATIONS

First, when discussing and assessing the proposals it is indispensable to highlight the regulatory approaches behind each instrument. Understanding their conceptual DNA allows us to test their compatibility with current developments and future conceptions of the AFSJ. Inconsistencies are easier to identify too. A newcomer to

3 *Meyer*, in: Böse/Meyer/Schneider, Conflicts of Jurisdiction in Criminal Matters, Nomos 2014, 169 (194).

4 Article 26 para 4 Regulation (EU) 2017/1939, OJ L 283/1; see also *Hans-Holger Herrnfeld* Choice of forum and case allocation in the EPPO regulation in Part II of this volume.

5 Insofar and unsurprisingly, Member States seem most concerned about the present state of affairs when they consider the outcome of an adjudication process in one Member State insufficient or where they fear limitations on their authority to prosecute all crimes that occurred on their soil.

this intricate field of research might mistake this plurality of options for a sign of intellectual indecisiveness or lack of direction. This would be an unfortunate misperception. The different instruments not only testify to the complexity of the problem. It is also reasonable to provide a toolkit of ideal-type instruments following different assumptions about the depth and direction of integration in the AFSJ, rather than imposing one specific path straight away. An inclusive and differentiated approach invites a broader discussion about the future course of integration and seems to be more in line with the mission of the ELI.

A second general strategic choice raises more doubts. The Working Group wisely chose a broad definition of the concept of 'conflict of jurisdiction', including negative and positive, abstract, and specific conflicts. The phenomenology of jurisdictional problems in the AFSJ is, indeed, too dynamic and complex to exclude any of these aspects. However, as interested readers of this book will notice, not all instruments are capable of solving all of these conflicts.

Few experts would challenge the idea that integrated solutions are required to resolve the many problems caused by multiple proceedings from a practical and a normative point of view. The proposed model, however, aims far beyond related proceedings. Their inclusion deserves special attention because the legal, in particular human rights, implications of multiple proceedings (regarding the same acts), and concentration of criminal proceedings that relate to different sets of facts are quite different. Joining cases across the EU therefore must be based on a different self-standing rationale. Concentration is not a value (or imperative legal principle) in and of itself. In search of a separate justification, the proposed instruments rely heavily on the principle of good administration of justice. A quantum of scepticism is warranted in this respect. The notion of 'good administration of justice' is quite vague in terms of substance and contours. European lawyers are perhaps better advised to refrain from moulding it into a new super-principle to drive far-reaching transformations that are at odds with the present legal landscape. Thus, more attention should be paid to the complex implications and preconditions of concentration.

First, it is interrelated with the concepts and purposes of criminal punishment. At the moment, it still matters very much where inside the AFSJ a case is tried; in particular in whose name justice is delivered and in which society a sanction is to serve a certain purpose.[6] The allocation of cases based on an administrative principle must convincingly explain whose (societal) interests will be served by concentration and whose justice and penal goals it is referring to when justifying concentration decisions. One is left to wonder whether the idea of good administration is really

6 See the contribution of *Angelo Marletta* on Forum Choice in the Area of Freedom, Security, and Justice in Part II of this volume.

strong enough to supersede countervailing national interests to mete out punishment autonomously, particularly where national societies reasonably expect punishment to take place in their courts. This leads to a second, interrelated objection. Concentration models more or less presuppose the existence of an integrated criminal justice system in the AFSJ within which cases can be moved freely, assuming that the interests of the aggrieved society can be served everywhere and that everywhere it is the same *ius puniendi* that is being enforced.[7] We should therefore be very wary of lending too much weight to good administration of justice. Justifications should be more specific and draw on fundamental rights and positive obligations. It is first and foremost the interests and rights of suspects that call for stronger concentration and that have to be balanced against state interests. There might even be a right to concentration (derived from the Charter of Fundamental Rights (CFR)). Attempts at justifying concentration should also distinguish between related and unrelated proceedings and differentiate between different types of crime; especially Euro crimes and non-Euro crimes. It will be easier to conceptualise concentration requirements for the former category.

Reverting to the general approach, the detour into the legal implications of concentration decisions should have made clear that it is crucial for any robust solution to elaborate on the various sources and types of legal obligations that come into play for the settlement of conflicts. Their pertinence for the legitimacy of allocation criteria (its legal status as incarnation of fundamental rights) and the question of judicial review cannot be overstated. It is of particular importance for the legal position of the individuals concerned. The project group follows a legality-oriented view and submits that a right to a judge (or lawful judge/gesetzlicher Richter) in the sense that unregulated processes of case allocation undermine the foreseeability of applicable national laws is recognised as a right to a reasonably foreseeable forum in the CFR. This position appears to be consolidating into the prevailing view among EU criminal law specialists.[8] However, I am not so certain whether this idiosyncratic concept can be extended into the transnational realm so easily. There would be other ways to achieve a similar result.[9] Secondly, much attention is paid to avoiding *ne bis in idem* situations.[10] Yet again, the normative core of this safeguard is still unclear. The Court

7 The solutions the project suggests presuppose that Member States drop their reservations against representational or subsidiary jurisdiction.

8 *Panzavolta*, Choice of Forum and the Lawful Judge Concept in Choice of Forum in Cooperation against EU Financial Crime, in: Luchtman (ed.), 162; *Luchtman*, Choice of Forum and the Prosecution of Cross-Border Crime in the European Union—What Role for the Legality Principle? in: Luchtman (ed.), 11; *Zimmermann*, Strafgewaltkonflikte in der Europäischen Union, 2015, 232 ff.

9 *Meyer*, in: Böse/Meyer/Schneider, Conflicts of Jurisdiction in Criminal Matters, Nomos 2014, 169 (202, 204).

10 See *Katalin Ligeti*, Fundamental Rights Protection Between Strasbourg and Luxembourg in Part II of this volume.

of Justice of the European Union (CJEU) has stretched its protective scope to cover transnational cases based on the freedom of movement without having answered what lies behind it. There are different conceptualisations in international and national law and each might play out differently in the context of solving conflicts of jurisdiction. Thirdly, the (supposedly) intimate connection between the architecture of allocation and settlement mechanisms on the one hand and the concepts and functions of criminal punishment in the AFSJ on the other remains astonishingly underexplored. Future research will hopefully bring more clarity.

Notwithstanding these modest demurs, the project marks a fundamental step ahead as both suspects and victims are recognised as holders of rights in the AFSJ that have to be taken into account. That all instruments provide for legal remedies is not only consistent but underscores this thrust. Legal review is a main and welcome building block of the overall approach. However, the remaining uncertainties surrounding the legal status of the individual will have ripple effects on the adjudication process. Scope and depth of review hinge on what human rights are at stake.

Finally, any settlement mechanism would be incomplete without effective implementation. The Working Group, compellingly, sets out to fill a gap of high practical importance. Member States have failed to agree on rules for the transfer of proceedings so far. All proposals make up for that shortcoming. With respect to the so-called rollback clauses, one may wish to consider whether the concept of final disposal should be specified or approximated beyond the CJEU's *ne bis in idem* case law. It is a crucial matter what decisions deserve unabridged recognition and settle a case for good. For instance, traditional powers to grant mercy or clemency would be considerably curtailed or even rendered meaningless if other jurisdictions retained the right to prosecute in such a scenario.

With these general observations in mind, some final comments on the specific instruments will conclude the preface.

III. INSTRUMENT 1

The so-called horizontal mechanism offers a settlement procedure-based consultation guided by a consolidated catalogue of criteria that does not stray too much from the Eurojust guidelines.[11] It is the most modest proposal, but, if adopted, it would still break new ground. The wording 'shall' underlines that the annexed criteria are supposed to be binding. Yet, it is difficult to determine their legal status. Some criteria might be or should be grounded in fundamental rights, whereas others are seemingly rooted in considerations of expediency. Status questions of this kind matter. They may have a profound impact on balancing processes. They also affect the provisions on judicial review of the (joint) allocation decision. Article 10 is not

11 Eurojust Guidelines, Europol Annual Report 2003, Annex, 60–66.

very satisfactory. It is understandable that Member States strongly dislike incursions into their judicial architecture but, without a minimum of harmonisation, it will be left to chance whether and how the consensus decision can be challenged. In the same vein, the draft proposal does not reveal what is subject to review and what a test of non-arbitrariness would entail. This holds particularly true for decisions concentrating multiple proceedings. Furthermore, the instrument does not address the question of parallel challenges and the treatment of successful challenges. Proceedings might therefore end up in legal limbo until all domestic remedies are exhausted or expired. It would be very optimistic to think that the CJEU will fix the situation and provide sufficient guidance promptly. Another problem for this instrument is the volatility of criminal investigations. Technically, introducing fixed time frames and pressing for an early decision is appealing. But the dynamic nature of investigations could turn out to be hardly compatible with rigid early decision requirements.

But the biggest problem, the elephant in the room, if you will, seems to be that early transfers often run counter to law enforcement interests. The wording of Article 8 para 2 opens the door for the continuation of present practices to run parallel proceedings until the cases are trial-ready.[12] Law enforcement agencies are afforded tremendous leeway. Onerous parallel proceedings in the investigative phase will therefore persist until the jurisdictions to prescribe themselves are limited. Even worse, the consultation process and settlement process could be ignored by Member States altogether if they decide to dispose of the case autonomously. This indicates the very weak position of the individual in this setting; although, admittedly, in some cases it might be the suspect who is primarily interested in pushing ahead to produce *ne bis in idem* in the more favourable system.

Finally, a transfer of evidence needs to be synchronised with the European Investigation Order. Evidence that could not have been taken in the receiving Member State is to be excluded; and a provision should be added that explains how the suspect may challenge the legality of investigative measures carried out in the transferring state after a transfer. The 'all in'-admissibility solution is particularly problematic in light of its interrelations with Article 8 and the time of allocation or concentration. The proposal invites prosecutors to gather all pertinent evidence available in their jurisdiction in line with their procedural rules before consenting to a transfer of proceedings. According to the proposal, their files could be transferred without limitations, even if they contained information such as secret evidence that is considered highly problematic in the receiving jurisdiction. This flexibility stands in stark contrast to the catalogue of allocation criteria that explicitly excludes

12 Not least in light of the remaining impediments of mutual legal assistance when criminal jurisdiction were to be concentrated in one state.

evidence standards. There is certain likelihood that the procedural flexibility would render this criterion virtually moot.

Overall, the horizontal approach leaves too many questions unanswered and shuns the root causes of conflicts of jurisdiction. An obvious response would have been a concerted effort to reduce the Member States' substantive scope of jurisdiction. The instrument does not touch this delicate issue. But it might still be the most likely to convince legislators.

IV. INSTRUMENT 2

The so-called vertical mechanism is not genuinely vertical since it neither foresees a proactive allocation of cases[13] nor regulates the scope of jurisdiction. It looks more like a dispute resolution stage attached to the horizontal mechanism. On the plus side, this legislative proposal intends to make Eurojust accessible for individuals and allow the agency to settle conflicts for good (which is, in essence, the new vertical element). Both outcomes would mark substantial progress. Also, paras 2 and 4 of Article 13 of the proposal appropriately realise the right to good administration in Article 41 CFR. It is unfortunate, on the other hand, that uncooperative Member States have the power to sideline Eurojust and establish a *fait accompli* simply by taking decisions with final effect. This might not happen very often, but it should not be possible at all.

The more robust legal framework and the emphasis on the Member States' duty of sincere cooperation with Eurojust's would nevertheless strengthen Eurojust's hand. And yet it is exactly Eurojust's current position and outlook that makes this proposal controversial. Anne Weyembergh has aptly dubbed this the 'this is not the right moment'-argument that stands in the way of conferring binding decision-making powers on Eurojust.[14] Admittedly, this should not stop us from weighing this option and push for a change of attitude among EU law-makers if necessary. But there are other objections. The proposal might lead to a conflation of roles (which will not be resolved through the establishment of a specialised structure). From the perspective of the suspect, the position of Eurojust is compromised owing to its coordinating and operative functions. In the future, the agency could play a stronger brokering role within the sphere of investigating and prosecuting agencies; but it would be very problematic to afford it binding powers vis-à-vis individuals and courts since it is not an independent judicial institution.

13 The proposal does not provide for an *ex officio* trigger. It, hence, offers no solution for negative conflicts of jurisdiction.

14 *Weyembergh*, An Overall Analysis of the Proposal for a Regulation on Eurojust, eucrim 2013, 127 (130).

Secondly, the explanatory notes envision Eurojust as an EU policy-maker that is supposed to devise and implement a European prosecutorial policy. One could well argue that Eurojust is not in a position to get this job done; and that it is not authorised to set a European policy for all cases that might come before it. In many cases, the crimes to be dealt with will not even be Euro crimes.

In terms of judicial review, its binding nature exposes the settlement decision to actions for annulment, which is beneficial for the suspect and a bare necessity if Eurojust were to render binding decisions. But its effectiveness suffers from the general malaise outlined above. Scope and depth of review are not sufficiently clear. Especially in the context of multiple proceedings, my contention would be that a test of arbitrariness would not live up to the complexity of the situation and the legal interests involved. For its lack of substance, Article 14 could be excised altogether.

V. INSTRUMENT 3

Instruments 1 and 2 make no attempt to limit Member States' almost unfettered jurisdiction to prescribe, although it is a root cause of the problem. Without rethinking the allocation of jurisdiction and the legitimacy of the traditional genuine links within the AFSJ, it is impossible to arrive at a more balanced jurisdictional architecture. The third truly vertical and harmonising instrument breaks new ground in this direction. It advocates a dramatic reduction of the scope of legitimate jurisdiction. Other studies have already shown that the abolition of most principles is, in fact, convincing for substantive reasons.[15] It would have been interesting to learn more specifically which legal considerations (which might turn out to be identical or close to the legal argumentation in prior studies) informed this proposal. In this context, the authors could have made a much stronger case for their proposal. The wording of Article 1 para 1 is too reluctant in that sense. It does not capture the gist of the matter. We should not be talking about the forum best placed on consideration of good and proper administration of justice, but the identification of the most legitimate forum based on fundamental principles and rights.

As regards the convincing focus on territoriality, one wonders whether the definition of 'territoriality' should be left to the Member States. This reservation is politically cautious but might produce problematic discrepancies down the road. Uniform definitions could be particularly pertinent with regard to crimes whose phenomenology diverges considerably from classic notions of territoriality; for example, cybercrime or other crimes with typically loosened territorial links.[16] Of course,

15 For instance, *Böse*, in: Böse/Meyer/Schneider, Conflicts of Jurisdiction in Criminal Matters, Nomos 2014, 43 ff.

16 See in Part II of this volume *Gavin Robinson*, Choice of forum and cybercrime.

focusing on territoriality alone does not settle the matter for good. The reality of cross-border crime or multi-territorial offences does not disappear by way of legislative fiat. The Working Group was mindful of that and has produced a viable solution for the regulation of multi-territorial offences in Articles 5 and 6. One could perhaps contemplate inserting another qualitative criterion in para. 3; namely where the most substantial harm materialised. Much more could be said about this proposal, in particular its fascinating Article 9 on the transfer of the exercise of jurisdiction which is, in fact, a micro-regulation on the transfer of proceedings. However, it is not details but the general direction of the proposal that matters most at this point and deserves to be emphasised. Looking back on the brief introductory analysis of the present crisis, it becomes clear that only the third instrument cuts to the core of the problem. While the other instruments might be the politically easier sell, it appears to be the third one that treats fundamental rights and principles in the AFSJ most seriously.

VI. FINAL REMARKS

I wish to conclude this *marche forcée d'horizon* with several words of praise for the contributors to this project. Despite some critical suggestions, the Working Group has done fascinating work and succeeded in tabling three thoughtful, well-crafted legislative proposals. Its drafting process has been accompanied by expert reports and public discussions in the best academic tradition. The project also testifies to the intellectual force and added value that the creation of the ELI has brought about. It is to be hoped that the ELI instrument will be well received by EU policy-makers and legislators. We are at a crucial moment in the constitutionalisation process of the AFSJ. Conflicts of jurisdiction are a long-term concern that should be seen and resolved in this context. The path ultimately chosen will create or stifle new momentum. Let us hope that it will be one that takes fundamental rights and principles seriously.

Draft Legislative Proposals for the Prevention and Resolution of Conflicts of Jurisdiction in Criminal Matters in the European Union

INSTRUMENT OF THE EUROPEAN LAW INSTITUTE

The European Law Institute (ELI) is an independent non-profit organisation established to initiate, conduct and facilitate research, make recommendations and provide practical guidance in the field of European legal development. Building on the wealth of diverse legal traditions, its mission is the quest for better law-making in Europe and the enhancement of European legal integration. By its endeavours, the ELI seeks to contribute to the formation of a more vigorous European legal community, integrating the achievements of the various legal cultures, endorsing the value of comparative knowledge, and taking a genuinely pan-European perspective. As such its work covers all branches of the law: substantive and procedural; private and public.

The ELI is committed to the principles of comprehensiveness and collaborative working, thus striving to bridge the oft-perceived gap between the different legal cultures, between public and private law, as well as between scholarship and practice. To further that commitment it seeks to involve a diverse range of personalities, reflecting the richness of the legal traditions, legal disciplines and vocational frameworks found throughout Europe. The ELI is also open to the use of different methodological approaches and to canvassing insights and perspectives from as wide an audience as possible of those who share its vision.

President: Christiane Wendehorst
Vice-President: Sjef van Erp
Treasurer: Denis Philippe
Speaker of the Senate: Reinhard Zimmermann

European Law Institute
Schottenring 16/175
1010 Vienna
Austria

Tel.: + 43 1 4277 22101
Mail: secretariat@europeanlawinstitute.eu
Website: www.europeanlawinstitute.eu

ISBN: 978-3-9503458-7-2

PRINCIPAL ABBREVIATIONS

AFSJ	Area of Freedom, Security and Justice
CFR	Charter of Fundamental Rights of the European Union OJ C 326, 26.10.2012, 391–407
CJEU	Court of Justice of the European Union
CoE	Council of Europe
DG	Justice European Commission Directorate-General for Justice
EAW	European Arrest Warrant, established with Council Framework Decision 2002/584/JHA
ECHR	European Convention of Human Rights
EIO	European Investigation Order, established with Directive 2014/41/EU
EJN	The European Judicial Network in criminal matters
EPPO	The European Public Prosecutor's Office
FD	Framework Decision
GC	General Court of the European Union
MPI	The Max Planck Institute
OLAF	The European Anti-Fraud Office
TEU	Treaty on European Union
TFEU	Treaty on the Functioning of the European Union

CONTENTS

EXPLANATORY NOTE

1. PROBLEM SETTING

When two or more states claim criminal jurisdiction to investigate, prosecute and adjudicate suspicious criminal conduct, a conflict between (legitimate) jurisdictions arises. Parallel criminal proceedings can endanger the 'interests' of the persons involved, who may face the risk of double prosecution and punishment, as well as different legal regimes that determine the safeguards and remedies available to reduce uncertainty and lack of foreseeability. If several countries exercise jurisdiction over the same facts, it leads to efforts and resources being wasted and potentially to arbitrary outcomes.

In the specific context of the EU, in particular, concurrence of jurisdiction coupled with the application of the principle of European *ne bis in idem* can result in the prosecution of specific offences being barred on a 'first come, first served' basis[1] if the authorities of one Member State finally dispose of the case, even though this Member State is not necessarily 'the best placed' to adjudicate the case. It is evident, therefore, that situations in which two or more states have concurrent jurisdictions over the same crime should be settled, or preferably, prevented.

2. TERMINOLOGY

In general, the concept of a conflict refers to:

'positive conflicts', i.e. when two or more Member States exercise or intend to exercise their jurisdiction over certain facts constituting a criminal offence.

'negative conflicts', i.e. when between several Member States having jurisdiction over certain facts constituting a criminal offence, none of them is willing to exercise its jurisdiction. It is important to note that negative conflict does not refer to situations in which no state has jurisdiction, but rather to the situation in which no state is willing to exercise it.[2]

1 The principle of European *ne bis in idem* is enshrined in art 54 of the Convention Implementing the Schengen Agreement of 1990, in art 50 of the Charter of Fundamental Rights and in Article 4 of Protocol n. 7 to the European Convention on the Protection of Human Rights and Fundamental Freedoms. The Court of Justice of the European Union recognised the relevance of the principle and its application on the 'first come, first served' basis in the seminal judgment Gözütok and Brügge (CJEU, 11 February 2003, C-187/01, joined cases Gözütok and Brügge; ECLI:EU:C:2003:87).

2 Similarly to the Anglo-American concept of *forum non conveniens* that allows for the discretion of courts to deny access when there is jurisdiction, also in criminal law there can be a gap between having jurisdiction and exercising it.

It is, however, disputed whether this phenomenon belongs to the conceptual framework of jurisdictional conflict.[3]

'parallel proceedings', i.e. criminal proceedings which are conducted or are about to be conducted in two or more Member States, against the same suspect or accused regarding the same facts; if both parallel proceedings continue, it will certainly lead to a *ne bis in idem* situation.

'multiple proceedings', i.e. criminal proceedings which are conducted or are about to be conducted in two or more Member States against the same suspect or accused in relation to different facts, or against different suspects or accused persons in relation to the same set of facts. Although multiple proceedings do not violate *ne bis in idem* as they concern different facts, in the case of organised crime for instance, in order to adjudicate the crime it could make sense to concentrate proceedings that relate to various individual acts that the perpetrator may have performed in different jurisdictions, but which are all related to the same organised criminal activity. Another example concerns similar but separate offences (e.g.: several thefts) committed by the same person in the territory of different Member States.[4] Due to the boundless reach of information technology, separate cybercrime offences in particular may cause harm across a great number of different jurisdictions (e.g. hate speech, training of 'lone wolf' terrorists, grooming of victims by sexual predators). In such cases, although not obligatory, a decision to concentrate proceedings in a single Member State may turn out to be opportune both in the interests of the suspect (possibility to attend a single trial and, in case of conviction, to serve the sentence in one Member State, potentially enhancing the chances of social rehabilitation) and of the good administration of justice (holding a single trial, possibility to adjudicate the whole series of crimes and, in case of conviction, to modulate the sentence in a proportionate way).

'actual conflicts', i.e. when concurrence of jurisdictions occurs *in concreto* and two or more parallel proceedings are actually run in two or more Member States.

'abstract conflicts', i.e. when concurrence of jurisdictions occurs only *in abstracto* since parallel proceedings are not yet started in two or more Member States.

3 Indeed, some authors have defined the denial of (the exercise of) jurisdiction as an enforcement gap requiring a totally different approach. See, for instance, the opinion expressed by A. Klip, What is a conflict? concept paper for the 2nd WG Group Meeting of the Project (March 2015).

4 A recent example is provided by the case of Melvin West, a UK national who was the subject of multiple European arrest warrants in connection with multiple thefts (of ancient and rare maps and valuable plates removed from atlases), all committed at libraries in three different Member States. See Case C-192/12 PPU *West v. Virallinen syyttäjä*, 28 June 2012, ECLI:EU:C:2012:404.

For the purposes of this instrument, the term **'criminal matter'** is understood as relating to the domain of criminal law *stricto sensu*. Accordingly, the proposed Instrument is to be applied in criminal cases. However, the Member States are free to broaden the circle of authorities which they would consider competent to apply the proposed rules. In line with the *Engel* jurisprudence of the ECtHR[5] that broadens the understanding of what is a 'criminal charge' and a 'criminal sanction' and also includes punitive administrative sanctions and 'quasi-criminal' proceedings,[6] it is up to the Member States to determine which authorities other than criminal justice authorities would be competent to apply the proposed rules.

Finally, the term **'multi-territorial offences'** refers to offences that concern or affect the territory of two or more Member States; e.g. trafficking offences committed through the territory of several Member States. Multi-territorial offences can often trigger positive conflicts of territorial jurisdiction.[7]

This project and the three draft legislative proposals presented further below apply a broad definition of the concept of 'conflict of jurisdiction' that covers:

- **Positive conflicts**: the proposed legal framework will limit its focus to positive conflicts of jurisdiction, excluding from its scope the settlement of negative conflicts. Addressing negative conflicts, in particular, would require reflection on the extent of the jurisdiction to prescribe and on the principle of mandatory prosecution. In this perspective, directly tackling this phenomenon would require the draft proposals to go beyond the scope of preventing and settling conflicts of 'exercise' of jurisdiction. The proposed legal framework will, nonetheless, to some extent allay the problem of negative conflicts by clarifying responsibilities in the exercise of criminal jurisdiction, including in situations where neither Member State wishes to prosecute.

5 ECtHR, *Engel and Others v. the Netherlands*, 8 June 1976, Series A no. 22; criteria at §§ 82–83.

6 ibid. The first criterion serves as a starting point: if domestic law classifies an offence as criminal, this is decisive. If not, the second criterion, which is considered more important (Jussila v. Finland [GC], § 38), is evaluated taking into consideration as appropriate the following factors: whether the legal rule in question is directed solely at a specific group or is of a generally binding character (*Bendenoun v. France*, § 47); whether the proceedings are instituted by a public body with statutory powers of enforcement (Benham v. the United Kingdom, § 56); whether the legal rule has a punitive or deterrent purpose (*Öztürk v. Germany*, § 53; *Bendenoun v. France*, § 47); whether the imposition of any penalty is dependent upon a finding of guilt (Benham v. the United Kingdom, § 56); and how comparable procedures are classified in other Council of Europe member States (*Öztürk v. Germany* §53). The second and third criteria are not necessarily cumulative; either the nature of the offence or the severity of punishment may invoke art 6 ECHR (*Lutz v. Germany*, § 55; *Öztürk v. Germany*, § 54). This third criterion is determined by reference to the maximum potential penalty attached to the relevant provisions (*Campbell and Fell v. the United Kingdom*, § 72; *Demicoli v. Malta*, § 34).

7 It emerged from the field research at Eurojust that the most frequent cases of conflicts of jurisdiction do actually arise from trafficking offences (drug trafficking, trafficking in human beings).

- **Parallel proceedings**: the definition of 'parallel proceedings' does in principle cover both the pre-trial and trial stage. Parallel investigations, however, should in principle be allowed as they might turn out to be necessary in order to acquire the full picture, also in the perspective of the resolution of a conflict. What is most relevant is that parallel investigations are conducted in a fair and coordinated way and, in particular, do not end up in multiple prosecutions. The proposed legal framework will therefore not focus on or rule out parallel investigations but rather parallel prosecutions.
- **Actual and abstract conflicts** of jurisdiction.
- **Multiple proceedings**.

Article 82(1)(b) TFEU refers to both the 'prevention' and the 'settlement' of conflicts of jurisdiction. This broad legal mandate has not been used to date in any concrete legislative proposal. This project is intended to provide options for legislative frameworks that could fill that legal gap.

3. LEGISLATIVE GAP IN EU LAW: THE BACKGROUND OF THE PROJECT

Although the problems described above also arise on a global scale, they increasingly pose a problem within the European Union. Article 3(2) TEU which states that 'the Union shall offer its citizens an area of freedom, security and justice without internal frontiers, in which the free movement of persons is ensured' and the idea of European citizenship, enshrined in the Charter on Fundamental Rights (CFR), entails the right to a natural judge in the AFSJ and thereby sets requirements in relation to regulating jurisdiction conflicts in criminal matters. Can individuals derive rights from Union Law (including the CFR and the related European Convention on Human Rights (ECHR)) when it comes to choice of jurisdiction or at least in order to protect themselves against double jeopardy in a transnational setting?

The issues of parallel proceedings and conflicting decisions have long been discussed and addressed in the field of international civil procedure. In countries belonging to the civil law tradition, such conflicts have traditionally been avoided through the doctrine of *lis pendens*, which forbids the court seized second of the same dispute to retain jurisdiction. In countries belonging to the common law tradition, such issues have been handled very differently through a variety of doctrines. The most prominent is *forum non conveniens*, which enables common law courts to compare courts and processes for the purpose of assessing which of the competing adjudicators is the most appropriate, and should therefore decide the dispute. In the EU, the civil law doctrine of *lis pendens* was adopted in civil and commercial matters as early as 1968. For 55 years, conflicts of jurisdiction have been successfully prevented or settled in civil and commercial matters by rules currently laid down in Regulation 1215/2012 (the Brussels I Regulation recast). Similar, although not identical, mechanisms have applied in matrimonial matters since the adoption of Regulation 2201/2003.

Today, even in the EU, there are no binding instruments establishing a mechanism to resolve conflicts of (exercising) jurisdiction in criminal matters. It is worth mentioning that as early as the 1960s experts within the Council of Europe (CoE) began work on a draft convention on conflicts of jurisdiction in criminal matters, dealing with competence, transfer of proceedings and *ne bis in idem*. As a result, in 1965 the Consultative Assembly of the CoE adopted Recommendation 420, establishing factors for a priority order of jurisdictions. Member States of the CoE, however, did not follow up on this recommendation, as they did not fully endorse the hierarchical order of jurisdictions as suggested in Recommendation 420.

Despite little support from European countries for an agreement on a mechanism for the prevention of jurisdiction conflicts in criminal matters, the CoE continued with its efforts to find an appropriate solution to the problem. In the 1970s, the CoE elaborated a Convention on the International Validity of Judgments (28 May 1970) and on the Transfer of Proceedings (15 May 1972). Although both conventions were forward-looking in their approach to resolving conflicts of jurisdiction, they received only a small number of ratifications.[8] Furthermore, they did not provide a shared, common and multilateral procedure for determining jurisdiction in criminal matters. Much more popular in the area of recognition of foreign judgements was the 1983 Convention on the Transfer of Sentenced Persons, to which no fewer than 65 states are party, including all Member States of the EU.

Even within the AFSJ, national authorities are free to initiate parallel national proceedings on the same case. In principle, national provisions on jurisdiction determine whether a Member State has the right to prosecute. However, important limits are set by the principle of *ne bis in idem*, enshrined in EU law and in the ECHR/CFR. It is especially the jurisprudence of the CJEU that has clarified this principle, and developed an autonomous transnational concept of *ne bis in idem*, independent from national laws of individual Member States.

Nevertheless, the principle of *ne bis in idem* has different features at the national and European levels. At the national level, it functions in a frame in which rules on jurisdiction are set and applied and it comes into play only if they lead to a conflict in which the suspect could be adversely affected. Conversely, at the European level

8 To date the 1970 CoE Convention on the International Validity of Criminal Judgments has been ratified by 23 Members of the Council of Europe, of which 13 are also Member States of the European Union (AT, BE, BG, CY, DK, EE, LV, LT, NL, RO, SI, ES, SE). To date, the 1972 CoE Convention on the Transfer of Proceedings in Criminal Matters has been ratified by 25 States of the Council of Europe. of which 13 are also Member States of the European Union (AT, BG, CY, CZ, DK, EE, LV, LT, NL, RO, SK, ES, SE).

there are no common rules on jurisdiction. However, several EU legal instruments requiring the criminalisation of certain conducts prescribe extraterritorial jurisdiction and thus trigger a potential conflict. This means that between different Member States, the risk of violation of *ne bis in idem* is much higher. The function of *ne bis in idem* converts into an instrument of jurisdiction priority on a 'first come, first served' basis (i.e. the first decision in one Member State bars a second prosecution against the same person on the same facts in another country). This rule is questionable to the extent that states competing in a race to be the first may not even be aware that they are in such a race. A case in point is provided by the criminal proceedings against M., in which investigations in Belgium and Italy ran in parallel and the final Belgian decision was taken 4 days before the trial in Italy started.[9] According to the CJEU, the Belgian decision that there was no ground to refer the case to a trial court effectively barred the Italian authorities from initiating and conducting their proceedings.

This, however, in no way addresses the question of which jurisdiction is the most appropriate for the prosecution and adjudication of a suspect in the European AFSJ.

It is worth mentioning that some EU instruments (namely the 1995 Convention on the protection of European Communities' financial interests, FD 2008/919/JHA on combating terrorism [2008] (OJ L330/21), and FD 2005/222/JHA on attacks against information systems) [2005] OJ L69/67 contain provisions suggesting coordination among the Member States in order to decide which of them will prosecute. However, they do not provide for any specific procedures in that regard.

Within the EU, the first effective attempt to provide for coordination in order to prevent conflicts of jurisdiction was developed by Eurojust. In 2003, Eurojust issued guidelines for deciding which jurisdiction should prosecute.[10] These guidelines set out certain factors to be applied when solving conflicts of jurisdiction between Member States' authorities. They are applied at the meetings, held at Eurojust, between the national authorities for investigation and prosecution involved in a given cross-border case. However, the main limitations of these guidelines are clearly visible. Above all, since they have no binding effect, Member States are not obliged to comply with them. Also, importantly, interested persons are not involved, so the 'forum choice' is essentially made by the prosecuting authority without notifying or consulting the interested persons, or taking into account their interests.

In 2005, the European Commission launched a consultation on conflicts of jurisdiction in criminal matters, including the principle of *ne bis in idem*. The result was the 'Green Paper on Conflicts of Jurisdiction and the Principle of *ne bis in idem* in

9 CJEU, 5 June 2014, Case C-398/12, Criminal proceedings against M; ECLI:EU:C:2014:1057.

10 Eurojust Guidelines for Deciding 'Which Jurisdiction Should Prosecute?', included in the Annex to the Eurojust Annual Report 2003 (The Hague, February 2004).

Criminal Proceedings', published on 23 December 2005.[11] The Green Paper, as well as the related working paper,[12] identified and analysed the main problems in this field, envisaging a mechanism of consultation among Member States leading to the potential solution of a conflict of jurisdiction.

The outcome of the Commission's efforts was the Council Framework Decision (FD) on prevention and settlement of conflicts of exercise of jurisdiction in criminal proceedings, adopted on 30 November 2009, just before the entry into force of the Lisbon Treaty. The FD establishes a procedural framework for reaching consensus on which Member States should investigate and prosecute a case. Where it is not possible to reach consensus, the matter shall, where appropriate, be referred to Eurojust. The adoption of this FD, however, is not sufficient to prevent conflicts of jurisdiction. First, no binding criteria are established[13] as to how the decision should be made when choosing the best place for prosecution. Second, the outcome of the consultation proceedings is not binding and the FD provides no instruments to enforce it. Third, there is the danger that the defendants and the victims are deprived of their rights, as there is no possibility to contest the final decision on jurisdiction.

In light of the existing legal framework, one may conclude that: a) even today there are no binding rules 'preventing' conflicts of jurisdiction nor mechanisms to solve conflicts of jurisdiction when parallel proceedings already exist in two or more Member States; b) the approach adopted so far at EU level has been strongly based on the concept of a 'nation state', its sovereignty to exercise criminal jurisdiction and to apply national law; c) the CJEU has elaborated the autonomous concept of transnational *ne bis in idem* in the AFSJ.

Although conflicts of jurisdiction have been kept out of both the Stockholm Programme[14] and the Post Stockholm Guidelines,[15] it is likely that this issue will re-emerge on the European agenda, as it is mentioned explicitly in Article 82 TFEU and linked to the mandatory objectives of the AFSJ, according to which 'the Union shall offer its citizens an area of freedom, security and justice without internal frontiers, in which the free movement of persons is ensured' (Article 3(2) TEU).

11 European Commission, Green Paper on Conflicts of Jurisdiction and the Principle of *ne bis in idem* in Criminal Proceedings, 23.12.2005, COM(2005) 696 final.

12 European Commission staff working document, Annex to the Green Paper on conflicts of jurisdiction and the principle of *ne bis in idem* in criminal proceedings, cit.

13 The current FD 2009/948/JHA refers vaguely to the Eurojust Guidelines in the recitals (Recital 9) but not in the enacting terms.

14 European Council, the Stockholm Programme – An open and secure Europe serving and protecting citizens, OJ C115/1, 4.5.2010.

15 European Council, 'Strategic guidelines for legislative and operational planning for the coming years within the area of freedom, security and justice', in European Council, Conclusions - 26/27 June 2014, EUCO 79/14 (Brussels, 27 June 2014).

In particular, three provisions are of utmost importance as regards conflicts of jurisdiction: First, Article 82 TFEU provides a legal basis for the European Parliament and the Council to adopt measures to prevent and settle conflicts of jurisdiction between Member States.[16] Second, Article 85 TFEU is dedicated to Eurojust's mission 'to support and strengthen coordination and cooperation between national investigating and prosecuting authorities in relation to serious crimes affecting two or more Member States or requiring a prosecution on common bases'. In this regard, future developments are foreseen: 'the European Parliament and the Council, by means of regulations adopted in accordance with the ordinary legislative procedure, shall determine Eurojust's structure, operation, field of action and tasks'. Among those tasks is the 'resolution of conflicts of jurisdiction'.[17] Finally, Article 86 TFEU provides for the establishment of a European Public Prosecutor's Office (EPPO) and the Commission presented the related proposal in 2013.[18] According to the current outcome of the negotiations, the EPPO shall, where several Member States' courts have jurisdiction for the case, choose as the forum for indictment the Member State where the 'focus of the criminal activity' is. However, the draft EPPO Regulation allows for the possibility of duly justified deviations from that principle, taking into account a sequential order of criteria (place of habitual residence of the suspect, nationality of the suspect and place where the main financial damage occurred).[19]

4. REQUIREMENTS TO COMPLY WITH FUNDAMENTAL RIGHTS

Given that post-Lisbon the CFR has assumed constitutional status, any legislative ambitions relating to the AFSJ, such as those emanating from this Instrument, ought to respect, reflect and foster its core provisions and values. Of those provisions, the right to an effective remedy and to a fair trial, set out in Article 47 CFR, is perhaps the most directly related to the proposals at hand. One of its core features is

16 Article 82(1)(b) TFEU provides for the possibility to adopt 'measures' on the prevention and settlement of conflicts of jurisdiction. The general reference to 'measures' potentially allows for the adoption of both directives and regulations and, differently from paragraph 2 of the same article, it is not limited to 'minimum rules'. Furthermore, the adoption of measures on conflicts of jurisdiction is not subject to the 'emergency brake' procedure provided by paragraph 3 of art 82 TFEU.

17 The Commission Proposal for a Regulation on Eurojust, COM (2013) 535 final, envisaged the possibility for Eurojust to adopt a written decision on conflicts of jurisdiction. In the course of Council negotiations, however, the non-binding nature of such a decision was agreed upon (see art 4(4) of the current negotiating text of the Regulation on Eurojust, Council Doc. 6643/15 of 27 February 2015).

18 European Commission, Proposal for a Council Regulation on the establishment of the European Public Prosecutor's Office, Brussels, 17 July 2013, COM(2013) 534 final.

19 See art 30 para 2 and 22 para 4 and 5 of the Council Doc. 112774/2/16 of 12 October 2016.

foreseeability: Article 47 provides *inter alia* that 'everyone is entitled to a fair and public hearing within a reasonable time by an independent and impartial tribunal previously established by law'. The latter clause—'tribunal previously established by law'—is of especial relevance in cases of parallel proceedings[20] where the jurisdiction in which a suspect is to be prosecuted is unclear and may remain undecided for an unacceptably long period of time.

In this regard, all three draft legislative models set out further below improve upon the limited approach of FD 2009/948/JHA notably by establishing a clear procedure with time-limits and, in the case of the vertical model, by envisaging a new role for Eurojust, which could include the power to adopt a binding decision on the choice of forum.

Foreseeability, moreover, could be relevant also in the perspective of substantive legality spelled out in Article 49 CFR. The core principle enshrined in Article 49 is that no one shall be held guilty of any criminal offence on account of any act or omission which did not constitute a criminal offence under national law or international law at the time when it was committed.[21] Insofar as the choice of jurisdiction determines the applicability of different national substantive provisions, a new clear framework for that choice would contribute to making the applicable substantive law reasonably foreseeable (including the concrete definition of the offence, the level of the penalties and of the other consequences of conviction[22]).

In addition to the rights laid down in the CFR, the Council adopted in 2009 the Roadmap for strengthening procedural rights of suspected or accused persons in criminal proceedings.[23] To date, the Roadmap has inspired the promulgation of three directives: Directive 2010/64/EU on the right to interpretation and translation in criminal proceedings [2010] OJ L280/1, Directive 2012/13/EU on the right to information in criminal proceedings [2012] OJ L142/1, and Directive 2013/48/EU on the right to access a lawyer in criminal proceedings and in European Arrest Warrant proceedings [2013] OJ L294/1.

20 On the relevance of foreseeability of the choice of jurisdiction within the Area of Freedom, Security and Justice, see M. Panzavolta, *Choice of Forum and the Lawful Judge Concept*, in M. Luchtman (Ed.), *Choice of Forum in Cooperation Against EU Financial Crime. Freedom, Security and Justice and the Protection of Specific EU-Interests*, Eleven, 2013, 159.

21 Article 49(1) CFR. The provision thereby impliedly prohibits retroactive criminalisation, as well as expressly prohibiting the retroactive increase of criminal penalties. Moreover, the severity of penalties must not be disproportionate to the criminal offence [art 49(3)].

22 On the relationship between substantive legality, foreseeability and choice of forum, see M. Luchtman, *Choice of Forum and the Prosecution of Cross-Border Crime in the European Union – What role for the Legality Principle?*, in M. Luchtman (Ed.), *Choice of Forum in Cooperation Against EU Financial Crime*, cit., 46.

23 Council Resolution of 30 November 2009, Roadmap for strengthening procedural rights of suspected or accused persons in criminal proceedings, OJ, 4 December 2009, C295/1.

The significance of these directives is often heightened in parallel proceedings involving – in addition to the Member State or nationality or residence of the suspect – at least one and frequently two or more unfamiliar foreign jurisdictions, where the ensuring of an adequate defence must clear a series of practical hurdles. All stages of proceedings, ranging from initial information about the accusation, through access to adequate legal representation, to grasping and influencing unfolding events in the courtroom can be greatly complicated by the involvement of judicial authorities from multiple Member States with different languages and divergent criminal laws.

Whilst the directives have already somewhat redressed these disadvantages, the draft legislative models set out further below provide for the involvement of the accused person in consultations underway in order to determine the appropriate jurisdiction, thereby further implementing the rationale of Directive 2012/13/EU. In addition, the suspect is entitled to submit written observations in the course of consultations on the choice of forum procedure. Finally, it is worth underlining that in the vertical mechanism the accused person may trigger the involvement of Eurojust in order to resolve a conflict of jurisdiction.

5. ADDED VALUE OF A NEW LEGISLATIVE INSTRUMENT

The construction of a tangible AFSJ in the EU entails the strengthening of the fundamental rights of people living in this area. Important among these fundamental rights is the right not to be prosecuted in different jurisdictions for the same facts. Furthermore, the good administration of justice would require a rational and non-arbitrary regulation of the exercise of jurisdiction. The abovementioned gaps and problems cast light on the need for new legislative solutions to conflicts of jurisdiction.

First, the added value of a new legal framework could be measured with regard to the interests of the good administration of justice in a broader sense: for the Member States, a coherent regulation of the exercise of jurisdiction could avoid the random and arbitrary effects of the principle of *ne bis in idem*. Indeed, currently the 'first come, first served' rule according to which the *ne bis in idem* principle operates does not take into account other relevant interests (e.g. state/national security interests or the interests of the victim) and may lead to a situation in which the first Member State acquits because of lack of evidence, where another Member State could have convicted.[24] A new legal instrument, instead, could provide a procedural framework to consider and balance the relevant interests before a *ne bis in idem* situation is irremediably determined.

Following the entry into force of the Lisbon Treaty and, in particular, the new constitutional role thereby acquired by the CFR, the current legal framework on

24 CJEU, Case C-467/04, *Gasparini and Others* [2006] ECR I-9199.

conflicts of jurisdiction needs to be aligned with the fundamental rights obligations stemming from EU law.

In this regard, a new legal instrument could also deliver added value with regard to the position of the suspect, providing more foreseeability and fairness by allowing for the involvement of the defence and the victim in the settlement of a conflict of jurisdiction. Such involvement is currently absent from the EU legal framework.

Second—and more specifically—a new legal instrument might also provide added value with regard to the existing FD 2009/948/JHA by overcoming the flaws of its horizontal and limited approach (open-ended and non-binding nature of the consultations, non-consideration of the issue of multiple proceedings) and by reinforcing the right to a judge 'previously established by law', meaning a right to a reasonably foreseeable forum.[25] In this perspective, a new role for Eurojust, which could include the power to adopt a binding decision on the choice of forum, could be envisaged and contribute to enhancing foreseeability.

6. PROJECT OBJECTIVES AND ELI'S MISSION

The Member States' approach to criminal justice is traditionally based on national sovereignty, by which there is a direct link between the national definition of the crimes and related criminal procedural provisions (the applicable law) and the jurisdictional competence (mostly based on territoriality). The European integration process and in particular the free movement of persons and the constitutional objective of developing an AFSJ goes beyond the idea of this exclusive link between national sovereignty, applicable law and criminal jurisdiction. The shared sovereignty in the EU legal order has consequences not only for the applicable law (through harmonisation) but also for existence of jurisdiction and the use of it.

By striving for a common European judicial space based on mutual trust[26] and European citizenship,[27] where rights and obligations can be enforced by Member State authorities with an EU-wide effect, as well as by EU bodies and agencies,

25 As required by art 47 para 2 CFR. On the relevance of foreseeability of the choice of jurisdiction within the Area of Freedom, Security and Justice, see M. Panzavolta, *Choice of Forum and the Lawful Judge Concept*, in M. Luchtman (Ed.), *Choice of Forum in Cooperation Against EU Financial Crime. Freedom, Security and Justice and the Protection of Specific EU-Interests*, Eleven, 2013, 159

26 See CJEU, Opinion 2/13 of the Court (Full Court) on Accession of the European Union to the European Convention for the Protection of Human Rights and Fundamental Freedoms, 18 December 2014, para 191; Cases: C-187/01 and C-385/01 *Gözütok* and *Brügge* [2003] ECR I-1345; Cases C-411/10 and C-493/10, *N. S. and Others* and *M. E. and Others* [2011] ECR I-13905; Case C-399/11 *Melloni* [2013] EU:C:2013:107; and Case C-129/14 *PPU Spasic* [2014] ECLI:EU:C:2014:739.

27 Ligeti, K. and Marletta, A. (2016), 'EU Criminal Justice Actors: Accountability and Judicial Review vis-à-vis the EU Citizen, *New Journal of European Criminal Law,* 2016(2): 175–189.

the exercise of criminal jurisdiction cannot be defined only on the basis of the prerogatives of sovereign nation states.

This project aims at elaborating a new legal framework for the Prevention and Resolution of Conflicts of Jurisdiction in Criminal Matters in the AFSJ. With particular regard to the legislative gaps underlined above, the Working Group considered a complex set of objectives for a new legal framework. A coherent solution for conflicts of jurisdiction within the AFSJ should at least: a) avoid that *ne bis in idem* remains the only rule to resolve jurisdictional conflicts; b) ensure a non-arbitrary choice of jurisdiction; c) avoid parallel prosecutions; and aim at d) ensuring the choice of the best forum.

In delivering such solutions, the project aims at improving EU Law and developing the AFSJ, thereby contributing to the ELI's objectives. The ELI's mandate to promote better law-making and to enhance European legal integration is fully mirrored in the project's philosophy. A genuine pan-European perspective and the value of comparative knowledge are embedded in the research design, which features a Working Group of experts coming from different legal traditions, as well as academic and professional backgrounds. Furthermore, the involvement of representatives from the European institutions and agencies (European Commission, European Parliament, Eurojust) and from civil society (European Criminal Bar Association) in the discussion was intended to ensure comprehensiveness and a broader understanding of the issue and of the interests at stake.

7. PROJECT METHODOLOGY: THREE LEGISLATIVE MODELS FOR THE EU

This ELI project was carried out at the University of Luxembourg in cooperation with the Max Planck Institute Luxembourg (MPI) by an international team composed of practitioners and academics, in both the private law and criminal law fields, coming from different EU countries.

Since the project began in June 2014, five Working Group meetings have been held (4–5 November 2014, 12–13 March 2015, 1–2 September 2015, 18–19 February 2016, 21–22 June 2016). The Working Group meetings:

- refined the project methodology;
- discussed the practical problems of conflicts of jurisdiction based on extensive field research carried out by the Working Group members in cooperation with Eurojust;
- carried out an in-depth comparison with international private law;
- elaborated the three proposed legislative models.

Several input papers prepared by the Working Group members enriched the discussions as well as the involvement of policy makers (in particular the representatives of DG Justice) and practitioners (in particular, Eurojust and the European Criminal Bar Association). In addition, the three project Reporters met three times in order to refine the drafts (2 December 2015; 11 May 2016; 15 July 2016).

The interim results of the project were presented to the ELI Members on four separate occasions:

- before the Members Consultative Committee on 4 September 2013 in Vienna;
- before the Members Consultative Committee on 26 September 2014 in Zagreb;
- before the Members Consultative Committee on 4 September 2015 (a meeting of the Working Group of the project took place in Vienna on the occasion of the ELI Annual Conference);
- before a meeting of the ELI Council on 12 February 2016 in Vienna.

Following extensive field research, expert consultations and comparisons with international private law, the project proposes **three legislative models** for preventing and solving conflicts of criminal jurisdiction in the AFSJ. All approaches only propose **building blocks** for a future legislative text. They are not blueprints for future legislation but contain, rather, the most important elements of the mechanism they represent and thereby offer various implementation options for the EU legislator. It is possible for the EU legislator to take an in-between step and develop a proposal that combines elements of, for instance, the horizontal and vertical mechanisms.

The three legislative models reflect different levels of approximation and thereby **three distinct policy options,** leaving the choice open to the EU legislator.

Each legislative model is an ideal-type with an inherent logic and each corresponds to a broader regulatory approach which it translates into a concrete legislative instrument. The three regulatory approaches underlying the prevention and settlement of conflicts of criminal jurisdiction in the AFSJ are as follows:

- **horizontal mechanism:** conflicts of jurisdiction are solved between the national criminal justice authorities of the concerned Member States. The horizontal mechanism relies on cooperation and coordination between national criminal justice authorities as to the exercise of their jurisdiction. Such coordination is based on the principle of mutual trust between the Member States. It implies the duty of national authorities to share information and to coordinate with each other as well as to notify each other about parallel proceedings in order to prevent and settle conflicts of jurisdiction.
- **vertical mechanism:** The vertical mechanism relies on a binding supranational decision in cases where coordination between the national criminal justice

authorities has failed. The vertical mechanism relies on the principle of sincere cooperation deriving from Union loyalty between national and EU authorities. It implies the duty of national authorities to share information and to coordinate with each other and with Eurojust, as well as to notify each other and Eurojust about parallel proceedings in order to prevent and solve conflicts of jurisdiction.

- **mechanism for the allocation of criminal jurisdiction in the AFSJ:** conflicts of jurisdiction are prevented by establishing uniform European rules on the allocation of the exercise of criminal jurisdiction in the AFSJ.

The three regulatory approaches **serve as an analytical framework** or ideal-type for developing the legislative models. Each regulatory approach entails a variety of normative options for its implementation. The project develops only one legislative model within each regulatory approach. The concrete features of the proposed legislative models are carefully chosen by the Working Group in order to best illustrate the spectrum of EU intervention. The horizontal mechanism requires only minimum approximation of national criminal laws: it primarily aims at coordinating non-approximated national criminal jurisdictions. Only the factors and the procedure for coordination are defined by EU rules. Conversely, the mechanism for the allocation of the exercise of criminal jurisdiction in the EU requires uniform EU rules on forum choice in the AFSJ and embodies a strong harmonisation. The vertical mechanism stands in between the two other regulatory approaches. Although it has lower ambitions in terms of approximation than the allocation mechanism, it empowers a supranational body with binding EU-wide decision-making powers for resolving conflicts of criminal jurisdiction. This supranational binding decision is a European decision motivated by a European prosecutorial policy. In that sense the vertical mechanism challenges national priorities in exercising criminal jurisdiction. The mechanism on the allocation of criminal jurisdiction has the broadest objective as it aims to prevent conflicts in the exercise of criminal jurisdiction in the AFSJ. It requires the development of a single unified set of factors for allocating jurisdiction, but it does not impact the Member States' jurisdiction to prescribe.

8. FACTORS FOR DECIDING BETWEEN COMPETING JURISDICTIONAL CLAIMS

Both the horizontal and vertical mechanisms provide for deciding between competing jurisdictional claims based on a set of factors. It is important to note that neither the horizontal nor the vertical mechanism seeks to establish a hierarchical list of jurisdictional claims. Nor does the proposed new legal framework for solving conflicts of jurisdictions in criminal matters follow the hard and fast private international law rule of *lis pendens alibi* as expressed in the Brussels I (recast) Regulation. Instead, the framework for criminal law is more akin to the *forum non conveniens* doctrine in Anglo-American private international law both as regards the distinction between having jurisdiction and exercising it and as regards the discretionary element to decide between competing jurisdictional claims.

The comparison with private international law highlighted the shortcoming of the *lis pendens* mechanism: it is rigid and open to abuse through so called torpedo actions started with the purpose of frustrating litigation elsewhere. Its rigidity may lead to a race to court, thereby frustrating attempts to reach a consensual solution. And the court being granted priority might not be the court best placed to deal with the case. In fact, the transnational *ne bis in idem* principle as developed by the CJEU has much in common with the drawbacks of the Brussels I system of *lis pendens*. Although the situation in criminal law is different, *inter alia*, because the decision to open a prosecution is not a decision of the parties (claimant), but the prerogative of the state, it seems that much of the criticism levelled at the rigidity of the *lis pendens* rule and of the transnational European *ne bis in idem principle* could also be raised in relation to a strict hierarchy of jurisdictional claims in criminal law.

A strictly hierarchical priority order, in the end, may not deliver a suitable solution for the domain of criminal justice, where different sets of interests (the public interest of the state in punishing crime while ensuring a fair trial, the opposing private interests of the defendant and the victims) may compete and require a case-by-case approach.

9. HORIZONTAL MECHANISM

This legislative model follows—as a starting point—the rationale of FD 2009/948/JHA. Accordingly, it is the primary responsibility of the Member States to resolve conflicts of criminal jurisdiction among each other within the framework of a consultation procedure. It can thus be immediately distinguished from both the vertical mechanism entailing a binding decision of a supranational body (Eurojust) on the choice of forum—when such horizontal consultations reach an impasse or inertia – and the allocation model which envisions the autonomous application of concrete rules for determining criminal jurisdiction without requiring—in principle—that any horizontal consultation take place.

The horizontal model offers several implementation options (9.1). The implementation options featured in the proposed legislative model (9.2) reflect certain choices made by the Working Group in order to best illustrate the features of the horizontal mechanism.

9.1. IMPLEMENTATION OPTIONS

9.1.1. Options for the objectives of the instrument

One may distinguish between three different objectives of the horizontal mechanism:

a) Avoiding that conflicts of jurisdiction are solved only by the *ne bis in idem* rule and thereby ensuring a non-arbitrary choice of the forum to prosecute: the Member State that finally disposes of a case first is not always the one actually better placed to adjudicate the case; for instance, an acquittal for lack of evidence might occur because witnesses are located on the territory of another Member State;

b) Avoiding parallel prosecutions;

c) Ensuring the choice of the best forum to prosecute: such a choice relates to the allocation of jurisdiction on the basis of an assessment of the various interests at stake. It might indeed occur that a Member State other than the territorial State is best placed to adjudicate the case: for instance when the crime has been committed during a short stay abroad (a holiday trip) and the suspect, the victim and the witnesses are citizens or residents of another Member State (a 'tourist scenario').

The first two objectives—avoiding conflicts of jurisdiction in order to ensure a non-arbitrary choice and avoiding parallel prosecutions—represent a baseline with a view to the objectives of Article 82 TFEU. The choice of the best forum to prosecute requires the resolution of a series of complex questions (what is the 'best forum', what should be the factors for the choice, etc . . .) that the project does not address in the horizontal mechanism.

9.1.2. Options for the concept of conflict

As explained above, the concept of a conflict covers both parallel and multiple proceedings. In addition, the implementation of the horizontal mechanism offers a narrow and a broad perspective:

a) The narrow perspective is limited to 'actual' conflicts, where two or more proceedings are run in parallel in different Member States;

b) The broader perspective could also address potential conflicts, where parallel proceedings might be conducted in different Member States (abstract conflicts). The broader approach would thus also have a clear preventive rationale.

9.1.3. Factors for deciding between competing jurisdictional claims

The horizontal mechanism relies on agreed European factors for deciding between Member States' competing jurisdictional claims. Currently, the relevant criteria are set out in the 2003 Eurojust Guidelines. In order to be in conformity with the CFR and the Lisbon Treaty, the project proposes to update these guidelines. The project proposes to restructure and streamline the Guidelines and to add a negative list of factors that may not be taken into consideration when determining the proper jurisdiction.

Taking into account the conclusions of the Eurojust Strategic Seminar on Conflicts of Jurisdiction,[28] the following amendments and updates are suggested:

- The factors should reflect the relevant instruments of mutual recognition such as the European Arrest Warrant (EAW)[29] and the European Investigation Order (EIO)[30] that have been adopted since 2003. These instruments impact some of the criteria listed in the Eurojust Guidelines;
- For instance, the EAW and FD 2008/909 on custodial sentences accord [2008] OJ L327/27, secondary importance to the location of the accused. Similarly, the entry into force of the EIO and the new opportunities it offers for video or telephone conferencing (Articles 24 and 25) make the attendance of witnesses unnecessary;
- Following a suggestion from Eurojust, the territoriality and personality factors could also be reworded to ensure that not only their quantitative dimension is duly considered, but also their qualitative dimension;
- The definition of territoriality, in particular, should not be limited to the place 'where the majority' of the criminality or loss occurred but should also allow for consideration of the place where the 'most important' part of the criminality or loss has taken place. We go beyond the traditional concept of territoriality and also include state interests;
- Similarly, where several co-defendants can be identified, not only should their number be relevant, but also their respective roles in the commission of the crime and their respective locations;
- The stage of proceedings in the Member States involved (relative 'trial-readiness') as a factor for deciding which Member State should continue is currently missing from the Eurojust Guidelines and should be taken into account. It is underlined that 'trial-readiness' is not to be construed as a general evaluation of the procedural efficiency of any given national system;

28 Eurojust Strategic Seminar, Conflicts of Jurisdiction, *Transfer of Proceedings and Ne Bis In Idem: Successes, Shortcomings and Solutions*, The Hague, 4 June 2015. See esp. Conclusions of Workshop 2, 7–8.

29 Council FD of 13 June 2002 on the European arrest warrant and the surrender procedures between Member States, 2002/584/JHA, OJ L190/1, 18 July 2002.

30 Directive 2014/41/EU of the European Parliament and of the Council of 3 April 2014 regarding the European Investigation Order in criminal matters, OJ L130/1, 1 May 2014.

- Finally, a 'negative list' could be inserted, including the inadmissible factors: following the current matrix of the Guidelines, such factors are 'evidential problems', 'legal requirements' and 'sentencing powers'.

It is important to underline that a decision to concentrate proceedings does not entail the admissibility of evidence transmitted from one jurisdiction to another. By the same token, the burden of proof in any given Member State shall not constitute a reason for the allocation a case. With this in mind, in order to discourage prosecutors from 'shopping around' for the most convenient forum from their perspective alone, the threshold of admissibility of evidence—as opposed to its *availability*—in any given Member State is included in the list of factors not to be considered in deliberations over the choice of forum (in Annex to each proposed model).

9.1.4. Regarding the transparency of the factors

In order to ensure the **transparency and clarity** of the factors applied by the national authorities in the consultation procedure, it is possible to:

- Leave the Eurojust Guidelines as soft law;
- Transform the Eurojust Guidelines into 'hard law' through inclusion in the legislative draft, albeit whilst maintaining a case-by-case assessment of the factors (no hierarchical list);
- Establish a hierarchical list of factors of case allocation.

9.1.5. As to formalising the consultation procedure

When **formalising the consultation procedure**, it is possible that the rules applicable to the consultation procedure:

- Do not provide for the involvement of the suspect or the victim as is the case currently pursuant to FD 2009/948/JHA;
- Provide for a limited involvement of the suspect or the victim;
- Provide for the full involvement of the suspect and the victim. This option would require, however, a higher degree of formalisation of the procedure (rules on access to the file and to information, or a formalised hearing within the consultation procedure).

9.1.6. Regarding the content of the consultation procedure

As for the content of the consultations, it is possible to imagine:

- A consultation about the determination of the Member State that should carry on the prosecution;

- A request from the judicial authority of one Member State to the judicial authority of another Member State to take over the prosecution of a case as the latter is better placed to do so.

9.1.7. Regarding the parties to the consultation procedure

The consultation procedure in the horizontal mechanism is by definition between the national authorities of the concerned Member States. It is possible that only the national authorities participate in the horizontal consultation. However, as the national authorities may ask Eurojust to help and to convene a consultation meeting, it is also possible under the current framework decision to involve Eurojust as a mediator.[31]

9.1.8. Regarding the outcome of the consultation procedure

As to the **outcome of the consultation procedure**, it is possible to:

- Make a generic reference to achieving 'any effective solution', without stipulating an obligation for the judicial authorities to reach consensus and without providing for consequences in case the consultation fails, as is the case today based on FD 2009;
- Make a reference to achieving a solution, whereby preference should be given to the concentration of the proceedings whenever possible and requiring a formal agreement, delineating the circumstances and the factors considered. This option would, however, not provide for consequences in case the consultation fails;
- To stipulate an obligation to issue a formal agreement, delineating the circumstances and the factors considered, whereby preference should be given to the concentration of the proceedings whenever possible. This option would include consequences in case the consultation fails.

9.1.9. Options for judicial review

As to **judicial review**, it is possible to:

- Avoid any express mention of judicial review. The silence of the new instrument on judicial review would, however, not impact the obligations of the Member States under Article 47(1) CFR to ensure the right to an effective remedy.
- Include a general reference in the new instrument on the need to ensure the judicial review of the decision by the national judge.

31 Currently, art 12 of the FD 2009/948/JHA and arts 6 and 7 of the Decision 2009/426/JHA (Eurojust Decision) allow for the involvement of Eurojust as a mediator when conflicts of jurisdiction arise or 'are likely to arise'.

9.2. PROPOSED LEGISLATIVE INSTRUMENT

Among the implementation options set out above, the Working Group decided to opt for the following choices:

- Its aim is to prevent *ne bis in idem* violations and ensure a non-arbitrary choice of forum;
- It covers both actual and potential conflicts;
- It addresses both parallel and multiple proceedings;
- It refers to the amended Eurojust Guidelines as guidance for the assessment of the specific circumstances of the individual case;
- It provides for a limited involvement of the suspect and the victim in the consultation procedure;
- It obligates the national authorities to conclude a formal agreement on the solution of the conflict, delineating the circumstances and the factors considered, whereby preference should be given to the concentration of the proceedings whenever possible;
- It clarifies the need for judicial review of the formal agreement before the national judge (of the Member State where the prosecution is eventually conducted). National law should determine the procedural rules for the review;
- It provides rules for the transfer of proceedings and of evidence.

9.3. ADDED VALUE OF THE PROPOSED HORIZONTAL LEGISLATIVE MODEL

This legislative model aims at a consultation procedure that improves the current state of affairs, providing for more consistency and legal certainty. It is not limited to 'Lisbonising' FD 2009/948/JHA. Although the system will remain horizontal, EU law will define both the procedure and the factors to be applied in the consultation procedure.

Most importantly, by explicitly referring to the Eurojust Guidelines in the proposed Directive, the application of those factors may be subject to judicial review. An effective remedy against arbitrary decisions will be granted to the defendant before the competent national courts.

In addition, unlike FD 2009/948/JHA the scope of the proposed instrument is not limited to parallel proceedings, but based on a broader understanding of the notion of 'conflict', it also addresses multiple proceedings.

Article 82(1)(b) leaves the choice between Regulations and Directives. The adoption of a Directive seems to be more consistent with the limited objective of this legislative model.

10. VERTICAL MECHANISM

The vertical mechanism goes beyond the horizontal philosophy of the current legal framework by involving Eurojust. It focuses on the settlement of conflicts of jurisdiction. Horizontal consultation between the national judicial authorities remains the first step, but will be complemented by a supranational procedure conducted by Eurojust in case of failure to reach an agreement to settle the conflict.

Eurojust's involvement, which may be triggered by either (or any) of the involved Member States or by the suspect, is the key distinguishing feature of the vertical model vis-à-vis both the horizontal and allocation models. The Eurojust decision on choice of forum is a binding judicial decision, taken in accordance with a detailed and transparent procedural framework provided in the model. It may be subject to judicial review before the CJEU.

10.1. IMPLEMENTATION OPTIONS

The implementation options of the vertical mechanism largely correspond to those of the horizontal mechanism outlined in 9.1. However, the supranational decision of Eurojust offers additional implementation options.

10.1.1. Regarding the involvement of Eurojust

For the **involvement of Eurojust**, it is possible

- To maintain the current role of Eurojust, i.e. coordination and assistance upon request of the involved national authorities;
- To develop the complementary role of Eurojust, providing for its *ex officio* intervention or empowering the Member States, the suspect or accused person and the victim with the possibility of triggering a decision by Eurojust in case the consultation between the concerned national authorities has led to no decision.

10.1.2. *Regarding the outcome of the intervention of Eurojust* As to the **outcome of Eurojust intervention**, it is possible:

- That Eurojust adopts a written and reasoned non-binding opinion or recommendation;
- That Eurojust takes a written and reasoned binding decision.

10.1.3. Options for judicial review

For the **judicial review** of the decision of Eurojust, the following possibilities are available:

- No judicial review of the non-binding opinion or recommendation of Eurojust, as it does not change the legal position of the affected person;[32]
- Limited judicial review of Eurojust's binding decision by the CJEU based on Article 263 TFEU. The CJEU can annul the decision if it was taken arbitrarily, but it cannot (re-) assess the facts of the case and decide on the jurisdiction to prosecute.[33]

In addition, Article 265(1) and (3) TFEU (action for failure to act) also applies to the vertical mechanism in case Eurojust fails to act.

10.2. PROPOSED LEGISLATIVE INSTRUMENT

Among the implementation options set out above, the project decided to opt for the following choices:

- It aims at preventing *ne bis in idem* violations and ensuring a non-arbitrary choice of forum;
- It maintains a preliminary horizontal consultation to allow judicial authorities to reach consensus on the basis of transparent and unambiguous factors;
- It empowers each of the involved authorities or the suspect with the power to trigger the decision of Eurojust when national authorities have failed to reach consensus in the horizontal phase;
- It provides for a procedure in front of a specialised structure within Eurojust for the adoption of a binding decision on jurisdiction to prosecute;
- It spells out a set of transparent factors for Eurojust's decision by referring to the amended Eurojust Guidelines as guidance for the assessment of the specific circumstances of the individual case;

32 This conclusion could rely on the current jurisprudence of the European Courts on the review of final reports of OLAF. According to consistent case law, only acts entailing 'a distinct change in the applicant's legal position' may be subject to an action for annulment *ex* art 263 TFEU. Such an effect is generally not recognised by the Court when the act adopted by the EU body or agency is formally not binding, i.e. when the addressed national authorities are potentially free to decide whether or not to provide for a follow-up to the act of the EU agency or body. See, in particular, Case T-193/04 *Tillac v. European Commission* [2006] ECLI:EU:T:2006:292.

33 According to art 264 TFEU, if the action for annulment is well-founded, the Court of Justice or the General Court shall declare the act void. Under an action for annulment, the EU Courts cannot substitute their own assessment to that of the author of the contested act nor issue orders, directions or injunctions to Union institutions, bodies, offices or agencies. See K. Lenaerts, I. Maselis, K. Gutman, *EU Procedural Law*, OUP, 2014, 411 ff. This restriction does not apply when unlimited jurisdiction is granted to the EU judicature according to art 261 TFEU: the conferral of unlimited jurisdiction, however, is admissible only in regard to the review of 'penalties'.

- It grants the suspect and the victims the right to submit their views by means of a written opinion before Eurojust adopts its decision;
- It provides for the judicial review of Eurojust's decision; in particular, pursuant to Article 263(5) TFEU it allows the national judicial authorities and the suspect to launch an action for annulment before the CJEU (or the GC). Such review will not entail a choice of jurisdiction made by the Court, but a control of the legality of the decision adopted by Eurojust;
- In case Eurojust should fail to act within the deadlines for the adoption of the decision on jurisdiction, the general rules set out in Article 265 TFEU apply.

10.3. ADDED VALUE OF THE PROPOSED VERTICAL LEGISLATIVE MODEL

The vertical mechanism enhances legal certainty and consistency in the determination of the jurisdiction to prosecute by spelling out the factors for the choice of forum and by involving Eurojust and empowering it with a binding decision.

This legislative model proposes a draft Regulation. Article 82(1)(b) TFEU allows for the adoption of either a Directive or a Regulation. Taking into account that this legislative model contains binding rules on the settlement of conflicts of jurisdiction in criminal cases—in particular the definition of the factors and the procedure as well as the role of Eurojust—a Regulation is preferred. In terms of subsidiarity and proportionality, this choice is justified. A binding decision by a European agency implies a vertical approach that can be better achieved by a Regulation than by a Directive. It would not be appropriate to make the instrument conditional on the national laws of implementation, as the main aim is not approximation of national criminal laws. It is worth stressing that Article 82 TFEU is not limited to the establishment of minimum rules, therefore—except the amendments to the competence of Eurojust—Article 82(1)(b) would allow for a comprehensive Regulation on solving conflicts of jurisdiction.[34]

In addition, as far as the role of Eurojust is concerned, the proposed Eurojust Regulation (COM (2013) 535 final, 2013/0256 (COD)) needs to be amended. This amendment can be drafted on the basis of Article 85 TFEU, as a separate legislative initiative.

34 Article 82(1) TFEU—differently from art 82(2) or art 83 TFEU—does not restrict the EU legislative intervention to the adoption of 'minimum rules' and allows the resort to both directives and regulations.

11. MODEL BASED ON THE ALLOCATION OF THE EXERCISE OF JURISDICTION IN THE AFSJ

Differently to both the horizontal model, which provides a mechanism for the resolution of jurisdictional conflicts between Member States through direct consultation, and the vertical model, which entails a supranational decision on choice of forum by Eurojust, the third legislative model aims to reduce the possibility of conflicts of jurisdiction from the outset. It therefore proposes a reshaping of the grounds to exercise jurisdiction in criminal matters within the AFSJ, based on territoriality. Within the AFSJ, Member States should no longer exercise jurisdiction on the basis of extraterritorial jurisdictional principles, such as active or passive nationality of the accused or the victim.

This legislative model essentially aims at preventing prosecution in more than one Member State, and not necessarily at forbidding parallel investigations. However, due to the fact that clear rules on jurisdiction apply, the concentration of investigations in the competent Member State is a likely consequence.

Whereas, as a consequence of the allocation of the exercise of jurisdiction to one Member State only, many current potential conflicts of jurisdiction will no longer exist, two challenges remain that are also addressed in the model:

- Multi-territorial offences (offences for which more than one Member State claims location in its territory). This model stipulates rules to allocate the exercise of jurisdiction to one Member State only;
- Good administration of justice may indicate that a Member State other than the territorial Member State should exercise jurisdiction. There are two such situations: single territorial offences and the multiple unrelated territorial offences committed in several Member States. In these situations, the model provides for a transfer of the right to exercise jurisdiction to the Member State that is better placed to handle the case.

11.1. IMPLEMENTATION OPTIONS

The implementation of the allocation of jurisdiction offers different options.

11.1.1. Options for defining territorial jurisdiction

As a general rule, this model identifies territoriality as the only jurisdictional ground in the EU. The first problem, therefore, is the definition of territoriality. It is possible:

- Not to define territoriality in the legislative instrument;
- To adopt a broad definition based on the theory of 'ubiquity';

- To adopt a narrow definition based on the place where the conduct or a relevant part thereof was committed;
- To adopt a definition based on the place where the event or the damage occurred.

11.1.2. Options for judicial review

Although in this model the case allocation should work automatically, judicial review should ensure the correct application of the factors. It is possible to:

- Provide for judicial review before the national trial court, with the possibility of a request to the CJEU for a preliminary ruling pursuant to Article 267 TFEU (objections about the risk of a 'pro-forum bias' of the national trial court, however, should be considered);
- Provide for a decision taken by Eurojust upon request of a dissenting national authority and subject to judicial review by the CJEU pursuant to Article 263 TFEU.

11.2. PROPOSED LEGISLATIVE INSTRUMENT

Among the implementation options set out above, the Working Group decided to opt for the following choices:

- It lays down a general rule on allocating jurisdiction based on territoriality;
- It tackles the issue of multi-territorial offences and provides for a consultation procedure and additional factors for the determination of the allocation of the exercise of jurisdiction in multi-territorial cases;
- It provides for judicial review of the determination of jurisdiction at the national level;
- It provides for the transfer of the exercise of jurisdiction when good administration of justice requires a Member State other than the territorial Member State to handle the case.

11.3. ADDED VALUE OF THE PROPOSED LEGISLATIVE MODEL FOR THE ALLOCATION OF JURISDICTION

This model primarily prevents conflicts of jurisdiction. In this case, no forum choice would be necessary because the forum is already pre-determined by the rules on jurisdiction. In cases of multi-territorial offences, however, rules for the determination of the only competent Member State are provided.

The model presents transfer of the exercise of jurisdiction to bring the effects of allocation of the exercise of jurisdiction, in line with the demands of good administration of justice.

This legislative model establishes uniform rules on the exercise of jurisdiction in the AFSJ. However, this instrument does not aim at a full harmonisation of the national approaches to jurisdiction, which will remain unaffected with regard to offences (partly) committed outside the Union.

These rules on the exercise of jurisdiction do not fall within the concept of 'definition of criminal offences' (covered by Article 83 TFEU), but only operate in the context of conflicts of jurisdiction. In this regard, Article 82(1) TFEU seems to allow the EU legislator to go beyond minimum rules, by including also some rules which - without being considered as approximation measures according to Article 82(2) or Article 83(1) TFEU - require Member States to adapt national provisions with regard to cross-border situations.[35] The proposed instrument is a Regulation.

35 Böse—M. Böse, 'Chapter 9: The legal basis (Art. 82 TFEU)', in M. Böse, F. Meyer, and A. Schneider, *Conflicts of Jurisdiction in Criminal Matters in the European Union*, Vol. II (Baden-Baden, Nomos, 2014) 367—argues that art 82 even 'empowers the Union to adopt rules on the ambit of Member States' criminal law and, thereby, to limit their jurisdiction to prescribe' (370), whereas art 83 'may serve as a supplementary basis if a category of offences calls for specific jurisdictional rules (e.g., in order to avoid a negative conflict of jurisdiction)' (373). art 82 also includes preventive measures: 'This broad interpretation corresponds to the general notion of jurisdiction and is further supported by the fact that, unlike art 83 TFEU, art 82 . . . is not limited to particular areas of criminal law, but provides for a general competence on conflicts of jurisdiction, irrespective of the nature of the offence' (369).

DRAFT TEXT

I. HORIZONTAL MECHANISM

Proposal for a

DIRECTIVE OF THE EUROPEAN PARLIAMENT AND THE COUNCIL on the settlement of conflicts of exercise of jurisdiction in criminal proceedings and the prevention of violations of the principle of *ne bis in idem*

THE EUROPEAN PARLIAMENT AND THE COUNCIL OF THE EUROPEAN UNION

Having regard to Article 82 paragraph 1(b) of the Treaty on the Functioning of the European Union,

Whereas:

(-) . . .

HAVE ADOPTED THIS DIRECTIVE:

CHAPTER 1
GENERAL RULES

ARTICLE 1
Objective

1. The objective of this Directive is to promote a closer cooperation between the competent authorities of two or more Member States conducting criminal proceedings, with a view to improving the efficient and good administration of justice in the Area of Freedom, Security and Justice.
2. Such closer cooperation aims to:
   (a) reach reasoned and non-arbitrary consensus as to the choice of forum in cases where parallel or multiple proceedings are being conducted or are about to be conducted; and
   (b) prevent situations where the same person is subject to parallel criminal proceedings in different Member States in respect of the same facts, where these might lead to the final disposal of the proceedings in two or more Member States, thereby constituting an infringement of the principle of '*ne bis in idem*'.

Explanatory note:
The objective of the new instrument is broader than that of FD 2009/948/JHA. Beyond the objectives of avoiding parallel prosecutions (parallel investigations are

allowed) and ensuring that ne bis in idem is not the only rule to resolve conflicts of jurisdictions, the new instrument will also cover multiple proceedings (see the definition under the new Article 3 (b)) and will aim, more generally, at ensuring a non-arbitrary choice of jurisdiction.

ARTICLE 2
Subject matter and scope

1. With a view to achieving the objectives set out in Article 1, this Directive provides for a framework on:
   (a) the procedure for establishing contact between the competent authorities of the Member States, with a view to detecting the existence of parallel or multiple criminal proceedings;
   (b) the exchange of information, through direct consultations, between the competent authorities of two or more Member States conducting parallel or multiple criminal proceedings;
   (c) the procedure to reach a reasoned consensus as to the choice of forum in cases where the existence of parallel or multiple criminal proceedings is detected.

Explanatory note:
The Directive maintains the horizontal philosophy of FD 2009/948/JHA and aims at formalising the consultation procedure between national competent authorities. As such, the Directive should enhance legal certainty.
The new instrument applies to criminal proceedings stricto sensu only. Not only competition law, but all other areas of quasi-criminal proceedings are outside the scope of the draft Directive.

ARTICLE 3
Definitions

For the purposes of this Directive:

(a) 'parallel proceedings' means criminal proceedings which are conducted or are about to be conducted in two or more Member States against the same suspect or accused in regard to the same facts;
(b) 'multiple proceedings' means criminal proceedings which are conducted or about to be conducted in two or more Member States against the same suspect or accused in relation to different facts, or against different suspects or accused persons in regard to a related set of facts;
(c) 'competent authority' means a judicial authority or another authority, which is competent, under the law of its Member State, to carry out the acts envisaged by Article 2 paragraph 1 of this Directive;

(d) 'contacting authority' means a competent authority which contacts another competent authority to confirm the existence of parallel or multiple criminal proceedings;

(e) 'contacted authority' means the competent authority which is asked by a contacting authority to confirm the existence of parallel or multiple criminal proceedings;

(f) 'forum' means the Member State whose courts may potentially adjudicate the relevant proceedings pursuant to a decision taken under Article 8 paragraph 3 of this Directive.

Explanatory note:
The new legal instrument addresses both parallel and 'multiple proceedings'. The notion of proceedings includes both investigations and prosecutions. The term multiple proceedings refers to situations where the principle of ne bis in idem does not apply since the underlying facts or the persons concerned are different, but in the interest of efficient and good administration of justice such proceedings should be concentrated – if possible – in one Member State. Multiple proceedings—differently from Article 30 of Regulation 1215/2012 (Brussels I Recast)—are not limited to related proceedings.

ARTICLE 4

Determination of competent authorities

1. Member States shall determine the competent authorities in a way that promotes the principle of direct contact between authorities.
2. In accordance with paragraph 1, each Member State shall inform the Commission which authorities under its national law are competent to act in accordance with this Directive.
3. Notwithstanding paragraphs 1 and 2, each Member State may designate, if it is necessary as a result of the organisation of its internal system, one or more central authorities responsible for the administrative transmission and reception of requests for information according to Article 5 and/or for the purpose of assisting the competent authorities in the consultation process. Member States wishing to make use of the possibility to designate a central authority or authorities shall communicate this information to the Commission.
4. The Commission shall make the information received under paragraphs 2 and 3 available to all Member States.

CHAPTER 2
EXCHANGE OF INFORMATION

ARTICLE 5
Obligation to contact

1. When a competent authority of a Member State has indications that parallel or multiple criminal proceedings are being conducted or are about to be conducted in another Member State, it shall contact the competent authority of that other Member State to confirm the existence of such parallel or multiple criminal proceedings, with a view to initiating a direct consultation as provided for in Article 7.
2. Such indications may include cases where a suspected or accused person or a victim notifies the competent authority that parallel or multiple proceedings in another Member State are being conducted or are about to be conducted, where a relevant request for mutual legal assistance by a competent authority in another Member State reveals the possible existence of such parallel or multiple proceedings, or where a police authority provides information to this effect.
3. If the contacting authority does not know the identity of the competent authority to be contacted, it shall make all necessary inquiries, including via the contact points of the European Judicial Network, in order to obtain the details of that competent authority.
4. Without prejudice to Article 7, the procedure of contacting shall not apply when the competent authorities conducting parallel criminal proceedings have already been informed of the existence of these proceedings by any other means.

Explanatory note:
The new instrument strengthens the obligation to contact by replacing the previous threshold ('reasonable grounds to believe that parallel proceedings are being conducted in another Member State') with a more precise set of 'indications'.

1. *The competent authorities of the Member States are obliged to contact one another in case of indications (examples of which are given in paragraph 2) that parallel or multiple criminal proceedings are being conducted or are about to be conducted in another Member State.*
2. *The indications are provided in a non-exhaustive fashion. They include the most typical ways in which the authorities may learn of the existence of parallel or multiple proceedings, such as reporting by the suspect or the victim, or requests for international cooperation. Suspects and victims can on an equal footing inform their national authorities and thereby trigger the obligation to contact.*

3. *The EJN has proven over the years to be an efficient and straightforward way to identify the competent authority in case of requests for international co-operation. National authorities involved in the consultation procedure may take advantage of the EJN.*
4. *Paragraph 4 sets out an exemption to the obligation to contact when the competent authorities are already aware of the existence of parallel or multiple proceedings. This exemption, however, does not affect the subsequent and autonomous obligation to enter into direct consultations provided under Article 7.*

ARTICLE 6
Obligation to reply

1. The contacted authority shall reply to a request submitted in accordance with Article 5 paragraph 1 by the deadline indicated by the contacting authority, or, if no deadline has been indicated, without undue delay and in any case within 30 days of receiving the request, and inform the contacting authority whether parallel or multiple proceedings are taking place in its Member State. In cases where the contacting authority has informed the contacted authority that the suspected or accused person is held in provisional detention or custody, the latter authority shall treat the request as a matter of urgency.
2. If the contacted authority is unable to provide a reply by the deadline set under paragraph 1, it shall promptly inform the contacting authority of the reasons therefore and indicate the time frame within which it shall provide the requested information.
3. If the authority which has been contacted by a contacting authority is not the competent authority under Article 4, it shall without undue delay transmit the request for information to the competent authority and shall inform the contacting authority accordingly.

Explanatory note:

1. *Similarly to Article 6 of the FD 2009/948/JHA the contacting authority can set a deadline for the reply.*

If no deadline has been indicated, without prejudice to a general rule of expediency ('without undue delay'), the maximum time frame is 30 days. This limit corresponds to the 30 days provided in Article 12 paragraph 3 of the Directive 2014/41 on the European Investigation Order and represents a reasonable length of time for the detection of the existence of parallel or multiple proceedings in the contacted Member State. There is no formal consequence if the contacted competent authority does not respond by the deadline. However, based on existing case law of the CJEU the obligation to reply remains intact even after the deadline has passed.

2. *The continuing obligation to reply and the principle of sincere cooperation imply that the contacted authority, when unable to comply with the deadline of 30 days, shall indicate a timeframe for its reply.*

CHAPTER 3
DIRECT CONSULTATION

ARTICLE 7
Obligation to consult and sincere cooperation

1. When it is established that parallel or multiple proceedings exist, the competent authorities of the Member States concerned shall enter into direct consultation in order to reach reasoned consensus on an effective solution to avoid the adverse consequences arising from parallel or multiple proceedings.
2. Such consensual solution shall be pursued in adherence with the principles of sincere cooperation and good administration of justice and should, in the case of parallel proceedings, lead to the concentration of the criminal proceedings in one Member State for the purpose of prosecution in accordance with Article 8. The same shall apply to multiple proceedings, where appropriate.
3. As long as the direct consultation is being conducted, the competent authorities concerned can take all necessary procedural measures and shall inform each other of any important procedural measures which they have taken in the proceedings.
4. Whenever reasonably possible a competent authority involved in direct consultation shall reply to requests for information from other competent authorities involved in such consultations, except where doing so could harm essential national security interests.

Explanatory note:

1. *This provision is based on Article 10 of FD 2009/948/JHA ('Obligation to enter into direct consultations'). The aim of the consultation is to avoid adverse consequences such as ne bis in idem.*
2. *Paragraph 2 stresses the relevance of the principle of sincere cooperation as an overarching obligation and defines the concentration of the proceedings in one Member State as a desirable outcome of the consultation. Whereas in case of parallel proceedings the proceedings should always be concentrated, the concentration of multiple proceedings is not always possible or desirable from the viewpoint of the proper administration of justice.*

3. *The opening of a consultation procedure does not rule out the adoption of procedural measures by the competent authorities. The competent authorities of the Member States may therefore continue parallel investigations, but only as long as this is necessary in order to establish the material facts of the case. They need inform each other only of important procedural measures taken (e.g. victim protection measures are important, whereas the award of legal aid is not important or relevant to the other Member State).*
4. *During the consultation procedure, the competent authorities should provide all necessary information to one another. However, this obligation does not apply where to provide the information would endanger national security interests.*

ARTICLE 8
Reasoned consensus and formal agreement on choice of forum

1. In order to reach a consensus on the concentration of proceedings including the final choice of forum, the competent authorities of the Member States shall assess the specific circumstances of the individual case in light of the factors for the choice of forum annexed to this Directive.
2. The competent authorities should aim to achieve such consensus as soon as possible and at the latest before either of the involved authorities presents the case to court for the purposes of prosecution or takes any measures which would have the effect of a final disposal of the case.
3. Where the competent authorities of the Member States agree that to do so would not jeopardise the investigation, they shall inform the suspect or accused and the victims of the existence of the consultation procedure and of the possibility to submit written observations within 15 days of the date of such notification.
4. When the competent authorities of the Member States concerned reach consensus, they shall conclude a formal agreement delineating the circumstances and the factors applied, and where to do so would not jeopardise the investigation, inform the suspect or accused and the victims thereof.

Explanatory note:

1. *Article 8 is a completely new provision. Differently from FD 2009/948/JHA, the new instrument will include as an Annex a set of factors for the choice of forum. Non-arbitrariness of the choice of the forum and the transparency of the factors applied are strictly interrelated. The requirement to reach a consensus on the final choice of forum—with the consequences stipulated in Article 9—does not prevent the national authorities from reaching provisional agreement at an early stage of the consultation.*

2. *In case of parallel proceedings and, where appropriate, in case of multiple proceedings, the consensus should be achieved before any of the authorities takes the case to court or takes other measures with the effect of finally disposing of the case. It is, however, not prohibited for both national authorities to go ahead with parallel proceedings even though this may eventually trigger the ne bis in idem principle.*
3. *The suspect or accused person and the victims should have the opportunity to submit their written observations in the course of the consultation procedure before consensus is reached. Although notification of the suspect or accused person and the victims is due only 'where the competent authorities agree that to do so would not jeopardise the investigation or the prosecution', this derogation is intended to be exceptional and must be applied narrowly.*
4. *In order to ensure non-arbitrariness and transparency, the consensus must be reasoned and formalised in a written agreement. It could be useful to develop a template annexed to the Directive for the use of national authorities.*

ARTICLE 9
Consequences of the agreement and transfer of proceedings

1. Following the agreement taken pursuant to Article 8 paragraph 4 to concentrate proceedings the national authorities of the other Member State shall transfer the file, refrain from taking further investigative or prosecutorial measures and close the case.
2. Any act with a view to proceedings taken in the transferring Member State before the conclusion of an agreement pursuant to Article 8 paragraph 4 shall be recognised in the receiving Member State as if it had been taken by the national authorities of that Member State, provided that such recognition does not give such an act a greater evidential weight than it has in the transferring Member State.
3. Any act which interrupts time limitation and which has been validly performed in the transferring Member State shall have the same effect in the receiving Member State and vice versa.
4. The transferring Member State regains the right to prosecute the case if the competent authority in the receiving Member State neither presents the case to a court for the purposes of prosecution nor takes other measures which would have the effect of a final disposal of the case.

Explanatory note:

1. *Article 9 is a new provision. It clarifies the consequences of the agreement and provides a legal basis to discontinue the proceedings at the national level and*

to transfer the file and the evidence to the other Member State. The provision is limited to parallel proceedings as multiple proceedings do not always lead to the concentration of the case.

2-3. *Drawing from the Convention on Transfer of Proceedings of the Council of Europe, the new provision also lays down rules on the equivalence of procedural acts interrupting time limitation periods and on the recognition of evidence.*

4. *If the receiving Member State does not prosecute the case following the transfer, the transferring Member State's right to prosecute revives.*

ARTICLE 10
Remedies

Any agreement concluded pursuant to Article 8 paragraph 4 is without prejudice to legal remedies under national law to request judicial review on the choice of forum.

Explanatory note:
Article 10 does not affect national remedies. It does not define whether only the suspect or also the victim has a right to challenge the choice of forum. Nor does it define the grounds for a challenge (the forum choice or closing of the case, etc.). This does not preclude the possibility to challenge the decision in the courts of each of the Member States concerned.

ANNEX A—FACTORS RELEVANT TO THE CHOICE OF FORUM

The competent authorities of the Member States shall determine the choice of forum in accordance with the following factors:

FACTORS TO BE CONSIDERED

1. TERRITORIALITY

In principle, territoriality shall determine the jurisdiction to prosecute.

In case of crimes affecting the territory of more than one Member State, the competent authorities shall take into account where the majority or the most important part of the criminality occurred or where the majority or the most important part of the harmful effect or loss was sustained when determining the choice of forum. Harmful effect also includes state interests (such as offences against state security).

2. STAGE OF THE PROCEEDINGS—TRIAL-READINESS

When determining the choice of forum, the competent authorities shall compare and consider the state and the trial-readiness of the different proceedings.

3. INTERESTS OF THE SUSPECT

The competent authorities shall take into account the interests of the suspect and whether they would be prejudiced if any prosecution were to take place in one jurisdiction rather than another. Interests of the suspect could relate to his or her effective links with the jurisdiction of a Member State, such as: the duration of his or her residence, the ability to understand the language spoken in the Member State, the degree of integration of the suspect in the society of one Member State, the possibility for him or her to access an effective legal defence, or the presence of dependent family members on the territory of another Member State. The vulnerability of the suspect and the possibility to ensure adequate safeguards should be carefully assessed.

4. INTERESTS OF VICTIMS

The competent authorities shall take into account the interests of victims and whether they would be prejudiced if any prosecution were to take place in one jurisdiction rather than another. Interests of the victims might include the possibility to avoid their secondary victimisation and to resort to protective measures, especially in the case of vulnerable victims or violent crimes. The possibility for the victim to obtain adequate compensation could also be considered.

5. NEED TO RESORT TO MUTUAL LEGAL ASSISTANCE AND MUTUAL RECOGNITION INSTRUMENTS

For example, where the majority of the evidence is located in one of the involved Member States.

6. NEED FOR CONCENTRATION OF PROCEEDINGS

In case of multiple proceedings, in determining the choice of forum, the competent authorities shall consider the possibility to concentrate the proceedings and the overall costs of the proceedings.

FACTORS NOT TO BE CONSIDERED

In determining the choice of forum, the competent authorities of the Member States are not to consider:

1. DIVERGING RULES ON EVIDENCE

Courts in different jurisdictions have different rules for the acceptance of evidence often gathered in very diverse formats. The potential admissibility and acceptance of evidence by a court cannot be considered as a factor to determine where the prosecution should take place.

2. LEGAL REQUIREMENTS

The competent authorities shall not decide to prosecute in one jurisdiction rather than another simply in order to avoid having to comply with the legal obligations that apply in one jurisdiction but not in another.

3. SENTENCING POWERS

The sentencing powers of courts and detention circumstances in the different Member States shall not be a factor in deciding the jurisdiction in which a case should be prosecuted. The judicial authorities should not seek to prosecute cases in a jurisdiction where the penalties are highest.

ANNEX B—DIAGRAM: HORIZONTAL MECHANISM

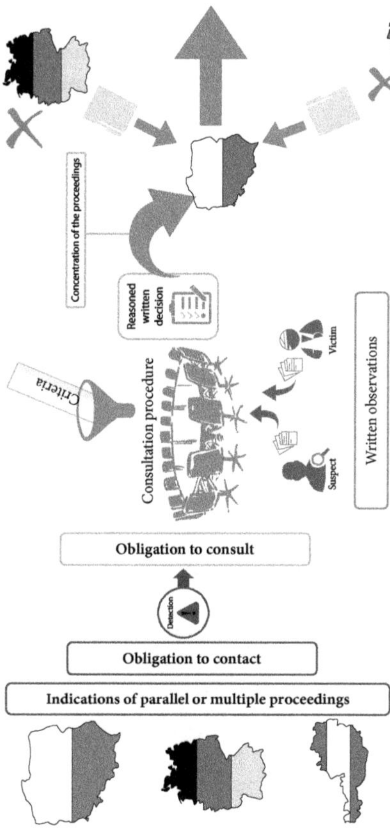

DRAFT TEXT

II. VERTICAL MECHANISM

Note:
The first 10 articles correspond to those of the horizontal mechanism.
Proposal for a

REGULATION OF THE EUROPEAN PARLIAMENT
AND THE COUNCIL
on the settlement of conflicts of exercise of jurisdiction in criminal proceedings and the prevention of violations of the principle of *ne bis in idem*

THE EUROPEAN PARLIAMENT AND THE COUNCIL OF THE EUROPEAN UNION

Having regard to Article 82 paragraph 1(b) of the Treaty on the Functioning of the European Union,

Whereas:

(-) . . .

HAVE ADOPTED THIS REGULATION:

CHAPTER 1
GENERAL RULES

ARTICLE 1
Objective

1. The objective of this Directive is to promote a closer cooperation between the competent authorities of two or more Member States conducting criminal proceedings, with a view to improving the efficient and good administration of justice in the Area of Freedom, Security and Justice.
2. Such closer cooperation aims to:
   (a) reach reasoned and non-arbitrary consensus as to the choice of forum in cases where parallel or multiple proceedings are being conducted or are about to be conducted; and
   (b) prevent situations where the same person is subject to parallel criminal proceedings in different Member States in respect of the same facts, where these might lead to the final disposal of the proceedings in two or more Member States, thereby constituting an infringement of the principle of *'ne bis in idem'*.

Explanatory note:
The objective of the new instrument is broader than that of FD 2009/948/JHA. Beyond the objectives of avoiding parallel prosecutions (parallel investigations are allowed) and ensuring that ne bis in idem is not the only rule to resolve conflicts of jurisdictions, the new instrument will also cover multiple proceedings (see the definition under the new Article 3 (b)) and will aim, more generally, at ensuring a non-arbitrary choice of jurisdiction.

ARTICLE 2

Subject matter and scope

1. With a view to achieving the objectives set out in Article 1, this Directive provides for a framework on:
   (a) the procedure for establishing contact between the competent authorities of the Member States, with a view to detecting the existence of parallel or multiple criminal proceedings;
   (b) the exchange of information, through direct consultations, between the competent authorities of two or more Member States conducting parallel or multiple criminal proceedings;
   (c) the procedure to reach a reasoned consensus as to the choice of forum in cases where the existence of parallel or multiple criminal proceedings is detected.

Explanatory note:
The Directive maintains the horizontal philosophy of FD 2009/948/JHA and aims at formalising the consultation procedure between national competent authorities. As such, the Directive should enhance legal certainty.
The new instrument applies to criminal proceedings stricto sensu only. Not only competition law, but all other areas of quasi-criminal proceedings are outside the scope of the draft Directive.

ARTICLE 3

Definitions

For the purposes of this Directive:

(a) 'parallel proceedings' means criminal proceedings which are conducted or are about to be conducted in two or more Member States against the same suspect or accused in regard to the same facts;
(b) 'multiple proceedings' means criminal proceedings which are conducted or about to be conducted in two or more Member States against the same suspect

or accused in relation to different facts, or against different suspects or accused persons in regard to a related set of facts;

(c) 'competent authority' means a judicial authority or another authority, which is competent, under the law of its Member State, to carry out the acts envisaged by Article 2 paragraph 1 of this Directive;

(d) 'contacting authority' means a competent authority which contacts another competent authority to confirm the existence of parallel or multiple criminal proceedings;

(e) 'contacted authority' means the competent authority which is asked by a contacting authority to confirm the existence of parallel or multiple criminal proceedings;

(f) 'forum' means the Member State whose courts may potentially adjudicate the relevant proceedings pursuant to a decision taken under Article 8 paragraph 3 of this Directive.

Explanatory note:
The new legal instrument addresses both parallel and 'multiple proceedings'. The notion of proceedings includes both investigations and prosecutions. The term multiple proceedings refers to situations where the principle of ne bis in idem *does not apply since the underlying facts or the persons concerned are different, but in the interest of efficient and good administration of justice such proceedings should be concentrated—if possible—in one Member State. Multiple proceedings—differently from Article 30 of Regulation 1215/2012 (Brussels I Recast)—are not limited to related proceedings.*

ARTICLE 4

Determination of competent authorities

1. Member States shall determine the competent authorities in a way that promotes the principle of direct contact between authorities.
2. In accordance with paragraph 1, each Member State shall inform the Commission which authorities under its national law are competent to act in accordance with this Directive.
3. Notwithstanding paragraphs 1 and 2, each Member State may designate, if it is necessary as a result of the organisation of its internal system, one or more central authorities responsible for the administrative transmission and reception of requests for information according to Article 5 and/or for the purpose of assisting the competent authorities in the consultation process. Member States wishing to make use of the possibility to designate a central authority or authorities shall communicate this information to the Commission.

4. The Commission shall make the information received under paragraphs 2 and 3 available to all Member States.

CHAPTER 2
EXCHANGE OF INFORMATION

ARTICLE 5
Obligation to contact

1. When a competent authority of a Member State has indications that parallel or multiple criminal proceedings are being conducted or are about to be conducted in another Member State, it shall contact the competent authority of that other Member State to confirm the existence of such parallel or multiple criminal proceedings, with a view to initiating a direct consultation as provided for in Article 7.
2. Such indications may include cases where a suspected or accused person or a victim notifies the competent authority that parallel or multiple proceedings in another Member State are being conducted or are about to be conducted, where a relevant request for mutual legal assistance by a competent authority in another Member State reveals the possible existence of such parallel or multiple proceedings, or where a police authority provides information to this effect.
3. If the contacting authority does not know the identity of the competent authority to be contacted, it shall make all necessary inquiries, including via the contact points of the European Judicial Network, in order to obtain the details of that competent authority.
4. Without prejudice to Article 7, the procedure of contacting shall not apply when the competent authorities conducting parallel criminal proceedings have already been informed of the existence of these proceedings by any other means.

Explanatory note:
The new instrument strengthens the obligation to contact by replacing the previous threshold ('reasonable grounds to believe that parallel proceedings are being conducted in another Member State') with a more precise set of 'indications'.

1. *The competent authorities of the Member States are obliged to contact one another in case of indications (examples of which are given in paragraph 2) that parallel or multiple criminal proceedings are being conducted or are about to be conducted in another Member State.*
2. *The indications are provided in a non-exhaustive fashion. They include the most typical ways in which the authorities may learn of the existence of parallel or multiple proceedings, such as reporting by the suspect or the victim, or*

requests for international cooperation. Suspects and victims can on an equal footing inform their national authorities and thereby trigger the obligation to contact.

3. *The EJN has proven over the years to be an efficient and straightforward way to identify the competent authority in case of requests for international co-operation. National authorities involved in the consultation procedure may take advantage of the EJN.*
4. *Paragraph 4 sets out an exemption to the obligation to contact when the competent authorities are already aware of the existence of parallel or multiple proceedings. This exemption, however, does not affect the subsequent and autonomous obligation to enter into direct consultations provided under Article 7.*

ARTICLE 6
Obligation to reply

1. The contacted authority shall reply to a request submitted in accordance with Article 5 paragraph 1 by the deadline indicated by the contacting authority, or, if no deadline has been indicated, without undue delay and in any case within 30 days of receiving the request, and inform the contacting authority whether parallel or multiple proceedings are taking place in its Member State. In cases where the contacting authority has informed the contacted authority that the suspected or accused person is held in provisional detention or custody, the latter authority shall treat the request as a matter of urgency.
2. If the contacted authority is unable to provide a reply by the deadline set under paragraph 1, it shall promptly inform the contacting authority of the reasons therefore and indicate the time frame within which it shall provide the requested information.
3. If the authority which has been contacted by a contacting authority is not the competent authority under Article 4, it shall without undue delay transmit the request for information to the competent authority and shall inform the contacting authority accordingly.

Explanatory note:

1. *Similarly to Article 6 of the FD 2009/948/JHA the contacting authority can set a deadline for the reply.*

If no deadline has been indicated, without prejudice to a general rule of expediency ('without undue delay'), the maximum time frame is 30 days. This limit corresponds to the 30 days provided in Article 12 paragraph 3 of the Directive 2014/41 on the European Investigation Order and represents a reasonable length of time for the detection of the existence of parallel or multiple proceedings in the contacted Member State. There is no formal consequence if the contacted competent authority does not respond by the deadline. However, based on existing case law of the CJEU the obligation to reply remains intact even after the deadline has passed.

2. *The continuing obligation to reply and the principle of sincere cooperation imply that the contacted authority, when unable to comply with the deadline of 30 days, shall indicate a timeframe for its reply.*

CHAPTER 3
DIRECT CONSULTATION

ARTICLE 7
Obligation to consult and sincere cooperation

1. When it is established that parallel or multiple proceedings exist, the competent authorities of the Member States concerned shall enter into direct consultation in order to reach reasoned consensus on an effective solution to avoid the adverse consequences arising from parallel or multiple proceedings.
2. Such consensual solution shall be pursued in adherence with the principles of sincere cooperation and good administration of justice and should, in the case of parallel proceedings, lead to the concentration of the criminal proceedings in one Member State for the purpose of prosecution in accordance with Article 8. The same shall apply to multiple proceedings, where appropriate.
3. As long as the direct consultation is being conducted, the competent authorities concerned can take all necessary procedural measures and shall inform each other of any important procedural measures which they have taken in the proceedings.
4. Whenever reasonably possible a competent authority involved in direct consultation shall reply to requests for information from other competent authorities involved in such consultations, except where doing so could harm essential national security interests.

Explanatory note:

1. *This provision is based on Article 10 of FD 2009/948/JHA ('Obligation to enter into direct consultations'). The aim of the consultation is to avoid adverse consequences such as ne bis in idem.*
2. *Paragraph 2 stresses the relevance of the principle of sincere cooperation as an overarching obligation and defines the concentration of the proceedings in one Member State as a desirable outcome of the consultation. Whereas in case of*

parallel proceedings the proceedings should always be concentrated, the concentration of multiple proceedings is not always possible or desirable from the viewpoint of the proper administration of justice.

3. *The opening of a consultation procedure does not rule out the adoption of procedural measures by the competent authorities. The competent authorities of the Member States may therefore continue parallel investigations, but only as long as this is necessary in order to establish the material facts of the case. They need inform each other only of important procedural measures taken (e.g. victim protection measures are important, whereas the award of legal aid is not important or relevant to the other Member State).*
4. *During the consultation procedure, the competent authorities should provide all necessary information to one another. However, this obligation does not apply where to provide the information would endanger national security interests.*

ARTICLE 8

Reasoned consensus and formal agreement on choice of forum

1. In order to reach a consensus on the concentration of proceedings including the final choice of forum, the competent authorities of the Member States shall assess the specific circumstances of the individual case in light of the factors for the choice of forum annexed to this Directive.
2. The competent authorities should aim to achieve such consensus as soon as possible and at the latest before either of the involved authorities presents the case to court for the purposes of prosecution or takes any measures which would have the effect of a final disposal of the case.
3. Where the competent authorities of the Member States agree that to do so would not jeopardise the investigation, they shall inform the suspect or accused and the victims of the existence of the consultation procedure and of the possibility to submit written observations within 15 days of the date of such notification.
4. When the competent authorities of the Member States concerned reach consensus, they shall conclude a formal agreement delineating the circumstances and the factors applied, and where to do so would not jeopardise the investigation, inform the suspect or accused and the victims thereof.

Explanatory note:

1. *Article 8 is a completely new provision. Differently from FD 2009/948/JHA, the new instrument will include as an Annex a set of factors for the choice of forum. Non-arbitrariness of the choice of the forum and the transparency of the factors applied are strictly interrelated. The requirement to reach a*

consensus on the final choice of forum – with the consequences stipulated in Article 9 – does not prevent the national authorities from reaching provisional agreement at an early stage of the consultation.

2. *In case of parallel proceedings and, where appropriate, in case of multiple proceedings, the consensus should be achieved before any of the authorities takes the case to court or takes other measures with the effect of finally disposing of the case. It is, however, not prohibited for both national authorities to go ahead with parallel proceedings even though this may eventually trigger the ne bis in idem principle.*
3. *The suspect or accused person and the victims should have the opportunity to submit their written observations in the course of the consultation procedure before consensus is reached. Although notification of the suspect or accused person and the victims is due only 'where the competent authorities agree that to do so would not jeopardise the investigation or the prosecution', this derogation is intended to be exceptional and must be applied narrowly.*
4. *In order to ensure non-arbitrariness and transparency, the consensus must be reasoned and formalised in a written agreement. It could be useful to develop a template annexed to the Directive for the use of national authorities.*

ARTICLE 9
Consequences of the agreement and transfer of proceedings

1. Following the agreement taken pursuant to Article 8 paragraph 4 to concentrate proceedings the national authorities of the other Member State shall transfer the file, refrain from taking further investigative or prosecutorial measures and close the case.
2. Any act with a view to proceedings taken in the transferring Member State before the conclusion of an agreement pursuant to Article 8 paragraph 4 shall be recognised in the receiving Member State as if it had been taken by the national authorities of that Member State, provided that such recognition does not give such an act a greater evidential weight than it has in the transferring Member State.
3. Any act which interrupts time limitation and which has been validly performed in the transferring Member State shall have the same effect in the receiving Member State and vice versa.
4. The transferring Member State regains the right to prosecute the case if the competent authority in the receiving Member State neither presents the case to a court for the purposes of prosecution nor takes other measures which would have the effect of a final disposal of the case.

Explanatory note:

1. *Article 9 is a new provision. It clarifies the consequences of the agreement and provides a legal basis to discontinue the proceedings at the national level and to transfer the file and the evidence to the other Member State. The provision is limited to parallel proceedings as multiple proceedings do not always lead to the concentration of the case.*

2-3. *Drawing from the Convention on Transfer of Proceedings of the Council of Europe, the new provision also lays down rules on the equivalence of procedural acts interrupting time limitation periods and on the recognition of evidence.*

4. *If the receiving Member State does not prosecute the case following the transfer, the transferring Member State's right to prosecute revives.*

ARTICLE 10
Remedies

Any agreement concluded pursuant to Article 8 paragraph 4 is without prejudice to legal remedies under national law to request judicial review on the choice of forum.

Explanatory note:

Article 10 does not affect national remedies. It does not define whether only the suspect or also the victim has a right to challenge the choice of forum. Nor does it define the grounds for a challenge (the forum choice or closing of the case, etc.). This does not preclude the possibility to challenge the decision in the courts of each of the Member States concerned.

CHAPTER 4
EUROJUST DECISION ON THE CHOICE OF FORUM

ARTICLE 11
Notification of Eurojust

1. Where no agreement on the choice of forum has been concluded within 60 days of the opening of the direct consultation pursuant to Article 7, any of the involved national authorities or the suspect may request that Eurojust exercise its competence to determine the choice of forum.
2. When a request pursuant to paragraph 1 has been submitted, Eurojust shall immediately notify the competent authorities of the other Member State concerned and, provided that the competent authorities of all Member States concerned agree that to do so would not jeopardise the investigation or the prosecution, also notify the suspects and the victims of the opening of a procedure to determine the choice of forum.

3. After the notification referred to in paragraph 2, the competent authorities of the Member States concerned shall transmit to Eurojust without delay all information which might be relevant for the determination of the choice of forum.

Explanatory note:

1. *Article 9 enables the competent national authorities involved in the horizontal consultation procedure as well as the suspect to trigger the binding decision of Eurojust where a decision on the choice of forum has not been adopted 60 days after the start of the consultation procedure. Eurojust cannot act ex officio.*
2. *When the request has been made by one of the national authorities involved, Eurojust shall immediately notify the other authority (-ies) and, if all concerned authorities agree that to do so would not jeopardise the investigation or the prosecution, also the suspect. This exception to the notification of the suspect must be interpreted narrowly. In particular, if the suspect had already been notified during the horizontal consultation, no objection can be raised to their notification by Eurojust.*
3. *The competent authorities shall provide Eurojust with all the information which might be relevant for the determination of the choice of forum. This should include, in particular, all the information considered in the horizontal consultation procedure.*

ARTICLE 12

Ongoing obligation and precautionary measures

Pending the decision of Eurojust, the competent authorities of the Member States concerned shall take appropriate investigative measures in consultation with Eurojust. They must also refrain from committing any act that may jeopardise the outcome of the procedure of Eurojust and, in particular, they must refrain from presenting the case to court for the purposes of prosecution or taking any measures which would have the effect of a final disposal of the case. The adoption of any coercive precautionary measure shall be immediately notified to Eurojust.

Explanatory note:

1. *This provision aims at ensuring the development and the outcome of the procedure conducted by Eurojust by preventing the national authorities from adopting any act that may jeopardise the outcome of the procedure. Subject to this proviso, national authorities may take investigative measures, but they must first consult Eurojust.*

2. *In particular, it prevents the national authorities from launching a prosecution in the proceedings referred to Eurojust. Such a standstill obligation is a concrete application of the principle of sincere cooperation. However, it does not prevent the national authorities from adopting coercive investigative or precautionary measures that are necessary and urgent. The adoption of any such measures must be promptly notified to Eurojust.*

ARTICLE 13

Eurojust's decision on the choice of forum

1. The Eurojust decision on the choice of forum should, in the case of parallel proceedings, lead to the concentration of the criminal proceedings in one Member State for the purpose of prosecution. The same shall apply to multiple proceedings, where appropriate.
2. In determining the choice of forum, Eurojust shall assess the facts and merits of the case in light of the factors set out in annex to this Regulation.
3. Within 15 days of notification pursuant to Article 11 paragraph 2, the competent authorities of the Member States concerned and, if they had been notified, the suspect and the victim, are entitled to submit written opinions.
4. If Eurojust deems the information transmitted pursuant to Article 11 paragraph 3 to be insufficient for determining the choice of forum, it shall request additional information from the competent authorities of the Member States concerned. This information shall be provided promptly and, at the latest, within 30 days.
5. Eurojust shall determine the choice of forum by issuing a written decision stating the reasons for the choice. The Eurojust decision on the choice of forum shall be binding upon the judicial authorities of the Member States concerned.
6. Following the adoption of the Eurojust decision on the choice of forum pursuant to paragraph 4 in case of parallel proceedings, the national authorities of the Member State(s) other than the one chosen shall transfer the file, refrain from taking further investigative or prosecutorial measures and close the case. The same applies in cases of multiple proceedings where the Eurojust decision on the choice of forum provides for their concentration.
7. Any act with a view to proceedings taken in the transferring Member State before the adoption of a decision pursuant to paragraph 4 shall be recognised in the receiving Member State as if it had been taken by the national authorities of that Member State, provided that such recognition does not give such an act greater evidential weight than it has in the transferring Member State.

8. Any act which interrupts time limitation and which has been validly performed in the transferring Member State shall have the same effect in the receiving Member State and vice versa.
9. The Eurojust decision on the choice of forum shall be adopted within 60 days of the opening of the procedure by Eurojust. When a request for additional information pursuant to paragraph 3 has been made this period can be extended by 30 days.
10. If the suspect is held in pre-trial detention during the Eurojust procedure, the period provided for the adoption of the Eurojust decision on the choice of forum under paragraph 9 is reduced to a maximum of 30 days. In the same circumstances, the extension allowed for the acquisition of additional information is limited to a maximum of 30 days.

Explanatory note:

Article 13 establishes a detailed procedural framework and the factors for the adoption of the decision on the choice of forum by Eurojust. Transparency, good administration of justice and sincere cooperation are the main principles inspiring the provision.

1. *The Eurojust decision on the choice of forum shall normally lead to concentration in the case of parallel proceedings in order to prevent a violation of the principle of ne bis in idem. In case of multiple proceedings, concentration may often not be the optimal solution but should be considered where appropriate in order to ensure the good administration of justice.*
2. *The second paragraph states the obligation for Eurojust to apply the factors for the choice of forum annexed to the Regulation. The Annex and the factors constitute an integral part of the instrument. The factors include priority factors, interest-based factors and factors not to be considered.*

3-4-9-10. Similarly to the horizontal procedure, where they have been notified of the choice of forum procedure the suspect and the victim are entitled to submit written observations. The procedure must progress speedily and deadlines are provided (60 days, extendable by a further 30 days where additional information is required). Stricter time limits apply in cases where the suspect is detained pending the outcome of the procedure.

5. *Eurojust's decision must provide reasons for the choice of forum. It is a judicial decision which is binding on the national authorities of the Member States; in particular, it implies the discontinuation of the proceedings in the Member State(s) other than the one recognised as competent by the Eurojust decision.*

6-7-8. *The proposed legal instrument regulates the consequences of the binding decision of Eurojust on the choice of forum. In case of parallel proceedings the need to concentrate the proceedings and the binding nature of the Eurojust decision require the Member State(s) other than that selected to close the case, transfer the file and to refrain from adopting any further investigative or prosecutorial measures. This provision applies to multiple proceedings only when the Eurojust decision provides for their concentration. In the same manner as for the horizontal procedure, paragraphs 7 and 8 lay down rules on procedural acts interrupting time limitation periods and for the recognition of evidence.*

ARTICLE 14

Judicial review of the Eurojust decision on the choice of forum

1. The suspect is considered to be directly affected in the sense of Article 263, paragraphs 4 and 5 TFEU. The Eurojust decision on the choice of forum is intended to produce legal effects in regard to the suspect.
2. The suspect and the national judicial authorities involved may launch an action for annulment against the Eurojust decision on choice of forum before the Court of Justice of the European Union pursuant to Article 263 paragraph 5 TFEU.

Explanatory note:

The binding decision of Eurojust on the choice of forum shall be reviewable before the Court of Justice of the European Union. An action for annulment can be launched by any of the Member States concerned or the suspect. The suspect, in particular, shall be considered fully entitled to have the decision annulled according to Article 263 paragraph 4 TFEU.

In case of inertia of Eurojust or failure to comply with the deadlines set under Article 13 the Member States concerned and the suspect are also entitled to launch an action for failure to act under Article 265 paragraph 1 TFEU.

ANNEX A—FACTORS RELEVANT TO THE CHOICE OF FORUM

The competent authorities of the Member States shall determine the choice of forum in accordance with the following factors:

FACTORS TO BE CONSIDERED

1. TERRITORIALITY

In principle, territoriality shall determine the jurisdiction to prosecute.

In case of crimes affecting the territory of more than one Member State, the competent authorities shall take into account where the majority or the most important part of the criminality occurred or where the majority or the most important part of the harmful effect or loss was sustained when determining the choice of forum. Harmful effect also includes state interests (such as offences against state security).

2. STAGE OF THE PROCEEDINGS—TRIAL-READINESS

When determining the choice of forum, the competent authorities shall compare and consider the state and the trial-readiness of the different proceedings.

3. INTERESTS OF THE SUSPECT

The competent authorities shall take into account the interests of the suspect and whether they would be prejudiced if any prosecution were to take place in one jurisdiction rather than another. Interests of the suspect could relate to his or her effective links with the jurisdiction of a Member State, such as: the duration of his or her residence, the ability to understand the language spoken in the Member State, the degree of integration of the suspect in the society of one Member State, the possibility for him or her to access an effective legal defence, or the presence of dependent family members on the territory of another Member State. The vulnerability of the suspect and the possibility to ensure adequate safeguards should be carefully assessed.

4. INTERESTS OF VICTIMS

The competent authorities shall take into account the interests of victims and whether they would be prejudiced if any prosecution were to take place in one jurisdiction rather than another. Interests of the victims might include the possibility to avoid their secondary victimisation and to resort to protective measures, especially in the case of vulnerable victims or violent crimes. The possibility for the victim to obtain adequate compensation could also be considered.

5. NEED TO RESORT TO MUTUAL LEGAL ASSISTANCE AND MUTUAL RECOGNITION INSTRUMENTS

For example, where the majority of the evidence is located in one of the involved Member States.

6. NEED FOR CONCENTRATION OF PROCEEDINGS

In case of multiple proceedings, in determining the choice of forum, the competent authorities shall consider the possibility to concentrate the proceedings and the overall costs of the proceedings.

FACTORS NOT TO BE CONSIDERED

In determining the choice of forum, the competent authorities of the Member States are not to consider:

1. DIVERGING RULES ON EVIDENCE

Courts in different jurisdictions have different rules for the acceptance of evidence often gathered in very diverse formats. The potential admissibility and acceptance of evidence by a court cannot be considered as a factor to determine where the prosecution should take place.

2. LEGAL REQUIREMENTS

The competent authorities shall not decide to prosecute in one jurisdiction rather than another simply in order to avoid having to comply with the legal obligations that apply in one jurisdiction but not in another.

3. SENTENCING POWERS

The sentencing powers of courts and detention circumstances in the different Member States shall not be a factor in deciding the jurisdiction in which a case should be prosecuted. The judicial authorities should not seek to prosecute cases in a jurisdiction where the penalties are highest.

ANNEX B—DIAGRAM: VERTICAL MECHANISM

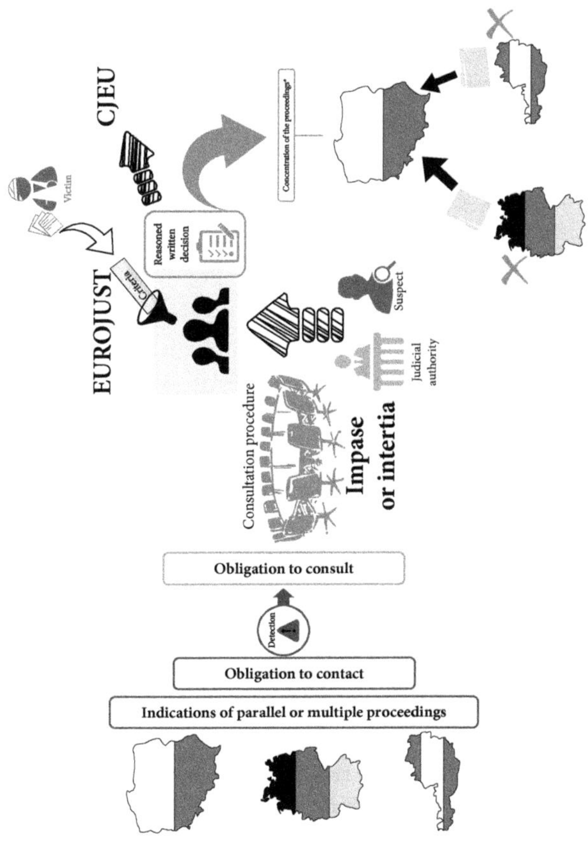

DRAFT TEXT

III. ALLOCATING THE EXERCISE OF JURISDICTION IN CRIMINAL PROCEEDINGS

Proposal for a

REGULATION OF THE EUROPEAN PARLIAMENT AND THE COUNCIL on the exercise of jurisdiction in the Area of Freedom, Security and Justice

The European Parliament and the Council of the European Union,

Having regard to the Treaty on the Functioning of the European Union, and in particular Article 82 paragraph 1 thereof,

Whereas:

(-) . . .

Have adopted this Regulation:

CHAPTER 1
GENERAL PROVISIONS

ARTICLE 1
Objectives

This Regulation aims at preventing and settling conflicts of jurisdiction through:

(a) ensuring the allocation to the forum best placed on consideration of good and proper administration of justice;

(b) reaching reasoned non-arbitrary consensus as to the choice of forum in cases where parallel or multiple proceedings are being conducted or are about to be conducted; and

(c) preventing situations where the same person is subject to parallel criminal proceedings in different Member States in respect of the same facts, where these might lead to the final disposal of the proceedings in two or more Member States, thereby constituting an infringement of principle of *'ne bis in idem'*.

Explanatory note:
The objective of the new instrument is threefold. It covers the prevention of violations of the principle of ne bis in idem, the guarantee of a non-arbitrary choice and also the allocation to the 'best placed' forum on consideration of the good and proper administration of justice by prioritising territorial jurisdiction. This latter additional objective substantially distinguishes the present instrument from the previous two.

The determination of the best placed forum is to be determined following the rules on the transfer in the interest of the good administration of justice (Article 9).

ARTICLE 2

Subject matter and scope

This Regulation aims at preventing and settling conflicts of jurisdiction through allocation of jurisdiction in relation to criminal offences committed within the Area of Freedom, Security and Justice.

ARTICLE 3

Definitions

1. For the purposes of this Regulation:

(a) 'parallel proceedings' means criminal proceedings which are conducted or about to be conducted in two or more Member States against the same suspect or accused in regard to the same facts;

(b) 'multiple proceedings' means criminal proceedings which are conducted or about to be conducted in two or more Member States against the same suspect or accused in relation to different facts, or against different suspects or accused persons in relation to the commission of the same offence;

(c) 'multi-territorial offence' means an offence the constitutive acts of which are committed over the territory of two or more Member States;

(d) 'competent authority' means a judicial authority or another authority, which is competent, under the law of its Member State, to carry out the acts envisaged by Article 2;

(e) 'contacting authority' means a competent authority which contacts another competent authority to confirm the existence of parallel or multiple proceedings;

(f) 'contacted authority' means the competent authority which is asked by a contacting authority to confirm the existence of parallel or multiple proceedings.

CHAPTER 2

RULES ON THE EXERCISE OF JURISDICTION

ARTICLE 4

Territorial jurisdiction

Within the Area of Freedom, Security and Justice, each Member State shall only exercise jurisdiction in respect of offences committed in its own territory as determined by national law.

Explanatory note:
Territoriality is the general rule for the allocation of exercise of jurisdiction in the Area of Freedom, Security and Justice. Extraterritoriality is therefore excluded. The definition of locus delict is left to national law. The same applies for the rules on the location of the conduct of accomplices, instigators and other participants.

ARTICLE 5

Multi-territorial offences

1. If more than one Member State has territorial jurisdiction in accordance with Article 4, the concerned Member States are obliged to allocate the exercise of jurisdiction to one Member State following the procedure pursuant Article 6.
2. When a competent authority of a Member State has indications that the proceedings conducted concern a multi-territorial offence, it shall contact the competent authority of that other Member State to confirm the existence of such parallel or multiple criminal proceedings, with a view to initiating a direct consultation as provided in Article 6.
3. Such indications may include cases where a suspected or accused person notifies the competent authority that he is subject to parallel or multiple proceedings in another Member State, or in case a relevant request for mutual legal assistance by a competent authority in another Member State reveals the possible existence of such parallel or multiple criminal proceedings, or in case a police authority provides information to this effect. When victims of crime have indications that parallel or multiple proceedings are being conducted in another Member State, the competent authority of a Member State shall upon request of the suspect or the victim contact the authorities of another Member State in accordance with Article 6.

Explanatory note:
Article 5 deals with multi-territorial offences, i.e. offences that are committed over the territory of different Member States (for instance, trafficking offences). In these cases the allocation of jurisdiction cannot work automatically and requires consultation between the various Member States involved.

2. *This paragraph establishes an obligation upon the judicial authorities to contact the corresponding authorities in the other concerned Member State(s) with a view to consultation. The trigger of the obligation is represented by 'indications' of parallel or multiple proceedings.*

ARTICLE 6

Consultation procedure and the allocation of the exercise of jurisdiction over multi-territorial offences

1. In order to allocate the exercise of jurisdiction in cases of multi-territorial offences, the competent national authorities of the Member States concerned

shall enter into direct consultations with a view to concentrating the proceedings in one Member State.

2. Where the competent authorities of the Member States agree that to do so would not jeopardise the investigation or the prosecution, they shall inform the suspect and the victims of the existence of the consultation procedure and of the possibility to submit written observations within 15 days from the date of notification.
3. In allocating the exercise of jurisdiction to one Member State, the competent authorities will take into account where the majority of the criminal activity took place, the interest of concentrating multiple proceedings in a single Member State, the number of suspects or accused persons involved, as well as post-offence facts, such as the location of evidence and of the suspect or accused person. In addition, factors such as residency of the suspect or accused person or victim and the prospect of resocialisation will be considered.
4. When the competent authorities of the Member States concerned reach consensus, they shall conclude a formal agreement delineating the circumstances and the factors applied.
5. The allocation of the exercise of jurisdiction as provided under this article is binding upon all Member States. The Member State to which the exercise of jurisdiction has not been allocated shall close the case.
6. The Member State that has not been allocated to exercise its jurisdiction retains an ongoing obligation to provide assistance to the Member State to which the exercise of jurisdiction has been allocated.
7. The Member State that has not been allocated to exercise its jurisdiction regains the right to prosecute the case if the Member State that has been allocated to exercise jurisdiction does not finally dispose of the case.

Explanatory note:

The consultation procedure is aimed at allocating jurisdiction by concentrating the proceedings for multi-territorial offences in a single Member State.

2. *This paragraph provides for a possible involvement of the suspect and the victim in the consultation by means of written observations. The notification and the potential involvement of the suspect and victim are however conditional: notification shall be made only when it would not jeopardise the investigation or the prosecution. This caveat leaves a margin of discretion to the judicial authorities; however, such discretion—limiting the right of the defence—shall be exercised narrowly.*

3. *This paragraph lays down the factors for the allocation. The list of factors is not hierarchical and encompasses pre- and post-offence factors as well as interest-based factors.*
5. *The outcome of the consultation procedure is binding upon all Member States. As a direct effect of the allocation, the non-selected Member States shall close their cases.*
6. *The closing of the cases does not exempt the non-selected Member States from their obligation to provide assistance to the selected Member State. This is a concrete application of the principle of sincere cooperation.*
7. *If the selected Member State does not finally dispose of the case following the transfer by bringing it to court or reaching an out-of-court-settlement, the non-selected Member State's right to prosecute revives.*

ARTICLE 7
Legal remedy

1. If an agreement on the allocation of exercise of jurisdiction has not been concluded 30 days after the suspect or accused person has been notified in conformity with Article 6, the suspect or accused person may make a request to the competent court in one of the Member States in which he is under investigation or being prosecuted concerning the same conduct, with a view to allocating the exercise of jurisdiction to one Member State. In doing so, the competent national court shall in particular apply the rules provided under Article 4 and 6 paragraph 3.
2. The agreement as provided under Article 6 is reviewable following the rules of the national system to which the exercise of jurisdiction has been allocated.
3. Member States shall provide a legal remedy on the exercise of jurisdiction for the suspect or accused person and victim in the event that a Member State neither exercises its jurisdiction nor transfers the exercise of jurisdiction to another Member State.

CHAPTER 3
TRANSFER OF EVIDENCE

ARTICLE 8
Transfer of evidence

The file and the evidence gathered before the exercise of jurisdiction has been allocated in accordance with Articles 5 or 6 shall be transferred to the Member State that will exercise jurisdiction.

CHAPTER 4
TRANSFER OF THE EXERCISE OF JURISDICTION

ARTICLE 9
Transfer in the interests of the good administration of justice

1. In the interests of the good administration of justice, the competent authorities of the Member States concerned may by agreement transfer the exercise of jurisdiction to another Member State in case of parallel and multiple proceedings.
2. Interests of good administration of justice are expressed by factors such as that:
   (a) the suspected person is ordinarily resident in another Member State;
   (b) the suspected person is a national of another Member State or that State is his State of origin;
   (c) the suspected person is undergoing or is to undergo a sentence involving deprivation of liberty in another Member State;
   (d) proceedings are underway in another Member State against the suspected person in relation to other offences;
   (e) transfer of the exercise of jurisdiction is warranted in the interest of arriving at the truth and in particular that the most important items of evidence are located in another Member State;
   (f) enforcement in another Member State of a sentence if one were passed is likely to improve the prospects for the social rehabilitation of the person sentenced;
   (g) the presence of the suspected person cannot be ensured at the hearing of proceedings in the Member State transferring the exercise of jurisdiction and that his physical presence at the hearing of proceedings in the other Member State can be ensured;
   (h) the transferring Member State considers that it could not itself enforce a sentence if one were passed, even by having recourse to surrender, and that the other Member State could do so.
3. Suspects or accused persons and victims may request that competent authorities reconsider the transfer in the interests of the good administration of justice as referred in paragraph 1.
4. Any act with a view to proceedings taken in the Member State transferring the exercise of jurisdiction before the adoption of a decision to transfer shall be recognised in the Member State accepting the exercise of jurisdiction as if it had been taken by the national authorities of that Member State, provided that such recognition does not give such an act a greater evidential weight than it has in the transferring Member State.

5. Any act which interrupts time limitation and which has been validly performed in the transferring Member States shall have the same effect in the receiving Member State and vice versa.

Explanatory note:

This Article implements the third objective of the instrument: ensuring the allocation of the exercise of jurisdiction to the best-placed forum. Such allocation operates by means of a transfer of both the proceedings and the jurisdiction when the best-placed forum is not territorially competent on its own (derivative jurisdiction). The benchmark for determining the better placement of a Member State is represented by the interests of the good administration of justice.

2. *The interests of the good administration of justice are expressed by a set of factors. The list is inspired by Article 8 of the 1972 CoE Convention on Transfer of Proceedings.*

ARTICLE 10

Repeal and replacement of Framework Decision 2009/948/JHA

1. FD 2009/948/JHA is hereby repealed and replaced.

PART II

PREVENTING AND RESOLVING CONFLICTS OF JURISDICTION IN EU CRIMINAL LAW

PREFACE TO PART II

PAULO PINTO DE ALBUQUERQUE

These are difficult times for European criminal law. Governments seem misguided by a strictly efficiency oriented approach to criminal law. This kind of reasoning is part and parcel of the now prevailing ideologically retrogressive policy mix composed of a purely retributivist approach to criminal law, a prosecution and police-interests driven strategy on criminal procedure, a purposefully hardened prison system and a truly repressive "crimmigration" process. Such liberticidal policy mix shows the worst face of Europe in recent criminal law history, as if *Dei Delitti e delle Pene* had never been written.

Retributivism is plain to see, for example, in the justification of the shoot-to-kill policy of the police in anti-terrorism action and the application of a subjective test to putative self-defence by police officers.[1] The same prosecution and police-interests driven strategy reigns in criminal procedure. The most eloquent example is the denial of the right of access to a lawyer without compelling reasons during the initial questioning of the suspect at the police station and the admission and assessment of the issuing incriminating evidence in trial.[2] The punitive effect of such policies is exacerbated by a purposefully hardened system of prison law. In a revival of the "just deserts" tactic to address serious crime, whole-life prisoners are deprived of an effective parole mechanism[3] and suspect offenders are interned indeterminately without judicial oversight.[4]

These policies also chime with an expansion of the use of criminal law in the field of migration law, with a view to maximise the potential repressive effect of the latter with the means of the former. The most powerful instrument of this new trend of "crimmigration" is evidently a toughened detention policy of asylum-seekers and unlawful migrants,[5] which is often articulated with a shamelessly implacable expulsion policy, including of terminally ill aliens.[6]

Meanwhile, the protection provided to crime victims, including those victims of serious offences, like torture, has seen no real improvement in the recent past, as demonstrated by the grant of State immunity[7] and of immunity to foreign State

1 See *Armani da Silva v. the United Kingdom* [GC], no. 5878/08, 30 March 2016.

2 See *Ibrahim and Others v. the United Kingdom* [GC], nos. 50541/08, 50571/08, 50573/08 and 40351/09, 13 September 2016.

3 *Hutchinson v. the United Kingdom (GC)*, no. 57592/08, 17 January 2017.

4 See *Hassan v. the United Kingdom* [GC], no. 29750/09, 16 September 2014.

5 *Abdullahi Elmi and Aweys Abubakar v. Malta*, nos. 25794/13 and 28151/13, 22 November 2016

6 *SJ v. Belgium* [GC], no. 70055/10, judgment of 19 March 2015.

7 *Al-Adsani v. the United Kingdom* [GC], no. 35763/97, ECHR 2001-XI.

officials concerning civil claims for torture[8] as well as the denial of forum of necessity or universal civil jurisdiction for civil claims for damages resulting from torture allegedly suffered in a third State.[9]

In this adverse context, it comes as no surprise that the *ne bis in idem* principle has been significantly watered down, since it is no longer the expression of a subjective right of the defendant, but a mere rule to guarantee the authority of the *chose jugée*, with the sole purpose of ensuring the punitive interest of the State and the impugnability of State adjudicatory decisions. More importantly, the *ne bis in idem* principle now applies to a lesser degree to sanctions falling outside the hard core of criminal law, such as tax penalties.[10] This evidently overlooks the fact that the content of a non-derogable Convention right, such as *ne bis in idem*, must not be substantially different depending on which area of law is concerned. By so doing, courts open the door to an unprecedented, Leviathan-like punitive policy based on multiple State-pursued proceedings, strategically connected and put in place in order to achieve the maximum possible repressive effect. It is no excuse to argue that, in an Article 4 of Additional Protocol No. 7 context, States should enjoy a wide margin of appreciation in this matter as long as the punishment appears to pursue a legitimate aim and does not entail an excessive or disproportionate burden for the defendant. The reason why this line of reasoning is wrong is plain to see: as framed by the mentioned Protocol 7, *ne bis in idem* is a non-derogable right and therefore States enjoy no margin of appreciation. For the same reason, there are two lines of argumentation that should be avoided in this context. As a matter of principle, it is wrong to invoke far-reaching, adverse and unforeseeable effects of penal law choices, without any concrete assessment of the concrete consequences of each choice. Such an *argumentum ad terrorem*, which plays the fear-appeal card, is not a legal argument and therefore should be given no credit whatsoever in a doctrinal discussion. The other example of an inadmissible fallacy is the argument that several European States which have opted for a certain specific penal law solution have pleaded for its maintenance, expressing views and concerns in a more or less concerted manner. This is called an *argumentum ad nauseam*, playing on the repetition of the argument by several interested stakeholders, and not on its merits. It should also be avoided, both when parliaments and governments legislate as well as when courts adjudicate.

These are some of the challenges with which the European Union is confronted when regulating the conflicts of jurisdiction in European Union criminal law. It is imperative that the liberal tradition of the continent is not sacrificed on the altar of

8 *Jones and Others v. the United Kingdom*, no. 34356/06 and no. 40528/06, 14 January 2014.

9 *Naït-Liman v. Switzerland* [GC], no. 51357/07, 15 March 2018

10 *A and B. v. Norway (GC)*, nos. 24130/11 and 29758/11, 15 November 2016.

the efficiency of the penal system. Today more than ever, it is important to recall that one major legacy left by the Enlightenment in Europe was precisely the liberalisation of criminal law. That is also the driving force of this book. This book presents a rich, multi-faceted overview of the many delicate topics related to the problem of regulating conflicts of jurisdiction and *ne bis in idem* in European criminal law. Let us hope that due attention is given, by the competent authorities, to this remarkable work of scientific research, and that significant progress is made in the establishment of a legal framework for the conflicts of jurisdiction in criminal law and the implementation of the *ne bis in idem* guarantee in Europe.

Paulo Pinto de Albuquerque
Judge at the ECHR
Full professor at the law faculty of the Catholic University, Lisbon
Strasbourg, 1 May 2018

INTRODUCTION TO THE ARTICLES

KATALIN LIGETI AND GAVIN ROBINSON

The chapters in this volume flesh out the insights, debates, and agreed principles which have steered the Project Working Group and core group along the road to the models for European Union (EU) legislation which we now propose. Whilst thorough treatment of conflicts of jurisdiction issues in criminal law in Europe is not novel (see in particular Max Planck Institute, Michiel Luchtman, and Böse/Meyer/Schneider), no such study has yet prompted legislative action at the EU level. This stands in contrast to comparable efforts to address conflicts of jurisdiction in private international law, spearheaded by our project partner the European Law Institute (ELI). By taking a fresh look at this multifaceted issue in the criminal law realm, beginning from the standpoint of a comparison with private international law, whilst anchoring the analysis on the explicit legal bases on hand following the Lisbon Treaty reforms, the research team behind the present proposals hopes to buck that trend and make a concrete—and in our view overdue—impact on EU policy.

In Part I of the volume, the legal and policy background, project methodology and milestones, and reasons for the (choices made within the) three distinct models have been set out within the ELI Instrument. Part II thus begins with a trio of chapters which discuss in greater detail both the project's formative empirical sources and the legislative routes available to its output. First, in Chapter 1 Angelo Marletta presents the results of field research carried out in cooperation with national desks at Eurojust. In Chapter 2, responding to the (by EU standards, relatively new) post-Lisbon arrangements mentioned above, Martin Wasmeier provides an analysis of the apposite legal bas(es) for the EU legislation aiming to prevent and resolve conflicts of jurisdiction in criminal law which the research aims to spur on. Insight gleaned from several national criminal justice systems also informed the Working Group's thinking. An example is found in Chapter 3, where Miguel Carmona Ruano, the Spanish Liaison Magistrate to the United Kingdom (UK), shares insights on conflicts of criminal jurisdiction in practice in Spain and the UK from a Spanish perspective.

The academic contributions herein are not intended as mere explanations of the choices made within the proposed models, but also to foster debate more generally as to the potential challenges, conditions, and limitations facing any attempt to take decisive action to prevent and resolve conflicts of criminal jurisdiction within the EU. In Chapter 4, Angelo Marletta sets the scene with a general discussion of forum choice in the Area of Freedom, Security and Justice, before Katalin Ligeti addresses one such challenge in Chapter 5: the growth of 'criminal administrative' sanctions—and the well-established practice in several European jurisdictions of combining such measures with criminal law sanctions *sensu stricto*—in a dual-track enforcement system. Whereas it was decided that the proposed models should focus on criminal law *au sens propre,* Ligeti directly addresses the challenge of extending *ne bis in idem* protection across administrative law and criminal law, with the emphasis on the latest developments in jurisprudence between the Strasbourg and Luxembourg courts.

Another scoping decision saw the Working Group 'limit' application of the models to conflicts of criminal jurisdiction across the board, thereby encompassing all criminal offences. Notwithstanding this, the question may be raised as to whether certain categories of crime require a tailored approach, especially where their very nature may be particularly liable to trigger overlapping claims to jurisdiction—or, indeed, challenge the very concepts (for instance, territoriality) upon which allocation has hitherto been organised. In this vein, in Chapter 6 Gavin Robinson explores conflicts of jurisdiction and forum choice in cyberspace.

As mentioned above, it was the comparison with solutions adopted in international private law which first triggered the Working Group's collaboration with the ELI. Thus, in addition to bolstering the proposed models for EU legislation, the fruits of this comparison are found in Chapters 7 and 8, where Pietro Ortolani and Aukje van Hoek respectively offer expert opinions and possible lessons from civil law.

What does it mean to be an EU citizen where multiple Member States are locked in a positive (or negative) conflict of criminal jurisdiction within the AFSJ? What role should the citizen-defendant play in the resolution of such conflicts, and to what extent should the outcome thereof be foreseeable? This theme is critically unpacked by Michiel Luchtman in Chapter 9. Whilst that chapter's focus is squarely on the defendant, in Chapter 10 Michele Simonato then shifts our focus onto the victim. Underlining that victims' interests as regards conflicts of jurisdiction are as multifarious as the very circumstances of their victimisation, Simonato couples a commentary on the forms in which victims are included in the procedural models set out in the project outcomes with an analysis of the justifiable limits of such involvement.

The volume closes by turning to arguably the most important related policy development coming fast down the track: the establishment of a European Public Prosecutor's Office (EPPO). As explained in Chapter 11 by Hans-Holger Herrnfeld, the EPPO mechanism for case allocation is based on a hierarchical list of criteria—differently to each of the models proposed by the present project.

Finally, the Working Group would like to express its sincere gratitude to the ELI, to the Luxembourg Fonds National de la Recherche (FNR), and to Oxford University Press for their crucial and constructive support throughout the process culminating in the present volume.

1

REPORT ON THE FIELD RESEARCH AT EUROJUST, FEBRUARY 2015

ANGELO MARLETTA

PRELIMINARY NOTE

Eurojust contributed to the three-year project entitled 'Prevention and Settlement of Conflicts of Exercise of Jurisdiction in Criminal Law', led by the University of Luxembourg. In this context, Dr Angelo Marletta also interviewed representatives from the Eurojust National Desks and the Secretary to the European Judicial Network, all of whom volunteered. These interviews took place in February 2015. The report is a summary of the field research, which is based on the interview transcripts. The transcripts should be considered raw material, neither verified nor edited, and not reflecting a Eurojust position. Also to be noted is that the Eurojust document, 'Guidelines for deciding "Which jurisdiction should prosecute?"', which was revised by Eurojust in 2016, after the interviews took place, is not reflected in the report.

I. INTRODUCTION

The three model frameworks on the prevention and settlement of conflicts of exercise of jurisdiction are based inter alia on the results of field research carried out at Eurojust. Through empirical research in the form of interviews, we acquired data on Eurojust's experience of the resolution of conflicts of jurisdiction. The aim was to enable us to find out the deficiencies in the current legal regime and the problems encountered by Eurojust with conflicts of jurisdiction in general and parallel proceedings in particular. In theory, Eurojust has been tasked with playing a major role in supporting European Union (EU) Member States to determine the appropriate jurisdiction (cf. Articles 82(1)(b) and 85(1)(c) TFEU[1]). The rationale behind the field research approach was to obtain a clearer picture on the criteria applied by Eurojust in settling conflicts of jurisdiction and to analyse the follow-up of the decisions taken by Eurojust on the matter.

1 Articles 82(1)(b) and 85(1)(c) TFEU refer to the tasks of Eurojust in preventing, settling, and resolving conflicts of jurisdiction.

Following the kick-off meeting of the project a questionnaire (annexed to this report) was developed by the Principal Investigator and the author of this report and discussed with the members of the Working Group and Eurojust's legal service that helped in preparing the interviews. The national desks at Eurojust were invited to participate in the field research and were presented with the questionnaire ahead of the interviews. Interviews were held in February 2015 with fourteen national desks[2] and the Secretary to the European Judicial Network (EJN) in criminal matters.

II. SUMMARY OF FIELD RESEARCH

The following section presents the main findings of the interviews, supplemented by the Report of Eurojust's Casework Experience in the Field of Prevention and Resolution of Conflicts of Jurisdiction.[3]

A. The legal role of Eurojust

In 2003, Eurojust issued guidelines for deciding which jurisdiction should prosecute.[4] These guidelines set out certain criteria to solve conflicts of jurisdictions between Member States' authorities. These guidelines are applied at the meetings held at Eurojust between the national authorities responsible for investigation and prosecution and who represent the Member States involved in a cross-border case. However, some limits of these guidelines are clearly visible. First, they do not have binding effect: Member States are not obliged to comply with them. Second, there is no hierarchy among these criteria. Third, interested persons are not involved, so the prosecuting authority essentially decides upon the choice of forum. This raises concerns as to Article 6 of the European Convention on Human Rights (ECHR), whereby the tribunal must be 'established by law', that is, by a law already in force at the time the crime is committed.

In 2005, the European Commission launched a consultation on conflicts of jurisdiction in criminal matters, including the principle of *ne bis in idem*. The result was the 'Green Paper on Conflicts of Jurisdiction and the Principle of *ne bis in idem* in Criminal Proceedings', published on 23 December 2005.[5] The Green Paper, as well

2 Interviews were conducted with the following national desks: Austria (AT), Belgium (BE), Czech Republic (CZ), Germany (DE), Denmark (DK), Spain (ES), France (FR), Ireland (IE), Italy (IT), The Netherlands (NL), Portugal (PT), Sweden (SE), Slovakia (SK), and United Kingdom (UK).

3 Eurojust, 'Report of Eurojust's Casework Experience in the Field of Prevention and Resolution of Conflicts of Jurisdiction' (4 June 2015) http://www.eurojust.europa.eu/Practitioners/operational/Pages/Guidelines-on-jurisdiction.aspx (last accessed 23 April 2018).

4 Eurojust, 'Guidelines for Deciding "Which Jurisdiction Should Prosecute?"'. These guidelines were revised in 2016 http://www.eurojust.europa.eu/Practitioners/operational/Pages/Guidelines-on-jurisdiction.aspx (last accessed 23 April 2018).

5 Commission of the European Communities, 'Green Paper on Conflicts of Jurisdiction and the Principle of ne bis in idem in Criminal Proceedings' COM(2005) 696 final.

as the related working paper, identified and analysed the main problems in this field, envisaging a mechanism of consultation among Member States leading to the potential solution of a conflict of jurisdiction.

Following the Commission's efforts, a proposal presented by a group of Member States in the Council led to the adoption of the Council FD on Prevention and Settlement of Conflicts of Exercise of Jurisdiction in Criminal Proceedings,[6] which was adopted on 30 November 2009, shortly before the entry into force of the Lisbon Treaty. The FD establishes a procedural framework for reaching consensus on which Member States should investigate and prosecute the case. Where Member States do not reach consensus, the matter shall, where appropriate, be referred to Eurojust.[7]

Pursuant to Articles 6(1)(a)(ii) and 7(1)(a)(ii) Eurojust Decision (EJD),[8] Eurojust may ask the competent authorities of the Member States concerned to accept that one of them may be in a better position to undertake an investigation or to prosecute specific acts. The College of Eurojust may also intervene in the resolution of a case of conflicts of jurisdiction when two or more national members cannot agree on how to resolve a case of conflict[9] and issue a written non-binding opinion on the case. Member States may decide not to comply with the above-mentioned request or the written opinion; under these circumstances and according to Article 8 EJD, they shall inform Eurojust of their decision and of the reasons for it.

Member States shall further ensure that their national members at Eurojust are informed of cases where conflicts of jurisdiction have arisen or are likely to arise, pursuant to Article 13(7)(a) EJD.

Beyond the EJD and the FD 2009/948/JHA, there are several other legal instruments in the area of criminal matters that may trigger Eurojust's involvement in questions of conflict of jurisdiction with the aim of centralising proceedings in a single Member State.[10]

6 Council FD 2009/948/JHA of 30 November 2009 on prevention and settlement of conflicts of exercise of jurisdiction in criminal proceedings [2009] OJ L328/42.

7 See art 12(2) of the FD.

8 Consolidated version of Council Decision 2002/187/JHA of 28 February 2002 setting up Eurojust with a view to reinforcing the fight against serious crime [2002] OJ L63/1; see Council Decision 2009/426/JHA of 16 December 2008 on the strengthening of Eurojust and amending Decision 2002/187/JHA setting up Eurojust with a view to reinforcing the fight against serious crime [2009] OJ L138/14.

9 See art 7(2) EJD. In this case and where the matter could not be resolved through mutual agreement between the national authorities concerned, the College shall be asked to issue a written non-binding opinion on the case.

10 For instance, the FD 2002/584/JHA of 13 June 2002 on the European arrest warrant (art 16(2)), the FD 2005/222/JHA of 24 February 2005 on attacks against information systems (art 10(4)) OJ L69/67, and the FD 2008/841/JHA of 24 October 2008 on the fight against organised crime [2008] OJ L300/42 (art 7(2)).

B. Parallel proceedings

1. The nature of parallel proceedings

Parallel investigations are common in the EU and most frequently occur in cases where the offence itself is of a cross-border nature. Thus, parallel proceedings are often encountered in relation to the trafficking of goods (in particular drugs) and human beings (THB).[11] In addition, most desks mentioned financial crimes such as VAT fraud, money laundering, and Euro counterfeiting as crimes that are very likely to generate parallel investigations. Owing to its ubiquitous nature, cybercrime has been identified as an emerging field of conflicts of jurisdiction, although not many cases have yet been encountered by the majority of desks. As of the date of the interviews, Eurojust was mainly concerned with traditional crimes that involved the physical crossing of borders of goods or human beings. The casework indicates that conflicts of jurisdiction are not restricted to specific criminal acts but arise in all kinds of crime, for instance where victims report a case in two Member States because the crime occurred whilst travelling, or where there are multiple victims in different Member States. It has been explained that increased movement of goods and persons goes hand-in-hand with an increase in conflicts of jurisdiction.

Almost all desks considered the existence of parallel investigations beneficial: they may smooth and intensify traditional mutual legal assistance (MLA) at an operational level. Several desks explained that in certain circumstances parallel investigations may be an express requirement for setting up joint investigations teams (JITs).

2. Detection of parallel proceedings

Parallel proceedings can be detected in numerous ways and at different stages of proceedings. Detection may even occur by mere coincidence before proceedings are brought to the attention of Eurojust. Parallel proceedings are often detected early in an investigation through police cooperation, at the execution of MLA requests or European arrest warrants (EAWs).[12] One desk explained that the Swedish initiative on the exchange of information between police authorities is the best option for identifying parallel proceedings.[13]

11 The totality of the interviewees mentioned trafficking offences.

12 As regards European arrest warrants, parallel proceedings can also be detected at Eurojust level when Eurojust is informed of competing warrants issued on the basis of FD 2002/584/JHA.

13 See Council FD 2006/960/JHA of 18 December 2006 on simplifying the exchange of information and intelligence between law enforcement authorities of the Member States of the European Union [2006] OJ L386/89.

At a later stage of investigations, defendants themselves or their counsel may also notify national authorities of parallel proceedings. Furthermore, the involvement of Europol/Interpol or requests under Article 13 EJD may lead to the detection of parallel proceedings. Although Article 13(7) EJD lays down a clear duty for Member States to inform their national members of all cases where conflicts of jurisdiction have arisen or are likely to arise, several interviewees questioned the effectiveness of that article. The number of cases reported to Eurojust on the basis of Article 13(7) EJD is very low.[14] National authorities seem to be reluctant to forward information to their national desks at Eurojust. Also, the secrecy of investigations in some Member States, when strictly applied, might be an obstacle in this context.

Some interviewees also attributed a lack of awareness of parallel proceedings to the data protection regime currently applied at Eurojust. Data retention within Eurojust's case management system is limited to a maximum period of three years, which is considered inadequate for the purpose of detecting parallel investigations and preventing conflicts of jurisdiction. Moreover, some desks even delete data immediately after the closure of a case and thereby jeopardise the identification of concurring proceedings. According to one interviewee, approximately 70 per cent of all cases are normally closed after one year, which renders it almost impossible to find a link between a closed case and potential parallel investigations in another Member State in Eurojust's case management system. Hence, even where information has been transmitted to Eurojust, parallel investigations may remain undetected.

Accordingly, there have been calls for more reliable information being available to facilitate the work of the national desks. In this context, various desks have suggested an inter-connection of existing national judicial databases to allow for a 'hit/no-hit' search tool at Eurojust. Such a remote search tool may facilitate the detection of parallel proceedings, while also providing information about the progress of investigations. A national desk suggested that by implementing a centralised searching point, data retention by Eurojust itself would be rendered obsolete, because remote searches would instantly show whether there is a hit (on a parallel investigation) in any of the connected national databases. If so, the respective national desks could then discuss the case even at a very early stage and start finding a solution. However, in practice this would require all Member States to operate a national database including all cases, which, for the time being, is not the case.

There is consensus that it is in everyone's interests to detect parallel proceedings as early as possible. The ideal situation would be that national investigating or prosecuting authorities proactively check the existence of parallel investigations whenever a case contains cross-border elements.

14 For instance, a total of 21 cases in 2013 and 28 cases in 2014. See Annex 2 to Eurojust, 'Report of Eurojust's Casework Experience' (n 3).

3. Parallel investigations and the role of JITs in the prevention of conflicts of jurisdiction

As previously stated, parallel investigations are commonly considered beneficial for combating crime in the EU as they inter alia smooth and intensify the traditional MLA at an operational level. However, this depends on parallel investigations being performed in a coordinated way. Coordination requires awareness of the existence as well as the progress of parallel investigations. Once parallel proceedings are identified, information exchange can be coordinated, for instance the sharing of evidence through letters of request (LoRs). Parallel investigations are particularly advantageous with regard to (complex) criminal organisations that operate across borders. Several autonomous investigations facilitate the capturing of the full picture of the criminal activity. In such cases, the disclosure of one investigation does not hinder the continuation in secret of another investigation.

Previous experience in cooperation with other Member States has been identified as a significant advantage for cooperation in future parallel investigations in the Member States concerned.

Once parallel investigations are detected, a JIT is generally seen as an excellent means for anticipating and avoiding conflicts. Several desks have pointed out that, under certain circumstances, the prior existence of parallel investigations is a condition for setting up a JIT.

Those that have previously been involved in JITs value them as a constructive way of anticipating potential problems, distributing tasks, and resolving disputes. Further, it has been explained that JITs allow for more intense discussions than a coordination meeting and facilitate subsequent decisions on which jurisdiction should prosecute.

Some desks have reported a history of JITs with particular Member States, which may indicate a reluctance of other Member States to engage in JITs. In fact, experience with JITs differs substantially. Notwithstanding the general positive reception of JITs, one desk reported that it is generally opposed to JITs and has no experience with them at all, whereas other desks report extensive experience. For instance, as of February 2015, the United Kingdom had had approximately 60 JITs since 2002, with a steady increase to the recent average of between twelve and thirteen each year. Some desks explained that they particularly encourage the setting-up of JITs. In contrast, one national desk stated that, although not opposed to JITs, it preferred classical MLA to cooperation through a JIT.

Almost all of the interviewees acknowledged that risks and drawbacks tend to arise when parallel investigations are uncoordinated. Non-coordination can be the result of a lack of awareness of parallel proceedings or ignorance of proceedings in a third state.[15]

15 For instance, where a Member State issues a LoR to another Member State and the latter opens its own investigation upon receipt of the LoR.

Possible drawbacks stemming from uncoordinated parallel proceedings have been generally related to *ne bis in idem* problems, waste of resources, and to the risk of mutually jeopardising the investigations (for instance through the execution of untimely arrests). Uncoordinated investigations may also place burdens on victims and witnesses, in the sense that it may be difficult for them to attend or follow investigations in more than one Member State.

One desk also expressed concerns that uncoordinated investigations may result in competition between the investigating authorities. In cases of organised crime, further concerns were raised in relation to a misunderstanding of the scope of the criminal group if the prosecutors involved only focus on their domestic part.

Finally, a concentration of previously uncoordinated proceedings at a later stage may lead to problems in terms of the admissibility of evidence gathered earlier on.

C. Resolution of conflicts of jurisdiction

1. Deciding on which jurisdiction should prosecute

If conflicts of jurisdiction arise, Eurojust is entitled to issue recommendations and non-binding opinions under Articles 6 and 7 EJD, defining which Member State is in a better position to pursue an investigation or to prosecute specific acts. The majority of desks have explained that they consider the 2003 Eurojust Guidelines for deciding 'which jurisdiction should prosecute?' to be very useful.[16] The flexibility of the guidelines and their 'reasonableness' are particularly welcomed, while the introduction of a list of binding criteria is generally opposed, for various reasons. The idea of inserting a flexible list of criteria in a binding legal instrument (Directive or Regulation) has not, however, been completely rejected. One reason is the overall satisfaction with the existing non-binding guidelines; another reason is the risks stemming from non-adherence to binding guidelines. Considering the appreciation of the existing guidelines, it is somehow surprising that—according to two desks—these guidelines are seldom applied.

Similarly, Eurojust rarely makes use of its powers under Article 7(1)(a)(ii) (formal recommendation by the College) or Article 7(2) (written non-binding opinions by the College) of the EJD. In fact, for the period 2003–2014 only four cases were registered on the basis of Article 7(1)(a)(ii),[17] while Article 7(2), to date, has never

16 The UK Crown Prosecution Service has even expressly adopted the guidelines in its own legal guidance on conflicts of jurisdiction http://www.cps.gov.uk/legal/h_to_k/jurisdiction/ (last accessed 3 June 2017).

17 These cases concerned a case of environmental crime, a fraud case, a murder case, and a VAT fraud case. See Eurojust, 'Report of Eurojust's Casework Experience' (n 3) 3, with further references.

been invoked.[18] The model in Article 7(2), under which the College shall be asked to issue a written non-binding opinion on the case, was criticised as being unworkable for Eurojust. One desk explained that this is primarily for diplomacy reasons: one party may feel insulted that the College was requested to issue a decision, rather than further negotiations taking place between the parties concerned. The receipt of a decision—although non-binding—by jurists 'coming from a different legal culture' is not considered very helpful. In sensitive cases, there may also be a national interest in refraining from disclosing details of the case as broadly as to the College.

Accordingly, conflicts of jurisdiction are preferably and commonly settled consensually between the national desks concerned during coordination meetings at Eurojust or in the framework of JITs and do not need the intervention of the College.[19] Although the Eurojust recommendation is not binding, there has been no controversy on the follow-up.

It has been stressed that consensus is far more easily achieved in cases of positive conflicts of jurisdiction than in cases of negative conflicts of jurisdiction. The latter refers to situations where either none of the Member States involved has jurisdiction, or where the Member States concerned are in principle competent, but refrain from investigation and/or prosecution. A Member State may prefer not to prosecute owing to a lack of resources or may argue that it has other priorities (principle of opportunity).

As a general perception, negative conflicts are less frequent than positive conflicts of jurisdiction, but they are far more difficult to solve.[20]

2. Criteria to determine jurisdiction

There is a general presumption that the Member State where the majority of criminality occurred, or the majority of loss was sustained, should prosecute. Hence, in the majority of cases, territoriality and active personality form the jurisdictional basis for prosecution. While territoriality remains a dominant criterion, other criteria such as the nationality and/or the place of residence of the defendant(s) and/or the victim(s), or the place where most evidence is present can also be of relevance in the assessment.

Further factors such as the interests of the victim, the interests of the defendant, the admissibility of evidence, the location of the suspect, and a concrete possibility

18 In the Report of Eurojust's Casework Experience (n 3) it has been stated that art 7(2) EJD has not been applied as yet.

19 This informal approach to address conflicts of jurisdiction is confirmed by the limited number of cases registered in Eurojust's case management system; cf. Annex 1 to Eurojust, 'Report of Eurojust's Casework Experience' (n 3).

20 For an example cf. Eurojust, 'Report of Eurojust's Casework Experience' (n 3) 4, with further references.

of having him or her surrendered may also be relevant in the assessment of who should prosecute. In each case, questions of jurisdiction have to be decided on a case-by-case basis by the Member States concerned.

As regards the admissibility of evidence as a criterion, the national desks have stressed that the choice of forum is generally made in favour of the jurisdiction of the Member State where the greatest part of the evidence is physically located and not in order to avoid or circumvent the stricter rules of admissibility of another jurisdiction.

The interests of the victim often play only a minor role in deciding who should prosecute. However, several desks have identified an increasing trend to exercise jurisdiction on the basis of passive personality in THB cases, where the victims are often very vulnerable. In these cases, the interests of the victim can become the deciding factor in transferring proceedings to the victim's home state.

According to the majority of the interviewees, the interests of the defendant are taken into consideration as one criterion in the decision on jurisdiction. One desk, however, highlighted that the interests of the defendant should receive more attention, while others denied that they were relevant at all. As regards the latter, it has been argued that it is not for the prosecutor to take the defendant's interests into account but for the defence counsel. In the majority view, the defendant's interests are duly respected when the trial is held in the defendant's state of nationality or residence, which facilitates the exercise of the rights of the defence.[21] Again, this can only be assessed on a case-by-case basis. The interests of the defendant are often used as an argument to split proceedings with multiple defendants from different Member States. The splitting of proceedings thus often occurs where the defendants have different nationalities or places of residence.

It should be noted that statutes of limitation are not usually assessed when determining jurisdiction.

3. In particular: the avoidance of *ne bis in idem* cases

The exchange of information through Eurojust also serves the prevention of *ne bis in idem* cases. Meetings at Eurojust can be used to assess at an early stage whether parallel investigations relate to the 'same acts' within the meaning of Article 54 of the Convention on the Implementation of the Schengen Agreement (CISA).[22] In the experience of the national desks, it can sometimes be challenging to determine whether an investigation or conviction concerns the same acts. As regards

21 The latter refers for instance to the fact that the defendant speaks the language of the trial.

22 The Schengen Acquis—Convention implementing the Schengen Agreement of 14 June 1985 between the governments of the states of the Benelux Economic Union, the Federal Republic of Germany and the French Republic on the gradual abolition of checks at their common borders [2000] OJ L239/0019.

the interpretation of the notion of 'same acts' under Article 54, some guidance can be derived from the Court of Justice of the European Union (CJEU) case law, for instance in the *Kraaijenbrink* case[23] relating to money laundering. However, the determination of 'same acts' remains difficult in practice.

Thus, it is not surprising that *ne bis in idem* has been identified as an increasing problem by one desk. In addition to the issues arising from the indefinite legal notion of 'same acts', Member States may be unaware of concurring investigations and trials, or lack knowledge as to the legal quality of certain acts in another jurisdiction.[24] So far, clarification in relation to which kind of acts/decisions are final decisions in the different legal systems can be achieved through Eurojust or the EJN, but this does not seem to be satisfactory for all desks.

To highlight the underlying problem the following example was brought forward which concerned a case of skimming in Member State A: the victims and suspects were nationals of Member State B, the proceedings were transferred to Member State B, but Member State B decided not to prosecute. Member State A then tried to clarify the nature of the decision not to prosecute with the Member State B desk and whether a decision to prosecute in Member State A would amount to a *ne bis in idem* case.

Conflicts of jurisdiction may also arise at the level of enforcement, meaning that two final decisions exist in parallel. These *ne bis in idem* situations may be detected when competing European arrest warrants for execution of a sentence exist. As of yet, conflicts of jurisdiction to enforce are very rare.

4. The actual transfer of proceedings

The transfer of proceedings is considered an indispensable means for solving conflicts of jurisdiction by all interviewees. Different opinions, however, were expressed about the need for a new legal instrument on transfer of proceedings at EU level. As of yet, there is no specific EU instrument dealing with the transfer of proceedings. An initiative for a framework decision in that regard was dropped when the Lisbon Treaty came into force. Some Member States apply the European Convention on the Transfer of Proceedings in Criminal Matters of 1972,[25] [26] although none of the interviewees specifically mentioned this instrument. In fact, not all EU Member States have ratified it.

23 Case C-367/05 *Norma Kraaijenbrink* ECLI:EU:C:2007:444.

24 For instance, whether a discontinuation by a prosecutor has the same effect as a judgment.

25 Council of Europe, European Convention on the Transfer of Proceedings in Criminal Matters of 15 May 1972, ETS No 73.

26 Cf. Eurojust, 'Report of Eurojust's Casework Experience' (n 3) 4.

Therefore, Article 21 of the Council of Europe Convention of 1959[27] remains the main instrument for transfers. In practice, the principle of reciprocity also serves as a legal basis in combination with relevant national provisions. The majority of desks consider the 1959 Convention as an adequate means; some other desks and the EJN, instead, would be in favour of an EU initiative to facilitate the procedure and to clarify some practical aspects, including the admissibility of evidence.[28] Critics of the current legal framework also claim that it lacks a duty to inform the transferring state of the follow-up and thus a transferring state may be unaware whether proceedings are pursued.

A common recurring issue on transfer of proceedings relates to the costs for translation of the file. Language is seen as a major problem in the transfer of proceedings. In practice, the parties involved might agree only to translate crucial parts of a file. Some desks have explained that they often have a consultation at Eurojust level to pre-check whether the other Member State concerned would in the end accept a transfer. This pre-check is considered to be very helpful to prevent unnecessary costs.

In sum, the majority of desks claim that the current legal framework on transfer of proceedings is unsatisfactory, with some expressing the need for a clear regulation of transfer of proceedings.

D. Summary

Most desks identified a lack of communication between judicial authorities and strive for more direct contacts between the authorities. There is a presumption that the promotion of direct cooperation would solve most problems encountered in parallel proceedings and conflicts of jurisdiction.

As of the date of the interviews, little or no experience existed with regard to the application of the Council Framework Decision on Prevention and Settlement of Conflicts of Exercise of Jurisdiction in Criminal Proceedings,[29] which establishes a procedural framework for reaching consensus on which Member States should investigate and prosecute cases. Some desks have complained that the Framework Decision is an unsatisfying instrument, in particular as it lacks a clear rule on the follow-up of the consultation. None of the desks reported experience of applying the Framework Decision. In fact, as of 2015, several Member States had not yet implemented the Decision. Conflicts are solved instead in coordination meetings.

27 Council of Europe, European Convention on Mutual Assistance in Criminal Matters of 20 April 1959, ETS No 30.

28 It has been expressed by one desk that any new European instrument should also address precautionary measures and EAWs.

29 Council FD 2009/948/JHA (n 6).

Critics also claimed that owing to its weaknesses the instrument can only be seen as a first step.

The interviews identified a strong preference for non-binding, flexible instruments such as the 2003 Eurojust Guidelines on who should prosecute. However, once an agreement is reached on who should prosecute, the responses to our questions suggest that an EU instrument governing the transfer of proceedings is desirable.

III. Annex: Questionnaire

1. How is the existence of a parallel proceeding in another Member State normally detected/discovered?
2. Which are the offences involved in the most common cases of parallel proceedings?
3. Are there risks or drawbacks stemming from parallel investigations?
4. Which are the jurisdictional bases involved in the most common cases of parallel proceedings? Have you ever dealt with conflicts arising from the exercise of purely extraterritorial jurisdiction by at least one of the Member States concerned (i.e. without any part of the conduct committed on its territory)?
5. Have you ever experienced cases in which the preliminary presumption in favour of the Member State 'where the majority of criminality occurred or the majority of the loss was sustained' has been rebutted? If yes, on the basis of which factors?
6. How are potential evidential problems evaluated? Can you describe a case in which the admissibility of evidence has also been taken into account in determining the competent jurisdiction?
7. How would you define the 'interests of victims'? And which consideration should be given to them? Can you describe a case where those interests have been expressly evaluated?
8. How would you define the 'interests of the defendant'? How are the defendant's interests evaluated in deciding on the competent jurisdiction? And which role is played by the location of the accused, his/her residence or nationality?
9. Is the risk of the crime being time-barred normally considered?
10. Would a list of binding criteria result in an advantage? And, in the affirmative case, why?
11. Can you describe at least one relevant occasion in which a case has been divided between two (or more) jurisdictions?
12. Which consideration is given to the ECJ case law on European *ne bis in idem* in deciding on the competent jurisdiction? Does Eurojust see as one of its tasks to prevent *ne bis in idem* violations when it deals with decisions on jurisdiction or with the coordination of MLA/MR requests?
13. Have you ever dealt with *ne bis in idem* cases involving two final decisions (conflicts of jurisdiction to enforce)?
14. Have you ever dealt with 'negative conflicts of jurisdiction'? Can you describe how they have been solved? Which role could be played by Eurojust in their regard?

15. How is the follow-up of Eurojust's recommendations monitored and ensured? Are you aware that national authorities dismissed a case after it had been assigned to their jurisdiction?
16. Does the FD 2009/948/JHA help you in solving conflicts of jurisdiction? Which are, in your opinion, the major benefits and shortcomings of this instrument? And how could it be improved?
17. To which extent could the transfer of proceedings facilitate the solution of conflicts of jurisdiction? Is the current legal framework on transfer of proceedings satisfactory?
18. What is, in your opinion, the most urgent problem concerning jurisdiction?

2

THE LEGAL BASIS FOR PREVENTING AND RESOLVING CONFLICTS OF CRIMINAL JURISDICTION IN THE TFEU

MARTIN WASMEIER*

I. INTRODUCTION

Since the European Union (EU) has received powers to adopt legally binding acts in the area of judicial cooperation in criminal matters, the Treaties expressly referred to conflicts of jurisdiction as one of the issues to be tackled. Under the Amsterdam Treaty, the Union could adopt decisions and framework decisions with the aim of 'preventing conflicts of jurisdiction between Member States' (ex-Article 31(d) of the Treaty on European Union (TEU)).[1] The Treaty of Nice (26 February 2001) added the coordination of prosecutions through Eurojust.[2]

The Lisbon Treaty has considerably extended the relevant legal basis. Article 82(1)(b) of the Treaty on the Functioning of the European Union (TFEU) calls now for 'measures to . . . prevent and settle conflicts of jurisdiction'. The term 'measures' comprises directives and regulations.[3] Moreover, Article 85(1)(b) extends the possible mandate for Eurojust to 'the coordination of investigations and prosecutions' and Article 85(1)(c) refers to 'the strengthening of judicial cooperation, including by resolution of conflicts of jurisdiction'. Under both articles, the ordinary legislative procedure (Article 289 TFEU) applies, with a number of procedural particularities foreseen in Title V, Chapters 1 and 4, of the TFEU.

One of the hallmarks of Union law is the principle of conferral, as expressed in Articles 4(1), 5(1), and (2) TEU. The Union can only legislate in areas where

* The views expressed in this chapter are exclusively those of the author and may not in any circumstance be regarded as expressing an official position of the European Commission.

1 FD 2009/948/JHA is based on ex-art 31(d) (and (b))TEU (the latter provided for action 'ensuring compatibility in rules applicable in the Member States' to improve judicial cooperation).

2 See ex-art 31(2)(a) TEU ('to facilitate proper coordination between Member States' national prosecuting authorities'). Eurojust was created in 2002, but the Nice Treaty enhanced its mandate to primary law.

3 The Treaties consistently use the word 'measures' when the Union legislator has a choice among the instruments mentioned in art 288 TFEU.

the Treaties confer upon it a competence to do so. In addition, it must respect the principles of proportionality (i.e. its action may not go beyond what is necessary to achieve the objectives of the Treaties, Article 5(4) TEU) and of subsidiarity (Article 5(3) TEU)[4]—acting 'only if and in so far as' the pursued objectives cannot be sufficiently achieved by the Member States. It has to respect the Member States' national identities, 'inherent in their fundamental structures, political and constitutional ...' (Article 4(2) TEU).

These principles are of particular relevance in the area of freedom, security and justice, where Article 67(1) TFEU underlines their importance and where specific rules and mechanisms are added: a requirement for strategic guidelines by the European Council (Article 68); a lower quorum for a 'yellow card' by national Parliaments (Article 69; Article 7(2) of Protocol No 2 [2016] OJ C202),[5] an exemption regarding the maintenance of law and order and internal security (Article 72 TFEU) and the right of a group of Member States to present legislative initiatives independently of the European Commission (Article 76(b) TFEU).[6]

In EU criminal law, approximation of laws and regulations is usually limited to 'minimum rules'. According to Article 82(2) TFEU, an approximation of procedural criminal law is only permitted where this is necessary to facilitate mutual recognition of judicial decisions and police and judicial cooperation. Rules concerning the definitions of criminal offences and sanctions may only be passed 'in the areas of particularly serious crime with a cross-border dimension resulting from the nature or impact of such offences or from a special need to combat them on a common basis' (Article 83(1)), or if they prove 'essential to ensure the effective implementation of a Union policy which has been subject to harmonisation measures' (Article 83(2)).[7]

Moreover, the Lisbon Treaty has introduced the possibility for an individual Member State to bring a related legislative process to a halt by pulling the 'emergency brake' foreseen in Articles 82(3) and 83(3) TFEU: any Member State can request that a draft be referred to the European Council and the procedure be suspended if it considers that it would affect 'fundamental aspects of its criminal justice system'.

These particularities of EU criminal law can largely be considered remnants from the former inter-governmental approach which dominated the so-called 'third

4 The principle of subsidiarity does not apply to areas which fall within the Union's exclusive competence (cf. art 3 TFEU), but the area of freedom, security and justice and esp. criminal law is a matter of shared competence (art 4(2)(j) TFEU).

5 On request by a certain quorum of votes from national parliaments, a Commission draft must be reviewed. Usually, this requires one-third of the votes, but for proposals in chapters 4 and 5 of Title V TFEU (cooperation in criminal matters), one-quarter is sufficient.

6 At least one-quarter of the Member States must require this.

7 The bar is even higher (unanimity) for the establishment of the European Public Prosecutor's Office (EPPO) (art 86(1) TFEU).

pillar' under the Treaties of Maastricht (ex-Article K.1 TEU), Amsterdam and Nice (ex-Articles 29 ff TEU), which have been kept in view of sensitive aspects of the Member States' sovereignty.

The priority given to mutual recognition (over approximation of laws) originates from a similar line of thinking. Mutual recognition is elevated to an overarching principle or *Leitmotiv* of EU criminal law, especially in Articles 67(3), 82, and 83 TFEU and in line with previous guidelines by the European Council[8] and related case law by the Court of Justice.[9] Restrictions to Union action are less severe where it mainly aims at facilitating or strengthening mutual recognition and judicial cooperation, while the most far-reaching restrictions and conditions (minimum rules, 'emergency brake') apply to harmonisation as such.[10]

II. ARTICLE 82(1)(B) TFEU—CONTEXT AND OBJECTIVES

Before this background, the wording and content of Article 82(1)(b) TFEU is remarkable: 'The European Parliament and the Council "shall" adopt measures to prevent and settle conflicts of jurisdiction'. Apparently, the authors of the Treaty considered the existence of conflicts of jurisdiction in an area of freedom, security and justice, which is based on mutual recognition, as a serious problem and saw a response by the Union as a necessary element of the Union's policy on criminal law. This can be concluded from three features of this provision:

First of all, the wording does not just provide a legal basis. It clearly expresses a mandate and duty for action, since throughout the Treaties the word 'shall' is only used where there is a legal obligation. Second, while one should not overlook the fundamental differences between civil and criminal law, this mandate clearly mirrors the approach on judicial cooperation in civil and commercial matters (Article 81(2) TFEU). In that area, rules on jurisdiction have formed an essential part of the common legal framework from the outset—even before judicial cooperation in civil matters became a Union competence.[11] Mutual recognition of judicial decisions and rules on 'conflicts of laws and of jurisdiction' have been regarded here as two sides of the same coin.[12]

8 See, in particular, the conclusions of the 1999 European Council of Tampere.

9 See the seminal ECJ judgment in Joined Cases C-187/01 and C-385/01 *Gözütok and Brügge* ECLI:EU:C:2003:87, para 33 and—after Lisbon—ECJ Opinion No 2/13 ECLI:EU:C:2014:2454, para 191ff (referring to a 'principle of mutual trust').

10 The terms 'harmonisation' and 'approximation' will be used here as synonyms (cf. André Klip, *European Criminal Law* (3rd edn, Intersentia 2016) 34 ff).

11 See Council Regulation (EC) No 44/2001 (Brussels I) [2001] OJ L12/1 (in particular, recitals (2), (5)–(6), (8)–(9), (11)), which builds on earlier international law agreements, the 1968 Brussels Convention [1972] OJ L299/32, and the 1988 Lugano Convention.

12 Cf. the contribution by Pietro Ortolani in this volume.

Third, instead of placing the legal basis for measures on jurisdiction into the second paragraph of Article 82 of the TFEU (i.e. in the context of harmonisation of procedural criminal law), the Member States decided to insert it in the list in the *first* paragraph of that article. Apparently, they considered that the measures in this list are by definition necessary to facilitate mutual recognition and judicial cooperation, as they exempted them from the additional test foreseen in Articles 82(2) and 83, as well as from the additional restrictions and conditions mentioned above (minimum rules, 'emergency brake', etc.).

This means that the Member States were convinced that measures to prevent and settle conflicts of jurisdiction are an essential element of an area of freedom, security and justice based on mutual recognition. In other words, there is an underlying assumption in the Treaty that such measures are a prerequisite for the good functioning of mutual recognition and judicial cooperation. The latter is also reflected in the wording of Article 85(1)(c) TFEU.

Indeed, it is difficult to imagine how a fully-fledged system of mutual recognition[13] could work smoothly without being complemented by a legal framework on how Member States should exercise their jurisdiction to adjudicate and/or to enforce where several of them have established a jurisdiction to prescribe. The mutual trust which is required for a full application of the principle of mutual recognition needs to be supported on several levels. Usually, the need for a harmonisation of procedural and substantive criminal law is at the centre of attention, but another relevant aspect is a need to ensure that all Member States concerned may have a say when it comes to the choice of a *forum*, that this choice is not arbitrary or based on inappropriate criteria, and that there is some form of accountability and judicial review.

In the absence of a related legal framework, it is not too surprising that the extent to which mutual recognition works out in practice is still controversial.[14] In any case, EU mutual recognition instruments provide for numerous possibilities to refuse mutual recognition on jurisdictional grounds. Such exceptions allow Member States to carry out their own prosecutions instead of recognising and enforcing acts taken by other Member States (especially, but not only for offences committed on their own territory). This is true, in particular, for Article 4(2) and (7) of the European Arrest Warrant (EAW),[15] Article 8(2)(f) of the Framework Decision on

13 Again, a parallel can be drawn with civil and commercial law, where there is now a fully-fledged system of mutual recognition, not least because the process has gone hand-in-hand with jurisdictional rules.

14 Cf. V. Mitsilegas, *EU Criminal Law After Lisbon* (Hart Publishing 2016) 151–52, 264; Steve Peers, *EU Justice and Home Affairs Law: Volume II: EU Criminal Law, Policing, and Civil Law* (4th edn, OUP 2016) 131–32.

15 FD 2002/584/JHA [2002] OJ L190/1.

Confiscation,[16] Article 7(2)(d) of the Framework Decision on mutual recognition of financial penalties,[17] or exceptions from *ne bis in idem* according to Article 55 of the Convention implementing the Schengen Agreement (CISA).[18] Such grounds for refusal of recognition could be reconsidered and perhaps be done away with if there were a Union framework on concurrent jurisdiction.[19]

This is not to say that a legal framework for the prevention and settlement of jurisdictional conflicts is the most important prerequisite for a judicial area based on mutual recognition, nor that mutual recognition could or should become an unconditional automatism if such a framework will be created. There are other important reasons for the occasional lack of mutual trust and/or for tendencies by national authorities to keep proceedings in their own hands, such as concerns with fair trial and other procedural rights. Nonetheless, the fact that Article 82(1) of the TFEU expressly refers to conflicts of jurisdiction, while other prerequisites for a good functioning of mutual recognition (e.g. those mentioned in Article 82(2)) are subject to additional conditions and limitations, clearly expresses a choice made in primary Union law.

A. Approximation of laws under Article 82(1)(b) TFEU?

The list of issues in Article 82(1) TFEU is exhaustive and very limited. In fact, a closer look at this list shows that jurisdiction conflicts (lit. b) are the only issue in this list where Union action is not limited to 'ensuring recognition' (Article 82(1)(a)), to mere 'support' (Article 82(1)(c)), or to 'facilitation' (Article 82(1)(d)). Thus, it is arguable that the provision's rationale is to enable the Union to create binding rules which may interfere with the Member States' laws and regulations, including the approximation of related national rules.

Non-binding measures can only contribute to the objective of preventing and settling jurisdiction conflicts to a very limited extent. This is more or less what the Council attempted by means of FD 2009/948/JHA, which provides for a duty to consult, but one that is hardly enforceable, since it neither provides for clear criteria on when a consultation is obligatory nor for any consequences if it is omitted.[20] But even an enforceable duty to consult could not prevent or settle an

16 FD 2006/783/JHA on the application of the principle of mutual recognition to confiscation orders [2006] OJ L328/59.

17 FD 2005/214/JHA [2005] OJ L76/16.

18 According to art 55(1)(a) CISA, Member States may declare that they do not apply the principle of *ne bis in idem* to offences committed on their territory (this can be problematic in view of art 50 Charter of Fundamental Rights (CFR)).

19 See Peers (n 14) 234.

20 Cf. in this context the ECJ judgment in Case C-129/14 PPU *Spasic* ECLI:EU:C:2014:586, paras 66 ff. Cf. also Peers (n 14) 234 ('disappointing'); Mitsilegas (n 14) 92.

enduring conflict. At least where differing opinions persist, ultimately a settlement will require binding rules on Union level.

The context and the wording of the provision does not leave much doubt that it is binding rules for the settlement or prevention of jurisdiction conflicts which are envisaged. Any measure at Union level that sets boundaries to the Member States' discretion on how to exercise their jurisdiction (be it in terms of procedure or of material criteria) necessarily interferes with national law and may entail a certain degree of approximation. Therefore, an exclusion of any approximating effect whatsoever would largely deprive the legal basis of its added value and effect. In view of its *effet utile*, Article 82(1)(b) of the TFEU should thus be interpreted as enabling the Union to adopt legally binding rules.[21]

This could perhaps be challenged by an *argumentum e contrario* from the first sub-paragraph in Article 82(1) TFEU, saying that approximation would be restricted to the areas 'referred to in paragraph 2 and in Article 83'. However, the structure of Article 82(1) TFEU suggests that the reference to Articles 82(2) and 83 expresses a principle rather than an exclusive reference and that the exceptions to that principle are listed in the second sub-paragraph of Article 82(1). Indeed, this list would be nearly devoid of purpose if there were no room for interference with national law—even more since mutual recognition instruments imply such interference, too: for their functioning, usually a common set of rules is required that superposes and approximates certain national rules (e.g. those on the form and contents of a EAW and its effects in national law). The ECJ has expressly acknowledged this.[22] In the same vein, a legal framework on conflicts of jurisdiction requires a certain approximation of national rules.

In addition, the genesis of Article 82 of the TFEU shows that the authors of the Treaty were aware of the numerous related proposals and initiatives within the Union and also in the Council of Europe.[23] Given the variety of models and approaches discussed and that nearly all of them implied some interference with national laws, it cannot be assumed that their intention was to restrain the legislator to a consultation or information mechanism. The idea was to extend the Union powers in this area (as ex-Article 31(1)(d) TEU only mentioned the prevention of conflicts).The 2005 Council and Commission Action Plan Implementing the Hague Programme referred to conflicts of jurisdiction under the heading of 'Approximation'.[24] This term

21 Peers (n 14) 229 refers to binding rules allocating jurisdiction as an 'obvious choice'.

22 See Case C-305/03 *Advocaten voor der Wereld* ECLI:EU:C:2007:261, paras 29, 38. Cf. Frank Meyer in Hans von der Groeben, Jürgen Schwarze, and Arnim Hatje (eds), *Nomos Kommentar Europäisches Unionsrecht* (*Commentary on TEU/TFEU*) (7th edn, Nomos 2015); art 82 AEUV Marginal No 19 ff.

23 See section I above.

24 [2005] OJ C198/1. In its s 4.2, the action plan referred to the Green Paper on conflicts of jurisdiction and double jeopardy (a) and a related legislative proposal (e). Cf. also COM(2005) 184 final.

can hardly have been used inadvertently, since Article III-270 of the Constitution for Europe (which had been signed the year before) was almost identical to Article 82 TFEU, taking the same stance on mutual recognition and approximation. Thus, it was accepted long before Lisbon that action on conflicts of jurisdiction may include the latter.

For all these reasons, it is submitted that Article 82(1)(b) of the TFEU allows for an approximation of laws complementing mutual recognition. The criterion to determine the dividing line between the first and second paragraph of Article 82 is not whether there is an interference with national law. Rather, it is to be found in the *objective* of the Union action: where the overall objective is to ensure and complement mutual recognition and/or judicial cooperation, a measure can be based on the first paragraph, even if it includes some (ancillary) elements of approximation. In contrast, where the dominating objective is a far-reaching harmonisation, it will have to be based on the second paragraph (or on Article 83).

In any case, even if Article 82(1) of the TFEU were to exclude approximation, the result would depend on what exactly is to be understood under this term. It seems that there is currently no uniform and entirely clear-cut definition. For some authors, 'approximation' only refers to Union law requiring a change of national rules applying to domestic situations, but not measures requiring an adaptation of rules that only deal with cross-border situations.[25] In this terminology, binding Union law on conflicts *between* Member States, as foreseen in lit. b would not be considered approximation of national rules.[26] While other authors use a wider notion of approximation, they acknowledge that binding rules closely connected with mutual recognition may be based on Article 82(1).[27] In the end, both approaches lead to very similar results.

As an example, one could refer here to a Union provision obliging Member States to provide for the discontinuation of prosecution with regard to proceedings in another Member State. Such a measure would enable national authorities to accept that the latter Member State is better placed to prosecute a case. This is crucial in legal systems

25 For instance, see Meyer (n 22); art 82 AEUV, Marginal No 16 (with further references); Peers (n 14) 137 also considers that art 82(1) TFEU sets out a power 'with a purely cross-border nature', but does not seek to assume that it excludes approximation.

26 It also seems to exclude conflicts of jurisdiction between a Member State and a third state.

27 Cf. Helmut Satzger in Rudolf Streinz (ed), *EUV/AEUV, Beck'sche Kurz-Kommentare* (*TEU/TFEU, Commentary*); art 82 TFEU Marginal No 20-21; Joachim Vogel and Jörg Eisele in Eberhard Grabitz, Meinhard Hilf, and Martin Nettesheim (eds), *Das Recht der Europäischen Union: EUV/AEUV* (60th loose-leaf edn, CH Beck 2016); art 82 TFEU Marginal No 50 (*enger Sachzusammenhang*), referring to the instructive example of art 10 of FD 2008/978/JHA on the European Evidence Warrant for obtaining objects, documents and data for use in proceedings in criminal matters ([2008] OJ L350/72). While Satzger suggests extending the 'emergency brake' by analogy to art 82(1) TFEU, Vogel and Eisele rightly object that this would mean to change the Treaty and suggest instead combining both legal bases (although this too might not be plain sailing).

applying the 'legality principle', that is, where prosecution of certain or most offences is obligatory, as the competent authorities might not be able to close their proceedings even where they would be willing to do so. While such a measure would require a change of national law (i.e. the provisions on when proceedings can be closed), this interference would only apply to cross-border situations.

All this leads us to the following conclusions: In procedural terms, the wording 'to settle conflicts' clearly implies that the Union can create a mechanism which may result in a decision that is binding for the Member States. This, however, is only possible by adopting a legal framework at Union level which, if need be, overrides national rules.[28] In material terms, an appropriate response could be the determination of criteria on where best to prosecute a case, including priorities or sequence among those criteria.[29]

B. The notion of 'conflicts of jurisdiction'

This leads us to the definition of 'conflicts of jurisdiction', the key concept in Article 82(1)(b) of the TFEU. In everyday language, a conflict is 'an active disagreement between people with opposing opinions or principles' or a 'competitive or opposing action of incompatibles'.[30] With this in mind, one could assume that a conflict only arises where authorities from different Member States disagree on where a case should be prosecuted. This would require a real dispute, or at least an *actual conflict*, as defined in the introduction to this book, that is, that parallel proceedings are actually run in several Member States.[31] However, several objections can be brought forward against such an interpretation:

First of all, if the intention were only to cover parallel (or subsequent) proceedings,[32] one may ask why the language does not say so clearly. Second, a consultation and/or decision-making process will be most effective if it starts *before* an actual conflict arises. Where proceedings have already been launched, it can be more difficult to convince a Member State to stop them in favour of another one.

28 Cf. the use of the word 'settlement' in art 81(2)(g), or in art 344 TFEU.

29 Cf. the approach in art 9 of the FD 2002/475/JHA on combating terrorism [2002] OJ L164/3 (now repealed and replaced by Directive 2017/541 of 15 March 2017 on combating terrorism and replacing Council FD 2002/475/JHA and amending Council Decision 2005/671/JHA [2017] OJ L88/6).

30 Cf. Cambridge Dictionary http://dictionary.cambridge.org/dictionary/english/conflict; Merriam Webster https://www.merriam-webster.com/dictionary/conflict (both last accessed 25 January 2017).

31 See section I above.

32 In this contribution, I use the term 'subsequent proceedings' for proceedings following a final decision barring further prosecution in one Member State in situations where the transnational *ne bis in idem* rule would exceptionally not apply. This may be the case, for instance, because of the enforcement condition in art 54 CISA or of declarations according to art 55 CISA (on the compatibility of these provisions with art 50 CFR see the contribution by Katalin Ligeti in this volume).

And even if avoiding parallel (or subsequent) proceedings were the only objective, it would hardly be understandable why a process with the aim of identifying the 'best place to prosecute' should not start before such a situation actually arises.[33]

Third, if the term 'conflict' were only to refer to parallel (and possibly subsequent) proceedings, several relevant problems could not be tackled. Different opinions on where a case should be prosecuted can even arise in situations where only one Member State has so far launched proceedings. A very narrow definition of the term 'conflict' would prevent the Union from dealing with such situations. To some extent, an extensive definition of 'parallel proceedings' could help here (e.g. by including situations where an authority is about to conduct proceedings[34]), but—leaving aside problems of legal certainty (when is an authority 'about to conduct' proceedings?)—this would still be rather restrictive.

An issue of choice of jurisdiction can even arise where no Member State has yet launched proceedings. The most well-known example is a so-called 'negative conflict'.[35] In the terminology used here,[36] a 'negative conflict' arises where no Member State is willing to exercise its jurisdiction. But the difficulties do not stop there. There can be other reasons, too, for a failure to take action. In particular, the competent authorities may not be aware of all relevant facts, circumstances and interests involved (e.g. interests of other Member States or of victims based elsewhere), or they simply deem another Member State better placed. Even if authorities are willing to prosecute, discretional considerations of efficiency, proportionality, or the 'opportunity principle' can lead to such situations.

Therefore, it makes sense to construe the term 'conflict of jurisdiction' as referring to any situation where two or more Member States have established jurisdiction on the same facts and the same person (which can be understood as an 'identity of material acts', or 'a set of facts which are inextricably linked together'[37]). In criminal matters, this would mean that at least two Member States have established jurisdiction to prosecute. We refer here to such situations as *abstract conflicts*.[38] In this sense, it is sufficient that parallel (or subsequent) proceedings may occur at a later stage.

33 FD 2009/948/JHA (which according to its art 1 aims at avoiding parallel proceedings) establishes a duty to contact if an authority has 'reasonable grounds to believe that' such proceedings are being conducted (art 5), ie not only when a dispute has arisen. However, a duty to consult comes only into play when it is established that parallel proceedings exist (art 10).

34 Cf. art 3(a) of the Draft Directive for a horizontal mechanism.

35 See section II.C below.

36 See section I above.

37 Cf. reply no 1 by ECJ in Case C-288/05 *Kretzinger*, ECLI:EU:C:2007:441 on *ne bis in idem*, according to art 54 CISA.

38 See section I above.

This interpretation is supported by a comparison with civil and commercial matters, where the term 'conflict of laws' is a synonym for private international law. A legal conflict in this sense does not necessarily refer to an active disagreement or to the existence of proceedings in several Member States. What is meant here is simply that there is a need to determine which national law applies in a situation with elements pointing to several states. It is in this sense that the term 'conflict' is used in Article 81(2)(c) of the TFEU.

Given that this provision mirrors Article 82(1)(b) of the TFEU in the area of judicial cooperation in civil matters, it seems obvious to take a similar interpretation of its *pendant* in the penal sphere. Despite all differences between civil and criminal law, the general difficulties regarding the forum choice (such as the risk of 'forum shopping') are rather comparable. In the absence of convincing arguments on why the same term should bear entirely different meanings in two neighbouring articles on judicial cooperation, it is reasonable to go for a comparable interpretation in criminal and civil law. Thus, the notion of conflict of jurisdiction in criminal law should simply refer to the fact that there is concurrent jurisdiction in several Member States, that is, a need to determine which one should or may exercise its jurisdiction.

One important difference is that Article 81 of the TFEU mentions also conflict of laws, in addition to conflicts of jurisdiction. But this difference can be easily explained: In civil and commercial matters, conflict of laws is a matter of almost daily practice for courts, with an established set of rules both in the Member States and on Union level. Under private international law, it is not rare that courts apply the law of another Member State than the one where the proceedings take place.[39] In contrast, criminal law is dominated by the *lex fori* rule, that is, in the vast majority of cases courts in the Member States will apply their own national law.[40] There is no need here to refer to conflicts of law, as the applicable criminal law will usually be the one of the Member State where the proceedings take place.[41] At the same time, this means that in criminal law the consequences of a choice of the forum are even more important.

Bearing this in mind, it would be beside the point to interpret the term 'conflict' in Article 82 of the TFEU in a narrower way than in Article 81. The objective

39 Cf. the contribution by Pietro Ortolani in this book.

40 Where there are exceptions, they usually rather complement the national law of the Member State where the proceedings take place. For an example in Swiss law, see Anna Petrig, 'The Expansion of Swiss Criminal Jurisdiction in Light of International Law' [2013] 9 Utrecht Law Journal 34, 48–49. On the relevance of foreign law for interpreting criminal law; see Anne Schneider in Martin Böse, Frank Meyer, and Anne Schneider (eds), *Conflicts of Jurisdiction in Criminal Matters in the European Union: Vol II: Rights, Principles and Model Rules* (Nomos 2014) 307 ff.

41 This is not to say that related measures under art 82 TFEU would be entirely excluded.

of Article 82(1)(b) is to enable the legislator to deal with any difficulties that can arise from concurrent jurisdiction. The rationale set out above, and the priority the Treaty attributes to the problem at stake, speak thus against a narrow interpretation. If Union action were to be limited to measures regarding actual conflicts, which are only a small part of the problem, the overall objective of strengthening mutual recognition and effective judicial cooperation in a common area of justice could hardly be met.

Moreover, it can be said that in criminal matters *actual* conflicts (i.e. active disagreements) are still relatively rare.[42] Equally or even more important are concerns regarding possibilities of forum shopping, a lack of transparency of the forum choice as well as the problem that authorities may tend to complete cases without taking into account the interests of other Member States and individuals based therein and/or without actively seeking information and evidence beyond national borders (which is all too understandable in a world of limited resources). Without rules on the exercise of jurisdiction, such problems are exacerbated by the 'first come, first served' effect resulting from *ne bis in idem*.

In an area of freedom, security and justice, there is a need to avoid any arbitrary choice of jurisdiction, which could violate fundamental rights and/or neglect legitimate interests of individuals or of other Member States. It is therefore submitted that the notion of 'conflict' in Article 82(1)(b) of the TFEU does not refer to actual conflicts and parallel proceedings alone, but also to abstract conflicts. Otherwise, as set out above, the provision would be deprived of its *effet utile* and practical relevance.

Having said this, under the principles of subsidiarity, proportionality, and respect for national legal orders, arguably the Union legislator may be held to target situations which bear a *potential* for actual conflicts, that is, which may lead to parallel or subsequent proceedings. In this vein, a line should probably be drawn between the right to establish jurisdiction (to prescribe) and the exercise of jurisdiction (to adjudicate and to enforce). It is reasonable to assume that the objective of the legal basis is to create a legal framework on the *exercise* of jurisdiction, rather than setting out detailed rules or conditions on the Member States' right to establish jurisdiction.

C. 'Negative conflicts' of jurisdiction and multiple proceedings

It has been discussed whether measures preventing or resolving so-called 'negative conflicts' could be based on Article 82(1) of the TFEU. As mentioned above, these are situations where no Member State is willing to prosecute a case. The Union

42 Although related statistical data are hardly available, this seems to be *communis opinio* among practitioners, as for instance can be seen in various responses to the Commission Green Paper COM(2005) 696 final.

acquis comprises a number of provisions providing that Member States can (or even have to) extend their jurisdiction for certain offences beyond territoriality.[43] They usually deal with the jurisdiction to prescribe, rather than the Member States' right or duty to *exercise* their jurisdiction. However, these provisions were adopted in the context of harmonisation of specific offences, which now falls under Article 83.[44] Thus, the historical context does not support an assumption that related measures could be based on the legal basis discussed here.[45] Neither does the wording, as one would have to stretch the meaning of the term 'conflict' to its very limits.

With regard to the objective of a high level of security in the area of freedom, security and justice (Article 67(3) TFEU), measures to alleviate the problem of impunity should not be excluded, especially when it comes to serious crime. The Union must be able to tackle related difficulties. Where the legislator considers certain measures appropriate for preventing and/or resolving 'positive' conflicts (e.g. a consultation mechanism, criteria, and if need be a binding decision) it should be possible to use the same measures in situations where no Member State seems to be willing to prosecute. The exact scope of such measures and their correct legal basis does not have to be determined here, as the proposals developed in this project do not focus on the problem of 'negative conflicts'.

Another question is whether Article 82(1) TFEU allows for action regarding *multiple proceedings*, as defined in the introduction (i.e. proceedings against the same person in relation to different facts[46]). This could be the case if the term 'conflict' were to be understood in the sense of an actual conflict, that is, opposing positions. However, as explained above, this does not seem to be the correct interpretation. The term usually refers (both in criminal and in civil law) to a set of facts regarding the same persons. It becomes clear here that the notion of an abstract conflict is not in all aspects wider than the one of an actual conflict. With regard to multiple proceedings, it is rather more restrictive than the latter.

Multiple proceedings can have undesirable effects both for the individuals concerned and for the courts and judicial authorities. However, many of these

43 For an overview see Peers (n 14) 225–26.

44 Accordingly, the new Directive 2017/541 on combating terrorism and replacing the FD 2002/475/JHA is based on art 83(1) TFEU. On jurisdiction see art 19 of this directive. Note that the Commission proposal COM(2015) 625 final was also based on art 82(2)(c) TFEU.

45 Cf. Peers (n 14) 218 (see also 67, 69): '[r]ules concerning the assertion of jurisdiction over a particular crime fall within the scope of . . . Article 83 TFEU, because such provisions are ancillary to the substantive criminal law powers and do nothing to prevent and settle conflicts of jurisdiction'. This argument would, however, not necessarily apply to measures limited to the stage of exercise of jurisdiction.

46 See section I above. It should be noted that in literature the term 'multiple proceedings' is sometimes also used as a synonym for what we call parallel proceedings.

effects and their reasons are rather of a factual than a legal nature. In particular, the principle of *ne bis in idem* does not apply here. A final decision in a Member State only excludes proceedings in another Member State if it refers to the same facts and the same person(s). The need for common rules at the Union level is therefore less compelling and obvious. It may be desirable to avoid multiple proceedings, since they can lead to difficulties when it comes to determining an appropriate penalty for related offences (in particular where national law provides for a cumulative sentence) and also with regard to an efficient use of resources, but this does not seem to be an indispensable element of a common judicial area. This is demonstrated by the fact that, even within Member States, multiple proceedings are not uncommon.

In conclusion, it is submitted that multiple proceedings should be regarded as an issue to be dealt with in the context of facilitating judicial cooperation. Related problems could be tackled via non-binding measures based on Article 82(1)(d) of the TFEU. *Mutatis mutandis,* this can also be said about proceedings against several persons which are factually connected.

III. SETTLEMENT OF CONFLICTS VIA EUROJUST—ARTICLE 85(1)(C) TFEU

The second legal basis referring explicitly to conflicts of jurisdiction is Article 85(1)(c) TFEU. Given its very similar wording and the close connection between both provisions, the interpretation of the notion of 'conflicts of jurisdiction' should be the same as in Article 82(1). There is no apparent reason why it should be construed differently in the context of Eurojust. Thus, to a large extent, the contents and scope of both provisions are overlapping. Essentially, they differ in the following points:

Firstly, Article 85 TFEU solely concerns Eurojust, the Union body created 'to support and strengthen coordination and cooperation' in criminal matters. The Union can confer tasks and powers on Eurojust within its general mandate, that is, 'in relation to serious crime affecting two or more Member States or requiring a prosecution on common bases . . . '. This rather flexible wording leaves a wide margin of discretion for the legislator. Member States can not only be 'affected' by the existence of parallel proceedings, but for instance also by a request for mutual assistance. It can therefore be said that they are affected if there is a need for co-ordination.[47] As concerns the expression 'serious crime', it is certainly wider than that of 'particularly serious crime' in Article 83(1) TFEU and can be understood as including any type of crime apart from misdemeanours or 'petty crime'.

47 It is not obvious what is meant by 'prosecution on common bases', but it is a rather safe assumption that this includes offences affecting the Union's financial interests (in the sense of art 325 TFEU).

Secondly, unlike Article 82(1), Article 85(1) only refers to the 'resolution' of jurisdictional conflicts. By looking at other linguistic versions of the Treaty, it becomes clear that 'resolution' is a synonym for 'settlement'.[48] So the main difference is that there is no reference to prevention. The reason for this is probably that Eurojust should deal with concrete casework, whereas preventative action is not in its core mandate. But even this difference should not be overestimated: the resolution of conflicts of jurisdiction is just one of several means for 'strengthening judicial cooperation', the overall objective of Article 85(1)(c), as expressed by the words 'including by . . . '. This supports an extensive interpretation, which does not exclude that Eurojust may also contribute to the prevention of jurisdictional conflicts.[49]

Thirdly, as to the type of legislative instrument, an important difference from Article 82 of the TFEU is that Article 85(1) explicitly requires the adoption of a regulation. A directive is not foreseen. The reason for this is that a directive would neither be appropriate for establishing the legal framework for a Union body, nor would it be possible to directly confer powers to such a body by a directive which needs to be put into concrete terms by national law.

Probably the most delicate question here is whether the Union legislator can bestow on Eurojust the power take binding decisions. At first sight, this seems to be in line both with the general objectives for judicial cooperation in criminal matters as set out in Article 82 and with the more specific ones in Article 85. Also, the word 'resolution' suggests that the legislator may, at least in certain circumstances, equip Eurojust with the power of taking a legally binding decision. Moreover, unlike in Article 85(1)(a), which differentiates between investigations and prosecutions, lit. c does not draw such a distinction. In any case, if Eurojust can determine the *forum* Member State,[50] this does not necessarily imply that a prosecution is to be initiated, as the national authorities can still come to the conclusion that an investigation can or must be closed.

However, Article 85(2) of the TFEU reserves 'formal acts of judicial procedure' to 'the competent national officials'.[51] Primarily, this means that Eurojust cannot

48 Most versions use the same root in both provisions, so that the only difference is the use of a verb or noun. See e.g. the German *beizulegen/Beilegung*, French *résoudre/résolution*, or Spanish text *resolver/resolución*.

49 Cf. Arts 6 ff of the current Council Decision on Eurojust (based on ex-art 31 TEU), which can be understood as including preventive action, also in view of considerations 4 and 10 of FD 2009/948/JHA.

50 In the present context, the term '*forum*' does not necessarily refer to court proceedings but simply to the Member State where an investigation (and, if so decided: prosecution) should take place.

51 The reason for this rather unusual wording ('officials' rather than 'authorities') could be the current structure of Eurojust: under current secondary law (Articles 2, 6, 9-9e of Council Decision 2002/187/JHA) [2002] OJ L63/1, the national members of Eurojust have the status of national officials. However, a binding decision on a conflict of jurisdiction would have to be taken by the Eurojust 'College' (or at least by several national members). Such a transnational decision would go beyond the notion of 'national officials'.

itself bring prosecutions against individuals or take related coercive acts.[52] It is controversial, however, whether Eurojust can be granted the power to *require* national authorities to begin or to end prosecutions. Arguably, this could render the reserve of the national competence set out in Article 85(2) ineffective.[53] But this is to be distinguished from a power to decide on the *forum* Member State. Such a decision would not necessarily imply a requirement to begin or end prosecution. In fact, a national authority would not per se be required to take a specific act of procedure (such as an indictment, opening, or closure of proceedings), as long as some discretion in this regard remains—and even more so if such a choice does not determine the competent court.

In this regard, a regulation based on Article 85(1) of the TFEU could clarify that the choice made by Eurojust is directed to the Member States as such (rather than a specific authority or the individuals concerned) and does not entail a concrete procedural measure, in order to make sure that the decision does not imply any formal act of judicial procedure, that is, that the consequences of a choice of forum remain a matter of national law and/or discretion.[54] A different, although related, issue is that of judicial review. If the decision is addressed to the Member States, they could challenge it under Article 263 of the TFEU. Depending on the details in the regulation, individuals may direct remedies against the relevant domestic decision, which may include an implicit review of the choice made by Eurojust—subject to a preliminary ruling according to Article 267 if a national court intends to set it aside.[55] However, given its important consequences for the individuals, it is also possible that the Eurojust decision could fulfil the criteria of Article 263(4); details of the procedure could then be set out according to paragraph 5 of that Article.

In any event, Eurojust is an obvious 'candidate' for a vertical approach on jurisdictional conflicts (and of course this is also true for the EPPO in its area of competence). While it does not seem to be excluded that the Union legislator may entrust related tasks and powers to another Union body or agency (based on Article 82(1) TFEU),[56] it

52 Peers (n 14) 218.

53 ibid 218–19.

54 This should apply both to the authorities of the 'chosen' Member State and to those of the other Member State(s). The latter may have several possibilities, eg to suspend, discontinue, or definitively close their proceedings (depending on the details of an EU regulation and of national law, a definitive closure might only be necessary in case of a final judgment). In the 'chosen' Member State it would have to be decided which prosecuting authority takes the case, whether the matter is to be brought to court and, if so, where.

55 Established case law, cf. case C-314/85 *Foto Frost* ECLI:EU:C:1987:452 (on legally binding acts); see also case C-322/88 *Grimaldi* ECLI:EU:C:1989:646, para 8 (regarding a recommendation). According to Koen Lenaerts, Ignace Maselis, and Kathleen Gutman (eds), *EU Procedural Law* (OUP 2014) 464, the principle developed in this case law accordingly applies to non-binding acts.

56 Böse (n 40) 374 arrives at a different conclusion (without explicit reasoning).

can be argued that regarding Eurojust Article 85(1)(c) of the TFEU is a *lex specialis*, as the more specific rule. Nonetheless, given that Articles 82(1) and 85 refer to the same legislative procedure, it seems possible to base such a regulation on both of them.[57]

IV. CONCLUSIONS REGARDING THE LEGISLATIVE MODELS DEVELOPED IN THIS PROJECT

After these explanations, it seems almost obvious that Article 82(1)(b) of the TFEU would be a sound legal basis for the first building block of this project, the *horizontal mechanism*. Its objectives are fully in line with this provision and the related legislative proposal does not affect the primary responsibility of the Member States to resolve conflicts of jurisdiction. It does not interfere with national rules applicable on purely domestic situations and therefore stays clearly within the limits set by the Treaty to an ancillary approximation of law. This is not only true for the baseline scenario, which aims at avoiding parallel prosecution and ensuring a non-arbitrary choice of forum, but also for the additional suggestions for a choice of the 'best forum', both in the 'narrow'[58] and in the 'broader perspective'.[59]

An additional update of the Eurojust guidelines[60] would not make them legally binding. But even an additional transposition of these guidelines into 'hard law' would not go beyond the scope of the legal basis. A catalogue of criteria such as the ones in the (extended) guidelines would certainly be an appropriate measure for the prevention and settlement of conflicts of jurisdiction. The catalogue would be limited to identifying the legitimate criteria (and/or possibly 'negative criteria') without imposing a strict order of priority. It would respect the Member States' legal systems and limit interference with national law. While national authorities and courts would have to add a transnational perspective to their existing conditions on where a case can be prosecuted, the internal mechanisms (for instance, criteria for local jurisdiction) would not be affected. Neither the procedural mechanism nor the catalogue of criteria would necessarily have direct effect, so that a directive would be sufficient.

The second building block, the *vertical mechanism*, would essentially build on Eurojust and considerably extend its tasks and powers and would thus mainly have to be based on Article 85(1)(c) of the TFEU (possibly in connection with

57 It is questionable whether there is a need for such an additional 'basing' on art 82(1) TFEU, but this is rather an academic issue (in favour of a double legal base: Peers (n 14) 217).

58 See Draft Legislative Proposals for the Prevention and Resolution of Conflicts of Jurisdiction in Criminal Matters in the European Union s 9(1)(2)(a).

59 ibid 9(1)(2)(b).

60 ibid 9(1)(3).

Article 82(1)(b)[61]). The proposed draft regulation remains within the general scope of Eurojust's mandate[62] and is in line with the objective of the 'resolution of conflicts'. It does not aim directly at the prevention of conflicts (which is not expressly mentioned in Article 85), even though the possibility of a binding decision by Eurojust may encourage consensual solutions at an earlier stage and thereby contribute to preventing disputes.

The acid test is to be found in Article 85(2) of the TFEU, that is, the rule that Eurojust cannot carry out formal acts of judicial procedure. The draft regulation within the project's second building block does not expressly provide for such acts. However, there is a need to examine carefully whether decisions adopted by Eurojust could have implications which would require national authorities to take certain concrete steps in this regard. A regulation would have to be drafted in such a way that the reservation for national competence in Article 85(2) will not be put into question.

In the draft regulation, it is foreseen that a Eurojust decision 'shall be binding upon the judicial authorities of the Member States concerned' and that in case of parallel proceedings it 'should' lead to a concentration of proceedings in one Member State and the authorities of other Member States 'shall transfer the file . . . and close the case'.[63] Since these obligations leave little discretion to national authorities, there is a possibility that they might be challenged in view of Article 85(2) of the TFEU. Therefore, some more fine-tuning might be advisable. For instance, it could be clarified that a Eurojust decision is solely directed to the Member States and that it is a matter of national law which procedural measures are to be taken.

With regard to judicial review, an open question is whether it is necessary and appropriate expressly to provide that the suspect 'is considered to be directly affected' in the sense of Article 263(4) of the TFEU.[64] While the qualification of an act as a formal act of judicial procedure must be distinguished from the question of judicial review (i.e. whether the act is of direct concern to a person), a provision such as Article 14 of the draft regulation could be construed as implying that Eurojust's decisions are directed to the individuals concerned. In any case, ultimately it is for the Court of Justice to decide on the interpretation of Article 263(4) TFEU.

The realisation of the third building block, a *mechanism for the allocation of jurisdiction*, touches on more complex legal questions. Generally, the related proposal, too, would remain within the rationale of Article 82(1)(b) of the TFEU,

61 See Böse (n 40) 374.

62 Arguably, it would have to be examined whether the proposal should be limited to 'serious crime'.

63 See art 13(4), (5), and (6) of the Draft Proposal (the same should apply to multiple proceedings).

64 Article 14 of the same Draft Regulation.

especially with a view to the prevention of conflicts of jurisdiction. However, it would test the limits of this legal basis, in particular the dividing line between Article 82(1) and 82(2). The proposed draft regulation would imply a much higher degree of approximation of national law than the ones under the first and second building block. It could be argued that it would go beyond what are 'minimum rules'. While the restriction to minimum rules does not apply to Articles 82(1), one could demur that this provision does not allow for a far-reaching harmonisation but rather for an approximation ancillary to judicial cooperation and mutual recognition. In view of the principles of subsidiarity and proportionality this could be an important objection.

Nonetheless, the envisaged approximation would effectively contribute to achieving the 'roof' objectives of Article 82 of the TFEU, that is, of complementing the principle of mutual recognition and strengthening the underlying mutual trust. The proposed draft regulation is limited to the exercise of jurisdiction between Member States and would not necessarily interfere with national law applicable to purely domestic situations. It could therefore be concluded that it can be based on Article 82(1)(b). If this is true, it would not have to undergo the specific, additional necessity test foreseen in Articles 82(2) and 83. Nonetheless, the instrument would have to pass the general tests on subsidiarity, proportionality, and respect of national identity.

For those who deem that the extent of approximation involved in this proposal would go beyond what Article 82(1) of the TFEU allows, there would be a need to consider whether the second paragraph of this article can serve as a legal basis. However, several problems would arise here. First, as stated above, the proposal would have to pass the additional tests foreseen therein. Second, it might go beyond mere 'minimum rules'. Third, since Article 82(2) does not contain an explicit reference to problems of concurrent jurisdiction, one would have to take resort to the general formula of 'other specific aspects of criminal procedure'. The Council would first have to identify the limits of exercising jurisdiction as such an aspect. Last but not least, it is far from obvious that jurisdiction is a procedural issue. In many Member States, this matter is rather considered in the context of substantive criminal law.[65]

Alternatively, one would have to examine whether related measures can be based on Article 83 of the TFEU. This article, however, is limited to the 'definitions of criminal offences and sanctions'. Even if one could interpret this in a very wide sense (as comprising even the exercise of jurisdiction), Article 83 is clearly aiming at rules

65 A possible approach would be to subsume the jurisdiction to prescribe under substantive criminal law, whereas the jurisdiction to adjudicate or to enforce has a strong procedural dimension. Cf. Böse (n 40) 23.

on *specific* offences.[66] A general mechanism could, thus, hardly be established on this legal basis.

In this context, it should also be recalled that in the area of criminal law the Treaty emphasises the need to respect the Member States' national identities (Article 4(2) TEU). In the area of freedom, security and justice, particular respect is to be paid to their different legal systems and traditions (Article 67(1) TFEU). In this regard, some Member States might be inclined to challenge the third building block, as it would considerably limit their right to exercise their jurisdiction to adjudicate. It would be rather difficult to forecast the result of such a challenge.

66 Cf. Böse (n 40) 373.

3

PREVENTION AND SETTLEMENT OF CONFLICTS OF JURISDICTION (SPANISH SYSTEM)

MIGUEL CARMONA RUANO

I. SETTLEMENT OF INTERNATIONAL CONFLICTS OF JURISDICTION IN SPANISH LAW

A. Traditional lack of rules about settlement of international conflicts of jurisdiction

Spanish law did not set up, until recently, any rules about either the prevention or the settlement of international conflicts of jurisdiction. These types of conflicts were not frequent at all in the context of Spain's international relationships in the days of the codification of Spanish law, in the last decades of the nineteenth century, when the main legal bodies were established. Broadly speaking, in those days there was little or no cross-border or transnational crime and, as a result, Spain saw little reason to legislate about concurrence of jurisdictions. The authors of the Ley de Enjuiciamiento Criminal (LECrim), the Criminal Procedure Law of 1882, which is still the principal legal text on the matter, would probably consider that the affirmation of the principle of territoriality would be sufficient. Therefore, in contrast to the detailed regulation of the conflicts of jurisdictions between the common and military courts or between secular and ecclesiastic courts, not a single word was devoted in the original text of this Law to possible international conflicts.

Over the following pages it will be demonstrated that legislation showed entrenched resistance to changes and little progress was made over more than a century, despite the changes that have taken place in the nature of criminality and in international relations and the ratification of multilateral conventions opening the door for extra-territorial jurisdiction, with the obvious possibility of criminal courts of different countries claiming their own jurisdiction over the same cases.

This lack of regulation extended to:

- rules for Spanish courts to claim or sustain their own jurisdictions against foreign ones
- rules for a Spanish court transferring away jurisdiction after the claim from a foreign one.

B. Lack of rules about transferring away of jurisdiction from Spanish courts

Certainly, it could be said that there were two precepts in the Spanish legal text that appear to deal with the transferring away jurisdiction in favour of foreign courts. These two norms are Article 65(3) of the Organic Law on Judicial Power (Ley Orgánica del Poder Judicial, or LOPJ), LO 6/1985, and Article 14 of Law 13/2006, of 26 May, on the Spanish National Member of Eurojust.

However, the analysis of these two precepts shows that their limited scope does not allow considering them as general rules aimed at the prevention and even less at the settlement of conflicts of jurisdiction.

The first of these two dispositions, Article 65(3) LOPJ, establishes that the Criminal Chamber of the National Court (Audiencia Nacional) is the relevant court for 'transfers of jurisdiction in criminal matters that can arise from compliance with international treaties to which Spain is a party'.[1]

The open wording of this rule would imply a provision to be applied in a general scope. However, as a matter of fact the origin of this rule shows that the authors of the bill had only a very limited situation in mind: the application of the Agreement on Defense Cooperation with the United States of America (USA), first signed in 1953, whose current text dates from 1988. In accordance with this agreement, Spain will facilitate the transfer of jurisdiction in criminal matters to the military courts of the USA in relation to crimes committed by members of the US Armed Forces and non-military staff when the US Command certifies that the facts in their origin were *acts of service*. In these cases, the relevant court to decide about this transfer of jurisdiction is the Audiencia Nacional.

Accordingly, when, out of this context, different courts have sent a case to the Audiencia Nacional asking for a possible decision on transferring away jurisdiction to a foreign country, the answer has always been that this Article 65(3) LOPJ is not to be applied to this situation and that the decision, where appropriate, must be taken by the ordinary court with territorial competence to handle the case.[2]

Yet, the only conclusion to be drawn from this precept is the internal assignation of this competence to the Audiencia Nacional instead of another court, but not any rule about how to act with regard to foreign authorities.

1 Article 65(3):º [*La Sala de lo Penal de la Audiencia Nacional conocerá*] *de las cuestiones de cesión de jurisdicción en materia penal derivadas del cumplimiento de tratados internacionales en los que España sea parte.*

2 However, two recent judgments of the Supreme Court, 745/2015 of 11 November 2015 and 828/15 of 14 December 2015, seem to contradict this traditional case law and to affirm the competence of the Audiencia Nacional for different situations, on the ground of this precept.

Much wider was the scope of the other cited rule contained in Article 14(2) of the Law 16/2006, on the Spanish National Member of Eurojust, a statute today repealed and replaced by Law 16/2015.

This Article provided for the attribution to the Fiscal General del Estado (Attorney General or FGE) of the faculty of receiving requests made by Eurojust encouraging the Spanish authorities to initiate or follow proceedings in Spain or, on the contrary, proposing recognition that another foreign jurisdiction was best placed to carry out a given investigation or prosecution of specific facts. After receiving this request from Eurojust, the FGE was obliged, in accordance with this precept, to decide whether to accept this proposal or not. When the proposal is accepted, the FGE will give the relevant order to the prosecutors, who are obliged to follow his or her instructions.

This precept was aimed at unifying the response of the Spanish public prosecution service when dealing with requests received from Eurojust. Article 7 of the Council Decision 2002/187/JAI, of 28 February 2002, setting up Eurojust, today Article 7(1)(a) after the amendments introduced by Council Decision 2009/426/JHA, establishes that the College of Eurojust may 'ask the competent authorities of the Member States concerned, giving its reasons: (i) to undertake an investigation or prosecution of specific acts; (ii) to accept that one of them may be in a better position to undertake an investigation or to prosecute specific acts'.

However, the apparently wide scope of this rule was in fact limited by the following four circumstances:

- The FGE is not obliged to follow the recommendation of the College of Eurojust but only to give reasons for his or her decision (Article 8 Eurojust Decision).
- The public prosecutor is a party in criminal proceedings, without the monopoly of the prosecution or the control of the decisions about jurisdiction. As a matter of fact, Article 14(2)(b) provided that, after receiving the instruction of the FGE, the relevant prosecutor must ask [the judge] the appropriate activity.
- Similarly, Article 16 of the same Law established that when the proposal of Eurojust estimates that it is Spain that has jurisdiction over the facts, the FGE '*may* call on the relevant Examining Judge (*Juez de Instrucción*) to initiate proceedings or to extend already existing proceedings so that they include new facts'. The final decision is from this moment on in the hands of the examining judge.
- Both the public prosecution service and the criminal courts must follow the principle of legality as opposed to the principle of opportunity. The proposal can only be accepted if the Spanish courts have jurisdiction over the case or over the new facts (Article 16(3)).
- Neither this Law nor any other can establish any rule or guide about how the potential conflict of jurisdiction could be prevented or settled in case of discrepancy or non-acceptance of the proposal.

Today, Law 16/2006 has been repealed and substituted by Law 16/2015. However, Article 27 of the new law retains the same system as that related to the functions of the FGE in the decision to be taken about the proposal from Eurojust of accepting jurisdiction, even though this new law reinforces the role of the FGE and introduces a more complex legal regulation, which will be considered below.

II. SETTLEMENT OF INTERNAL CONFLICTS OF JURISDICTION

As stated above, in contrast to the lack of regulations about international conflicts, Spanish law did provide for detailed rules of prevention and settlement of conflicts between the judiciary and other branches, namely the administration, as well as between different jurisdictions, including between common criminal courts and military criminal courts.

The existing rules are made up of:

- Jurisdiction Conflicts Act 2/1987 (Ley de Conflictos de Jurisdicción 2/1987) (LCJ)
- Articles 38 to 41 of the LOPJ of 1985
- several articles of the LECrim.

In these three legal bodies, the usual proceedings for settlement of conflicts follow a similar pattern:

(i) Decision of claiming or of transferring jurisdiction adopted after hearing the opinion of the parties and of the public prosecutor office.

(ii) Communication with the jurisdiction deemed appropriate.

(iii) Decision of this latter body, after hearing the parties and the public prosecutor's office, on whether to accept or not the claim or the transfer of jurisdiction.

(iv) In the event of discrepancy, communication to the former body and deferral of the dispute to a common superior (e.g. a special chamber of the Supreme Court formed by judges of the criminal and military chambers) or a mixed body.

III. THE DEFINITION OF SPANISH JURISDICTION IN CRIMINAL MATTERS

The definition of Spanish jurisdiction in criminal matters exactly follows the model defined by Professor Vervaele: 'National rules on jurisdiction are not designed to prevent or solve a conflict of jurisdiction between countries or in a common area.

They are designed to claim competence, authority, *Strafgewalt, ius puniendi*, in a unilateral way by one State'.[3]

The Spanish law in this field follows this scheme:

- affirmation of territoriality as the basic criterion
- cases of extra-territorial jurisdiction by reason of the person involved
- cases of extra-territorial jurisdiction based on objective principles
- cases of universal jurisdiction of Spanish courts.

The principle of territoriality as the basic and general criterion of attribution of jurisdiction to Spanish courts is affirmed in Article 23(1) LOPJ: 'Spanish courts have jurisdiction over crimes and misdemeanours committed in Spanish territory or committed aboard ships or aircraft flying the Spanish flag'.

However, this same Article 23(1) establishes at the same level the reference to the priority of international conventions: '[w]ithout prejudice to the provisions of international treaties to which Spain is a party'.[4] This headline reference to the international treaties is also proclaimed in Article 21(1) (amended by Organic Law 7/2015) related to civil courts as the first and paramount criterion: 'Spanish civil courts will deal with lawsuits arising in Spanish territory in accordance with treaties and international conventions to which Spain is a party, with . . . Law and with Spanish Law'.[5] It should be borne in mind that, in accordance with Article 96(1) of the Spanish Constitution, international treaties, once officially published in Spain, form part of the internal legal order, and their provisions *may only be repealed, amended, or suspended in the manner provided in the treaties themselves or in accordance with the general rules of international law*. In section 4 below we will see the potential strength of this constitutional provision.

After this affirmation of the principle of territoriality as the basis for criminal jurisdiction, the law includes two main extensions: the first related to the person involved, the second on the objective criteria of protection of Spanish public interest.

This first extension is outlined in Article 23(2) LOPJ:

2. Spanish courts also have jurisdiction for crimes committed outside the national territory when those criminally responsible are Spanish citizens or foreigners

3 See John Vervaele, 'European Territoriality and Jurisdiction: The Protection of the EU's Financial Interests in Its Horizontal and Vertical (EPPO) Dimension' in Michiel Luchtman (ed), *Choice of Forum in Cooperation Against EU Financial Crime* (Eleven Publishing 2013) 171.

4 *1. En el orden penal corresponderá a la jurisdicción española el conocimiento de las causas por delitos y faltas cometidos en territorio español o cometidos a bordo de buques o aeronaves españoles, sin perjuicio de lo previsto en los tratados internacionales en los que España sea parte.*

5 *1. Los Tribunales civiles españoles conocerán de las pretensiones que se susciten en territorio español con arreglo a lo establecido en los tratados y convenios internacionales en los que España sea parte, en las normas de la Unión Europea y en las leyes españolas.*

who acquired Spanish citizenship after the commission of the act and the following requirements are also fulfilled:

a. The facts are punishable in the country of execution, unless, under an international treaty or of an act of an international organisation to which Spain is a party, that condition is not necessary . . .

b. The victim or the public prosecutor files a complaint before the Spanish courts.

c. The offender has not been acquitted, pardoned or punished abroad, or, in the latter case, has not served the sentence. If the sentence has been only served in part, this part will be taken into account to proportionally reduce the penalty.

It must be taken into account that Spanish law does not follow, on this point, an extension of the principle of territoriality based on the protection of Spanish citizens for crimes committed against them abroad. The principle is based on active, not passive, personality. The perpetrator's nationality rather than the victim's is what defines the extension of the jurisdiction on the basis of those criteria.

To close the circle, the principle of protection of the Spanish public interest follows, in Article 23(3) LOPJ:

3. Spanish courts will also have jurisdiction over acts committed by Spaniards or foreigners outside the country when they can be classified according to the Spanish penal law as any of the following offences:

   a. Treason or crimes against the peace and independence of the State.
   b. Crimes against the King or Queen, his or her Consort, his or her successor or the Regent.
   c. Rebellion and sedition.
   d. Counterfeit of the royal signature or stamp, of the stamp of State, of the signature of Ministers and of public or official seals.
   e. Counterfeit of the Spanish currency and issue of false currency.
   f. Any other forgery that directly harms the reputation or interests of the State, and the introduction or delivery of the counterfeit.
   g. Attacks against Spanish authorities or public officials.
   h. Crimes and offences committed in the exercise of their functions by Spanish officials residing abroad and crimes against the Spanish Public Administration.
   i. Crimes relating to exchange control.

However, the most controversial (and evolving) clause of definition of the jurisdiction of Spanish criminal courts comes from universal jurisdiction over certain types of crimes. The evolution, changes, and cases relating to this principle will be dealt with separately.

IV. THE PRINCIPLE OF UNIVERSAL JURISDICTION AND ITS EVOLUTION IN SPANISH LAW

As stated above, Articles 21 and 23 LOPJ stipulate that treaties or international conventions to which Spain is a party are the primary law to define the extension of the jurisdiction of Spanish courts, either civil or criminal.

As a matter of fact, several international conventions, prior or subsequent to the Organic Law of 1985, establish the universal jurisdiction of every state party for the investigation, prosecution, and adjudication of the crimes they are dealing with.

The principle of universal jurisdiction over certain types of crimes is by no means recent. There are facts that, by reason of their own nature and of their transnational execution, have been traditionally defined as international crimes. This happens, for instance, in cases of piracy and trafficking of slaves.[6] The basis of this principle is that there are crimes that by reason of their nature and consequences affect not only a limited physical space or number of persons but the whole of humanity and this circumstance entitles and obliges the international community to investigate and prosecute the perpetrator(s), regardless of the specific place where the crime has been committed. We are speaking of crimes against humanity, genocide, war crimes, or torture.

In other cases, conventions such as the Vienna Convention on Drug Trafficking (20 December 1988) also establish the same international obligation to block and intercept the traffic and to prosecute the persons responsible, considering that these crimes are by nature transnational crimes.

The transposition of this principle of universal jurisdiction into the internal law, established when the LOPJ was enacted in 1985, did not contemplate any restriction for Spanish criminal courts over these crimes.

The original wording of Article 23(4) LOPJ was very generous when defining the jurisdiction of Spanish courts:

6 See opinion of Chief Justice Marshall in *United States v Klintock* (1820), quoted by Ana Isabel Pérez Cepeda, 'Principio de Justicia Penal Universal versus principio de jurisdicción penal internacional' in Ana Isabel Pérez Cepeda (ed), *El principio de Justicia Universal. Fundamento y límites* (Tirant lo Blanch 2012).

Spanish courts also have jurisdiction over crimes committed by Spaniards or foreigners outside Spanish territory when such crimes could be typified, according to Spanish law, as:

a. Genocide
b. Terrorism
c. Piracy and illegal hijacking of aircraft
d. Forgery of foreign currency
e. Crimes relating to prostitution
f. Illegal trafficking of drugs
g. Any other crime that must be prosecuted in Spain in accordance with conventions or treaties to which Spain is a party.

This initial list was extended by successive amendments of 1999 (LO 11/1999) to include sexual assault against minors, 2005 (LO 3/2005) on female genital mutilation, and 2007 (LO 13/2007) to include trafficking of human beings.

Under this regulation, Spanish courts initiated proceedings relating to events that had happened in the territory of countries such as Chile (the well-known *Pinochet* case),[7] Argentina,[8] or Guatemala.

A claim related to crimes committed in Chile under the dictatorship prompted the issue by a central examining court of a request for the extradition of General Augusto Pinochet, who happened to be in London at the time. The request was accepted by the United Kingdom (UK) courts, even if eventually the Secretary of State for the Home Department decided to reject the rendition on the ground of illness.

The second case, concerning Argentina, gave rise to the trial, conviction, and sentence of an ex-member of the Argentinian army, Adolfo Scilingo, for crimes of genocide, terrorism, and torture committed in the notorious Escuela de Mecánica de la Armada (ESMA) during the military dictatorship.[9]

Nevertheless, the latter, related to Guatemala, provided the opportunity for the revision of the scope of this principle. The Central Examining Magistrate's Court (Juzgado de Instrucción) had accepted in 1999 the claim of the Nobel Peace Prize recipient Rigoberta Menchú against the general Efraín Ríos Montt and others for crimes committed during the military dictatorship. However, first the Audiencia

7 Ruling of the Audiencia Nacional of 4 November 2000, declaring the jurisdiction of Spanish courts.

8 Ruling of the Audiencia Nacional of 5 November 2000, with similar content.

9 Judgment of the Audiencia Nacional of 19 April 2005, after the affirmation of the jurisdiction by a ruling of the Supreme Court of 15 November 2004.

Nacional[10] and afterwards the Supreme Court[11] rejected the jurisdiction of the Spanish Court in this case, introducing the requirement of the existence of a 'relevant connection' with Spain. These decisions were overruled by the Constitutional Court in Judgment 237/2005 of 26 September upon the basis that this requirement was neither expressed nor implicit in the legislation and, accordingly, its introduction represented an undue and unconstitutional restriction of the right to access to courts guaranteed by the Constitution. The Audiencia Nacional obviously abided by this constitutional judgment[12] and so did the Supreme Court, which followed suit in the judgments of 11 December 2006, case *Couso*, relating to Iraq, and 18 July 2007, case *Cavallo*, relating to Argentina.

Another judgment of the Constitutional Court of 22 October 2007 on the case *Falun Gong* regarding China reaffirmed this case law, based on the absence of supplementary requirements attached to the jurisdiction of the Spanish courts over the list of crimes established by the legislation.

However, juridical and political debates had already started and this led to the first restriction through the amendment of the LOPJ by Organic Law 1/2009. The fact that triggered the amendment was the opening of committal proceedings related to war crimes supposedly committed by the Israeli army. It seems likely that intense pressure exerted by Israel, the USA, and other states induced the Cortes Generales (Spanish Parliament) to introduce an amendment to Article 23(4) of the LOPJ, requiring some 'relevant connection' with Spain for the universality principle to operate.[13] In fact, during the parliamentary debate representatives of the two main political parties referred to the need to 'solve some problems compromising our international relations and creating diplomatic conflicts'. According to the new wording of Article 23(4) LOPJ, the recognition of Spanish jurisdiction in these cases required at least one of the following additional conditions to be met:

- the supposed perpetrator is located in Spain or
- the victims are of Spanish citizenship or
- there is some other relevant connection with Spain.

10 Ruling of 13 December 2003.

11 Judgment of 25 February 2003.

12 Ruling of 16 February 2006.

13 The text introduced in art 23(4) is:

> *Sin perjuicio de lo que pudieran disponer los tratados y convenios internacionales suscritos por España, para que puedan conocer los Tribunales españoles de los anteriores delitos deberá quedar acreditado que sus presuntos responsables se encuentran en España o que existen víctimas de nacionalidad española, o constatarse algún vínculo de conexión relevante con España y, en todo caso, que en otro país competente o en el seno de un Tribunal internacional no se ha iniciado procedimiento que suponga una investigación y una persecución efectiva, en su caso, de tales hechos punibles.*

It was also required that no other country with territorially preferential jurisdiction or an international court were carrying out proceedings relating to the same case.

On the other hand, the new text added crimes against humanity to the list of crimes of universal jurisdiction as a consequence of the entry into force the Statute of Rome of the International Criminal Court.

Nonetheless, the amendment did not put an end to the 'problems compromising our international relations', which the legislation sought to avoid. The above-mentioned reference to the international treaties and conventions and the force of these international instruments in Spain's legal system, in accordance with the Constitution, led to a new string of proceedings applying this principle and relating particularly to Guantánamo, Gaza, and Tibet, apart from the following up of the already initiated proceedings over the *Couso* case (a Spanish photo-journalist killed by a missile launched from an American battle tank at the Palestine Hotel in Baghdad) or Guatemala once again.

A new and stronger embarrassing diplomatic conflict led in this case to the second amendment of the LOPJ, enacted in this case by the current Organic Law 1/2014, of 13 March, on universal justice.

On this occasion, the introduction of a new, more restrictive amendment was prompted by criminal investigations carried out against the President, the Prime Minister and other relevant political figures of the People's Republic of China for war crimes and crimes against humanity in Tibet between 1950 and 1979. The National Court had first accepted the claim in 2006. However, after the entry into force of the Organic Law 1/2009, the examining magistrate's court decided to close the proceedings, as the facts had neither a relevant connection to Spain nor had Tibet in past or current times historical, cultural, political, or, indeed, any other sort of relations with Spain. The judge also considered that in this case neither the conventions against genocide (even if deemed not applicable) nor the international law on crimes against humanity established a clear obligation for Spain to prosecute on these facts. This ruling was backed by the Audiencia Nacional, which dismissed the appeal lodged by the claimants, and eventually by rulings of the Supreme Court dated 6 October 2011 and 25 October 2012.

Nevertheless, another claim, this one referring to other facts even if also related to the Chinese occupation of Tibet, provided the occasion for a second set of committal proceedings carried out by a different examining judge of the Audiencia Nacional. In this case, after a first decision of the examining judge and the Audiencia Nacional rejecting the acceptance of the criminal claim lodged before them by several human rights organisations, the Supreme Court, by judgment 645/2006 of 20 June, had overruled these decisions and ordered the acceptance. After many vicissitudes, international arrest warrants were issued against the individuals holding the positions of President of the People's Republic of China, Prime Minister, Secretary General of the Communist Party and members of the Chinese Government over the relevant period of time. A third criminal claim was lodged on 16 April 2014, alleging torture and crimes against humanity committed against Buddhist Tibetan monks.

This embarrassing situation for Spanish diplomacy provided the opportunity for the Spanish government to present a new bill including a further restriction of the reach of this principle in the jurisdiction of Spanish courts. According to this amendment, passed as Organic Law 1/2014, the acceptance of jurisdiction in these cases of universal jurisdiction included in Article 23(4) LOPJ requires the presence of cumulative points of connection with Spain and, even so, the acceptance must be triggered by the *fiscal* (Public Prosecutor).

The new requirements are, in short:

- In genocide, crimes against humanity, or war crimes, the legal proceedings must be carried out against a Spanish national, or against a foreign citizen with habitual residence in Spanish territory if the demand for extradition was initially rejected.
- In torture or enforced disappearance, the legal proceedings must be carried out against a Spanish national or the victim be a Spanish national *and* the perpetrator is on Spanish territory.
- In other crimes such as terrorism, piracy, drug trafficking, trafficking of human beings, or corruption in international contracts the requirements vary but always refer to the Spanish nationality of the perpetrator or the habitual residence in Spanish territory or the Spanish nationality of the victim, in this latter case when the perpetrator is also located on Spanish territory.

Even in these cases, the jurisdiction of Spanish courts must be denied if an international court has accepted the investigation and prosecution and the jurisdiction must also be transferred to the country where the crimes have been committed if this country is investigating or prosecuting them, except in the event of lack of will or of capacity for the investigation and prosecution. The decision as to what constitutes this lack of will or capacity is reserved for the Supreme Court.

As a further measure directly devoted to overcoming these diplomatic embarrassments, the final Schedule (*disposición final*) of the Law ordered the entry into force of this amendment on the day after its publication, on 13 March 2014.

Finally, as a sort of counter-balance for the negative image that this reform would cast, the new law introduced some new offences falling into the extra-territorial jurisdiction of the Spanish criminal courts, such as the abovementioned corruption in international contracts, as well as corruption among individuals or in international economic transactions, or offences covered by the Council of Europe Convention of 28 October 2011 on counterfeit medical products and crimes that threaten public health, and, last but not least, the much-praised inclusion of offences related to violence against women and domestic violence, with a reference to the Council of Europe Convention of 11 May 2011.

The list of crimes which must be prosecuted in Spain in accordance with conventions or treaties to which Spain is a party was also completed with the specific mention of each one of these conventions. A final general and open clause completes the list, referring to '[a]ny other offence whose prosecution is mandatorily imposed by a Treaty to which Spain is a party, or in other normative acts of an international organisation to which Spain is a member, in the circumstances and conditions determined by these norms'.

The final result is a relatively long list of twenty-one different types of crimes, but always accompanied by detailed requirements of nationality of the supposed perpetrators, effects on the territory or the interests of Spain or extended to Spain, and, more particularly, the possibility itself of investigation and/or prosecution of the crimes when the perpetrators are in Spain and so the proceedings can be carried out against them.

After this Amendment of 2004, the Audiencia Nacional, by ruling 38/2014 of 2 July adopted in plenary session, decided to close the case related to Tibet because of the lack of jurisdiction of the Spanish courts over the facts at issue. Several other court rulings followed suit soon afterwards, thereby putting an end to the outstanding proceedings related to universal jurisdiction and accordingly to the controversy about its extent. Among them can be mentioned ruling 215/2014 of 15 July 2014 on *Falun Gong*, or ruling 215/15 of 25 November 2015 on the previously cited *Couso* case.

But once again the above-mentioned force of international treaties and conventions guaranteed in the Spanish Constitution kept the juridical debate open. This same cited ruling of the Audiencia Nacional in plenary formation of 2 July 2014, on Tibet, included the dissenting opinion of five judges, who maintained the prevalence of the obligation of every jurisdiction to prosecute war crimes in accordance with the Geneva Conventions of 1949, and particularly Article 146 of the fourth Geneva Convention. In addition, a new ruling of a central examining court, relating to the *Guantánamo* case, reaffirmed its jurisdiction over possible crimes of torture and war crimes on grounds of the Spanish nationality of one of the victims, the prevalence of the obligations to prosecute imposed by the Geneva Conventions and the Convention against torture, and the lack of any effective investigation of these crimes by the territorial jurisdiction whose authorities did not respond to the request for information. On this last point, the examining judge acknowledged the existence of some administrative investigation and, in accordance with the regulation introduced by the above-mentioned Organic Law 1/2014, referred the decision concerning the existence and sufficiency of the proceedings carried out by the preferential territorial jurisdiction to the Supreme Court. Another case closely related to this one, about the stopovers in Spain of some flights with prisoners during the so-called extraordinary renditions, was closed by the judge in a ruling that was confirmed by the Audiencia Nacional, but not without a dissenting vote.

Even jurisdiction over cases relating to drug trafficking has been the subject of debate after this Organic Law 1/2014. In two initial rulings (with dissenting votes), the Audiencia Nacional followed the literal wording of the new text and decided that Spain did not have jurisdiction over ships without a Spanish flag sailing the open seas. But the Supreme Court, in plenary session, accepted the appeals lodged by the public prosecutor and overruled these decisions in judgments 592/2014 and 593/2014, both of 24 July. Later judgments (755/14, 810/14, 847/14, 866/14, 168/15, 628/16, and 730/16) confirmed these precedents and declared their own jurisdiction in cases of seizure of drugs on ships outside Spanish territorial waters carrying the flags of Turkey, Sierra Leone, or other countries. These decisions affirmed Spanish jurisdiction in these types of cases, applying the Vienna Convention of 1988 on drug trafficking and the United Nations Convention on the Law of the Sea of 1982 (Montego Bay Convention).

To close this chapter, it is necessary to make reference to another ruling of the Audiencia Nacional, No 256/2014 of 4 July, which affirmed the jurisdiction of the Spanish court over crimes allegedly committed by Moroccan armed forces in Western Sahara. The Spanish jurisdiction over these facts, supported also by the Public Prosecution Service, was grounded in the reason that Spain is, de iure even if not de facto, the administering power for this territory and accordingly obliged by Articles 73 and 74 of the Charter of the United Nations (26 June 1945) to give jurisdictional protection to the citizens residing there. A new diplomatic conflict, this time with Morocco, was looming.

Yet, even with these doubts, a string of recent judgments of the Supreme Court, in particular judgments 296/2915, of 6 May 2015 on *Tibet*, 297/2015 of 8 May 2015 on *Falun Gong*, 551/2015 of 24 September 2015 on *Rwanda*,[14] and, more recently, 797/2016 of 25 October 2016 on the *Couso* case, and 869/2016 of 18 November 2016 on *Guantánamo*, have eventually put an end to the legal debate. In these judgments, the Supreme Court affirmed that the amendment of the LOPJ by Organic Law 1/2014 provided for a limited model of universal jurisdiction, which excludes, as a general rule, the investigation and prosecution of these types of crimes *in absentia*, and introduces the need for a relevant link with Spain. According to the Supreme Court, the different treaties signed by Spain in this field do not impose an absolute and unconditional model of universal jurisdiction and its exercise must be subject to the limits of the relevant national law. The Supreme Court in these judgments also rejected the demand of the claimants to refer the legal point to a preliminary ruling of the Constitutional Court.

V. CONVENTION NO 73 OF THE COUNCIL OF EUROPE ON THE TRANSFER OF PROCEEDINGS

The above-mentioned lack of regulation in the internal Spanish law of conflicts of jurisdiction was balanced with the existence of norms of other origin to be applied to the transfer of proceedings.

14 In this case a high-ranking general of the Rwandan Army had been arrested in London as a result of the EAW issued by Spain.

The most important of these legal instruments is the European Convention No 73 of the Council of Europe of 1972 on the Transfer of Proceedings in Criminal Matters.

According to Article 3 of this Convention, any contracting state having competence (jurisdiction) under its own law to prosecute an offence may, for the purposes of applying this Convention, waive or desist from proceedings against a suspected person who is being or will be prosecuted for the same offence by another contracting state. Having regard to Article 21(2), any such decision to waive or to desist from proceedings shall be provisional, pending a final decision in the other contracting state.

On the other hand, a contracting state may request another contracting state to commence proceedings in the circumstances listed in Article 8, which enumerates the reasons to deem preferential the jurisdiction of another state more closely related to the case or being in a better position to investigate, prosecute, and adjudicate the crime giving rise to the proceedings.

The Convention neither obliges a contracting state to agree to the request, nor obliges another state to accept or waive its jurisdiction; merely to communicate the decision taken. Should the states concerned agree, the transfer of jurisdiction must take place through the central authorities designated by the contracting states, usually through the respective Ministries of Justice.

However, this Council of Europe Convention has not yet been ratified by all the Member States of the European Union (EU), and Finland, France, Germany, Ireland, Malta, Poland, and the UK are not parties to this instrument. Other countries have expressed important reservations.

A similar regulation can be found in Article 19 of the Convention on Mutual Assistance in Criminal Matters between the European Union and the United States of America of 25 June 2003 and transposed in Spain by agreement of 17 December 2004. According to this norm, in cases of concurrent jurisdiction each state can demand that the other initiate the criminal prosecution of the facts. The demand must be transmitted through the central authorities and must be settled by the required states applying their own principles.

VI. LAYING OF INFORMATION, ARTICLE 21 OF CONVENTION NO 30 OF THE COUNCIL OF EUROPE ON MUTUAL ASSISTANCE IN CRIMINAL MATTERS 1959

Far less reduced is the scope of Article 21 of the European Convention on Mutual Assistance in Criminal Matters, Convention No 30 of the Council of Europe of 20 April 1959.

According to this Article, one contracting party may lay information to another contracting party with a view to proceedings in the courts of the latter.

The only provision of the Convention on this point is that the laying of information shall be transmitted between the Ministries of Justice and that the requested party shall notify the requesting party of any action taken on such information and shall forward a copy of the record of any verdict pronounced.

VII. CASES OF TRANSFER OF JURISDICTION

What has been said so far does not necessarily lead to the conclusion that this lack of regulation has represented an insurmountable obstacle to the existence of cases of transfer of jurisdiction in both directions: from a Spanish court to a foreign one and from a foreign jurisdiction to Spain.

An example case of a transfer from the Spanish jurisdiction can be seen in the settlement agreed in the operation named 'Pleasure' between the courts of Alicante in Spain and Manchester in the UK.

The case began with a joint investigation team (JIT) operating in both England and Spain to investigate a British organisation dealing with drug trafficking (hashish resin), to be transported from Spain to the UK.

The fruit of the work of this JIT, with undercover British agents operating in Spain, was the seizure of 300 kg of hashish resin and the arrest of six UK citizens in Denia, Alicante, and the simultaneous arrest of two more suspects in the UK, also British citizens. As a result, both jurisdictions initiated proceedings.

In the UK, the two arrested suspects pleaded guilty before the Manchester Crown Court and a European arrest warrant (EAW) was issued for the surrender of the six people arrested in Spain. At the same time, the UK Crown Prosecution Service made a request to transfer the proceedings from Spain to the UK. It is worth noting that Spain is a contracting party to the European Convention of the Council of Europe of 1972 on the Transfer of Proceedings in Criminal Matters but, as stated above, the UK is not.

Nevertheless, after consultations between the two concurrent jurisdictions, the examining judge of Denia, who was carrying out the committal proceedings in Spain, decided to waive jurisdiction and to transfer the proceedings to the UK. This decision, challenged by two of the defendants, was backed by the Provincial Criminal Court (Audiencia Provincial) of Alicante, which by ruling 425/2013 dismissed the appeal and confirmed the ruling of the examining judge of Denia.

The grounds of the decision of the judge, backed by the Audiencia Provincial, were the better position of the British jurisdiction to prosecute and adjudicate the crimes at issue, owing to the fact that:

- the organisation was based in the UK
- the suspects were all British
- the criminal proceeds would be recovered in the UK

- two of the members of the organised group had already appeared before the court in Britain and pleaded guilty
- the unity of proceedings in the same facts demanded the adjudication of all of the defendants by the same British court.

On these grounds, the judge concluded that the best place for the adjudication of the entire case was in the Manchester Crown Court.

As a matter of fact, this possibility of transferring away jurisdiction had already been applied to Chile before any amendment of the LOPJ, and on other occasions the Spanish courts have waived their own concurrent jurisdiction, considering other countries best placed for the adjudication of the facts at issue. An example of this type of situation can be found in a ruling of the Audiencia Nacional of December 2008, when the court accepted the rendition to France of a person against whom a EAW had been issued. The defendant tried to resist the surrender, invoking the concurrent jurisdiction of the Spanish court over the facts of drug trafficking and money laundering, the object of the warrant. But the court rejected the allegation, arguing that drug trafficking is a crime of international prosecution committed in the territory of the common space of freedom, security and justice of the EU with four possible jurisdictions involved (Spain, France, the Netherlands, and Switzerland) and that the jurisdiction which issued the warrant, France, was best placed for the prosecution, as both drugs and money had been seized there.

More recently, the Supreme Court in the above-mentioned judgments 745/2015 of 11 November 2015 and 828/15 of 14 December 2015 confirmed the decision of the Audiencia Nacional and of the central examining judge to order the transfer of proceedings to Portugal in a case dealing with a seizure of drugs carried out by the Spanish authorities on the high seas when boarding a vessel flying the Portuguese flag, after receiving a request from the Portuguese authorities. It should be noted that, in this case, the Spanish courts invoked the bilateral treaty between Spain and Portugal on the combat against illicit drug trafficking on the high seas, a treaty made in Lisbon on 2 March 1998, which gave preference in this case to the Portuguese courts.

Other cases of acceptance of the jurisdiction transferred by a foreign court can be found in Spanish case law. Examples of these acceptances include:

- Judgment 20/2013, Audiencia Nacional, of 12 July 2013 (conviction of a Spanish woman for a crime of injuries caused in Slovakia where the prosecution was initiated and transferred to Spain. No question over Spanish jurisdiction was raised in this case).
- Ruling of the Supreme Court of 26 September 2013 in a case of trafficking of human beings initiated in Cologne, Germany and transferred to Spain.

VIII. FRAMEWORK DECISION ON PREVENTION AND SETTLEMENT OF CONFLICTS OF JURISDICTION AND ITS TRANSPOSITION INTO SPANISH LAW

The state of play changed when the Spanish Parliament passed the above-mentioned Law 16/2015 of 7 July 2015 on the Statute of the Spanish National Member of Eurojust, Conflicts of Jurisdiction, International Cooperation Networks and members of the Ministry of Justice posted abroad in the Foreign Service.

The antecedents of this legal instrument in the Council of Europe and in the EU are the object of other works and there is no need to reproduce them here. It is only necessary to recall that, after the failure of the Greek proposal for the adoption of a Framework Decision establishing a consultation procedure and setting a list of preferential criteria to determine the more relevant jurisdiction in criminal cases, the European Commission published in 2005 a Green Paper reiterating the need to establish criteria for the choice of the jurisdiction.

Eventually, in 2009, the EU adopted the Council FD 2009/948/JHA of 30 November 2009 on Prevention and Settlement of Conflicts of Exercise of Jurisdiction in Criminal Proceedings. However, as has often been repeated, the scope of this legal instrument is limited to providing for mechanisms of mutual information and consultation in case of parallel proceedings, without establishing criteria for the choice of jurisdiction.

Spanish Law, at the time of transposing this framework decision into the national law, went a step further and included some criteria that, to a considerable extent, follow the guidelines drawn up by the Eurojust College in 2003.

The FWD 2009/948/JHA was transposed into Chapter V of the aforesaid law as Articles 30 to 32. The system is very simple and closely follows Article 5 *passim* of the Framework Decision, in that a Spanish judicial authority which considers that a possible conflict may exist must send a proposal of contact (*solicitud de contacto*) providing the available information and which, after receiving the response, must 'promote a consensus', with the possible help of Eurojust. Eventually, should the relevant authorities not reach any agreement, the Spanish judicial authority, after hearing the public prosecutor and the parties, will decide about its own jurisdiction. The same procedure must be followed after receiving a similar communication from a foreign judicial authority about possible parallel proceedings. The judicial authority is obliged in both cases to inform the National Member (NM) of Eurojust.

Article 30 contains a detailed regulation of the content of the communication to be sent to the foreign authorities in this 'proposal of contact'. This communication must include:

(a) A detailed description of the facts that are the object of the proceedings carried out in Spain.

(b) Criminal classification and potential punishment of these offences under Spanish law.

(c) Identification of suspects and information about whether they are in custody or any other supervision measures that may have been adopted.

(d) Identification, if relevant, of the victims and possible protection measures adopted.

(e) Stage of the proceedings with a certified copy of the decisions already adopted about the communication of charges or indictment.

(f) Contact details of the examining judge carrying out the judicial proceedings or the public prosecutor carrying out preliminary investigations as well as, if applicable, of the contact point of the European Judicial Network (EJN) or the National Member of Eurojust helping out in the contacts.

(g) Details as to which Spanish authorities can provide additional information about evidence or investigations already undertaken or any foreseen difficulties for the investigation or prosecution in Spain.

Article 31 deals with the obligation to respond to the requests of contact coming from judicial authorities of other countries, providing, if necessary, the above-mentioned information about the proceedings underway in Spain.

In both cases, of active or passive initiative, the law provides for the disclosure and participation of the parties, except if secrecy has been imposed, and how to take the relevant judicial decisions for the proposal of contact.

After the contact has been established, the law, following the framework decision, encourages the Spanish authorities to try to reach an agreement with their counterpart in other jurisdictions.

On this point, the law goes further than the framework decision and includes criteria to decide about the jurisdiction. These criteria are:

a. residence and nationality of the defendant

b. place where most of the facts or the most substantial facts have been committed

c. jurisdiction under whose rules the evidence has been obtained or where it is more likely to be obtained

d. interest of the victim

e. localisation of the proceeds or effects of the offence and the jurisdiction which demanded their freezing

f. phase of the different proceedings

g. criminal classification of the facts in the law and penalties applicable in the states in conflict.

Nevertheless, these criteria are not ranked and, accordingly, no hierarchy or preference is established among them, and no rule is provided for weighing them.

If we compare this list with the criteria listed by the College of Eurojust in 2003, there appears to be a striking absence of any reference to a general principle akin to the initial one proclaimed by the Eurojust guidelines that the prosecution should take place in the jurisdiction 'where the majority of the criminality occurred or where the majority of the loss was sustained'. There is also a lack of any reference to costs and resources, to the possibility of dividing the prosecution between two or more jurisdictions, or even to the protection of witnesses.

In addition, the new law repeals and replaces the system provided for in Law 16/2006 related to the proposals received from the NM or the College of Eurojust to waive or to accept jurisdiction.

The new system seems at first glance only slightly different from the former one, already seen, of Articles 14 and 16 of Law 16/2006. However, there are significant differences.

First, in Article 22 of the new Law, the NM of Eurojust will communicate directly with the national coordinator of Eurojust in Spain or with the relevant authority. However, the requests of the NM must be addressed to the FGE insofar as they deal with the initiation of an investigation in Spain or the transfer abroad of some proceedings carried out in Spain. In these cases, the FGE must take a decision within ten days and, if the proposal is accepted, must request that the relevant judge adopt the appropriate activity.

For its part, Article 27 of the new law deals with the transfer of proceedings to Spain from another Member State of the EU. Repeating substantially the wording of the precedent Article 22, when a judicial authority of another Member State of the EU has decided to transfer a proceeding initiated abroad on the grounds that Spain is in a better position to prosecute, the Eurojust College or the Eurojust NM may urge the relevant authorities to undertake such investigations. Only if the demand refers to the initiation of a new procedure in Spain will they forward the request to the FGE.

The acceptance of the transfer depends on whether or not the Spanish courts have jurisdiction in accordance with the domestic law.

However, the question of the absence of regulation about the way to settle the possible conflict still stands. As stated above, the new law provides for a mechanism of consultations and promotes the search for a consensus. If this consensus is not reached directly between the relevant authorities of the states in conflict, the Spanish judicial authority *can* refer the case to Eurojust seeking an agreement between the national members and, as a last resort, the case *can* be referred to the College, asking for a non-binding opinion. But, eventually, should all these mechanisms fail and the relevant authorities not reach any agreement, the Spanish judicial authority, after hearing the public prosecutor and the parties, will decide about its own jurisdiction.

It is necessary to clarify, furthermore, that according to the consistent case law of the Spanish Supreme Court, Spanish law does not allow the Spanish court to maintain a conflict of jurisdiction with a foreign court. The doctrine of the Supreme Court was established through the judgment of 25 February 2003, and confirmed by the judgment of 18 July 2007 (the *Argentina* case) and, more recently, by a ruling of 24 November 2010. The latter did not accept the defendant's appeal asking the court to declare the lack of jurisdiction of the Spanish court and to transfer the case to its Portuguese counterpart. According to the Supreme Court (TS), the Articles of the LECrim invoked in that case by the defendant by no means refer to international conflicts of jurisdiction but to internal ones. The TS concludes its rationale declaring that an international negative conflict of jurisdiction could not arise from a decision of a Spanish court, given that 'there is no body to settle the possible conflict nor the possibility of a unilateral attribution of jurisdiction to a foreign court as there is no rule allowing this transfer'.

A more recent judgment of the Supreme Court, No 118/2014 of 18 February, confirms this position. The defendant in a case of money laundering demanded, on appeal, the waiving of the Spanish jurisdiction in favour of that of the USA, where allegedly a district court of Florida was dealing with some proceeding concerning the same facts. The transfer had been denied by the Audiencia Nacional. According to the Supreme Court, the proposed waiving of jurisdiction was not possible as neither had a transfer request been received from the American authorities nor had any decision been taken by the Spanish central authority (Ministry of Justice) whose competence was reserved by the bilateral convention.

Certainly, this case law has been produced before the Law 16/2015. But the state of play has not changed after the new statute.

IX. CONCLUSION

1. In the past and until recently Spanish law did not provide for any mechanism of prevention or of settlement of conflicts of jurisdiction.
2. The definition of the jurisdiction of the Spanish courts in the Organic Law on the Judicial Power provides for cases of extraterritorial jurisdiction as well as for the exercise of universal jurisdiction over several types of crimes, even though this universal jurisdiction was severely limited in 2014.
3. Spain has transposed the Council FD 2009/948/JHA of 30 November 2009 on prevention and settlement of conflicts of exercise of jurisdiction in criminal proceedings through Law 16/2015 of 7 July.

4. The new law closely follows the mechanisms of consultations provided for in the framework decision and encourages reaching a consensus with the authorities of other countries so as to prevent possible conflicts of jurisdiction. These mechanisms consist of exchange of communications and of data with the authorities of another Member State of the EU in order to trace or confirm the existence of possible parallel proceedings and to try to reach an agreement about the jurisdiction.
5. However, the Spanish judge or court must take their own decision on the ground of the domestic law and there is no mechanism foreseen for the settlement of international conflicts of jurisdiction.
6. The law also provides for the response to a request coming from Eurojust or from the authorities of another Member State of the EU to accept proceedings initiated abroad, to accept the request to initiate an investigation in Spain, or to transfer criminal proceedings underway in Spain to another country.
7. Again, the decision to initiate or to carry on a criminal investigation or prosecution in Spain will be unilateral and it depends exclusively on the definition of the extent of the jurisdiction of the Spanish courts in accordance with the domestic law.
8. There is a reference in Article 32(4) of the new law to the possibility for Spanish courts to waive their own jurisdiction and transfer abroad proceedings initiated in Spain. This decision can obviously be taken when the Spanish court has no jurisdiction. However, the law does not provide any support to a possible decision by Spanish courts to waive their own jurisdiction in the very frequent cases of transnational offences where both countries can claim it in accordance with the respective domestic law.
9. According to the consistent case law of the Supreme Court, the Spanish courts cannot raise a conflict of jurisdiction with the judicial authorities of another country.

4

FORUM CHOICE IN THE AREA OF FREEDOM, SECURITY, AND JUSTICE

ANGELO MARLETTA

I. INTRODUCTION: JURISDICTION, CONFLICTS, AND CHOICES IN THE AREA OF FREEDOM, SECURITY, AND JUSTICE

The European Union (EU), as unprecedented institutional and polity project, is responsible for the fulfilment of a set of policy goals that go beyond the mere sum of the interests of its Member States. The establishment of an 'area of freedom, security and justice without internal frontiers, in which the free movement of persons is ensured in conjunction with appropriate measures with respect to . . . the prevention and combating of crime'[1] is probably one of the most demanding goals of the integration process, whose fulfilment requires commitment to coherent action on several levels: vertically, between the EU and the Member States, through incorporating the implementation of the Treaty objectives in the development of their respective criminal policies, and horizontally, between the Member States themselves, by developing mutual trust.

The prevention and settlement of conflicts of criminal jurisdiction is an essential element of the action to establish and maintain an area of freedom, security and justice (AFSJ) and, at the same time, represents one of the strongest challenges to the old conceptions of Westphalian sovereignty. After the adoption of the Lisbon Treaty, the mandate to the EU legislator to deal with jurisdictional conflicts is, nonetheless, clear. Two legal bases are indeed provided in the Treaty: the first one in Article 82(1)(b) TFEU to regulate both the prevention and the settlement of jurisdiction and the second in Article 85(1)(c) TFEU for what concerns the potential role of Eurojust, the European Union's Judicial Cooperation Unit in the 'resolution' thereof.[2]

At this point, a preliminary terminological clarification is needed. The Treaty language adopts the terms 'settlement' or 'resolution' of conflicts of jurisdiction, while this contribution resorts to the concept of 'choice of forum' to better highlight the existence of a margin of discretion in the settlement—or resolution—of a positive

1 Article 3(2) TEU.

2 For the analysis of the current legal bases on jurisdictional conflicts see the contribution of M. Wasmeier, 'The Legal Basis for Preventing and Resolving Conflicts of Criminal Jurisdiction in the TFEU', in this book at 100.

conflict of jurisdiction. Thus, 'choice of forum', for the purposes of this analysis, has to be intended as the result of the resolution of a conflict between two or more claims of *ius puniendi*, by way of an agreement between the concerned Member States or by means of an authoritative decision by an external, third, 'decider'.

That being said, this contribution will provide a critical analysis of the current state of the art on the choice of forum in the AFSJ, considering the pre-Lisbon-Era framework, the fundamental rights and principles enshrined in the EU Charter of Fundamental Rights (EU CFR) and the results of the research project 'Prevention and Settlement of Conflicts of Exercise of Jurisdiction in Criminal Law' (CJCL Project) carried out at the University of Luxembourg between June 2014 and August 2017.[3]

II. PRE-LISBON APPROACH AND AD HOC CONSULTATION PROCEDURES

Conflicts of jurisdiction made their way into EU primary law for the first time in 1997 with the Amsterdam Treaty, which—together with the concept of 'Area of Freedom, Security and Justice' (AFSJ)—introduced their prevention as an objective of the common action under former Article 31(d) of the Treaty on the European Union. Nonetheless, the pre-Lisbon approach of the EU legislator to criminal jurisdiction was more prone to promote potential overlaps—and then risk of conflicts—than to prevent them.[4] In line with the trend endorsed by several international[5] and Council of Europe conventions[6] addressing the most serious forms of criminality, several EU legal instruments aiming at approximating the definition of certain types of offences have indeed also expressly encouraged the EU Member States to establish or extend their extra-territorial jurisdiction over these same offences.

3 The author of this contribution participated in the CJCL Project as a research associate.

4 See P. Caeiro, 'Jurisdiction in Criminal Matters in the EU: Negative and Positive Conflicts, and Beyond', in *KritV*, 4/2010, 366 ff and also A. Klip, *European Criminal Law. An Integrative Approach* (3rd ed, Intersentia 2016) 217 ff.

5 See for instance art 5 of the 1979 UN Convention on taking of hostages; art 5 of the 1984 UN Convention against torture; art 6 of the 1997 UN Convention for the suppression of terrorist bombings; art 15 of the 2004 UN Convention against transnational organised crime. S. Z. Feller, 'Concurrent Criminal Jurisdiction in the International Sphere' (1981) *Israel Law Review* 43 observed that from the perspective of international law the potential concurrence of multiple criminal jurisdiction may be desirable 'for two reasons: to ensure that every offender receives his appropriate punishment, and to allow the pluralistic approach of the states in determining the scope of incidence of the criminal law norms according to the locus of the crime'.

6 See e.g. art 5 of the 1998 CoE Convention on the Protection of the Environment through Criminal Law; art 17 of the 1999 CoE Convention on Corruption; art 22 of the 2001 CoE Convention on Cybercrime; art 14 of the 2005 CoE Convention on the Prevention of Terrorism; art 25 of the 2007 CoE Convention on the protection of children against sexual exploitation and sexual abuse.

Dating back to the Convention on the Protection of Financial Interest of 1995, both the active personality principle[7] and various forms of the protective principle have been promoted as additional bases of jurisdiction in several EU instruments dealing with corruption,[8] the counterfeiting of the Euro,[9] terrorism,[10] trafficking in human beings,[11] immigration offences,[12] drug trafficking,[13] organised crime,[14] cyber-crime (attacks against information systems),[15] sexual exploitation of children, and child pornography.[16] From a theoretical standpoint, such an expansive approach was essentially justified by the need to fill potential jurisdictional gaps with regard to cross-border criminality and to avoid impunity in an area where internal borders have been abolished and free movement of persons—and potentially also of offenders—is granted.[17]

While the promotion of extra-territorial jurisdiction represented a clear trend of the approximating efforts of the EU legislator, the side-effects of such jurisdictional overlaps—potential positive jurisdictional conflicts—were inconsistently addressed

7 The active personality principle—or the principle of active nationality—is a classical and generally accepted ground for jurisdiction which confers extraterritorial reach to the criminal laws of the state of nationality of the offender. In force of this principle, the citizen will be subject to the jurisdiction of his State of nationality also if the conduct has been completely committed outside the territory of that state. This, of course, can create a potential concurrence between the jurisdiction of the territorial state and the state of nationality. The principle of active personality relies on a variety of theoretical justifications, including the idea of a general duty of allegiance embedded to the status of citizenship. More recently, the principle has been promoted to support the principle *aut dedere aut iudicare* in cases where the extradition of nationals is not possible. See C. Ryngaert, *Jurisdiction in International Law* (OUP 2008) 90 and A. Chehtman, *The Philosophical Foundations of Extraterritorial Punishment* (OUP 2010) 59.

8 Article 7 of the Corruption Convention of 1997; with regard to the corruption in the private sector, see art 7 of FD 2003/568/JHA, [2003] OJ L192/54.

9 Article 9 FD 2000/383/JHA, [2000] OJ L140/1.

10 Article 9 of FD 2002/475/JHA [2002] OJ L164/3. Today, this instrument has been replaced by Directive 2017/541/EU.

11 Article 6 of FD 2002/629/JHA, [2002] OJ L203/1, now replaced with substantial amendments by art 10 of the Directive 2011/36/EU.

12 Article 4 of FD 2002/946/JHA, [2002] OJ L328/1.

13 Article 8 of FD 2004/757/JHA, [2004] OJ L335/8.

14 Article 7 of FD 2008/841/JHA, [2008] OJ L300/42.

15 Article 10 of FD 2005/222/JHA, [2005] OJ L69/67, today replaced by Directive 2013/40/EU.

16 FD 2004/68/JHA, [2004] OJ L13/44, art 8, now replaced with substantial amendments by art 17 of Directive 2011/92/EU.

17 See M. Luchtman, 'Towards a Transnational Application of the Legality Principle in the EU's Area of Freedom, Security and Justice?' (2013) *Utrecht Law Review* 16.

under the pre-Lisbon legislative framework.[18] Most of the above-mentioned EU legal instruments indeed provided for a consultation mechanism between the authorities of the Member States in case of a positive conflict of jurisdiction[19] but only a few of them indicated criteria to solve the conflict and, what is more, endorsing very different approaches. The no longer in force FD on terrorism, for instance, contained a list of criteria to be taken in 'sequential account' when determining which of the Member States potentially having concurrent jurisdiction should prosecute the case. The presence of the adjective 'sequential'—no longer reproduced in the corresponding provision of the 2017 Directive on combating terrorism[20]—suggested a hierarchical nature of the criteria listed in the FD.[21] Within a hierarchical model, the jurisdictional criteria are ranked and applied following a pre-determined priority order and—at least in theory—there is no margin for discretionary choices:[22] the lower criterion may be applied only if the higher one cannot be determined; the determination of the prosecuting Member State is therefore highly foreseeable but also rigid. The 2008 FD on organised crime, on the contrary, adopted a more flexible approach: the criteria listed under Article 7(2) (territoriality, nationality, or residence of the perpetrator, nationality of the victims, territory where the perpetrator was found) have only to be taken in 'special' but not 'sequential' account by the national authorities.

Those two examples are an expression of the 'piecemeal' attitude of the EU legislator towards the issue of conflicts of jurisdiction in the pre-Lisbon era. An attitude which combined a panoply of *ad hoc* consultation procedures scattered across the various EU legal instruments approximating criminal law, a variable indication (or

18 Caeiro, 'Jurisdiction in Criminal Matters in the EU' (n 4) 366 critically argues that 'the duty of the European Union (EU) to prevent positive conflicts was plainly violated by framework decisions that have multiplied, with no apparent need, mandatory and optional principles of jurisdiction'.

19 See art 9(2) of FD 2002/475/JHA, today replaced by art 19(3) of Directive 2017/541/EU (terrorism); art 10(4) of the no longer in force FD 2005/222/JHA, a provision that has not been reproduced under the Directive 2013/40/EU (cybercrime); art 7(2) of the FD 2008/841/JHA (organised crime) OJ L300/42.

20 In the new Directive 2017/541/EU (art 19(3)) the list of criteria has been maintained but the adjective 'sequential' has been removed.

21 However, H. H. Herrnfeld, 'Mechanisms for Settling Conflicts of Jurisdiction' in M. Luchtman (ed), *Choice of Forum in Cooperation Against EU Financial Crime. Freedom, Security and Justice and the Protection of Specific EU-Interests* (Eleven Publishing 2013) 190 argued that since para 5 of the same article was not excluding the exercise of jurisdiction by a Member State in accordance with its national legislation, the 'sequential' account had to be intended as not actually entailing a binding character.

22 In the text of the FD 2002/475/JHA the criteria were ranked giving priority, in first place, to the territorial Member State, followed by the Member State of nationality or residence of the perpetrator, the Member States of 'origin' of the victims, and finally the Member State where the perpetrator was found.

the complete lack) of criteria to decide how to settle a jurisdictional conflict, and, starting from 2002, the reduction of the issue of conflicts of jurisdiction into a purely operational problem allocated to Eurojust in the absence of any binding power.

For the sake of completeness, however, it must be recalled that, before 2009 and under the pressure of the developing case law of the Court of Justice of the European Union (CJEU) on the principle of transnational *ne bis in idem*,[23] two attempts towards the establishment of a general mechanism to deal with conflicts of jurisdiction had actually been made: the first, in 2003, with the Greek Initiative on *ne bis in idem*[24] and the second, in 2005, with the Commission Green Paper on Conflicts of Jurisdiction and the Principle of *ne bis in idem* in Criminal Proceedings.[25]

Neither of the two initiatives eventually resulted in EU legislation but, interestingly, the 2005 Green Paper tackled several key aspects of conflicts of criminal jurisdiction, which still remain unaddressed by the current legal framework and have been extensively discussed in the course of the CJCL Project.

The Green Paper, indeed, sketched the main features of a rather advanced procedural mechanism to settle jurisdictional conflicts, including the perspective of entrusting an EU body with the power to issue a binding decision in cases where the consultations between the national authorities had failed.[26] More significantly, the Green Paper considered the possibility of involving the individuals concerned in the procedure, when this would not have jeopardised the prosecution or affected the rights of victims and witnesses.[27] Those proposals, as stated, were quite advanced but remained a dead letter and no legislative initiative followed up until 2009, when, just before the entry into force of the Treaty of Lisbon,[28] a Proposal for a FD on

23 The interpretation provided by the Court of Justice of the European Union of the principle of transnational *ne bis in idem* provided under art 54 of the Convention Implementing the Schengen Agreement (CISA) represented the strongest 'push factor' for taking conflicts of criminal jurisdiction seriously. The first judgment of the Court on the principle in the case *Gözütok and Brügge* (CJEU, 11 February 2003, Case C-187/01 *Gözütok and Brügge* ECLI:EU:C:2003:87) provided a protective conception of the principle, based on a 'first come, first served' basis. For an analysis of the relationship between conflicts of jurisdiction and the principle of transnational *ne bis in idem*, see the contribution of K. Ligeti in this volume, at 100–81.

24 Initiative of the Hellenic Republic with a view to adopting a Council FD concerning the application of the *ne bis in idem* principle, OJ 2003 C100/24.

25 See COM(2005) 696 final.

26 The possibility of a binding decision by an EU body was actually considered 'in the long run' with the further caveat that such an additional step would have been 'very difficult to realise' under the previous Treaty framework.

27 See COM(2005) 696 final, 6.

28 The Treaty of Lisbon entered into force on 1 December 2009. The FD 2009/948/JHA was adopted on 30 November 2009.

conflicts of jurisdiction was presented by a group of Member States[29] and approved in the form of the current FD 2009/948/JHA.

III. THE CURRENT EU LEGAL FRAMEWORK: FD 2009/948/JHA

The general mechanism for the 'prevention and settlement of conflicts of exercise of jurisdiction in criminal proceedings' in the AFSJ is currently represented by the FD 2009/948/JHA,[30] the last legal instrument being adopted under the institutional framework of the former Third Pillar on 30 November 2009. Similarly to directives, framework decisions needed to be implemented into national law and, nowadays, the implementation process of the FD 2009/948/JHA is almost complete: according to the latest available survey, twenty-four Member States out of twenty-eight implemented the instrument in their legal systems.[31]

Despite its ambitious title, the FD does not actually deal with the prevention of conflicts of jurisdiction but only with their settlement in cases where parallel proceedings may lead to violations of the *ne bis in idem* principle.[32] It establishes a horizontal mechanism based on consensus between the competent national authorities and aims at reaching 'any effective solution' able to avoid 'the adverse consequences arising from parallel proceedings'.[33]

Parallel proceedings are defined as criminal proceedings, in the pre-trial or trial phase, conducted in two or more Member States against the same person in regard to the 'same facts':[34] a definition clearly pointing out at European *ne bis in*

29 The initiative (Proposal) was presented by the Czech Presidency, Poland, Slovenia, Slovakia, and Sweden.

30 FD 2009/948/JHA on prevention and settlement of conflicts of exercise of jurisdiction in criminal proceedings, OJ 2009 L328/42.

31 See the data sheet on the status of implementation of the FD 2009/948/JHA European Judicial Network available at https://www.ejn-crimjust.europa.eu/ejn/libdocumentproperties.aspx?Id=941. To date—20 July 2017—only Bulgaria, Greece, and the United Kingdom have not implement the FD. Luxembourg is in the process of passing an implementation law.

32 The objectives of the FD are spelled out under art 1.

33 Article 1(2)(b) FD.

34 On the definition of 'same facts' for the purposes of European *ne bis in idem*, see CJEU, 9 March 2006, Case C-436/04, *Van Esbroeck* ECLI:EU:C:2006:165, where the Court affirmed the irrelevance of the legal qualification given by two different legal orders, and stated as the only relevant criterion to identify an *idem factum* 'the identity of material acts, understood in the sense of the existence of a set of concrete circumstances which are inextricably linked together' (para 36). The approach of the CJEU on transnational *ne bis in idem* was endorsed by the ECtHR in its later judgment in ECtHR, 10 February 2009, *Zolotukhin v Russia*, App No 14939/03. More generally, on the concepts of *idem* and *bis* in the case law of the CJEU and ECtHR see J. Vervaele, 'Schengen and Charter-Related Ne Bis in Idem Protection in the Area of Freedom, Security and Justice: M. and Zoran Spasic' (2015) *Common Market Law Review* 1339 ff.

idem situations and the need to prevent the violation of such principle. The FD 2009, indeed, addresses conflicts of jurisdiction in the sole perspective of European *ne bis in idem*. Multiple proceedings—meaning criminal proceedings for different facts conducted against the same suspect or relating to the same set of facts against different suspects—have been left out of the scope of the FD. Such a choice is certainly consistent with the objective of preventing the breach of *ne bis in idem* (since multiple proceedings do not fall under the prohibition), but represents a clear limit in the broader perspective of determining the most adequate jurisdiction to prosecute and, ultimately, to build up an adequate procedural mechanism for the AFSJ.[35] The key elements of the mechanism are represented by the direct contact between the competent authorities[36] and three autonomous obligations: to contact, to reply, and to enter into direct consultations. Thereby, the obligations to contact[37] and to reply[38] represent the basic building blocks of the mechanism. The obligation to contact, according to the FD, arises when the competent authority of a Member State has 'reasonable grounds to believe' that parallel proceedings are being conducted in another Member State. The reasonable grounds are not defined in the FD, but Recital (5) provides a non-exhaustive exemplification of 'sources' and 'circumstances' from which they may be inferred. These include cases where a suspect or accused person reports and provides details on the existence of a parallel proceeding in another Member State or when a request for mutual legal assistance discloses the possible existence of such proceedings or, finally, if police authorities provided information in that same regard.[39] If such reasonable grounds exist, the competent authority has an obligation to contact the competent authority of the other Member State(s)[40] where the parallel proceedings are supposed to be conducted and to provide certain 'minimum information' in order to allow the contacted authority to identify and, being the case, confirm the existence of such proceedings.

35 The CJCL proposal, as will be explained in further detail below, considered such limitation of the current legal framework and extended the scope of its models to include multiple proceedings.

36 According to art 3(b) of the FD 2009/948/JHA, a 'competent authority' is defined as a 'judicial authority or another authority, which is competent under the law of its Member State, to carry out the acts envisaged by art. 2 (a) of this Framework Decision'. The acts referred to in the definition are the procedure for establishing contact and the conduction of direct consultations. Important to notice, the judicial nature of the authority is not a necessary requirement for the purposes of this instrument.

37 Article 5 FD.

38 Article 6 FD.

39 Field research conducted in the context of this project confirmed that these three are the most common 'sources' of detection of parallel proceedings.

40 Article 2(2) of the FD 2009/948/JHA expressly addresses the case in which the identity of the other competent authority is not known to the contacting authority and refers to the possibility to resort to the European Judicial Network and its contact points.

The contacted authority is also under an obligation to reply within 'any reasonable deadline' set by the contacting authority and in any case 'without undue delay'. Worth mentioning, contrary to the approach endorsed for mutual recognition instruments, the FD on conflicts of jurisdiction avoided to include precise deadlines for carrying out the procedure, leaving the timeframe of the mechanism more flexible but also far more vague.[41] If the reply of the contacted authority confirms the existence of the parallel proceeding, a bilateral obligation to enter into direct consultations arises upon all the competent authorities concerned.[42] The consultation phase represents the 'core' of the mechanism and also its most under-regulated part.

As for the general objective, the consultation phase should aim at a consensual solution of the conflict in order to avoid 'the adverse consequences arising from' parallel proceedings. The type of solution is left undetermined: according to the FD, consensus can be reached on 'any effective solution' and concentration of proceedings is not required, but merely indicated as an option to be considered 'where appropriate'.[43] Bearing in mind the focus of the FD on *ne bis in idem* situations, however, concentration should ordinarily be 'appropriate' in the most part of the cases.

Beyond the obligation to enter into direct consultations, the procedural rules for reaching consensus are rather minimal and essentially concerned with the exchange of information between the competent authorities in the course of the consultations.[44] In particular, it seems important to highlight that the legislator avoided to spell out in the enacting terms of the FD any clear reference to the criteria to be applied in the course of consultations in order to decide how to solve the conflict of jurisdiction: only a spare reference to the Eurojust Guidelines—which will be addressed in the following paragraph—is contained in a recital and drafted in terms of a mere 'suggestion' or a 'reminder' to the competent authorities involved in the consultations.[45] The original proposal for the FD,[46] actually, contained a reference to

41 The original Proposal for the FD, actually, contained a strict set of time limits (15 days extendable for another 15 days). This provision was deleted in the course of the negotiations. See art 10 of the Initiative for a Council Framework Decision on prevention and settlement of conflicts of jurisdiction in criminal proceedings, OJ 2009 C39/2.

42 Article 10 of FD 2009/948/JHA.

43 ibid.

44 See art 10(2) of FD 2009/948/JHA establishing an obligation for the competent authorities to inform each other pending the consultations of any important procedural measure which they have taken in the national proceedings and art 10(3) stating that a request for information coming from a competent authority should be answered 'whenever reasonably possible' and provided that the disclosure of the information requested do not harm 'essential national security interests' or risk to jeopardise the 'safety of individuals'.

45 See Recital 9 of the FD 2009/948/JHA. The text of the recital states that: 'In order to reach consensus, the competent authorities should consider relevant criteria, which may include those set out in Guidelines which were published in the Eurojust Annual Report 2003 [. . .]'.

46 See art 15 of the original proposal, OJ 2009 C39/6.

a general presumption in favour of the territorial Member State, which would have been rebuttable in the presence of 'other sufficiently significant factors . . . strongly pointing' in favour of another jurisdiction.[47] In the course of the negotiations of the instrument, however, the insertion of specific criteria or any ranking of jurisdictional grounds resulted in political controversy and ended up in the compromise solution of Recital (9), which ultimately leaves the choice to the national legislators in the implementing phase. Although some national implementing laws (like the Spanish[48] and the Italian[49] ones) did provide for certain criteria to be followed by their national competent authorities in the course of the consultations, the lack of any clear indication in the FD in this regard appears problematic in terms of consistency and legal certainty.

Finally, it has to be highlighted that the FD text defines the instrument as 'complementary' to the Eurojust Decision: in the horizontal philosophy of the FD, however, such complementarity implies that the involvement of Eurojust is only optional, as a 'mediator' where the national competent authorities could not reach consensus on a solution.[50]

IV. THE CURRENT LEGAL FRAMEWORK: THE EUROJUST DECISION AND THE EUROJUST GUIDELINES

A. The Eurojust decision

The Eurojust Decision represents the 'second pillar' in our analysis of the legal framework on conflicts of jurisdiction and choice of forum. As a matter of fact, considering the delays in the implementation of the 2009 Framework Decision as

47 See art 15(1) of the original Proposal for the FD. In the original text of the Proposal the presumption in favour of the territorial Member State was based on a 'narrow' conception of territoriality (referred only to the factual conduct and not also to the damage, which was considered) separately as a potential other significant factor to rebut the presumption. The 'other sufficiently significant factors', on the other hand, were listed under art 15(2) in a rather articulated way and included: location of the suspect and the possibility of obtaining his surrender; his nationality or residence; the territory of the Member State where most of the damage occurred; significant interests of the victims and of the accused persons; the location of important evidence; the protection of vulnerable witnesses; the residence of the most important witnesses; the stage of the proceedings; the existence of ongoing related proceedings; and the economy of the proceedings. On the contents of the proposal see Steve Peers, 'The Proposed Framework Decision on Conflict of Jurisdiction in Criminal Proceedings: Manipulating the Right to a Fair Trial, Statewatch analysis, 12 March 2009, 3.

48 See art 32(5) of the Ley 16/2015 of 15 July 2015.

49 See art 8(4) of the Legislative Decree no 29 of 15 February 2016.

50 See art 12 2009 FD.

well as its rather modest objectives, to date Eurojust's[51] role in the matter is central. Eurojust's competence and practice on conflicts of jurisdiction dates back to its establishment in 2002[52] and, by 2003, it had adopted specific Guidelines for deciding which jurisdiction should prosecute when two or more Member States have jurisdiction over the same case falling under Eurojust competence.

In 2008,[53] this specific ambit of competence was reinforced by providing for an obligation upon the national judicial authorities to inform Eurojust of all the 'cases where conflicts of jurisdiction have arisen or are likely to arise'[54] and enabling the College of Eurojust to adopt a non-binding opinion 'where two or more national members cannot agree on how to resolve a case of conflict of jurisdiction as regards the undertaking of investigations or prosecution'.[55]

Currently, however, the Eurojust functions in regard to the settlement of conflicts of jurisdiction and choice of the forum to prosecute are of a non-authoritative nature: Eurojust National Members act through the method of consensus, while the College opinion is expressly qualified as non-binding. In practice, the consensual method based on coordination meetings and the consultations between the Eurojust National Members and the relevant national authorities[56] is the only method for the solution of conflicts of jurisdiction concretely resorted at Eurojust; to date, indeed, the College has never been requested to exercise its competence to issue a (non-binding) opinion under Article 7(a)(ii) of the Eurojust Decision.

Most importantly, the procedural framework for the resolution of conflicts of jurisdiction in the context of coordination meetings at Eurojust is flexible and

51 Eurojust is the European body in charge of 'stimulating, improving and supporting' the coordination of investigations and prosecutions conducted by the competent authorities of the Member States against serious cross-border crimes. The objectives of Eurojust are stated in art 3 of the current consolidated Eurojust Decision: for the consolidated version of the Eurojust Decision see Council Doc. 5347/3/09 REV 3 of 15 July 2009.

52 The original Council Decision establishing Eurojust 2002/187/JHA already provided for the possibility to Eurojust acting through its National Members (art 6(a)(iii)) or the College (art 7(a)(ii)) to ask national competent authorities to 'accept[ing] that one of them may be in a better position to undertake an investigation or to prosecute specific acts'.

53 In 2008 the Council adopted a Decision to strengthen Eurojust: see Council Decision 2009/426/JHA.

54 See art 13(7)(a) of the Consolidated Eurojust Decision.

55 See art 7(2) of the Consolidated Eurojust Decision.

56 Eurojust operational and coordination activities (including the settlement of conflicts of jurisdiction) are based on the so called coordination meetings. Coordination meetings, in Eurojust practice, are divided in three different levels, depending on the complexity of the issue at stake: normally, Level 1 meetings involve the 28 National Members and take the form of a general discussion within College meetings; Level 2 meetings are restricted to the concerned National Members, while Level 3 meetings are extended to the judicial and/or police authorities of the Member States concerned.

deformalised and, by its nature—Eurojust to date being still largely an intergovernmental structure—limited to the consultation of authorities involved in the conflict. In the current setting, the suspect/accused person and the victims are not able to submit their views or observations on the choice of forum to Eurojust.

In principle, however, a different approach, including the attribution of binding powers to the College *as extrema ratio*, would not be excluded in the post-Lisbon framework. The importance of Eurojust's role in this field has indeed been acknowledged by the Treaties under Article 85(1)(c) TFEU, which placed the resolution of conflicts of jurisdiction within the mandate of the Agency, thus providing an additional and complementary legal basis to the above-mentioned Article 82(1)(b) TFEU.[57] Article 85 TFEU does not set express limits to the nature of Eurojust intervention in the resolution of jurisdictional conflicts and a more ambitious role of the Eurojust College could be conceived in situations where a consensual solution was not possible. Nonetheless, the post-Lisbon reform of Eurojust currently under negotiation seems to move in the direction of reaffirming the non-binding nature of the College's opinion,[58] preferring a less intrusive approach and the preservation of the current working method of the agency based on consensus.[59]

B. The Eurojust guidelines

The Eurojust Guidelines were first adopted as an Annex to the Eurojust Annual Report 2003.[60] In December 2016, following the outcome of the discussions at the Strategic Seminar held in 2015, Eurojust released an updated version of the Guidelines,[61] which will constitute the reference of our analysis. Both the original and the updated Guidelines are soft law instruments, lacking binding force. This circumstance is clearly acknowledged in the text of the Guidelines and represented a central point of discussion in the course of the CJCL Project.[62]

57 For the analysis of the legal bases on conflicts of jurisdiction provided by the Treaties, see the contribution of M. Wasmeier in this book.

58 See art 4(4) of the Council's General Approach on the Proposal for a Regulation on the European Union Agency for Criminal Justice Cooperation (Eurojust) adopted on 27 February 2015; see Council Doc. 6643/15.

59 The Vertical Model of the CJCL proposal, instead, tried to develop a more ambitious role, elaborating a procedural framework and criteria for the adoption for a binding decision of Eurojust in case the horizontal consultations between the national judicial authorities did not achieve a consensual solution of the jurisdictional conflict.

60 Available at http://eurojust.europa.eu/doclibrary/corporate/Pages/annual-reports.aspx.

61 See Eurojust Guidelines for Deciding 'Which Jurisdiction Should Prosecute?' Revision 2016, available at http://www.eurojust.europa.eu/Practitioners/operational/Pages/Guidelines-on-jurisdiction.aspx.

62 The models elaborated in the CJCL Project opted in favour of annexing the amended guidelines to the different legal instrument proposed, providing such criteria with the legal status and binding force of EU secondary law.

The Guidelines are conceived in the perspective of a flexible, case-by-case, assessment of the 'best jurisdiction to prosecute'. starting from a preliminary, rebuttable, presumption in favour of the territorial Member State. Thus, in principle, the best placed jurisdiction should be the one in which 'the majority—or the most important part—of the criminality occurred or in which the majority—or the most important part—of the loss was sustained'.[63]

The definition of territoriality endorsed is rather broad and, after the 2016 revision, also includes a 'qualitative' dimension through the reference to the 'most important part' of either the conduct or the damage. Both the dimensions—qualitative and quantitative—have to be duly considered. Therefore, the identification of the territorial jurisdiction and the application of the presumption do already incorporate a balancing exercise in itself, since the competent authorities will have to determine which part of the conduct may be considered the 'most important' according to the findings of the parallel investigations.

The presumption in favour of territoriality, as already mentioned, is rebuttable. For this purpose, the Guidelines provide for a set of factors to be balanced against each other and against the presumption, in a comprehensive assessment. These factors are: (a) connecting factors relating to the suspect or accused person and his/her location; (b) the availability and admissibility of evidence; (c) the protection of witnesses; (d) the interests of victims; (e) the stage and length of proceedings; (f) the respect of legal requirements; (g) the available sentencing powers; (h) the availability of freezing and confiscation powers; (i) costs and resources; and (j) Member States' priorities.

Compared to the original version of 2003, the 2016 revision of the Guidelines introduced some novelties, but it did not substantially alter the definition of the factors and their flexible nature. For the purposes of this contribution, some considerations have to be made with regard to the criteria belonging to the connecting factors between the accused and his/her location, the availability and admissibility of evidence, the availability of sentencing powers, and Member States' priorities.

The connecting factors between the suspect and his location refer to a number of 'elements' to be considered when deciding the 'best place to prosecute'. These elements are represented by the place in which the suspect (or accused) person was found, his nationality or usual place of residence, the possibility of securing his/her surrender through a European arrest warrant, or to transfer the proceedings. Compared to the 2003 version, the 2016 revision added a significant additional element in the basket: 'the possible strong personal connections with one Member State or other significant interests of the suspect/accused person'. This periphrasis

63 See the 2016 Eurojust Guidelines, 3.

substantiates the concept of the 'interests of the suspect' and should include considerations such as the existence of family ties, the relative degree of integration in the society of one Member State rather than another, and other relevant interests that could be subsumed to the respect of private and family life under Article 8 of the European Convention on Human Rights (ECHR) and Article 7 of the EU CFR.

This addition introduces in the balancing exercise of the Guidelines a 'protective' element which, on the one hand, seems to acknowledge the impact that conducting a criminal trial in a certain jurisdiction rather than another may have a detrimental effect on the fundamental rights of the suspect and, on the other, appears functional to the resocialisation and reintegration of the person in case of a future conviction. However, one may wonder to what extent the assessment of this kind of interests can be effectively—and fairly—performed in a unilateral way by the prosecutorial authorities without any room for the interested person to present his/her view on the point and to present elements for a correct assessment. The factual circumstances to perform this kind of assessment properly does not, normally, constitute part of a criminal investigation and relevant personal circumstances may well remain unknown to the prosecutorial authorities if they are not put forward by the suspect or his/her lawyer. The CJCL Project, in the context of the proposed models, tried to formulate a balanced solution to this issue, which will be discussed in the final paragraph.

As for the criteria relating to evidence, the 2016 Guidelines expressly recall—similarly to the 2003 original version—the perspective admissibility of evidence as one of the elements for the choice of the best placed jurisdiction to prosecute.[64] While the physical availability of evidence does not seem to raise particular problems, considerations on the comparative admissibility of evidence may appear controversial and be perceived as a drift towards *forum shopping*. In my perspective, however, the criterion of admissibility needs to be read in connection with the other criterion of the respect of legal requirements recalled by the same Guidelines; this further criterion indeed states that:' judicial authorities should not decide to prosecute in one jurisdiction rather than another simply to avoid complying with legal obligations that apply in one jurisdiction but not in another'. Thus, a combined reading of the two criteria prevents a choice of one jurisdiction made in order to secure the admissibility of means of evidence which would have been otherwise excluded because irregularly gathered *ab initio* (according to the *lex loci* of the Member State where the investigative measures were performed). In the absence of provisions on the mutual admissibility of evidence,[65] the choice of forum cannot be

64 Under the heading 'availability and admissibility of evidence' the 2016 Eurojust Guidelines state that 'the location and availability of evidence in the proper form as well as its admissibility and acceptance by the court should be considered'.

65 Article 82(2)(a) TFEU provides a legal basis for an instrument on the mutual admissibility of evidence. Directive 2014/41/EU on the European Investigation Order does not contain provisions

resorted to turn inadmissible evidence into admissible. On this specific point, the CJCL Project adopted a neat solution preventing the consideration of the diverging rules on evidence as a factor for the forum choice.[66]

With regard to the availability of sentencing powers, the 2016 Guidelines expressly forbid a preference of one jurisdiction 'simply because the potential penalties available are higher than in another'. This negative criterion was already present in the 2003 version of the Guidelines and represents an essential aspect to ensure the fairness of the forum choice. As will be explained in more detail later, the reasonable exercise of discretion in making a choice which may entail the application of different criminal penalties is part of respect of the principle of substantive legality under Article 7 ECHR.[67]

Finally, a mention must be made of the Member States' priorities. The 2016 Guidelines gave more visibility to this criterion, which essentially prevents Member States' authorities from refusing a case under their jurisdiction simply because it is not considered a priority under their national prosecution policy. In the new structure of the Guidelines, this negative criterion is symmetrical to the principle—already expressed in the preamble of the FD 2009/948/JHA[68] and restated in the introduction of the new Eurojust Guidelines—that the principle of mandatory prosecution 'should be considered fulfilled when any Member State ensures the prosecution of a particular criminal offence'.

Both the irrelevance of national prosecutorial priorities and the 'equivalent fulfilment' of the principle of mandatory prosecution in the context of forum choice can be read as expression of the principle of loyal cooperation and joint responsibility of the Member States in the realisation of the objectives of the AFSJ, and a first surfacing of an 'European interest' when dealing with conflicts of jurisdiction.[69]

on the mutual admissibility of evidence but only with the simplification of its cross-border gathering in the perspective of facilitating 'cooperation between judicial or equivalent authorities of the Member States', according to art 82(1)(d) TFEU.

66 See the Annexes to the Horizontal and Vertical Models. Under 'Factors not to be considered' it is clearly stated that: 'The potential admissibility and acceptance of evidence by a court cannot be considered as a factor to determine where the prosecution should take place'.

67 See below under the heading 'Choice of forum as a process: the importance of procedural safeguards'.

68 See Recital 12 of the FD 2009/948/JHA.

69 See J. Vervaele, 'European Territoriality and Jurisdiction: The Protection of the EU's Financial Interests in Its Horizontal and Vertical (EPPO) Dimension' in M. Luchtman (ed), *Choice of Forum in Cooperation Against EU Financial Crime. Freedom, Security and Justice and the Protection of Specific EU-Interests* (Eleven Publishing 2013) 172.

V. ASSESSMENT OF THE CURRENT LEGAL FRAMEWORK IN LIGHT OF THE RELEVANT FUNDAMENTAL RIGHTS STANDARDS

Forum choices are not merely technical or operational activities concerning state authorities: as will be better explained in the following paragraphs, such choices are, on the contrary, an exercise of discretionary power that can substantially alter/modify the legal position of the individual as a suspect or defendant in criminal proceedings, even if the individual is not prima facie the direct addressee of the decision taken by the judicial authorities involved in the jurisdictional conflict. In a transnational and pluralistic (non-unified) legal order, indeed, the choice of forum inevitably determines the applicable procedural rules and, most importantly, the applicable substantive criminal law. While a certain amount of discretion in dealing with transnational forum choices is probably unavoidable, the legitimate exercise of such a discretion cannot be untied from the respect of fundamental rights and from the existence of certain minimal safeguards to avoid arbitrariness. In particular, a fundamental principle comes into play: the principle of the 'lawful judge', which has been recognised both under the ECHR and the EU CFR.

A. Choice of forum and the principle of the lawful judge

Article 47(2) of the EU CFR states that 'everyone is entitled to a fair and public hearing within a reasonable time by an independent and impartial tribunal previously established by law'. This article of the EU CFR largely recalls Article 6(1) of the ECHR[70] and the principle of the 'lawful judge', common to the constitutional traditions of several Member States. In its essence, the principle implies that the judge who will adjudicate a case has to be established by law, meaning that his determination cannot be completely left to the unfettered discretion of the executive power and that the individual should be able to reasonably foresee which tribunal will adjudicate his case.

70 Article 6 ECHR, first period states: 'In the determination of his civil rights and obligations or of any criminal charge against him, everyone is entitled to a fair and public hearing within a reasonable time by an independent and impartial tribunal established by law . . .'. It is worth recalling that according to art 52(3) of the EU CFR, in so far as the Charter contains rights 'which correspond to rights guaranteed' by the ECHR, the 'meaning and the scope' of those rights shall be the same, always provided the possibility for EU law to provide a more extensive protection. In regard to this latter possibility, it is worth noting that the definition of the right to a lawful judge under art 47(2) EU CFR includes the adverb 'previously', which adds a temporal element not present in the ECHR provision. On this point, see M. Panzavolta, 'Choice of Forum and the Lawful Judge Concept' in M. Luchtman (ed), *Choice of Forum in Cooperation Against EU Financial Crime. Freedom, Security and Justice and the Protection of Specific EU-Interests* (Eleven Publishing 2013) 159.

The principle of the 'lawful judge' as acknowledged by Article 47(2) EU CFR is relevant and applies to the choice of jurisdiction in the AFSJ; indeed, when the national authorities act under the FD 2009/948/JHA or apply the *ad hoc* consultation procedures provided by the different FDs mentioned above or, again, when, together with the support and coordination of Eurojust, they determine the forum to prosecute under the provisions of the Eurojust Decision and the Eurojust Guidelines, they are properly 'implementing' EU law in the meaning of Article 51 of the EU CFR and they are, accordingly, bound by the rights and principles contained in the Charter.

As pointed out in the literature, in case of parallel proceedings in different Member States 'to choose jurisdiction means also to choose rules and context';[71] even if there is no right as such for the suspect to have his/her trial held in a specific jurisdiction,[72] holding a criminal trial in one Member State rather than another is not neutral for his legal position: as previously mentioned, the choice of forum, indeed, determines the procedural rules applicable and, most importantly, the substantive criminal law applicable. Different procedural and substantive rules may entail very different trial outcomes and, from the defendant's perspective, different defence chances and choices. This, in turn, implies that the minimal core of legality—a reasonable level of foreseeability, which in our view seems particularly emphasised in Article 47(2) EU CFR by the use of the adverb 'previously'[73]—must be guaranteed to the individual in the context of forum choice. Reasonable foreseeability, of course, does not mean that exercise of discretion should not be allowed in forum choices or that the individual should have since the very beginning the absolute certainty about which jurisdiction will eventually adjudicate his case; more realistically, reasonable foreseeability would imply that the criteria for exercise the choice should have a decent legal basis and that certain minimal procedural safeguards for the suspect—such as the possibility to be heard or at least submit his point of view to the authorities in charge of deciding—should be in place with regard to the choice of forum as 'a process'.

The current EU secondary law on the prevention and settlement of conflicts of jurisdiction does not seem in line with the standards required by the EU CFR: as for the criteria for the choice, it must be recalled that the Eurojust Guidelines are only a soft law instrument which have no binding value and that the criteria referred in certain pre-Lisbon approximating instruments are not true examples of legal clarity; as for the procedural guarantees, both the FD 2009/948/JHA and the current Eurojust Decision do not provide any room for the involvement of the suspect's point of view in the choice/settlement process.

71 See Panzavolta (n 70) 160.

72 See Vervaele, 'European Territoriality and Jurisdiction' (n 69) 180.

73 See Panzavolta (n 70).

B. Choice of forum as a process: the importance of procedural safeguards

In our view, the importance of an adequate procedural framework and procedural safeguards is a central point in aligning the mechanism for choice of forum. If it is true, as it actually is, that a certain degree of case-by-case discretion in forum choices is inevitable in a transnational setting, then clear procedural rules are needed to ensure that such discretion is reasonably exercised and that the individual is put in the position to reasonably foresee the potential outcome of a forum choice.

In this perspective, the argumentation developed by the ECtHR in *Camilleri v Malta* of 2013[74] and analysed in the contribution of Luchtman in this volume seems relevant.[75]

Camilleri essentially concerned a Maltese legislation leaving broad discretion to the public prosecutor in choosing between two different courts (the criminal court or the magistrates' court) to present the accused for trial, with such a choice determining the potential application of substantially different penalties (far more severe before the criminal court).[76] Even if, in this specific case, the Strasbourg Court revised the choice of forum from the perspective of the substantive legality of the penalties under Article 7(1) ECHR (*nulla poena sine lege certa*)[77] rather than the right to a lawful judge under Article 6 ECHR, it seems not without meaning the connection that the same Court drawn between the acceptable 'reasonable' exercise of prosecutorial discretion and the need for procedural safeguards.[78]

In an adequate procedural mechanism for determining which jurisdiction should prosecute, therefore, the suspect or accused person should, at least where this would not jeopardise the investigation, be put in the position to express its view before the choice is made. Providing for a 'tailored' version of the right to be heard would serve both the respect for defence rights and the legitimacy of the choice.

Another basic procedural safeguard that should be carefully considered and, at present, is not specifically addressed by the relevant EU legal instruments relates to the right to an effective remedy against the decision on the forum choice. While it could reasonably be argued that the 'natural venue' for the review of the choice

74 See ECtHR, 22 January 2013, *Camilleri v Malta*, App No 42931/10.

75 See M. Luchtman, 'Choice of Forum, European Citizenship and Fundamental Rights: The Position of the Defendant' in this volume, at 251–82.

76 See para 15 of the judgment.

77 Article 7(1) ECHR provides that: 'No one shall be held guilty of any criminal offence on account of any act or omission which did not constitute a criminal offence under national or international law at the time when it was committed. Nor shall a heavier penalty be imposed than the one that was applicable at the time the criminal offence was committed'. The principle of legality of offences and penalties is provided under art 49 of the EU CFR.

78 See para 43 of the judgment.

should be identified in the national court where the subsequent trial takes place, the argument is not entirely convincing when the choice of the forum resulted from the intervention of a supranational/EU body, such as Eurojust. In those cases, the 'natural venue' for such a review would be a European Court. To date, however, the formal lack of binding nature of Eurojust intervention (taking place through recommendations and non-binding opinions), would probably prevent the possibility of a review by the Court of Justice of the European Union, on the basis of similar arguments developed in the case law on the inadmissibility of action for annulment against the final reports adopted by the European Anti Fraud Office (OLAF).[79] Lacking binding effect, Eurojust recommendations and opinions would probably not be considered 'of direct and individual concern' to the suspect for the purposes of the admissibility of an action for annulment.[80] Although it is disputable that a decision settling a jurisdictional conflict and choosing the forum of the prosecution does not entail 'a distinct change on the legal position' of the suspect, probably, only a legislative intervention would allow to overcome this obstacle to the admissibility of an action for annulment.

VI. CONCLUSION: SOME CONSIDERATIONS ON THE CJCL PROPOSALS

In light of the considerations expressed above and without overlying on the Explanatory Note accompanying the CJCL Proposal, I would conclude my contribution with a few general remarkson the three models.

As mentioned above, despite the efforts towards ensuring more clarity through the Eurojust Guidelines, the current legal framework on the settlement of conflicts

79 See General Court, 4 October 2006, T-193/04, *Tillack v Commission*, paras 68 and 69. According to this case law, only acts entailing 'a distinct change in the applicant's legal position' can be considered of 'direct and individual concern' and subject to an action of annulment *ex* art 263 TFEU. In regard to OLAF reports the effect of bringing about a distinct change in the legal position of the individual was denied by the Court owing to the lack of binding force of such reports and recommendations. Following this line of reasoning, since the national authorities addressed by OLAF remain free to follow up or not the recommendations, the act actually affecting the individual's legal position would be the one adopted by the national authority under its own responsibility and not the acts adopted by OLAF. In this regard, see J. Inghelram, *Legal and Institutional Aspects of the European Anti-Fraud Office (OLAF). An Analysis with a Look Forward to a European Public Prosecutor's Office* (Europa Law Publishing 2011) 206. More recently, see K. Ligeti, G. Robinson, 'Transversal Report on Judicial Protection' in M. Luchtman and J. Vervaele (eds), *Investigatory Powers and Procedural Safeguards: Improving OLAF's legislative framework through a comparison with other EU Law Enforcement Authorities* (ECN/ESMA/ECB 2017) 219 ff.

80 See art 263(4) TFEU, according to which: 'Any natural oflegal person may, under the conditions laid down in the first and second paragraphs, institute proceedings against an act addressed to that person or which is of direct and individual concern to them, and against a regulatory act which is of direct and individual concern to them and does not entail implementing measures'.

of jurisdiction does not seem yet in line with the requirements of the EU CFR. In particular, the absence in EU secondary law of clear criteria to operate the choice between different jurisdictions appears problematic in ensuring the respect of the principle of the 'lawful judge' in a transnational setting and a reasonable degree of foreseeability for the individuals concerned. The reform of Eurojust still under negotiation does not seem—at the current stage—to announce substantial changes in this field.

On the basis of these premises and following extensive field research at Eurojust, the CJCL Project developed an articulate proposal to address the current *lacunae*, conjugating the academic methodology and the perspective of practitioners, while carefully considering the different policy ambitions in the development of the AFSJ.

The CJCL proposal is composed of three models, which express different regulatory approaches but which all aim at reconciling the EU secondary law with the principle of the lawful judge and, more generally, the respect of the right to a fair trial.

With regard with the three aspects addressed above (namely, the foreseeability of the criteria for the choice, involvement of the suspect in the procedure for the choice of forum, and the guarantee of the right to an effective remedy against the decision on the forum), it is worth highlighting that:

- All three models incorporate the criteria for the choice in their respective legal instruments (Directive for the Horizontal Mechanism, Regulation for the Vertical Mechanism, and the Allocation Model), thereby conferring on them legal value and the foreseeability of EU secondary law.
- All three models included in their different procedural modules the opportunity for the suspect and the victims to present their point of view in the settling procedure by submitting written observations within a reasonable deadline.[81] Such involvement, of course, is not unconditional: it can be restricted when there is a risk of jeopardising the investigations. However, in all three models, it appears clearly that involvement is the rule, while the restriction shall be interpreted strictly.
- With regard to right to an effective remedy, the three models present the most differences: while the Horizontal Mechanism provides only for a 'non-affection clause', leaving the effectiveness and the very existence of a remedy to the variable geometry of the national systems, the Vertical Mechanism and the Allocation Model took a much bolder position on the issue. Both the solution endorsed (possibility of an action for annulment before the CJEU in the Vertical Mechanism and right to a legal remedy before a national court in the Allocation Model) seem adequate in the logic of the respective models. However, in the

81 See art 8(4) of the Horizontal Mechanism, art 13(3) of the Vertical Mechanism, and art 6(2) of the Allocation Model.

view of the author, the possibility of a direct control of the CJEU through actions for annulment would probably guarantee a greater consistency in the interpretation and application of the criteria, at least, in the shorter run.

In the view of this author, the above-mentioned points represent the most important and forward looking elements of the CJCL proposal, which could provide a valuable basis for a future legislative action aimed at filling the *lacunae* in the current legal framework and thereby developing a crucial aspect of the AFSJ.

5

FUNDAMENTAL RIGHTS PROTECTION BETWEEN STRASBOURG AND LUXEMBOURG

Extending Transnational *ne bis in idem* Across Administrative and Criminal Procedures

KATALIN LIGETI

I. INTRODUCTION

Since long before the entry into force of the Charter of Fundamental Rights of the European Union (CFREU), the two highest courts in Europe, the Court of Justice of the European Union (CJEU) and the European Court of Human Rights (ECtHR) have sought to develop their respective jurisprudence in such a way as to ensure a strong protection of individual rights, whilst avoiding clashes between the decisions taken in Luxembourg and Strasbourg. An important statement in this regard is provided by the *Bosphorus* judgment,[1] in which the Grand Chamber of the ECtHR recognised the existence of a presumption of equivalent protection of fundamental rights under EU law.[2] The presumption is rebuttable, but expresses the trustful attitude (and a certain degree of deference) of Strasbourg towards the ability of EU law (and of the CJEU) to protect Convention rights.

A key example of the European Courts' ambition to strengthen the fundamental rights position of individuals, whether in the EU or European Convention on Human Rights (ECHR) signatory states and whilst avoiding clashes, is found in their extensive case law on *ne bis in idem*—the prohibition on repeated prosecution or sanction in relation to the same unlawful conduct. A dialogue between the Courts in Luxembourg and Strasbourg has emerged, throughout which each has inspired developments in the jurisprudence of the other.

Two distinct phases of this evolution can be identified. First, and through analysis of the very rationale(s) underpinning *ne bis in idem* protection, the choice of a

1 ECtHR, 30 June 2005, *Bosphorus Hava Yollari Turizm v Ireland*, App no 45036/98.

2 ibid para 165.

broad, factual interpretation of the facts upon which putatively repeated sanctions are deemed to be based—and thus censured—has expanded its scope. Second, and through the adoption of an autonomous notion of a 'criminal charge' capable of drawing administrative punitive sanctions into the protection from double jeopardy provided by *ne bis in idem*, more recent refinements of the case law before the European Courts have dealt with the conditions under which administrative and criminal procedures may be deemed to constitute together a coherent whole. Where this is so, since there is no *repetition* of punishment in relation to the same conduct, there can be no *bis* and therefore no violation of extended (administrative—criminal) *ne bis in idem* protection.

It is this extended application of *ne bis in idem* which is the topic of the present chapter. How, and in which circumstances, may a punitive administrative procedure bar criminal prosecution either in a purely national or in a cross-border setting? The chapter begins, therefore, by analysing the conceptual roots of extended *ne bis in idem* protection and, in particular, how the concept of 'criminal charge' developed by the ECtHR impacts the interpretative outcomes of the CJEU and the ECtHR respectively. The chapter will then present the specific case law of the two Courts on extended *ne bis in idem*, including the latest developments, and will offer an assessment of the consequences of this jurisprudence for transnational cases in the Area of Freedom, Security and Justice (AFSJ). In particular, the transnational application of extended *ne bis in idem* requires a reconceptualisation and rethinking of the legal framework for preventing and resolving conflicts of criminal jurisdiction in the AFSJ.

II. EUROPEAN *NE BIS IN IDEM*: LEGAL FRAMEWORK AND RATIONALES

Ne bis in idem protection has developed in the European legal space over recent decades through a complex patchwork of intertwining provisions. The different legal expressions of the principle also reflect the composite rationale at its normative core: the prohibition of repeated prosecution or sanction in relation to the same unlawful conduct—also known as 'double jeopardy'. In order to lay the groundwork for an analysis of extended *ne bis in idem* in section III, the constituent parts of the relevant legal framework along with the long-established rationales for such protection are briefly evoked in the ensuing section.

At the EU level, the principle of *ne bis in idem* makes a crucial contribution to ensuring the freedom of movement of citizens of the Union through the protection it offers them from multiple prosecutions in different Member States. It has become a key element of the AFSJ, especially since the entry into force of the Lisbon Treaty. The Lisbon reforms marked a significant change in the status and scope of the protection afforded by the principle, with Article 50 of the CFREU establishing *ne bis in idem* as a fundamental individual right, which is now guaranteed by primary EU law.

Article 50 CFREU stipulates: 'No one shall be liable to be tried or punished again in criminal proceedings for an offence for which he or she has already been finally acquitted or convicted within the Union in accordance with the law'. The provision is clearly based on the wording of Article 4 of Protocol 7 of the ECHR, but features a larger (pan-EU) territorial scope than the (older) ECHR provision, which addresses only 'domestic' cases of *ne bis in idem*: where there is an attempt to start successive trials or sanctions within the same jurisdiction. The protection offered by Article 50 CFREU, in contrast, also applies where different EU jurisdictions duplicate trials or sanctions for the 'same criminal offence'. Whereas this second, broader form of protection was already laid down in various instruments of secondary EU law, such as Article 54 of the Convention implementing the Schengen Agreement (CISA),[3] provisions in mutual recognition instruments, or conventions dealing with legal assistance that applied in the transnational context only,[4] post-Lisbon primary EU law now additionally provides for *ne bis in idem* protection in cases that affect a single Member State insofar as the application of EU law is concerned.[5]

With the entry into force of the CFREU, therefore, *ne bis in idem* protection became a denser legal patchwork: although Article 50 CFREU is a primary source of Union law, it now co-exists with both the transnational *ne bis in idem* set out in Article 54 CISA[6] and the domestic *ne bis in idem* of Article 4 of Protocol 7 ECHR. This raises several questions not only as to the hierarchy of norms,[7] but also as to the rationale and scope of *ne bis in idem* protection.

3 Article 54 of the CISA states: 'A person whose trial has been finally disposed of in one Contracting Party may not be prosecuted in another Contracting Party for the same acts provided that, if a penalty has been imposed, it has been enforced, is actually in the process of being enforced or can no longer be enforced under the laws of the sentencing Contracting Party'.

4 In the context of mutual recognition instruments, transnational *ne bis in idem* is usually considered as a (mandatory or optional) ground for refusal. See e.g. art 3(2) of FD 2002/584/JHA (European Arrest Warrant); art 9(1)(c) of FD 2008/909/JHA (Mutual recognition of custodial sentences) OJ L327/27; art 15(1)(c) of FD 2009/829/JHA on mutual recognition of supervision measures as an alternative to provisional detention [2009] OJ L294/20 (European Supervision Order); art 11(1)(c) of FD 2008/947JHA (Mutual recognition of probation measures) [2008] OJ L337/102; art 11(1)(d) of Directive 2014/41/EU (European Investigation Order).

5 According to art 51(1) CFREU, the Charter applies to institutions, bodies, and agencies of the Union and to the Member States. In regard to the Member States, however, the same provision specifies that the CFREU applies 'only when they are implementing Union law'.

6 As to the historical development of art 54 CISA see Bas van Bockel *The Ne Bis in Idem Principle in EU Law* (Kluwer Law International 2010) 19 ff.

7 See Wolfgang Schomburg, 'Criminal Matters: Transnational Ne Bis in Idem in Europe—Conflict of Jurisdictions—Transfer of Proceedings' (2012) 13 ERA Forum 311, 314 ff.

In its classical 'domestic dimension', the principle of *ne bis in idem* traditionally presented a composite rationale, accommodating different individual and super-individual interests.[8] As an individual guarantee (the human rights rationale of the principle), *ne bis in idem* has traditionally been intended as protection from possible abuses by the state of its *ius puniendi*[9] (through repeated attempts to convict an individual for the same offence) and a safeguard against disproportionate punishment. As a super-individual or systemic principle (the rule of law rationale), *ne bis in idem* is traditionally connected to the legitimacy of the legal system, especially in view of guaranteeing legal certainty and *res judicata*.[10] Economic considerations, involving the prevention of costly multiple prosecutions and incentives for the efficient coordination between prosecutors, are often also considered in this perspective.[11]

The co-existence of (and interaction between) the human rights and the rule of law rationales is equally present as regards the transnational application of *ne bis in idem:* however, for transnational cases the CJEU identified the free movement of citizens as an additional *sui generis rationale*. In more than a dozen judgments starting with its seminal decision in *Gözütok and Brügge*,[12] the CJEU stated that the objective of *ne bis in idem*—as enshrined in Article 54 CISA—is "to ensure that no one is prosecuted on the same facts in several Member States on account of his having exercised his right to freedom of movement".[13] In other words, once a person is threatened with a new prosecution on the same facts merely because the offence is transnational, his or her right to move freely within the EU is not honoured.[14]

8 See Juliette Lelieur, '"Transnationalizing" Ne Bis in Idem: How the Rule of Ne Bis in Idem Reveals the Principle of Personal Legal Certainty' (2013) 9(4) Utrecht Law Review 198.

9 See van Bockel (n 6) 25.

10 From the point of view of legal certainty, all European Member States recognise that once ordinary appellate remedies have been exhausted, or the relevant time limit for appeal has expired, a conviction or acquittal is to be regarded as irrevocable, acquiring the quality (or force) of *res judicata*.

11 See van Bockel (n 6) 27 and Petter Asp, *The Procedural Criminal Law Cooperation of the EU* (Stockholms universitet skriftserie 2016) 101.

12 CJEU, 11 February 2003, Joined Cases C-187/01 and C-385/01, *Gözütok and Brügge* ECLI:EU:C:2003:87.

13 ibid para 38.

14 Alongside the free movement rationale, the CJEU has also identified a concurring 'security rationale' underlying transnational *ne bis in idem* and stemming from the objectives of the AFSJ established by the Treaties. art 67(3) TFEU, indeed, embeds also the objective of ensuring a 'high level of security through measures to [prevent] and combat crime within the AFSJ'. In several cases this rationale has been employed by the Luxembourg Court to interpret and limit the application of transnational *ne bis in idem*. For the most recent cases focusing on the 'security rationale' see CJEU, 27 May 2014, Case C-129/14 PPU *Spasic* ECLI:EU:C:2014:586 (on the validity of the so-called 'enforcement condition' under art 54 CISA) and CJEU, 29 June 2016, Case C-486/14 *Kossowski* ECLI:EU:C:2016:483 (on the possibility to consider a prosecutorial dismissal for lack of evidence as a decision triggering transnational *ne bis in idem*).

These rationales are of pivotal importance to interpreting *idem* and *bis* and consequently for defining the scope of protection offered by the principle. As mentioned above in section I, both of these elements and the underlying rationales of *ne bis in idem* protection have been the subject of extensive jurisprudence before both European Courts, resulting in a dialogue between the two Courts through which they have mutually inspired each other's jurisprudence.

Amongst the many interesting aspects of the respective jurisprudence is the fact that both Courts have referred to the autonomous concepts of '*matière pénale*' and 'criminal charge' developed by the ECtHR in relation to the fair trial rights enshrined in Article 6 ECHR when delineating the scope of protection offered by the *ne bis in idem* principle. In doing so, both Courts have recognised that punitive administrative procedures that qualify as criminal for the purposes of the application of fair trial rights may, according to the same logic, also be considered as a final disposal of the case for the application of the *ne bis in idem* principle. Transposing the notion of 'criminal charge' into the *ne bis in idem* field is motivated by the ambition of the ECtHR and the CJEU to contribute to extending the human rights rationale and strengthening the fundamental rights character of the principle.

III. THE CONCEPTUAL ROOTS OF EXTENDED *NE BIS IN IDEM*

In order to introduce the specific case law of the two Courts on the issue, in the following section, the conceptual roots of the extended application of *ne bis in idem* will be briefly presented. These two specific roots are the '*Engel* doctrine' (the autonomous definition of what constitutes a 'criminal charge') and the factual and broad interpretation of the *idem* element, which has been adopted under the supranational human rights framework.

A. The *Engel* doctrine and the concept of a 'criminal charge'

For a *bis* to arise, a final decision or, to use the wording of Article 54 of the CISA, a decision 'finally disposing of' the case must already have been taken. Such a (final) decision is the trigger of the *ne bis in idem* preclusion. The characteristics of decisions that qualify as 'final decision' have been fleshed out by the CJEU in relation to transnational *ne bis in idem*[15] and by the ECtHR in relation to domestic *ne*

15 In the context of the transnational application of the principle under art 54 CISA, the CJEU had to deal several times with the issue of what kind of decisions may have been considered to finally dispose of the case for the purposes of triggering *ne bis in idem* protection. See, particularly, the CJEU cases *Gözütok and Brügge* (CJEU, 11 February 2003, Joined Cases C-187/01 and C-385/01 *Gözütok and Brügge* ECLI:EU:C:2003:87); involving an out-of-court settlement imposing the payment of a monetary sum as a condition for a prosecutorial dismissal); CJEU, *Miraglia* (CJEU, 10 March 2005, Case C-469/03 *Miraglia* [2005] ECR I-2009; involving a prosecutorial dismissal

bis in idem.[16] The rich case law of the two Courts assesses a series of different kinds of proceedings, including transactions and other prosecutorial case endings, out-of-court settlements, acquittals for lack of evidence, and other types of decisions in light of the *bis* requirement of the principle. In this context, both Courts had the possibility to go beyond specific forms of national criminal procedure and consider the more conceptual questions related to the very nature of the procedure. Both Courts have thus reflected on the question of what kind of proceedings are to be considered criminal for the purposes of *ne bis in idem* protection.

Since the second half of the 1970s, the ECtHR has developed autonomous concepts of '*matière pénale*' and of 'criminal charge' in the context of Article 6 ECHR and the right to a fair trial. By resorting to these autonomous concepts, the ECtHR has extended the application of fair trial guarantees of the Convention beyond the formal boundaries of criminal proceedings *stricto sensu* to proceedings which are not formally labelled criminal under the relevant national law but, nonetheless, can be considered 'criminal in nature', according to a set of criteria known as the *Engel* criteria.[17] In order to determine the 'criminal nature' of a proceeding, they require an assessment of the formal classification of the offence under national law (but only as a first, indicative, criterion), of the very nature of the offence and, finally, of the degree of severity of the penalty. By applying the *Engel* criteria, punitive administrative proceedings have been recognised as 'criminal in nature' and, therefore, been subject to the application of the guarantees of Article 6 ECHR. This has notably

based on the sole ground that a criminal proceeding for the same acts and against the same defendant had been started in another Member State following the coordination between the judicial authorities concerned; in this case the *bis* effect was excluded); CJEU, *Van Straaten* (CJEU, 28 September 2006, Case C-150/05 *Van Straaten* [2006] ECR I-9327, recognising *bis* nature of a court acquittal for lack of evidence); CJEU *Gasparini* (CJEU, 28 September 2006, Case C-467/04, *Gasparini* [2006] All ER (D) 141 (Sep), recognising the *ne bis in idem* effect of a court decision declaring the offence time barred); CJEU, *Turansky* (CJEU, 22 December 2008, Case C-491/07, *Turansky* ECLI:EU:C:2008:768, concerning a decision taken by a police authority dismissing an investigation for lack of evidence; in this case the *bis* effect was excluded); CJEU, *M.* (CJEU, 5 June 2014, Case C-398/12, *M.* ECLI:EU:C:2014:1057, involving a pre-trial decision of *non-lieu*); CJEU, *Kossowski* (CJEU, 29 June 2016, C-486/14, *Kossowski* (n 14), considering a prosecutorial dismissal for lack of evidence; in this case, the Court seemed to recognise the *bis* effect of such a decision only where it follows a "detailed investigation" into the merits of the case). For an overview of the case law see A Weyembergh and I Armada, 'The Principle of ne bis in idem in Europe's Area of Freedom, Security and Justice' in V Mitsilegas, M Bergström, and T Konstadinides (eds), *Research Handbook on EU Criminal Law* (Edward Elgar Publishing 2016) 199 ff.

16 For the ECtHR case law, see ECtHR, 10 February 2009, *Zolotukhin v Russia*, App No 14939/03, paras 107 and 108; ECtHR, 20 July 2004, *Nikitin v Russia*, App No 50178/99, para 37.

17 See ECtHR, 8 June 1976, *Engel and Others v Netherlands*, App Nos 5100/71, 5101/71, 5102/71, 5354/72, and 5370/72, para 85.

been the case of administrative proceedings aiming at the levying of tax surcharges, and antitrust proceedings conducted by national administrative authorities.[18]

The consequences of the *Engel* doctrine drawing a large part of proceedings considered as administrative by the national legal systems into the requirements set by Article 6 ECHR are potentially very broad. In order to limit this spread, the ECtHR has in its subsequent jurisprudence nuanced its approach, most significantly in distinguishing between proceedings aiming at the application of "the hard core of criminal law" and other punitive administrative proceedings deemed 'criminal in nature' according to the *Engel* criteria.[19] In *Jussila v Finland*,[20] the Court thus referred to the different and lesser "degree of stigma" carried by certain punitive administrative proceedings as a reason to distinguish the modalities of application of criminal law guarantees, implying the possibility of a less stringent application of fair trial guarantees in relation to this category of proceedings.[21]

The question of whether the *ne bis in idem* principle is to be applied on the same terms and with the same protective scope both for procedures that concern the hard core of criminal law and other punitive procedures is particularly important to the many European legal systems which feature a so-called 'double-track' enforcement

18 See ECtHR, 20 September 2011, *Menarini Diagnostics v Italy*, App No 43509/08.

19 ECtHR, 23 November 2006, *Jussila v Finland*, App No 73053/01.

20 ibid, in particular at para 43, where the Court noted that: 'Notwithstanding the consideration that a certain gravity attaches to criminal proceedings, which are concerned with the allocation of criminal responsibility and the imposition of a punitive and deterrent sanction, it is self-evident that there are criminal cases which do not carry any significant degree of stigma. There are clearly "criminal charges" of differing weight. What is more, the autonomous interpretation adopted by the Convention institutions of the notion of a "criminal charge" by applying the Engel criteria have underpinned a gradual broadening of the criminal head to cases not strictly belonging to the traditional categories of the criminal law, for example administrative penalties (*Öztürk*, cited above), prison disciplinary proceedings (*Campbell and Fell v the United Kingdom*, 28 June 1984, Series A no. 80), customs law (*Salabiaku v France*, 7 October 1988, Series A no. 141-A), competition law (*Société Stenuit v France*, 27 February 1992, Series A no. 232-A), and penalties imposed by a court with jurisdiction in financial matters (*Guisset v France*, no. 33933/96, ECHR 2000-IX). Tax surcharges differ from the hard core of criminal law; consequently, the criminal-head guarantees will not necessarily apply with their full stringency (see *Bendenoun and Janosevic*, para 46 and para 81 respectively, where it was found compatible with Article 6 para 1 for criminal penalties to be imposed, in the first instance, by an administrative or non-judicial body, and, *a contrario, Findlay*, cited above)'.

21 The '*Jussila* solution', nonetheless, is not uncontroversial: see, in particular, the partly dissenting opinion presented in the same case by judges Loucaides, Zupancic, and Spielmann; the three judges stressed, in particular, the difficulty in distinguishing between what actually belongs to the "hard core of criminal law" and what falls out of this category and the problematic choice of making the application of fair trial guarantees conditional on such a distinction. In this regard, see also Nicholas Croquet, 'The European Court of Human Rights' Norm-Creation and Norm-Limiting Processes: Resolving a Normative Tension' (2011) Columbia Journal of European Law 307, 333.

system, prescribing both punitive administrative and criminal sanctions for the same unlawful act. Whereas the *Engel* doctrine suggests that the accumulation of criminal and punitive administrative proceedings may constitute a violation of the *ne bis in idem* principle, the distinction developed in *Jussila* would tend to permit 'double-track' enforcement systems to operate unhindered.

Before analysing the respective arguments of both Courts, it is important to note, however, that the contours of the extended application of *ne bis in idem* depend not only on the definition of the nature of the proceeding (*bis*), but are also strongly linked to the interpretation of *idem*.

B. The broad, factual concept of *idem*

The first constitutive element of *ne bis in idem* is whether the proceedings in question relate to the same 'offence' (*idem*). A variety of approaches exists to ascertain whether the offence for which an individual has been prosecuted is indeed the same as the one in respect of which he or she has already been finally convicted or acquitted.[22] *Idem* has long been interpreted in different ways by national and European jurisdictions.[23] The dispute has traditionally hinged on the question of whether this notion refers only to the material facts, to their legal classification, or to the protected legal interest.[24]

The consequences of the choice of whether *idem* ought to be understood as *idem factum* (literally, the same fact) or *idem crimen* (the same offence) are particularly relevant, since the same material facts may qualify as different offences under several national laws.[25] To consider protected legal interests, on the other hand, may also significantly narrow down the applicability of *ne bis in idem* since the same material conduct could affect different legal interests, the protection of which may require different (criminal or administrative) legal responses. For example, the same material conduct may be punished with an administrative sanction for drunk driving (considering road safety as an autonomous legal interest) as well as a criminal sanction for the offence of causing death by negligence (identifying the legal interest in the protection of human life).

This variety of approaches gave rise to a level of legal uncertainty which was incompatible with the protection of a fundamental right.[26] At the same time, the legal texts recognising the principle of *ne bis in idem* at the supranational level did not clarify the issue. Whilst Article 50 CFREU takes up the wording of Article 4 of

22 For an overview of the various approaches see *Zolutukhin* (n 16) paras 31 ff.

23 John Vervaele, 'Ne Bis in Idem: Towards a Transnational Constitutional Principle in the EU?' (2013) Utrecht Law Review 211, 212.

24 Cf. CJEU, 9 March 2006, Case C-436/04 *Van Esbroeck* ECLI:EU:C:2006:165, paras 25 ff.

25 Lelieur (n 8) 198, 205.

26 See in this sense *Zoluthukin* (n 16) para 78 and van Bockel (n 6) 190.

Protocol 7 ECHR referring to the same 'offence', suggesting that the legal classification of the conduct should be taken into account, Article 54 of the CISA speaks of 'the same acts', seeming to point towards a factual material approach to the concept of *idem*.

The definition of *idem* had also long been dealt with in a rather inconsistent way by the ECtHR in several cases concerning Protocol 7[27] by the time the CJEU first addressed transnational *idem* in 2006. In its landmark decision *Van Esbroeck*, the CJEU declared that *idem* should be understood as *idem factum*,[28] relying on the concept of mutual recognition and on freedom of movement in order to hold that the only relevant criterion for the purposes of Article 54 CISA was the "identity of the material facts, understood in the sense of the existence of a set of concrete circumstances which are inextricably linked together"[29] "in time, in space and by their subject matter".[30] The Court went on to emphasise that: "[b]ecause there is no harmonisation of national criminal laws, a criterion based on the legal classification of the acts or on the protected legal interest might create as many barriers to freedom of movement within the Schengen territory as there are penal systems in the Contracting States".[31]

Looking at the problem from the perspective of free movement and mutual recognition, the CJEU deliberately opted for an autonomous interpretation of Article 54 CISA that did not depend on the national criminal laws of the Member States: such an autonomous interpretation was enabled only by the endorsement of a factual approach that clearly gave *idem* a broad meaning that favours the accused. Ultimately, the factual understanding of the concept of *idem* was justified by the need to grant *effet utile* to Article 54 of the CISA and was consistent with the free movement rationale underpinning the very idea of transnational *ne bis in idem*.

Nonetheless, the solution was subsequently endorsed by the ECtHR in the *Zolotukhin* case with regard to domestic *ne bis in idem* under Protocol 7 ECHR. The case concerned an administrative conviction (for minor disorderly acts) and

27 The different approaches adopted by the ECtHR are summarised in the Grand Chamber judgment in *Zolotukhin v Russia* (n 16). A purely factual/material approach was initially endorsed by the Court in the case of *Gradinger v Austria* (ECtHR, 23 October 1995, App No 15963/90); in the subsequent case law, however, different approaches—focusing on the 'essential elements' of the relevant offences were adopted. See e.g. the case of *Fischer v Austria* (ECtHR, 29 May 2001, App No 37950/97) and the admissibility decision in the case *Garretta v France* (ECtHR, 4 March 2008, App No 2529/04).

28 CJEU, *Van Esbroeck* (n 24) paras 27, 32, and 36.

29 CJEU, *Van Esbroeck* (n 24) para 36.

30 ibid para 38. This approach has subsequently been confirmed in e.g. Case C-467/04 *Gasparini* (n 15) para 54; Case C-150/05 *Van Straaten* (n 15) para 48; Case C-367/05 *Norma Kraaijenbrink* ECLI:EU:C:2007:444.

31 CJEU, *Van Esbroeck* (n 24) para 35.

a subsequent criminal prosecution (charges: disorderly acts and resisting a public official) in relation to conduct during an interrogation at a police station. The applicant claimed a violation of Protocol 7, arguing that the criminal charges relating to disorderly acts (and which resulted in acquittal) had been based on the same material facts as the prior administrative conviction. The Russian government did not challenge the criminal nature of the two sets of proceedings (i.e. it conceded *bis*) but contested the existence of *idem* by referring to the ECtHR case law on *concours idéal d'infractions* and on the identity of 'essential elements'.[32] According to the government, whereas the administrative offence of minor disorderly acts responded to "merely the deviation from established social and moral norms", the criminal offence "implied the use of violence and resistance against a public official".[33]

Acknowledging the need to harmonise its previous case law on the point,[34] the ECtHR made an express reference to the findings of the CJEU in *Van Esbroeck*[35] and deemed the *idem factum* approach both a practical and an effective way to ensure the respect of the principle. To hold the contrary (i.e. to opt for the formal criterion of the legal qualification), according to the Court, would have been "too restrictive on the rights of the individual".[36] The ECtHR thus took the view that "Article 4 of Protocol 7 must be understood as prohibiting the prosecution or trial of a second 'offence' insofar as it arises from identical facts or facts which are substantially the same" and thereby opted for the *idem factum* approach.[37] This means that the Court's inquiry should "focus on those facts which constitute a set of concrete factual circumstances involving the same defendant and inextricably linked together in time and space, the existence of which must be demonstrated in order to secure a conviction or institute criminal proceedings."[38] Endorsing the factual approach in *Zolotukhin,* the ECtHR thereby clearly strengthened the fundamental rights aspect of *ne bis in idem* and also enhanced the convergence between the internal and the transnational *ne bis in idem*.

Moreover, when such a broad interpretation of *idem* based on the consideration of the sole factual conduct is combined with the consolidated case law of the Strasbourg Court on the autonomous interpretation of the concept of 'criminal

32 See ECtHR, 29 May 2001, App no 37950/97, *Franz Fischer v Austria*, para 25 and ECtHR, 30 July 1998, App no 84/1997/868/1080, *Oliveira v Switzerland.*

33 ibid para 66.

34 In *Zolutukhin* (n 16), the ECtHR recognised the existence in its case law of at least three different approaches to the '*idem*' element and acknowledged the need for harmonisation of the concept. See para 78.

35 ECtHR, *Zolotukhin* (n 16) para 37.

36 ibid para 81.

37 ibid para 82.

38 ibid para 84.

charge' in light of the Engel criteria, an especially wide protection of *ne bis in idem* is the result. This represents a potentially serious challenge to the foundations of several national enforcement systems, which regularly ally administrative to criminal penalties. Although it does not rule out two-pronged enforcement systems, the ECtHR's approach in *Zolotukhin* effectively demands some form of coordination between both prongs in order to avoid arbitrary outcomes.[39]

IV. THE TWO COURTS AND THE DEVELOPMENT OF EXTENDED *NE BIS IN IDEM*

A. *Åkerberg Fransson* and *Grande Stevens*: applying the *Engel* criteria in the context of *ne bis in idem*

First of all, it should be recalled that neither Article 50 of the CFREU nor Article 4 of Protocol 7 nor Article 54 of the CISA mention administrative proceedings within the scope of *ne bis in idem*. Instead, the text of the CFREU refers to 'criminal proceedings' and Article 4 of Protocol 7 refers to 'penal procedure'. Relying on the strict wording, therefore, administrative proceedings would fall outside the scope of application of *ne bis in idem*. As already seen in relation to the jurisprudence on Article 6 ECHR, however, the issue arises whether an assessment of the criminal nature of a proceeding in light of the *Engel* criteria—and therefore the assessment of the actual punitive nature of a proceeding—should be performed also in applying the prohibition of *ne bis in idem*.

In *Zolothukin*, the ECtHR had expressly applied the *Engel* criteria in regard to Protocol 7,[40] highlighting that the legal characterisation of the procedure under national law cannot be the sole criterion of relevance for the applicability of *ne bis in idem* as this would mean leaving such application to the discretion of the Member States. In the same vein, the accumulation of a criminal sanction and an administrative sanction was addressed for the first time by the CJEU in *Bonda*,[41] three years after *Zolotukhin*. The case concerned a criminal sanction and the administrative exclusion from a subsidy in the field of the common agricultural policy.[42] In the specific circumstances of the case, the Court found that the administrative exclusion under Regulation 1973/2004/EC was not of a punitive nature, but in reaching

39 The importance of coordination has also been stressed by the CJEU in its most recent judgments on extended *ne bis in idem* (*Menci, Di Puma*, and *Garslsson*; see section IV.C).

40 ibid para 53. The Court recalled previous case law, which had already applied the *Engel* criteria in the context of *ne bis in idem* and Protocol 7, in particular ECtHR *Storbråten v Norway* (dec.) App No 12277/04.

41 CJEU, 5 June 2012, Case C-489/10 *Bonda* ECLI:EU:C:2012:319.

42 ibid para 37.

this conclusion it expressly applied the *Engel* criteria and endorsed the extended approach to *ne bis in idem* developed by the ECtHR.

This approach was subsequently explicitly confirmed by the CJEU also in relation to the interpretation of Article 50 CFREU in the *Åkerberg Fransson*[43] ruling. In *Åkerberg Fransson*, the CJEU reaffirmed that Member States are free in principle to impose both an administrative penalty and a criminal sanction for the same conduct, but that they are bound to the respect of Article 50 CFREU and the principle of *ne bis in idem*. Duplication through formally criminal proceedings, therefore, is forbidden under EU law, where the tax penalty is "criminal in nature for the purposes of Article 50 of the Charter" and the decision is final.[44] Importantly, in determining the nature of the tax penalty, the CJEU referred again to the threefold *Engel* criteria on punitive sanctions.[45] As such, the CJEU broadened the scope of *ne bis in idem* protection under EU law by aligning its interpretation to that of the ECtHR and expanding it to cover punitive administrative proceedings.[46]

This dialogue between the two Courts and cross-fertilisation between their respective bodies of case law were further perpetuated in the subsequent ECtHR judgment in *Grande Stevens and Others*,[47] in which it expressly referred back to the CJEU's solution in *Åkerberg Fransson* in order to substantiate its reasoning that a state cannot impose a double penalty (administrative and criminal) in respect of the same facts if the first penalty is criminal in nature.[48] The case concerned administrative fines and criminal convictions for market manipulation, all drawing on a press release issued by the applicants in which they had not mentioned the renegotiation

43 CJEU, 26 February 2013, Order in Case C-617/10 *Hans Åkerberg Fransson* ECLI:EU:C:2013:280.

44 ibid para 34.

45 ibid para 35.

46 In *Åkerberg Fransson*, the CJEU left to the national court the task of applying the *Engel* criteria and assessing the existence of a violation in the concrete case (ibid para 36). In the *Bonda* case, however, the Court itself had applied the *Engel* criteria to the relevant provisions excluding their 'criminal nature'. These different approaches followed by the CJEU have been criticised in literature (see Vervaele (n 23) 225; it is, however, important to highlight that the provisions at stake in *Bonda* were laid down in an EU Regulation and not in an implementing national law). In the most recent judgments on extended *ne bis in idem* in the fields of VAT and market abuse and manipulation (CJEU, *Menci*, *Di Puma*, and *Garlsson*, on which more in detail see section IV.C below), the Court restated that it is for the national Court to assess the respect of the principle of *ne bis in idem* in the individual case but, at the same time, to provide thorough guidance to the national judge through an extensive analysis of the national provisions.

47 ECtHR, 4 March 2014, *Grande Stevens and Others v Italy*, App Nos 8640/10, 18647/10, 18663/10, 18668/10, and 18698/10.

48 ibid para 229. The Court also rejected the Italian government's argument that, in order to ensure the proportionality of the penalty to the accusations, the Italian criminal courts were able to take into account the prior imposition of an administrative penalty and to reduce the criminal penalty. See para 218.

of an equity swap with Merrill Lynch in order to avoid being subject to a takeover bid. The Italian Stock Exchange Commission (CONSOB) imposed fines of varying amounts (the largest €5 million) on the applicants, before criminal charges were successfully brought.

Before the ECtHR, the applicants claimed an infringement of both Article 6 ECHR and *ne bis in idem*, focusing on the press release as the common source of all proceedings. The Italian government, having briefly contested the existence of *idem* by referring to pre-*Zolotukhin* case law on *concours idéal d'infractions*, focused on *bis* by asserting the non-criminal nature of the CONSOB administrative fine.[49] Before it addressed *idem* equally briefly (by restating the findings of *Zolotukhin* and recognising the identity of the material conduct underlying the two types of proceedings), the Court confirmed the criminal nature of the CONSOB proceedings in a detailed application of the *Engel* criteria.[50]

In Strasbourg, *Grande Stevens* launched a new line of case law under which the ECtHR established a violation of the *ne bis in idem* principle where a second set of criminal or administrative proceedings were initiated and a punitive sanction imposed following an acquittal[51] or conviction[52] in a prior proceeding based on the same conduct (*idem factum*). Tensions, however, seemed to emerge early on between this line of case law and the widespread practice of 'double-track enforcement' (especially, but not only, in tax matters) in several Member States.

B. Engines astern? The new approach of the ECtHR to extended *ne bis in idem* in *A and B v Norway*

At this point, it should be recalled that, in general terms, Article 4 of Protocol 7 does not per se prohibit the imposition of a criminal and an administrative sanction for the same set of facts, provided that the administrative sanction is not criminal in nature. On the other hand, as mentioned above, starting with the *Jussila* judgment,[53] the ECtHR opened a possibly diversified application of fair trial guarantees in proceedings which may qualify as 'criminal in nature' under the *Engel* criteria, yet which do not belong to the 'hard core of criminal law' (such as proceedings in antitrust

49 In doing so, it also attempted to rely on a reservation made by Italy to Article 4 of Protocol 7, which limited its applicability to offences, procedures, and decisions classified as criminal under Italian law. The Court held this claim to be inadmissible as the reservation failed to meet the criteria set out in art 57 ECHR, which notably prohibits reservations 'of a general character' (art 57(1)) paras 209–11.

50 ibid paras 94–101.

51 See e.g. *Sismanidis and Sitaridis v Greece*, App Nos 66602/09 and 71879/12; *Lucky Dev v Sweden*, App No 7356/10.

52 See e.g. *Kapetanios and Others v Greece*, App Nos 3453/12, 42941/12, and 9028/13; *Milenkovic v Serbia*, App No 50124/13.

53 See ECtHR, *Jussila v Finland* (n 19) para 43.

matters, customs matters, or proceedings for 'regulatory offences'). In this perspective, the question may arise whether such a differentiation is also relevant for the application of *ne bis in idem*.

Having regard to the Strasbourg case law, after *Grande Stevens* in 2014 several other cases addressed the extended application of *ne bis in idem* in the context of 'double-track' enforcement systems in tax matters. In the 2015 case of *Kapetanios and Others*, the ECtHR explicitly reiterated the CJEU judgment in *Åkerberg Fransson* and noted a convergence in the two Courts' jurisprudence with regard to the assessment of the criminal nature of tax proceedings and the implementation of the *ne bis in idem* principle in tax and criminal matters.[54]

However, in another series of tax cases, the ECtHR seemed willing to limit the expansive trend on extended *ne bis in idem* inaugurated with *Grande Stevens* by excluding a violation of the principle where parallel criminal and administrative proceedings show a "sufficiently close connection in substance and time".[55] Comparable reasoning also emerged in relation to road traffic offences. For example, *Boman v Finland*[56] concerned the imposition of a driving ban under administrative law, which presupposed that a person had already been found guilty of a traffic offence and did not entail a separate examination by the police of the offence or conduct at issue. The two sets of proceedings were considered as intrinsically linked and thus as a single set of proceedings for the purpose of Article 4 of Protocol No 7 to the Convention. Similarly, where an administrative authority could only depart from a prior criminal judgment under certain limited conditions, the Court held in *Rivard v Switzerland*[57] that the administrative (withdrawal of licence) and criminal (fine) procedures were bound by a sufficiently close material and temporal link to be considered as two aspects of a single system, and that there had not been two separate procedures or sets of proceedings. The case law thus indicates that the Court began to place the emphasis on a 'sufficiently close connection' in order to allow states a 'second' punitive sanction in a second or parallel proceedings. These fluctuations in the case law of the ECtHR, which reflected the tensions with established national practices of double track enforcement in certain regulatory fields, continued until November 2016, when the Grand Chamber delivered its judgment in *A and B v Norway*.[58]

54 See *Kapetanios and Others v Greece* (n 49) para 73.

55 See, in particular *Lucky Dev v Sweden* (n 48) paras 60–62. In May 2014, in *Nykanen v Finland* the Court had recalled the said condition but on that occasion a violation of the *ne bis in idem* principle was found.

56 ECtHR, 17 February 2015, *Boman v Finland*, App No 41604/11).

57 ECtHR, 4 October 2016, *Affaire Rivard v Suisse*, App No 21563/12 (judgment available in French only).

58 ECtHR, 15 November 2016, *A and B v Norway*, App Nos 24130/11 and 29758/11.

In *A and B v Norway*, the Grand Chamber of the ECtHR once and for all limited the findings of *Grande Stevens* by further specifying the features of the *bis* element in the extended dimension of *ne bis in idem*.

In particular, the Court stressed that Article 4 of Protocol 7 does not as such exclude the conduct of dual proceedings, provided that certain conditions are fulfilled. According to the ECtHR, for the accumulation of administrative and criminal proceedings to be acceptable, the following four substantive conditions must be satisfied: (1) the proceedings must pursue complementary aims and address different aspects of the social misconduct at issue; (2) the duality of proceedings must be a foreseeable consequence of the same impugned conduct (*idem*); (3) there must be no duplication of the collection and assessment of evidence; and (4) an offsetting mechanism designed to ensure that the overall amount of any penalties imposed is proportionate must be in place.[59]

This approach is underpinned by the rationale that states "should be able legitimately to choose complementary legal responses to socially offensive conduct (such as non-compliance with road-traffic regulations or non-payment/evasion of taxes) through different procedures forming a coherent whole so as to address different aspects of the social problem involved, provided that the accumulated legal responses do not represent an excessive burden for the individual concerned".[60] The ECtHR argues that the object of Article 4 of Protocol 7 is not to "outlaw legal systems which take an 'integrated' approach to the social wrongdoing in question, and in particular an approach involving parallel stages of legal response to the wrongdoing by different authorities and for different purposes".[61]

This very detailed judgment, to date, clearly distances the Strasbourg Court from the approach of the Luxembourg Court in *Åkerberg Fransson*. On the other hand, as highlighted in the articulate dissenting opinion of Judge Pinto de Albuquerque attached to the judgment, by reshaping the contours of the *bis* element in *A and B v Norway*, the ECtHR seemed to a certain extent also willing indirectly to limit its previous extensive approach to *idem* launched in *Zolotukhin v Russia*. Assessing the complementarity of the aims pursued by administrative and criminal enforcement in tackling different aspects of the same social misconduct—as suggested by the first condition laid down in *A and B v Norway*—is "intrinsically a substantive issue" that belongs more to the concept of *idem* than to that of *bis*.[62]

The *A and B* approach was subsequently confirmed and refined in *Johannesson and Others v Iceland*,[63] where the Court eventually found a violation of *ne bis in idem*

59 ibid para 132.

60 ibid para 121.

61 ibid para 123.

62 ibid. See, in particular, points 50 ff of the Dissenting Opinion of Judge Pinto de Albuquerque.

63 ECtHR, 18 May 2017, *Johannesson and Others v Iceland* (App no 22007/11).

under Article 4 of Protocol 7. The case related, again, to a hypothesis of double-track tax enforcement in which criminal proceedings lasting several years were brought after the adoption of a final administrative tax surcharge for the same facts (the same failure to declare income).[64] On this occasion, the ECtHR confirmed that double-track enforcement is not prohibited as such by Protocol 7 ECHR and specified the condition of the 'sufficiently close connection'. The Court denied the existence of a 'sufficiently close connection' between the two proceedings in the concrete case since their "overall length"[65] totalled over nine years, placing a "disproportionate prejudice" upon the applicants and determining a violation of *ne bis in idem in concreto*.[66] Owing to the peculiar circumstances of the case, the judgment in *Johannesson* attached a particular weight to the 'time' element of the 'sufficiently close connection', specifying that "the weaker the connection in time the greater the burden on the State to explain and justify any such delay as may be attributable to its conduct of the proceedings".[67] Interestingly, the Court also mentioned as an additional circumstance contributing to the violation of the principle the "largely independent collection and assessment of evidence", highlighting its detrimental impact on the overall length of the proceedings. Thus, although the tenets of the restrictive approach of *A and B v Norway* are confirmed, *Johannesson* seems also to place a greater emphasis on the need for trans-procedural coordination.

C. Case closed? The CJEU and extended *ne bis in idem* in the aftermath of *A and B v Norway: Menci, Di Puma*, and *Garlsson*

Shortly after judgment was reached in *A and B v Norway*, the CJEU was confronted with the issue of compatibility between systems of double track enforcement and the principle of *ne bis in idem* under Article 50 CFREU in three Italian cases:[68]

64 The identity of the facts (same) and the criminal nature of the tax surcharges were not contended by the parties; see paras 44 and 47of the *Johannesson* judgment (n 63).

65 See para 50 of the *Johannesson* judgment (n 63). The Court recalled para 134 of *A and B v Norway* (n 58), which stated that 'the connection in time must be sufficiently close to protect the individual from being subjected to uncertainty and delay and from proceedings becoming protracted over time . . ., even where the relevant national system provides for an "integrated" scheme separating administrative and criminal components'.

66 See para 56 of the *Johannesson* judgment (n 63).

67 ibid para 50.

68 The three cases all concern internal or 'domestic'—as opposed to transnational—*ne bis in idem*. The applicability of the Charter and art 50 CFREU was recognised by the Court since, in all the situations concerned, the Member States were 'implementing Union law' within the meaning of art 51(1) CFREU. In regard to VAT enforcement, the connection with EU law had already been acknowledged in *Åkerberg Fransson* under the umbrella of the protection of the EU's financial interests and art 325 TFEU (see paras 26–27 of the *Åkerberg Fransson* judgment (n 44)). In the cases

Menci,[69] *Di Puma*,[70] and *Garlsson Real Estate*.[71] The three cases presented partly different backgrounds, *Menci* being a case of double-track enforcement in the field of VAT collection, while *Di Puma* and *Garlsson* related to the accumulation of criminal and administrative proceedings for insider dealing and market manipulation.[72] Nonetheless, they all revolved around the same fundamental legal question and were assigned to the Grand Chamber "in view of the importance of the questions raised by that judgment of the European Court of Human Rights with regard to the interpretation of Article 50 of the Charter".[73]

relating to market abuse and market manipulation (*Di Puma* and *Garlsson*), the applicability of the CFREU was recognised by the Court since the relevant Italian legislation was expressly enacted in implementation of the no longer in force Directive 2003/6/EU (the old Directive on insider dealing and market abuse [2003] OJ L96/16, now replaced by Directive 2014/57 on criminal sanctions for market abuse (Market Abuse Directive) [2014] OJ L173/179 and Regulation 596/2014) [2014] OJ L173/1. On this latter point see the Opinion of AG Campos Sánchez-Bordona in *Garlsson* (ECLI:EU:C:2017:669) at paras 36–39 and the Court's judgment in *Garlsson* (see n 71 below) at para 23.

69 *Menci* was originally joined with the cases of *Orsi and Baldetti* (CJEU, 5 April 2017, Joined Cases C-217/15 and C-350/15 *Orsi and Baldetti* ECLI:EU:C:2017:264) relating to the double application in Italy of fiscal (administrative) and criminal penalties for unpaid VAT. If VAT has wrongfully not been paid, Italian law (art 1(1) of Legislative Decree No 471 of 18 December 1997) foresees a tax penalty in the form of an administrative penalty. Additionally, the omission of VAT payment can qualify as a criminal offence (see art 10a of Legislative Decree No 74/2000 of 10 March 2000). The Italian court was therefore asking whether art 50 of the CFREU would have precluded the possibility of conducting criminal proceedings concerning an act (non-payment of VAT) for which a definitive administrative penalty had already been imposed on the defendant. The reason for disjoining *Menci* from *Orsi and Baldetti* lay in the fact that, while both cases related to the accumulation of administrative and criminal proceedings for the non-payment of VAT, in the case in *Orsi and Baldetti* the tax proceedings were carried out against a company with autonomous legal personality, and thus the solution of the case was deemed less problematic owing to the fact that the subjects of legal proceedings were legally distinct (in this sense see also ECtHR, 20 May 2014, App no 35232/11 *Pirittimaki v Finland*. *Orsi and Baldetti* was decided on 5 April 2017, excluding a violation of *ne bis in idem*). On the contrary, in *Menci* both the tax and the criminal proceedings were brought against the same natural person, posing the same issues as in *A and B v Norway* (n 58).

70 Joined Cases C-596/16 and C-597/16 *Di Puma and Zecca v CONSOB* ECLI:EU:C:2018:192. In this case, *Di Puma* and *Zecca* had been finally acquitted in a criminal proceedings for insider dealing, but the parallel punitive administrative proceedings for the same facts were not discontinued. The preliminary question was raised by the Italian Court of Cassation in the context of an appeal against the fining decision adopted in those punitive administrative proceedings.

71 Case C-537/16 *Garlsson, Ricucci and Magiste v CONSOB* ECLI:EU:C:2018:193. In this case, the same person was subject to a criminal conviction for market manipulation which had become final before the conclusion of a parallel punitive administrative proceeding for the same conduct. The criminal conviction, nonetheless, had been extinguished by the subsequent application of a pardon.

72 Those cases presented a legal background similar to the one addressed by the ECtHR in *Grande Stevens* (n 49).

73 Case C-524/15 *Menci* (order of the court).

After the assignation of *Menci* to the Grand Chamber, Advocate General Campos Sánchez Bordona delivered his opinion in September 2017.[74] This Opinion (which constituted the blueprint for the two opinions delivered by Advocate General Sánchez Bordona in *Di Puma* and *Garlsson*) is particularly significant since it recognised the restrictive intent underlying the *revirement* of the Strasbourg Court in *A and B v Norway*[75] and, most importantly, advocated for an autonomous and more protective interpretation of Article 50 CFREU than that offered under Article 4 of Protocol 7 ECHR in regard to extended *ne bis in idem*.[76] The autonomous approach of the Advocate General presents two interesting points that it might be worth presenting briefly, before moving to the analysis of the CJEU judgments. In the first place, the Advocate General seems to conduct an analysis of the 'criminal nature' of punitive administrative proceedings and sanctions for the purposes of Article 50 CFREU based on the application of the *Engel* criteria, without introducing any distinction as suggested by the *Jussila* case law.[77] As observed above, the reference to *Jussila*—distinguishing punitive proceedings by virtue of their belonging to the 'hard core of criminal law'—represented an important element of the reasoning of the Strasbourg Court in *A and B v Norway*: to a certain extent, it could be argued that the *revirement* of the ECtHR and the limitation of the scope of *ne bis in idem* in this latter judgment rely conceptually on the possibility of differentiating between various 'shades of punitiveness' for the purposes of adapting criminal law guarantees.[78]

The fact that the *Jussila* argument is not used in the Opinion is significant here: the Advocate General clearly considered that limitations of the principle of *ne bis in idem* should not be construed on a blurred distinction.[79]

Secondly, and more explicitly, the AG affirmed that under EU law the legitimacy of limitations of Article 50 CFREU should not be tied to the vague criterion of the

74 See the Opinion of the Advocate General Campos Sánchez-Bordona delivered on 12 September 2017 in Case C-524/15 *Menci* ECLI:EU:C:2017:667.

75 See, in particular, ibid para 60.

76 ibid paras 71–72 and 74–77.

77 See section III.A above.

78 See para 133 of the ECtHR judgment in *A and B v Norway* (n 58), where the Strasbourg Court openly states that: "the extent to which the administrative proceedings bear the hallmarks of ordinary criminal proceedings is an important factor . . . The additional factor that those proceedings do not carry any significant degree of stigma renders it less likely that the combination of proceedings will entail a disproportionate burden on the accused person".

79 At para 89 of the Opinion the AG stresses that: "There is nothing to prevent the Member States from imposing both criminal and administrative penalties in respect of the same acts where the administrative penalties are not of a criminal nature. In my view, that should be the focus of the discussion. Rather than blur the clarity which should imbue the right protected by the principle *ne bis in idem*, by making it subject to disproportionately complex assessments, it is sufficient to retrace the steps which led to the treatment of pecuniary penalties imposed by the tax authorities as being criminal in nature".

substantive and temporal connection between the two types of proceedings as spelt out in *A and B v Norway* but rather tested in light of the 'horizontal limitation clause' of Article 52(1) CFREU.[80] This provision of primary EU law permits a limitation of the rights and freedoms under the CFREU only where it is provided by law, respects the essence of the rights and freedoms, and complies with the principle of proportionality, meaning that the restriction is strictly necessary and 'genuinely meets the objectives of general interest recognised by the Union or the need to protect the rights and freedom of others'.[81]

In regard to the criterion of 'strict necessity', the Advocate General concluded that the duplication of punitive administrative proceedings and criminal proceedings for the same facts, admitted by the ECtHR under the *A and B v Norway* approach, would fail the test of Article 52(1) CFREU, inasmuch as it would not meet the necessity requirement of the proportionality test set out by the provision. In other words, the restrictions to the principle of *ne bis in idem* represented by dual-track (punitive administrative/criminal) enforcement systems would generally be disproportionate and "unnecessary".[82] The non-necessity of such a restriction of the principle of *ne bis in idem*, according to the Advocate General, finds support precisely in the fact that not all of the EU Member States implement double-track enforcement systems; on the contrary, several other Member States have adopted single-track (*una via*) systems.[83]

In answering the preliminary questions, the Court followed the methodology suggested by the Advocate General and performed an analysis of the limitation of *ne bis in idem* under the criteria of Article 52(1) of the CFREU[84] but, eventually, achieved a result which seems substantially in line with *A and B v Norway*. The judgment in *Menci*, indeed, concluded that a limitation to the principle of *ne bis in idem* deriving from the accumulation of punitive administrative and criminal proceedings for the same facts may be admitted under arts 50 and 52(1) CFREU

80 The scheme of art 52(1) CFREU to assess the legitimacy of the limitations to art 50 CFREU was already adopted by the CJEU in the context of transnational *ne bis in idem*, when testing the validity of the so-called 'enforcement condition' under art 54 CISA in the case *Spasic* (CJEU, 27 May 2014, Case C-129/14 PPPU *Spasic*). The AG refers to *Spasic* expressly in his Opinion.

81 See art 52(1) CFREU.

82 See para 82 of the Opinion.

83 ibid paras 82–86.

84 Similarly to the AG, the Court stressed the methodological autonomy of its reasoning from that of the ECtHR in *A and B v Norway*. With regard to the 'corresponding rights' (meaning those rights provided under the CFREU that correspond to rights under the ECHR and that, according to art 52(3) of the CFREU, are to have the same meaning and scope of those under the Convention), the Court remarked that its role is to "ensure the necessary consistency between the Charter and the ECHR, without thereby adversely affecting the autonomy of Union law". See para 23 of the *Menci* judgment and para 25 of the *Garlsson* judgment (n 71).

under a set of conditions which are in substance identical to those considered by Strasbourg.[85] According to the CJEU, duplication of administrative and criminal proceedings may be admitted if such a possibility is: (1) provided by law, (2) pursues an objective of general interest, (3) is necessary to pursue additional (and complementary) objectives, (4) subject to rules on coordination aimed at limiting the disadvantage for the person concerned "to what is strictly necessary" (5) subject to rules that ensure the proportionality of all the penalties imposed (essentially, an offset mechanism/application of the accounting principle).

Differently to the Opinion of the Advocate General and similarly to the ECtHR in *A and B v Norway* the Court, therefore, did not rule out double-track enforcement but admitted its compatibility with the principle of *ne bis in idem* subject to the above-mentioned conditions.[86]

The concrete assessment of the conditions in *Menci* were ultimately left to the referring national court,[87] while a more stringent analysis was performed in the two other decisions in *Di Puma* and *Garlsson*.

Especially in the latter case (*Garlsson*), the CJEU seems to have endorsed a strict proportionality assessment[88] in opting to scrutinise in depth the Italian legislation on market manipulation. As a result, the Luxembourg judges observed that the Italian legislation on market manipulation appears to go beyond what is strictly necessary to achieve the objective of protecting the integrity of financial markets.[89] More specifically, the Court pointed out that "in the event of a criminal conviction" under the Italian provision on market manipulation,[90] the possibility

85 See para 63 of the *Menci* judgment.

86 See para 47 of the judgment, where the Court stated that: "In the absence of harmonisation of EU law in the matter, the Member States have therefore the right to provide either for a system in which VAT offences may be subject to proceedings and penalties only once, or for a system authorising the duplication of proceedings and penalties. In those circumstances, the proportionality of national legislation, such as that at issue in the main proceedings, cannot be called into question by the mere fact that the Member State concerned made the choice to provide for the possibility of such a duplication, as otherwise that Member State would be deprived of that freedom of choice".

87 Although the Court acknowledged—prima facie—that the Italian legislation on double-track enforcement in the field of VAT seems not in contrast with the principle of *ne bis in idem* under art 50 CFREU (interpreted in light of art 51(1) CFREU). See para 57 of the judgment in *Menci*.

88 Apparently, also in *Garlsson* (n 71) the last word is left to the national judge (para 59). However, the analysis performed by the Court over the Italian provisions seems to leave very little leeway to the national judge.

89 See para 61 of the *Garlsson* judgment (n 71).

90 Article 185 of the Italian Consolidated Law on Financial Intermediation (Testo Unico delle Disposizioni in Materia di Intermediazione Finanziaria, TUF) provides criminal sanctions (imprisonment between one and six years and a criminal fine from €20,000 to €5 million) for the offence of market manipulation.

of bringing or continuing punitive administrative proceedings for the same facts should be considered to exceed what is strictly necessary, "in so far as that criminal conviction is such as to punish the offence committed in an effective, proportionate and dissuasive manner".[91] Additionally, the Court noted the inadequate offsetting of penalties in the Italian provisions applied in the two types of proceedings: an obligation to take into account the previously inflicted sanction (administrative or criminal), whilst provided by the law, is limited to the pecuniary fine and does not extend to criminal imprisonment.[92]

V. CONCLUSIONS: TRANSNATIONAL APPLICATION OF EXTENDED *NE BIS IN IDEM* AND CONFLICTS OF JURISDICTION

In light of the latest developments in the supranational case law of Strasbourg and Luxembourg on the issue of extended *ne bis in idem*, some general considerations can be offered in regard to its relevance for conflicts of jurisdiction.

Extended *ne bis in idem* has so far been addressed both in Strasbourg and in Luxembourg in regard to purely domestic cases: all of the cases brought before the two Courts have pertained to the dual-track enforcement systems of a single state. Notwithstanding this, the extended application of the principle—also if reconfirmed under the limited and conditional approach of *A and B v Norway*—may have a transnational dimension.

Theoretically, combining the factual conception of *idem* endorsed by the CJEU in the transnational application of the principle with the application of the *Engel* criteria in defining the *bis* element, a final decision delivered in punitive administrative proceedings in Member State A may bar criminal prosecution on the same facts in Member State B. A concrete example in this regard, provided by Vervaele,[93] is the fallout from the *Fortis* financial scandal, where parallel criminal and administrative proceedings for suspicions of market manipulation and market abuse were carried out separately by the (uncoordinated) Dutch and Belgian authorities against both the legal persons and the leading individuals. In such cases, while the risk of infringement of *ne bis in idem* (in its extended and transnational configuration) may

91 See para 57 of the *Garlsson* judgment (n 71). The CJEU assessed the proportionality of the national legislation *in abstracto*, considering irrelevant (at para 62 of the judgment) the application of a pardon which had completely extinguished the penalty in the concrete case.

92 See para 60 of the *Garlsson* judgment (n 71).

93 See J. A. E. Vervaele, 'European Territoriality and Jurisdiction' in M. Luchtman (ed), *Choice of Forum in Cooperation Against EU Financial Crime* (Eleven Publishing 2013) 168, with regard to the *Fortis* case.

be particularly high, on the other hand, a random application of the principle on a 'first come, first served' basis may lead to arbitrary outcomes.

The solution, however, cannot be to deny the application of a fundamental right, but rather to prevent its infringement from the outset. In this perspective, the 'sufficiently close connection in substance and time' between the parallel proceedings required by the Strasbourg Court (and its further requirement of 'an adequate interaction between the authorities involved') and the existence of rules on coordination between proceedings considered by the CJEU in *Menci*[94] may promote the extension of a mechanism for the prevention and settlement of conflicts of jurisdiction beyond the circle of *stricto sensu* criminal justice actors in order to include the activities of punitive administrative enforcers.

Although the proposed models put forward by the present research project focus on criminal law actors only, the analysis set out here supports the view that the EU legislator ought to keep the extended perspective in mind in the course of its future endeavours. Of course, this could represent a demanding challenge for the EU legislator, since punitive administrative enforcement in a transnational setting may actually present a higher level of fragmentation than in the field of criminal justice, where the actors of judicial cooperation are more easily-identifiable. Moreover, it remains unclear how much of the reasoning developed in relation to domestic cases of extended *ne bis in idem* might extrapolate to the transnational arena. In *Rivard*, for example, the ECtHR held there to be no duplication of punishment (no *bis*) as regards criminal (a fine for speeding) and administrative (withdrawal of driving licence) proceedings: a 'material link' between procedures was deemed to exist inter alia since each authority had distinct, non-overlapping remits and the outcome of the criminal procedure had a bearing on that of the administrative one.[95] Tailored common European criteria would be essential to a coherent analysis of the *unicité* of proceedings in the cross-border extended *ne bis in idem* scenario; their elaboration presents a formidable challenge. Nonetheless, in order to respect the principle of *ne bis in idem* as a fundamental right, whilst ensuring a coherent exercise of jurisdiction in the AFSJ, this challenge should be accepted.

94 See the judgment in *Menci*, para 63. The Court requires the existence of "rules ensuring coordination which limits to what is strictly necessary the additional disadvantage which results, for the persons concerned, from a duplication of proceedings".

95 See *Affaire Rivard v Suisse* (n 57), *lien matériel*, para 31. The Court went on to note that the long-standing practice in question was based on a Swiss law dating from 1959, subject to both consistent jurisprudence and regular political debate: "*il est donc largement connu*". At present, any convincing application of each of these pieces of supporting reasoning across borders at the EU level would appear doubtful.

6

CHOICE OF FORUM AND CYBERCRIME

GAVIN ROBINSON

I. IS CYBERSPACE CONFLICT-PRONE?

A. Definitions of cybercrime

In the words of the chair of the drafting committee behind the Council of Europe Convention on Cybercrime (Budapest Convention; CCC), cybercrime 'is a term of 'hype' and not a legal definition'.[1] For Clough, there are 'almost as many terms to describe cybercrime as there are cybercrimes'.[2] The 'cyber' element is, of course, a first crucial characteristic; as Walden recalls, much of the illicit activity which qualifies as cybercrime is a (novel) subset of computer crime. Infect a computer with a virus through a floppy disk or CD, for example, and this would lack the cyber element.[3] Some attempts at defining the phenomenon have hitched developments in cybercrime to the development of the internet itself—as is the case for 'e-crime 1.0' and 'e-crime 2.0'.[4] Alternatively, a focus on the victim or target is used: crimes against computers; crimes against property; illicit content; and (comparatively new—take cyber-harassment, for instance) offences against the person with a cyber element.[5]

In the United States (US), the United Kingdom (UK), and in Australia and Canada, some variant of a twofold classification between 'cyber-dependent' and 'cyber-enabled' crimes has been adopted. The first term refers to crimes that can only be committed through the use of ICT devices, where the devices are both the tool for committing the crime and the target of the crime, such as hacking, malware, and denial-of-service attacks, whilst the second refers to crimes that may be

1 See H. W. K. Kaspersen, 'Jurisdiction in the Cybercrime Convention' in B.-J. Koops and S. W. Brenner (eds), *Cybercrime and Jurisdiction: A Global Survey* (T.M.C. Asser Press 2006) ch 2, 9.

2 Inter alia, 'computer crime', 'computer-related crime', 'crime by computer', 'high technology crime', '(inter)net crime', 'digital crime', 'electronic crime', 'IT crime', and so on; see J. Clough, *Principles of Cybercrime* (Cambridge University Press 2015) at 9–10.

3 I. Walden, *Computer Crimes and Digital Investigations* (2nd edn, Oxford University Press 2016) at 2.04 ff.

4 M. Yar, 'E-crime 2.0: The Criminological Landscape of Social Media' (2012) 21 *Information and Communications Technology Law* 207–19.

5 See A. A. Gillespie, *Cybercrime: Key Issues and Debates* (Routledge 2016), a leading textbook on cybercrime structured in these four parts.

committed without ICT devices, such as fraud and theft, but which are changed significantly by the use of ICT in terms of scale and reach: financial loss online, mass-marketing frauds, phishing emails, and myriad other types of scam.[6] More extensive sub-categorisations further distinguish criminal activities that are created by computer-mediated communication (hacking, digital piracy, information espionage, cyber-terrorism) from traditional criminal activities that are either expanded or enhanced by the internet on the one hand (criminal exploitation of ATM machines, industrial espionage and reverse engineering) or generalised and 'radicalised' by the internet (money laundering, drug smuggling, cyber-pornography, online gambling) on the other.[7]

These two categories—albeit not all crimes falling within them—are reflected in the core provisions of what is still the leading international law instrument in the field: the Budapest Convention, from 2001.[8] Thus, perhaps the most intuitive forms of cybercrime are found in Articles 2 to 6 of the CCC: the so-called 'CIA' offences (offences against the confidentiality, integrity, and availability of computer data and systems), in other words 'any crime directed against computer systems and networks and their information content'.[9] Such activity would simply not materialise without computers: the technology created the possibility of the wrongdoing. Into the broader category of age-old crimes given a new lease of life by the same technology go cyber-boosted property offences (Article 7—computer-related forgery; Article 8—computer-related fraud). Offences against the person such as cyber-bullying and cyber-stalking are also relevant here, but—having not generated much concern at the time the CCC was drafted[10]—are not included in its provisions. On the other hand, the Convention does require the establishment of content-related offences (Article 9; child pornography) and offences related to infringements of intellectual property rights (Article 10). Finally, at the opposite end of the spectrum from the 'CIA offences', it also binds state parties to ensuring that procedural measures are in place for the investigation of '[any] other criminal offences committed by means of a computer system'[11] and, further still, for the 'collection of evidence in electronic

6 HM Government, *National Cyber Security Strategy 2016–2021* (November 2016) Annex 2, Glossary, 'Cyber crime' https://www.gov.uk/government/publications/national-cyber-security-strategy-2016-to-2021; see also M. McGuire and S. Dowling, *Cyber Crime: A Review of the Evidence* (Home Office Research Report 2013) 75.

7 See B. Sandywell, 'On the Globalisation of Crime: The Internet and New Criminality' in Y. Yewkes and M. Yar (eds), *Handbook of Internet Crime* (Willan Publishing 2010), 38–66 at 46 and the sources cited therein.

8 Council of Europe, Convention on Cybercrime, Budapest, 23.XI.2001, CETS No. 185.

9 Kaspersen, 'Jurisdiction in the Cybercrime Convention' (n 1) at 9.

10 Gillespie, *Cybercrime* (n 5) at 262.

11 CCC, art 14(2)(b).

form of a [thus, any] criminal offence'[12]—identified elsewhere as a third, broad category of 'computer-supported crimes'.[13]

B. A generator of multiple claims to jurisdiction

The objective here is not to debate the relative—and at best partial—accuracy of the extant definitions, which are mentioned only insofar as they serve to underline those aspects of (the comprehensive worldwide criminalisation of) cybercrime which are plausibly liable to multiply tenable claims of material criminal jurisdiction. In keeping with the overarching goals of the present research project, the chapter focuses on material (or 'substantive') jurisdiction only; although related, procedural, investigative and enforcement jurisdiction fall outwith its scope.[14]

For Clough, cybercrime is marked by five key intertwining issues: the sheer scale, accessibility and global reach of the internet, the possibility to easily commit crimes—to a degree—anonymously, and the portability and transferability of electronic evidence of criminal wrongdoing.[15] Each of these challenges to the enforcement of criminal laws in cyberspace shows, it is commonly argued, a propensity to multiply such claims. Indeed, however defined—and despite not constituting a type of crime in a traditional criminal law or criminological sense—the global reach of computer networks makes it difficult not to concur that cybercrime is 'apart from exceptions, in principle a cross-border crime'.[16] Yet unlike cross-border real-world crimes, where the commission of a single offence or a single course of conduct typically takes place in one or a handful of (often contiguous or close—as with drug trafficking) jurisdictions, cybercrime offences can multiply exponentially both the

12 ibid, art 14(2)(c).

13 M. Kowalski, 'Cyber-Crime: Issues, Data Sources, and Feasibility of Collecting Police-Reported Statistics' (Canadian Centre for Justice Statistics, Catalogue No. 85-558-XIE 2002) 6.

14 Whilst material or substantive jurisdiction is closely linked to both jurisdiction to prescribe (a sovereign entity's authority 'to make its law applicable to the activities, relations, or status of persons, or the interests of persons in things . . . by legislation, by executive act or order, by administrative rule . . . or by determination of a court'; *Third Restatement of the Foreign Relations Law of the United States*, vol. 1 (14 May 1986), § 401(a)) and jurisdiction to adjudicate ('to subject persons or entities to the process of its courts or administrative tribunals'; *Third Restatement*, § 401(b)), procedural jurisdiction overlaps with jurisdiction to enforce at either the investigative or judicial phase ('to induce or compel compliance or to punish noncompliance with its laws or regulations, whether through the courts or by use of executive, administrative, police, or other nonjudicial action'; *Third Restatement*, § 401(c)). For a discussion of ongoing EU-level developments in the latter context see K. Ligeti and G. Robinson, 'Transnational Enforcement of Production Orders for Electronic Evidence. Beyond Mutual Recognition' in R. Kert and A. Lehner (eds), *Vielfalt des Strafrechts im internationalen Kontext: Festschrift für Frank Höpfel zum 65. Geburtstag* (NWV 2018), 625–44.

15 Clough, *Principles of Cybercrime* (n 2) at 5 ff.

16 H. W. K. Kaspersen, 'Cybercrime and Internet Jurisdiction' Discussion paper (draft) for Project on Cybercrime (Council of Europe, 5 March 2009) 12.

number of plausible claims to jurisdiction and the distance between claimants. In even the most basic of scenarios, if malware is launched or 'spear-phishing' carried out from Member State A, remotely targeting victims in Member States B, C, D, and E, based on the traditional territoriality principle each of those countries may have a valid claim to prosecute the perpetrator(s). Contemporary ICT is able to boost such wrongdoing beyond all recognition, as in cases such as the Dridex botnet, which by 2015 had breached tens of thousands of organisations across twenty-seven countries causing losses of £20 million in the UK alone.[17]

In such cases, however, a proviso is called for. Does the generation of multiple plausible claims to jurisdiction necessarily imply—as we are accustomed to thinking in relation to offline crime—that those claims are likely to conflict with each other? Unauthorised access to a computer system, for example, may conceivably be considered to physically take place (at least in part) either where the perpetrator is at the moment when access occurs, where the system or network accessed is located, or where the internet switches used in the process of gaining access are located.[18] As Brenner puts it, large-scale cybercrime activity such as mega-hacks tend to produce 'a factually and legally severable criminal transaction'[19] in each country affected, victimising citizens of each country, and which is unique to that country.[20] There is as such no conflict between the competing claims to jurisdiction, since the offence committed in each jurisdiction is discrete; a by-product of the sheer range and complexity of cyber-offending. Of course, conflicts in the *exercise* of jurisdiction are nonetheless liable to arise in such cases, not least where victims reside in tens of affected countries, rendering sequential prosecutions—even where lawful, in the absence of *idem*—practically difficult and of an importance which is likely to shrink as punishment accumulates and time passes.

Whether or not a perpetrator is considered to have acted at a certain location depends in the first place on the legal definition of the crime. In this respect, the reactions of distinct national legal systems to the ubiquity of cybercrime have inevitably varied. As will be seen in detail below, EU law has as yet made no great effort to facilitate the decisive allocation of territorial jurisdiction to one Member State or another in relation to cybercrime offences. On the contrary, instruments such as the

17 Hitting the UK, US, and France especially hard. See 'FBI takes down Dridex botnet, seizes servers, arrests suspect' *The Register* (14 October 2015) https://www.theregister.co.uk/2015/10/14/dridex_botnet_takedown/.

18 Kaspersen, 'Jurisdiction in the Cybercrime Convention' (n 1) at 10–11.

19 S. W. Brenner, 'The Next Step: Prioritizing Jurisdiction' in B.-J. Koops and S. W. Brenner (eds), *Cybercrime and Jurisdiction: A Global Survey* (T.M.C. Asser Press 2006) ch 17 at 334–35.

20 Gillespie, too, recognises that with cross-border cybercrimes, 'we are likely to be speaking about multiple jurisdictions rather than concurrent jurisdiction'; Gillespie, *Cybercrime* (n 5) at 29.

'Integrity Directive'[21] clearly demonstrate a wide-net approach aimed at ensuring that multiple jurisdictional claims exist whilst leaving the definition of jurisdiction to national law. Insofar as attempts have been made at the European level to reduce the risk of conflicts of jurisdiction in criminal matters and to prevent and resolve such conflicts, these have been of general application and have not treated cybercrime differently to any other offence. Underpinning the ensuing analysis, therefore, is the open question of whether cybercrime deserves or requires a distinct approach—and if so, what that approach might look like.

Whether and to what extent conflicts of jurisdiction do materialise in practice—in relation to cybercrime as for other offences—remains unclear due to a lack of empirical data. Still, in theory it seems likely that serious cybercrimes will lead to 'positive' competition between affected states, whereas cases of diffuse damage caused for instance by widespread viruses may tip the scales of the public interest in no single country—a 'negative' conflict of jurisdiction leaving justice unserved and victims unprotected.[22] Building on that premise, section II begins with a discussion of the problematic application of traditional grounds for substantive criminal jurisdiction to offences committed in or through cyberspace (section II.A). The modest existing initiatives to confront conflicts of criminal jurisdiction in cybercrime cases are then addressed, along with an assessment of recent evidence on the current extent of European judicial cooperation on cybercrime (section II.B). The chapter concludes by addressing how the models proposed in the present research project might contribute to improving forum choice in cybercrime cases from the perspectives of law enforcement, defendants, and victims (section III).

II. CONFLICTS OF SUBSTANTIVE JURISDICTION IN CYBERSPACE

Of the traditional international law bases of substantive jurisdiction,[23] most[24] are found in the main binding and non-binding international and regional instruments

21 Directive 2013/40/EU of the European Parliament and of the Council of 12 August 2013 on attacks against information systems and replacing Council FD 2005/222/JHA, OJ L218, 14.8.2013, 8–14.

22 S. W. Brenner and B.-J. Koops, 'Approaches to Cybercrime Jurisdiction' (2004) 4(1) *Journal of High Technology Law* 1 at XVII.A.

23 Territoriality; active nationality; passive personality; protective principle: see I. Brownlie, *Principles of Public International Law* (6th edn, Oxford University Press 2003) 306.

24 The universality principle, applicable to offences deemed to constitute crimes against humanity such as genocide, is widely considered unsuitable for the vast majority of offences grouped under the banner of cybercrime, which are considered less serious. For that reason, it is not discussed here.

aiming to regulate cybercrime.[25] Jurisdiction had been identified as a key concern from the very genesis of the CCC: when the European Committee on Crime Problems (CDPC) decided in November 1996 to set up a committee[26] to draft a Convention on Cybercrime, its terms of reference included 'the question of jurisdiction in relation to information technology offences, e.g. to determine the place where the offence was committed (*locus delicti*) and which law should accordingly apply, including the problem of *ne bis in idem* in the case of multiple jurisdictions and the question how to solve positive jurisdiction conflicts and how to avoid negative jurisdiction conflicts'.[27] The final text of the Convention seeks to ensure that Member States are able to assert jurisdiction in relation to cybercrime offences committed on their territory and/or by their nationals whether at home or abroad, that Member States which refuse extradition instead assert jurisdiction themselves, and it also foresees consultations between state parties where competing claims to jurisdiction emerge.[28]

Although the focus here is firmly on the international, the CCC has also made a profound impact on the main bases for jurisdiction applied to cybercrime at the national level, both as regards the application of pre-existing jurisdiction principles to crimes qualifying as cybercrime in national systems and in paving the way for the introduction of tailored domestic rules on jurisdiction for specific cybercrime offences. Whatever the makeup and application of national rules, however, the core bases for jurisdiction in cybercrime cases are common worldwide.[29] These include, in the first place, different modalities of territoriality:

- commission of crime partly/wholly on the territory;
- effects/damages within the territory;

25 Apart from the CCC, other notable regional instruments include the Arab Convention on Combating Information Technology Offences (21 December 2010) and the (non-binding) COMESA Cybersecurity Draft Model Bill. The influence of the CCC is visible in all of the latter instruments; see United Nations Office on Drugs and Crime (UNODC), *Comprehensive Study on Cybercrime* (Draft—February 2013) 70, 190 ff.

26 The Committee of Experts on Crime in Cyber-space (PC-CY).

27 See CCC, Explanatory Report to the Convention on Cybercrime (23 November 2001), at para 11. The principal aims of the CCC are (1) to harmonise domestic criminal substantive law elements of cybercrime offences, (2) to provide for domestic criminal procedural law powers necessary for the investigation and prosecution of such offences as well as others committed by means of a computer system or evidence in relation to which is in electronic form, and (3) to set up a fast and effective regime of international cooperation; at para 16.

28 See CCC art 22, and discussion below. The provisions in art 22 have since been replicated, with offence-relevant adjustments, in additional Council of Europe instruments: the Convention on the Protection of Children against Sexual Exploitation and Sexual Abuse (art 25); the Convention on Action against Trafficking in Human Beings (art 31); and the Convention on the Prevention of Terrorism (art 14). The jurisdiction-related provisions in the CCC, in other international legal instruments, and in EU legislation will be addressed where appropriate in the ensuing analysis.

29 The cited bases are from UNODC (n 25) at 191 ff.

- computer/programme/data used for the commission of the crime located within the territory.

There follows the main dimension of recognised principles founding extraterritorial jurisdiction on the nationality of actors involved in or affected by a criminal offence:

- active nationality: perpetrator is a national or is habitually resident in the state;
- passive personality: victim is a national or is habitually resident in the state.

Finally, extraterritorial jurisdiction may also exceptionally arise in light of:

- the protective principle, or a 'protective nexus'[30] allowing exercise of jurisdiction where a national interest of the forum state is at stake.
- *Aut dedere aut judicare* or the 'representation principle': where a state is required to establish and exert jurisdiction over its own national due to its inability under domestic law to extradite to the requesting state where the crime was committed.

In the following section, the application in the relevant international and European legal instruments of first territorial and then extraterritorial grounds for jurisdiction to offences committed in cyberspace is examined.

A. Rules founding substantive cyber-jurisdiction

1. Territoriality

The territorial ambit of national criminal law naturally derives from state sovereignty.[31] Over time, the base notion of territoriality has expanded from acts physically committed in a certain jurisdiction to include within the locus of the crime acts committed abroad but which produce an effect in the claimant jurisdiction: the so-called 'objective territoriality principle' or 'effects doctrine', which is closely related to the passive personality principle to the extent that 'effect' in a jurisdiction will, depending on the offence, signify victims in that jurisdiction.[32]

30 R. August, 'International Cyber-jurisdiction: A Comparative Analysis' (2002) 39(4) *American Business Law Journal* 531.

31 A. Cassese and others, *Cassese's International Criminal Law* (3rd edn, Oxford University Press 2013) 15.2.1. See also Ortolani, in this volume, arguing at section III.A that, whereas jurisdiction in modern civil law resembles more 'a service provided by State courts in a competitive international market, blurring the public/private divide in a quest for efficiency', jurisdiction in criminal law and the state's monopoly on the repression of criminal activities can be seen as 'an epiphenomenon of sovereignty'.

32 Walden, *Computer Crimes and Digital Investigations* (n 3) at 5.27.

The territoriality principle is found in all international or regional cybercrime instruments that contain a jurisdiction clause.[33] Article 22(1)(a) of the CCC thus provides that '[e]ach Party shall adopt such legislative and other measures as may be necessary to establish jurisdiction over any offence established in accordance with Articles 2 through 11 of this Convention, when the offence is committed . . . in its territory'.[34] Reflecting in 2006 on their earlier sample survey of cyber-jurisdiction rules in the CCC and seven selected jurisdictions worldwide (three of which were EU Member States), Brenner and Koops found that 'perhaps surprisingly, territoriality still turns out to be a prime factor, despite the non-physical nature of the bits and bytes that usually constitute a cybercrime'.[35] On the other hand, perhaps given the wealth of possible composite acts of even the simplest cybercrime offence (targeted hacking; uploading child abuse material) it is less surprising that different jurisdictions would find divergent interpretations of 'territorial connections',[36] in addition to local variations in the use of the protective principle in the name of state interests.

Despite the putative uniqueness of cyberspace, the territoriality principle remains by far the predominant ground for asserting jurisdiction in relation to cybercrime. Yet precisely because of this continued attachment to territory, cybercrime is particularly liable to spawn conflicts of jurisdiction since it is extremely difficult to decisively 'anchor'[37] wrongful acts 'committed online' exclusively to one part of the physical world. For example, with regard to content-related offences, might the making available of universally-criminal material fall under the territorial jurisdiction of all of the approximately 190 national legal systems in the world?[38] The CCC does not provide rules or criteria on how to determine *locus delicti* with regard to cybercrimes, leaving the matter to national law and jurisprudence save for an indication in its Explanatory Report that 'for example, a Party would assert territorial jurisdiction if both the person attacking a computer system and the victim system

33 See UNODC (n 25) 191.

34 Furthermore, the accepted competence in international law of states to establish territorial jurisdiction in relation to conduct on board a ship flying the flag of that state or an aircraft registered under its laws is converted into an obligation to establish jurisdiction by arts 22(1)(b) and (c).

35 B.-J. Koops and S. W. Brenner (eds), *Cybercrime and Jurisdiction: A Global Survey* (T.M.C. Asser Press 2006) 6.

36 Koops and Brenner (n 35) 45.

37 Translation of the Spanish *anclaje* in I. Flores Prada, 'Prevención y solución de conflictos internacionales de juridicción en materia de ciberdelincuencia' (2015) (17–20) *Revista Electrónica de Ciencia Penal y Criminología* 1, at 9–11.

38 U. Sieber, 'Cybercrime and Jurisdiction in Germany. The Present Situation and the Need for New Solutions' in B.-J. Koops and S. W. Brenner (eds), *Cybercrime and Jurisdiction: A Global Survey* (T.M.C. Asser Press 2006) ch 9, at 186.

are located within its territory, and where the computer system attacked is within its territory, even if the attacker is not'.[39]

Territory is also interpreted along these lines in the most relevant EU legislation. The Directive on Child Exploitation, for instance, requires Member States to establish jurisdiction *inter alia* where a relevant offence is 'committed in whole or in part within their territory'[40] and specifies that 'Member States shall ensure that their jurisdiction includes situations where an offence . . . is committed by means of information and communication technology accessed from their territory, whether or not it is based on their territory'.[41] The Integrity Directive, meanwhile, echoes the CCC guidance in providing that when establishing whether an offence has been committed 'in whole or in part within their territory'[42] Member States shall ensure that they have jurisdiction 'where (a) the offender commits the offence when physically present on its territory, whether or not the offence is against an information system on its territory; or (b) the offence is against an information system on its territory, whether or not the offender commits the offence when physically present on its territory'.[43]

The interpretation of whether an information system is located on, or data is stored or controlled from 'on its territory' thus falls to the national level, where broad provisions are found in Member States' domestic laws. Indeed, at times the criterion of a territorial link is stretched to virtual redundancy.[44] In France, for example, *la compétence territoriale* is construed to cover the 'quasi-totality' of cybercrime offences with a link to France not only through the territorial character of

39 CCC, Explanatory Report, para 233. One explanation for the silence of the CCC is that the creation of a special regime for weighing competing claims to jurisdiction in cybercrime cases would have raised the question of its applicability to other crimes; see Kaspersen (n 1) 11.

40 Article 17(1)(a).

41 Article 17(3).

42 Article 12(1)(a).

43 Article 12(2)(a).

44 See in this vein Koops and Goodwin's (2014) thorough exploration of the possible (partial) abandonment of territoriality in relation to investigations in cyberspace in favour of an adapted version of one of a series of exceptions to territoriality which already exist in other contexts (common heritage of mankind; high seas and flag jurisdiction; piracy as an analogy for [certain types of] cybercrime; the right to acquire remote sensing imagery and the principle of Open Skies; common concern of mankind): B.-J. Koops and M. Goodwin, 'Cyberspace, the Cloud, and Cross-Border Criminal Investigation: The Limits and Possibilities of International Law' Study commissioned by WODC, Ministry of Security & Justice (Netherlands), December 2014) 69 ff. Possible routes to international agreement on measures surrendering national sovereignty in such a way—at least in relation to universally-abhorred crimes—include the CCC context (at 83) and the UN General Assembly (at 79). Cf. Clough, *Principles of Cybercrime* (n 2), who highlights a clear division of opinion at the UN on the topic of a new international convention (at 24 ff) and Gillespie, *Cybercrime* (n 5), who argues that the lack of respect shown to physical borders by the internet differs little from that of communications by telephone or radio.

a constitutive element of the wrongdoing, but also by blending in active nationality (including accomplices) and passive personality.[45] Article 337E of the Maltese Criminal Code, meanwhile, provides that where an offence is committed outside Malta that, had it been committed in Malta, would have constituted an offence, it shall 'if the commission affects any computer, software, data or supporting documentation which is situated in Malta or is any way linked or connected to a computer in Malta, be deemed to have been committed in Malta'.[46]

2. Extraterritorial jurisdiction

Under international criminal law, it may be possible—depending on the offence—to exert extraterritorial jurisdiction through the principles of active nationality, passive personality, universality, and the protective principle (state interests). As regards cybercrime, nearly all of the relevant existing international and regional instruments include active nationality as a ground for establishing extraterritorial jurisdiction,[47] whilst one instrument adds the protection of state interests.[48]

Article 22(1)(d) of the CCC envisages the assertion of jurisdiction by a state party where the offence is committed 'by one of its nationals, if the offence is punishable under criminal law where it was committed or if the offence is committed outside the territorial jurisdiction of any state'. Although this provision is optional,[49] leading to the entering of numerous reservations by state parties, the Integrity Directive has effectively rendered it mandatory EU-wide in relation to the relevant offences by requiring that Member States establish jurisdiction where such an offence is committed 'by one of their nationals, at least in cases where the act is an offence where it was committed'.[50] This particular attempt to close the jurisdictional loop vis-à-vis remote and/or mobile perpetrators, first introduced with the CCC in 2001, has taken some time to reach the domestic law of non-civil law countries less accustomed to using active nationality in order to trigger extraterritorial jurisdiction.[51] The UK, for example, took until 2015 (having agreed the Integrity Directive) to amend its Computer Misuse Act 1990 to cover such situations.[52]

45 GENVAL Report, France, at 5.4.1.

46 GENVAL Report, Malta, at 5.4.1.

47 See UNODC (n 25) 190.

48 The Arab Convention on Combating Information Technology Offences, art 30(1)(e): 'If the offence affects an overriding interest of the State'.

49 CCC, art 22(2).

50 Article 12(1)(b).

51 As acknowledged in the *Explanatory Report* to the CCC, at para 236.

52 Computer Misuse Act 1990, s. 5(1A). In practice, in respect of cybercrime offences committed by a UK national abroad British prosecutors may still struggle to clear the public interest hurdle in order to reach trial; Walden, *Computer Crimes and Digital Investigations* (n 3) at 5.32.

Similarly, Article 17(1)(b) of the Directive on Child Exploitation obliges Member States to establish extraterritorial jurisdiction in relation to the relevant offences where the offender is a Member State national, irrespective of the *locus* of the crime. Moreover, it goes further than the Integrity Directive in envisaging (although not requiring) the broadening of active nationality to habitual residents,[53] the triggering of passive personality with regard to both nationals and habitual residents,[54] and the establishment of jurisdiction where an offence is committed abroad 'for the benefit of a legal person established in [the Member State's] territory'.[55] In December 2016, the Commission reported that twenty-one of twenty-eight Member States had put in place legislation transposing the Child Exploitation Directive's binding provisions on territoriality and active nationality.[56] This indirect codification of active nationality in respect of child exploitation in particular represents a significant dose of EU-wide harmonisation vis-à-vis extraterritorial cyber-jurisdiction. Most Member States also decided to implement the optional passive personality provision (nineteen of twenty-eight), whereas fewer of them decided to trigger jurisdiction in respect of offences committed for the benefit of a legal person established in their territory (eleven of twenty-eight).[57] The Directive further requires Member States to ensure that neither double criminality[58] nor any requirement of a victim report[59] may constitute conditions for the establishment of extraterritorial jurisdiction. As of December 2016, twenty-one Member States either provide for specific exceptions to double criminality in relation to the relevant offences or have no double criminality clause in their domestic law, whilst most Member States have legislation transposing the non-requirement of a victim report.[60]

Returning to the CCC, the principle of *aut dedere aut judicare* ('extradite or prosecute') is also included as a mandatory provision in Article 22(3) of the Convention, which requires state parties to establish jurisdiction over alleged offenders present on their territory who cannot (on nationality grounds) be extradited to the requesting

53 Article 17(1)(c).

54 Article 17(2)(a): 'A Member State shall inform the Commission where it decides to establish further jurisdiction over an offence . . . committed outside its territory, inter alia, where the offence is committed against one of its nationals or a person who is an habitual resident in its territory'.

55 Article 17(2)(b).

56 For the seven remaining Member States, information was inconclusive. See Report from the Commission to the European Parliament and the Council assessing the extent to which the Member States have taken the necessary measures in order to comply with Directive 2011/93/EU of 13 December 2011 on combating the sexual abuse and sexual exploitation of children and child pornography [2011] OJ L335/1, COM/2016/0871 final, at 2.1.15.

57 ibid.

58 Applicable to selected offences targeted by the Directive; see art 17(4).

59 Applicable to all offences targeted by the Directive; see art 17(5).

60 COM/2016/0871 final (n 56) at 2.1.15.

state. Furthermore, it is worth underlining that the CCC expressly provides that it does not exclude any criminal jurisdiction exercised by a state party in accordance with its national law.[61] In sum, whilst the European legal framework on the assertion of jurisdiction in relation to cybercrime offences is one of the most comprehensive, any real uniformity of approach across the Member States would appear a distant prospect as national courts continue to settle cases according to their own methodologies and legal traditions.[62]

B. Existing efforts to confront conflicts of jurisdiction

1. International and European initiatives

As of yet, there is no specific international initiative dedicated to confronting the problem of conflicts of jurisdiction in the cybercrime context. Indeed, there is no UN convention on cybercrime: the closest thing in the field to a truly global instrument remains the CCC which, although its roots are European, has been signed and ratified by non-Members of the Council of Europe including the USA, Canada, Australia, and Israel.[63]

It was seen earlier that the terms of reference for the committee charged with drafting the CCC specifically envisaged taking steps in order to solve positive conflicts of jurisdiction and avoid negative conflicts of jurisdiction. Article 22(5) of the CCC thus provides that '[w]here more than one Party claims jurisdiction over an alleged offence established in accordance with this Convention, the Parties involved shall, where appropriate, consult with a view to determining the most appropriate jurisdiction for prosecution'. The obligation to consult reflects the need for international comity,[64] the international law requirement that the assertion of jurisdiction ought to be reasonable,[65] and the importance of showing 'mutual respect for the sovereignty of other States and refraining from unjustified interference in the internal affairs of those states'.[66] Nonetheless, it is not absolute: instead, state parties must consult each other 'where appropriate'. According to one drafter of the Convention, this refers not to 'situations where one Party estimates that the expected outcome of the consultation is apparent', but rather to 'situations where one of the parties involved has already announced it will not take further action, or where a Party fears that prosecution in the other Party state would jeopardize its

61 Article 22(4).

62 See C. Velasco, 'Cybercrime Jurisdiction: Past, Present and Future' (2015) 16(3) *ERA Forum* 331, at 339.

63 See Council of Europe, 'The Budapest Convention on Cybercrime at 15: Achievements and Challenges' (November 2016) https://rm.coe.int/16806b7f24.

64 Clough, *Principles of Cybercrime* (n 2) at 485.

65 Third Restatement of the Foreign Relations Law of the United States, § 403.

66 See generally Council of Europe, European Committee on Crime Problems (1992).

own investigation or prosecution'.[67] Communication and coordination would thus appear central—yet no procedure or criteria forming the basis of such consultations are provided in the CCC itself.

The provision is in fact similar to an earlier clause in the UN Convention against Transnational Organized Crime (TOC) providing that: '[i]f a State Party exercising its jurisdiction . . . has been notified, or has otherwise learned, that one or more other States Parties are conducting an investigation, prosecution or judicial proceeding in respect of the same conduct, the competent authorities of those States shall, as appropriate, consult one another with a view to coordinating their actions'.[68] However, whereas the TOC provision expressly addresses the investigative phase, the CCC mechanism appears trial-focused: its Explanatory Report specifies that such consultations aim to 'avoid duplication of effort, unnecessary inconvenience for witnesses, or competition among law enforcement officials of the States concerned, or to otherwise facilitate the efficiency or fairness of the proceedings', whilst envisaging both the choice of a single venue for prosecution and the dividing up of 'participants' between state parties as possible outcomes.[69] In particular, it has been argued that the selection of an *appropriate* jurisdiction in light of the 'fairness of proceedings' must refer not only to practical issues but also to inherent legitimate interests of witnesses and suspects.[70] Although it is possible to read victims of cybercrime into the reference to 'participants' in criminal proceedings, this may risk stretching the drafters' intentions too far. We return to defendants and victims below in the context of the models developed through this research project.

Turning now to the EU legal framework, the limited, slow, and uneven progress it has made in relation to preventing and resolving conflicts of jurisdiction in criminal law generally since the CCC's finalisation in 2001 is addressed in depth elsewhere in this volume.[71] It suffices to recall here that the FD 2009/948/JHA (the FWD) provides that the competent authorities 'shall consider the facts and merits of the case and all the factors which they consider to be relevant'[72] and for the possible involvement of Eurojust should agreement prove elusive, where appropriate.[73] The FWD contained, therefore, no specific guidance on factors or

67 Kaspersen (n 1) 18.

68 Article 15(5).

69 CCC, Explanatory Report, at para 329.

70 According to Kaspersen, 'Cybercrime and Internet Jurisdiction' (n 16) para 59.

71 In April 2014, more than a year after the implementation due date, the Commission reported that thirteen of twenty-eight Member States had not taken steps to transpose the obligations in the Framework Decision; COM(2014) 313 final, at 1.4 and see esp. Marletta, 'Forum Choice in the Area of Freedom, Security and Justice', in this volume, 4–7.

72 Article 11.

73 Article 12(2) and recital 14; the FWD also encourages Member States to use inter alia the Eurojust Guidelines of 2003, discussed below.

criteria to be used in weighing competing claims.[74] This stands in contrast to the previously-adopted Council Framework Decision on combating terrorism,[75] which focused on the concentration of proceedings, envisaging to this end recourse by the Member States to any body or mechanism established within the European Union in order to facilitate cooperation between their judicial authorities and the coordination of their action, and providing that sequential account shall be taken of the territory where an offence is committed, active nationality, passive nationality, and the territory where a perpetrator is found.[76] In the new 2017 Terrorism Directive,[77] the same four factors are set out in Article 19(3), save for one difference: the 'sequential' qualifier is gone, having been negotiated out from the Commission proposal.[78] The 2009 Framework Decision, however, remains the principal EU legislation on conflicts of jurisdiction for the vast majority of cybercrime offences which do not qualify as cyber-terrorism.[79]

2. European judicial cooperation on cybercrime

In the recent GENVAL evaluations,[80] of the seventeen Member States for which reports are available only a handful shared details of conflicts of jurisdiction in cybercrime cases. The majority either merely referred to their (often fairly new and as-yet-unused) domestic provisions implementing the FWD on conflicts of jurisdiction, made generally positive remarks on the assistance of Eurojust in resolving potential conflicts,[81] reported that there are no conflicts of jurisdiction in practice in cybercrime cases or did not mention conflicts of cyber-jurisdiction at all. This general impression is supported by the outcomes of interviews conducted under

74 Although recital 9 to the FWD encouraged Member States to make reference inter alia to the (non-binding) Eurojust Guidelines of 2003, discussed below.

75 OJ L164, 22 June 2002, 3–7.

76 ibid art 9(2).

77 Directive (EU) 2017/541 of the European Parliament and of the Council of 15 March 2017 on combating terrorism and replacing Council FD 2002/475/JHA and amending Council Decision 2005/671/JHA, OJ L88 (31 March 2017), 6–21.

78 Article 21(2), COM(2015) 625 final, 2 December 2015.

79 As things stand, the confrontation of conflicts of jurisdiction specifically in the cybercrime context has emerged only at a policy level; see the work of the AIDP (Association Internationale de Droit Pénal) discussed below.

80 All reports are accessible at http://www.coe.int/en/web/octopus/blog/-/blogs/genval-evalutation-reports-on-cybercrime, (sic) (6 June 2016).

81 For instance, Greece remarked that the assistance of Eurojust is 'very significant since, by the organisation of Coordinative Groups between the Judicial or/and the Police Authorities of the States involved, in cases that concern several States-Members, the solution of the problem of any parallel jurisdiction is achieved as well as the avoidance of several prosecutions starting against the same perpetrator for the same criminal acts in the cyber space'. See GENVAL, Greek report, at 5.4.

the aegis of the present research project with several National Desks at Eurojust: the agency had been mostly concerned with traditional crimes involving goods or human beings physically crossing borders.[82]

Some of the GENVAL reports hint at high levels of coordination across the EU—for example, Romania stated that it cannot open a cybercrime investigation if a competent authority in another Member State has done so; the FWD has been implemented in Romania, but in practice there are no conflicts of jurisdiction.[83] France reported that since its implementation of the FWD it had never had to contact Eurojust to solve a conflict, relying instead on mutual legal assistance (MLA) measures such as *dénonciations officielles* and spontaneous transmissions of information.[84] Only three (potential) conflicts of jurisdiction were reported. In one of these Hungary, having detected a potential conflict with the UK over a child pornography investigation, initiated consultations at Eurojust, following which the US joined the UK and Hungary for a coordination meeting. Since the territory was unclear, the UK and Hungary began setting up a joint investigation team (JIT), and Hungarian judicial authorities sent MLA requests to the US Department of Justice for IP addresses stored on iCloud and GoogleDrive.[85] The UK report mentioned a cybercrime case involving Scotland, two other Member States and two third states: amicable multilateral discussions led to the concentration of proceedings. The UK also noted that where linguistic or practical obstacles have arisen, Eurojust meetings have been called to discuss the matter further. Lastly, Spain reported having set up a JIT with Bulgaria within the Eurojust framework before eventually transferring proceedings to Bulgaria.[86]

What is not divulged by Member States when reporting as part of GENVAL is which specific criteria (if any) are used—and how those criteria are weighted—in the course of such consultations. The involvement of Eurojust would nonetheless tend to suggest that the agency's own guidelines are to some extent employed.[87] Partially emulating earlier—unsuccessful—proposals made within Council of Europe bodies,[88] the non-binding 2003

82 See Marletta, 'Report on the Field Research at Eurojust, February 2015', in this volume, at II.B.1.

83 GENVAL, Romanian report, at 5.4.

84 GENVAL, French report, at 5.4.

85 GENVAL, Hungarian report, at 5.4.

86 GENVAL, Spanish report, at 5.4.

87 See also Marletta, 'Forum Choice' in this volume, identifying from interviews with Eurojust national desks a strong preference for non-binding, flexible instruments such as the (then) 2003 Guidelines; at II.D.

88 Despite a recommendation to that effect from the Consultative Assembly at the Council of Europe, no such criteria had been included in the 1972 European Convention on the Transfer of Proceedings in Criminal Matters, with the Explanatory Report adjudging that 'the assumption

Guidelines[89] suggested 'a preliminary presumption that, if possible, a prosecution should take place in the jurisdiction where the majority of the criminality occurred or where the majority of the loss was sustained'.[90] In doing so, the original Guidelines differed from one contemporaneous project seeking to elaborate criteria for deciding the forum which had limited itself to prescribing an 'aggregate balance' of all listed factors.[91] All the same, they were of general application, with no specific attention paid to cybercrime—which is putatively especially (and increasingly) liable to create conflicts of jurisdiction.

According to the Guidelines, the territorial presumption was to be weighed on a case-by-case basis alongside, in the first place:

- the location of the accused;
- whether extradition, surrender or transfer of proceedings are possible, and the feasibility of dividing the prosecution into cases in two or more jurisdictions;
- the attendance, and the protection, of witnesses;
- interests of victims, which may include the possibility of claiming compensation;
- the availability and admissibility of evidence and its acceptance by the court ('factors which prosecutors must consider').[92]

that it is normally most appropriate to prosecute an offence where it has been committed is not justified', reasoning *inter alia* that since prospects of rehabilitation and securing of evidence will vary from case to case, it would be unwise to bind state parties to 'a prior acceptance of a system restricting their power to impose sanctions'. See Explanatory Report, at 18, and Luchtman, in this volume, at 2.

89 Eurojust, *Guidelines for deciding 'which jurisdiction should prosecute'* (2003, revised 2016) http://www.eurojust.europa.eu/doclibrary/corporate/eurojust%20Annual%20Reports/Annual%20Report%202003/Annual-Report-2003-EN.pdf (2003 version) and http://www.eurojust.europa.eu/Practitioners/operational/Documents/Operational-Guidelines-for-Deciding.pdf (2016 version).

90 ibid 2003 version, at 62.

91 Princeton Principles on Universal Jurisdiction, Principle 8—Resolution of Competing National Jurisdictions: 'Where more than one state has or may assert jurisdiction over a person and where the state that has custody of the person has no basis for jurisdiction other than the principle of universality, that state or its judicial organs shall, in deciding whether to prosecute or extradite, base their decision on an aggregate balance of the following criteria: (a) multilateral or bilateral treaty obligations; (b) the place of commission of the crime; (c) the nationality connection of the alleged perpetrator to the requesting state; (d) the nationality connection of the victim to the requesting state; (e) any other connection between the requesting state and the alleged perpetrator, the crime, or the victim; (f) the likelihood, good faith, and effectiveness of the prosecution in the requesting state; (g) the fairness and impartiality of the proceedings in the requesting state; (h) convenience to the parties and witnesses, as well as the availability of evidence in the requesting state; and (i) the interests of justice'.

92 2016 Guidelines (n 89) at 65.

Of secondary importance—in the sense that a forum choice should not be based on any such factors alone—were the avoidance of legal obligations, the relative sentencing powers in the contending jurisdictions, and the more effective recovery of proceeds of crime. Finally, only when all other factors were balanced should the envisaged duration of proceedings and the resources and costs of prosecuting also be considered. An update of the Guidelines in 2016 retained all of these factors, expanding upon most of them and in places slightly changing the calibration between them.[93] However, again no specific attention is paid to settling jurisdiction as regards offences committed in cyberspace. In the ensuing concluding section I begin to ask how such treatment might look, where appropriate by reference to the potential added value of the models proposed in this research project.

III. IMPROVING FORUM CHOICE IN CYBERCRIME CASES

A. Investigation and prosecution

Taking a global perspective, Walden insists that as cybercrime inevitably and increasingly involves parallel and competing jurisdictions, future determinations of which jurisdiction should prosecute will involve a much more difficult decision-making process than the initial question of whether an offence has been committed.[94] Yet several of the GENVAL national reports underline how, from a law enforcement point of view, overlapping jurisdictions in cybercrime cases within the EU can be anything but conflictual: the Slovak authorities, for example, emphasised that, on the whole, positive conflicts of jurisdiction 'enable parallel securing of evidence, which particularly in the context of the short period for data retention and technical capabilities of the perpetrators may lead to identification and punishment of perpetrators of this crime'.[95] The usefulness of parallel investigations (as opposed to parallel prosecutions) was also highlighted by Eurojust national desks in interviews run by the Working Group,[96] whilst Luchtman notes in this volume that the increased cooperation potentially facilitated by overlapping competences may allow certain Member States 'to correct incompetence or inactivity by authorities of other states', and, certainly once facilitated by such institutions as Eurojust, play a role in the development of a truly transnational legal area.[97]

93 See further Marletta, 'Forum Choice', in this volume, at 4.2.

94 Walden, *Computer Crimes and Digital Investigations* (n 3) at 5.43.

95 GENVAL, Slovak report, at 5.4.

96 See Marletta, 'Report on Field Research at Eurojust', in this volume, at II.B.1. See further Simonato, in this volume, discussing the vision of 'collective responsibility' in cases of trafficking in human beings evoked by the European Court of Human Rights in Rantsev; at V.C.

97 See Luchtman, in this volume, at 2.1.

Like the Eurojust Guidelines, the models proposed in this volume establish that in principle, territoriality shall determine the jurisdiction to prosecute, whilst the horizontal and vertical models replicate the wording of the reworked Guidelines by including quantitative and qualitative aspects: 'where the majority or the most important part of the criminality occurred or where the majority or the most important part of the harmful effect or loss was sustained'.[98] As with the Guidelines, the factors proposed in the models consciously avoid a separate treatment of any category of criminal offence; as Kaspersen has cautioned, any attempt to develop specific common criteria for the resolution of conflicts of jurisdiction in cybercrime offences would require in-depth analysis of very divergent decisions of national courts determining *locus delicti*[99]—a task far beyond the remit of the present project. The same author has also envisaged the gradual development and refinement of cybercrime-specific criteria potentially allied to a (binding) ruling by the CDPC,[100] whilst others have explored the idea of addressing jurisdictional issues in the context of a new international convention on cybercrime.[101] The former vision chimes in particular with the vertical model proposed in this volume, which has the potential to provide space for the gradual elaboration of practical solutions to establish priority through its solid procedural framework and the binding decisional power it ascribes to Eurojust.

How any chosen factors are conjugated in the context of any individual set of forum choice negotiations will depend in the first place on the category of cybercrime offence on the table. So far, the establishment of rules capable of stemming the potential for conflicts of jurisdiction have been explored at a policy level—for example, in the Resolutions of the Nineteenth International Congress of Penal Law, which recognised that the territoriality principle produces adverse effects when applied to offences in cyberspace in that it de facto allows states to localise offences on their territory almost on a universality basis, leaving individuals in doubt as to which states may claim jurisdiction. The Resolutions thus urged states to 'exercise restraint in exercising jurisdiction in situations in which the effect is not 'pushed' by a perpetrator into a state, but 'pulled' into it by an individual in that state'.[102] When determining effects, they also encouraged states to 'consider the existence of

98 See Annex A to both Horizontal and Vertical Models, 'Factors to be considered', 1. Territoriality.

99 Kaspersen, 'Jurisdiction in the Cybercrime Convention' (n 1) at 21.

100 Kaspersen, 'Cybercrime and Internet Jurisdiction' (n 16) at 66 and 67.

101 Concerning malware-related crimes, see R. Rahman, 'Legal Jurisdiction over Malware-related Crimes: From Theories of Jurisdiction to Solid Practical Application' (2012) 28 *Computer Law and Security Review* 403, esp. at 2.1 ff.

102 Resolutions of the Nineteenth International Congress of Penal Law, Rio de Janeiro (31 August–6 September 2014) (AIDP Resolutions), Section IV Res. 3.

a particular nexus with the offence, such as the intent of the perpetrator as it may appear from the use of a given language, the provision of domestic payment facilities, a service offer in specific cities, etc'.[103] The formalised 'ante-forum' envisaged by the first two models may provide a valuable venue for the gradual elaboration of cybercrime-specific criteria along these lines.

B. Defendants in cybercrime cases

Limits on (or rules intended to channel) prosecutorial discretion are inextricably linked to the interests of the defendant. In this regard, it is worth highlighting several of the proposed models' innovations. The first two models eschew a hierarchical and/or sequential approach to factors relevant to forum choice in favour of a somewhat novel[104] 'binary' approach, identifying both positive factors which must be assessed (territoriality; stage of the proceedings—trial-readiness; interests of the suspect; interests of victims; need to resort to MLA and mutual recognition instruments; the need for concentration of proceedings) and negative factors which must not be taken into account (diverging rules on evidence; legal requirements; sentencing powers).[105] This last negative factor, especially when formalised in the context of a binding decision by Eurojust as envisaged by the vertical model, is excluded in order to ward off the danger of the process of negotiation resulting in jurisdictional arbitrage, with severity of sentence and its resultant deterrence value being considered relevant factors.[106]

A more constructive vision would strive not only to allay fears of arbitrage but above all to lay the groundwork for greater foreseeability of the potential consequences of one's actions, at the time of action, and from an EU-wide perspective. So it is that Luchtman, in this volume, argues forcefully that interferences with

103 ibid Res. 4.

104 Although the Eurojust Guidelines (n 89) include indications that certain aspects (e.g. relative sentencing powers) 'should not be a determining factor' in deciding in which jurisdiction a case should be prosecuted, the exclusion set out by the first two proposed models is both firmer ('Member States are not to consider') and more explicit, in the sense that positive and negative factors are unambiguously separated in the text; see Annex A to both the horizontal and vertical models, 'Factors not to be considered'.

105 The approach proposed by the project also contrasts with that envisaged by the latest draft Regulation on the establishment of a European Public Prosecutor's Office (EPPO), which provides in relation to PIF-crimes that 'as a rule', investigations shall be initiated and handled by a European Delegated Prosecutor from the Member State 'where the focus of the criminal activity' is—construed as location of the activity, rather than the damage it causes—subject to certain deviations on duly justified grounds taking into account *in order of priority* the following criteria: habitual residence of suspect or accused person, nationality of suspect or accused person, and the place where the main financial damage has occurred'; art 26, draft EPPO Regulation. See further Herrnfeld, in this volume, at III.B.

106 As Walden, *Computer Crimes and Digital Investigations* (n 3) warns at 5.43.

the rights of EU citizens must meet certain standards of accessibility and foreseeability in order to adequately reflect the concept of citizenship of a European Union which aspires to encompass a unified Area of Freedom, Security and Justice.[107] The alternative to foreseeability (the arbitrariness of judicial enforcement decisions), Luchtman writes, is constituted not by the defendant's inability to predict or choose where the trial will take place, but by the fact that 'the content and scope of the procedural framework under which they are tried—their procedural rights and duties—is *de facto* chosen by their direct adversaries in the same proceedings',[108] jeopardising the principle of equality of arms. Given its quintessentially cross-border nature and the potential for remote victimisation, such a risk would seem particularly acute for cybercrime offences; it is not difficult to think of examples of online crime where the question of a suspect's or defendant's 'effective links with the jurisdiction of a Member State' may prove decisive.[109] Moreover, as Wasmeier underlines, also in this volume, without rules on the exercise of jurisdiction the problems of forum-shopping and non-transparent choices of jurisdiction for prosecution are presently exacerbated by the 'first come, first served' effect produced by *ne bis in idem*.[110] In this regard, the enhancement of the procedural position of the defendant envisaged by the models[111] ought to function as a helpful corrective. Moreover, the development over time of a common language for the localisation of offences within a particular state's borders, enabled—as evoked previously—by the opportunity for (or, as the case may be, the obligation on) Member States to deliberate upon the choice of forum subject to the binding decision of Eurojust may contribute to ensuring that it is credibly compatible with the reasonable expectations of defendants.[112]

107 Luchtman, in this volume, at III.

108 Luchtman, in this volume, at IV.B.1.

109 See Factor 3, which lists for example the duration of his or her residence, the ability to understand the language spoken in the Member State, the degree of integration of the suspect in the society of one Member State, the possibility for him or her to access an effective legal defence, or the presence of dependent family members on the territory of another Member State. Furthermore, the 'vulnerability of the suspect and the possibility to ensure adequate safeguards should be carefully assessed'; this may be of particular relevance in cases such as that of Scottish hacker Gary McKinnon, accused of the 'biggest military hack of all time' (*BBC News*, 'Profile: Gary McKinnon', 30 July 2008), whose extradition order (to the USA) was quashed by UK Home Secretary Theresa May in 2012 on the grounds of mental illness.

110 Wasmeier, in this volume, at II.B.

111 See arts 8(3), 8(4), and 10 of the horizontal and vertical mechanisms, along with arts 11(1), 11(2), 13(3), 13(10), and 14 of the vertical model, and arts 6(2), (3), 7(1)–(3), and 9(3) of the allocation model.

112 See for instance AIDP Resolutions, Res. 5: 'When a state localizes the effects of an offence within its borders, the principle of legality requires that the perpetrator could have had a reasonable expectation that his or her conduct would cause effects in that country'.

C. Victims in cybercrime cases

The remoteness of perpetrators of much of the criminal activity carried out online cuts both ways: not only suspects but victims too may be distant and extremely difficult to identify, locate, and contact. In relation to the core 'CIA' offences, especially widespread attacks on computer systems and data stored therein (for instance botnets or phishing)—which may often not be directed against any victims in particular—the relevance of the victim criterion in the weighing of competing claims to jurisdiction is likely to be minimal.[113] On the other hand, concerning targeted hacking, content related to child sexual exploitation and child sexual abuse, as well as online crimes against the person such as cyber-harassment or cyber-stalking, in particular the location of (the greatest number of, or the most badly-impacted) victims may be a significant factor in forum choice for both state and victim.

Although victims' interests can often overlap with the interests of prosecutors (the truth of events; proportionate punishment efficiently delivered), their views—if any—on the suitable forum for prosecution, just as their needs and expectations, are so variegated as to defy comprehensive analysis.[114] Multiple investigations—and indeed sequential prosecutions—may in some cases be welcomed by victims where prosecution has faltered in a given jurisdiction.[115] Nonetheless, it is entirely plausible that the hypothetical victim of cybercrime may have a preference as regards the suitable forum for prosecution. For example, whilst several Eurojust National Desks interviewed for the present research project identified a growing trend of allocating jurisdiction on the basis of passive personality in respect of victims of trafficking in human beings on the basis of their especial vulnerability,[116] depending on the specific facts (take the stalking or bullying of online groups of particularly vulnerable individuals residing in multiple Member States) similar considerations may arise in relation to crimes against the person committed in cyberspace.[117]

To the extent that the latter do arise, the formalised involvement of victims in the procedure for determining the appropriate forum for prosecution as proposed

113 Kaspersen, 'Cybercrime and Internet Jurisdiction' (n 16) at 64. That is not to say that the possibility of claiming compensation may not be worth considering, say for example where extensive damage is done to computer networks owned and operated in State A by nationals of State B.

114 Simonato, in this volume, at IV.

115 ibid.

116 Marletta, 'Field Research at Eurojust', in this volume, at II.C.2.

117 Although, admittedly, the avoidance of secondary victimisation as well as the issue of protective measures (as mentioned in Factor 4 'to be considered', 'Interests of Victims' in Annex to the horizontal and vertical models) in cyberspace are a more complex matter than, for instance, ensuring physical distance between aggressor and victim is maintained in future. See also art 6(3), allocation model.

in the models,[118] although more limited than that of defendants,[119] ought in general to contribute to creating a more transparent space for the expression of victims' preferences and increasing the likelihood of their accepting the decision ultimately taken.

118 Articles 5(2), 8(3), 8(4) of both the horizontal and vertical mechanisms, arts 11(2), 13(3), (4), and (9) of the vertical mechanism, and arts 5(3), 6(2), 7(3), and 9(3) of the allocation model.

119 Article 14 of the vertical mechanism proposal clarifies that judicial review of the Eurojust decision on the choice of forum is available only to the suspect and the national judicial authorities; welcomed by Simonato, in this volume, at VI.

7

CONFLICTS OF JURISDICTION IN CRIMINAL LAW

Lessons from European Civil Procedure

PIETRO ORTOLANI*

I. INTRODUCTION

One of the main purposes of private international law is the resolution of conflicts of jurisdiction in civil matters. In the European Union (EU), this goal is pursued by an articulate body of regulations, forming part of what is usually labelled as 'European procedural law' or 'European civil procedure'. In criminal law, by contrast, no such system exists: although Eurojust aims at resolving conflicts of jurisdiction by facilitating the identification of the jurisdiction that should prosecute cross-border crimes,[1] no hard-law instrument regulates this matter in a binding fashion.

Having noted this legislative gap, in January 2013 the European Law Institute accepted a project proposal dealing with the prevention and settlement of conflicts of jurisdiction in criminal law. One of the tasks of the Working Group focusing on this project was a comparison between private international law and criminal matters, so as to assess whether and to what extent the solutions adopted in the former field could be successfully transposed to the latter. This chapter presents some reflections of the topic, triggered by the Working Group's meetings and discussions.

The chapter proceeds in three parts. The first part preliminarily highlights some fundamental differences between civil and criminal justice, which must be taken into account. As the chapter will show, the differences at hand constrain, to a certain extent, the feasibility of a cross-sectoral comparative exercise, but they by no means make it impossible. The second part looks at private international law in general and argues that some of its basic principles should be adopted in the field of conflicts of jurisdiction in criminal law too. Finally, the third part draws some specific lessons from European civil procedure in particular.

* The author would like to thank the Members of the European Law Institute Working Group for the many fruitful discussions and Marloes van Wijk for her insights on the nature of criminal justice.

1 See section II.C.

II. SCOPE AND LIMITS OF THE COMPARISON: STRUCTURAL DIFFERENCES BETWEEN CIVIL AND CRIMINAL JUSTICE

Before attempting a comparison between criminal law and private international law, it is necessary to highlight some fundamental limits to the feasibility of such an exercise. Civil and criminal justice serve largely different purposes and are governed by different procedural architectures. For this reason, the comparison cannot result in abrupt 'legal transplants': it would be simply impossible to transpose the mechanisms for the resolution of conflicts of civil jurisdiction existing in EU civil procedure to the field of criminal justice.

Despite the above-mentioned limits, a cross-sectoral study of conflicts of jurisdiction can yield interesting results, from at least two points of view. First, as section III of this chapter will illustrate in detail, the evolution of private international law has been marked by the progressive emergence of some core concepts, concerning the coordination of national judicial authorities in cross-border cases. Private international law, hence, can serve as a useful 'conceptual repository' for criminal lawyers who aim at addressing the same topic in their own field of study and practice. In this respect, while private international law cannot provide ready-made solutions for criminal justice, it can certainly trigger a process of cross-fertilisation and thus impact positively the further development of judicial cooperation in criminal matters.

A second, fundamental viewpoint for the comparison at hand is the specific setting of European civil procedure. This area is characterised by a particularly articulate and successful variety of mechanisms for the resolution of conflicts of jurisdiction. European civil procedure dates back to the 1968 Brussels Convention and today comprises several instruments, whose relevance will be scrutinised in section IV of this chapter. Without ignoring the many differences, thus, it will be possible to draw some direct lessons from the solutions adopted in the field of civil litigation.

The first step of our comparative exercise must necessarily be a brief overview of the most relevant differences existing between civil and criminal justice, which can have an impact on the topic of jurisdiction conflicts. This synthetic review will serve as a general framework, within which the comparative analysis carried out in the remainder of the chapter will develop.

A. Procedural architecture and party impulse

In principle, a conflict of jurisdiction can be either 'hypothetical' or 'actual'. In the former case, two different states lay claim upon the jurisdiction to adjudicate a certain dispute. In other words, given a dispute with certain features, the courts of two (or more) states have potentially the power to resolve it. In the latter case, instead, this hypothetical conflict materialises: proceedings dealing with the same subject matter are commenced in more than one jurisdiction. The actual conflict must be resolved, in order to avoid the risk of parallel proceedings leading to potentially irreconcilable outcomes.[2]

The existence of a hypothetical conflict of jurisdiction depends exclusively on the contents of the law allocating jurisdiction: if under the applicable law more than one national court is competent to hear a certain case, a hypothetical conflict exists. By contrast, the emergence of actual conflicts hinges on party impulse: the conflict can only exist inasmuch as the parties have commenced parallel proceedings in more than one state.

Against this background, we can note a first, fundamental difference between civil and criminal justice. On the one hand, in civil justice, the parties are generally both private (natural or legal) persons: they are put on an equal footing and it is up to them to decide whether to commence proceedings or not. On the other hand, criminal cases can only be initiated by certain categories of parties, performing prosecutorial tasks. Therefore, the dynamics whereby an actual conflict of jurisdiction emerges in civil and criminal cases are fundamentally different.

Along the same lines, an additional difference between civil and criminal justice is that the latter is characterised by a certain fragmentation of the national laws governing the standing to commence proceedings. In particular, according to some systems of criminal procedure, only certain subjects (such as the Public Prosecutor) have the power to initiate the procedure. By contrast, other systems provide for more extensive standing, allowing e.g. the victim to start the case. Furthermore, some national systems enshrine the principle of prosecutorial discretion, whereby the Public Prosecutor can decide whether or not to commence the proceedings, while other states are based on a mechanism of obligatory prosecution.

Such a fragmentation, which obviously cannot be explored in detail in this chapter, does not exist in the field of civil litigation. In a civil case, each party generally has the power to access the competent court and trigger the start of the proceedings. For this reason, it can be concluded that the way conflicts of jurisdiction materialise is structurally different in civil and criminal cases.

B. Relevance of the problem of inactivity

As already mentioned, it is up to each party to access courts and initiate civil proceedings. This feature of civil justice has an obvious corollary: if none of the parties commences proceedings, the courts will not be seised of the matter and, hence, will not render a decision. Inasmuch as private rights are concerned, this is normally

2 It must be noted that, according to art 45(1)(c) and (d) of the Brussels I bis Regulation (and analogous provisions in other instruments) the irreconcilability of decisions is a ground for refusal of recognition of judgments. European civil procedure, therefore, tries to prevent the situation where parallel proceedings lead to potentially irreconcilable judgments. On the Brussels I bis Regulation see, in detail section IV below.

(but with some exceptions)[3] not perceived as problematic. Let us consider, for instance, a contract concerning commercial rights concluded by two corporations. If neither of the corporations brings a claim, this is generally interpreted as a sign that substantive law is operating satisfactorily and no judicial intervention is needed. The same rationale, of course, cannot be transposed to criminal matters.

While the inactivity of civil courts is normally not problematic, the passivity of criminal courts raises some obvious concerns. If cross-border criminal activities are not met with any judicial reaction in any of the states concerned, this may create a risk of impunity. Hence, any attempt to implement a mechanism for the resolution of conflicts of jurisdiction in criminal law must confront the problem of prosecutorial inactivity.

The issue of prosecutorial inactivity can potentially be tackled in very different fashions. On one end of the spectrum, it could be argued that any system for the allocation of jurisdiction in criminal matters should fight the risk of impunity. Following this line of reasoning, it should be desirable to provide that, in cases where the state having jurisdiction fails to prosecute the crime, proceedings could be commenced in a different state in a subsidiary fashion (*forum necessitatis*).[4] On the opposite end of the spectrum, it could also be argued that, inasmuch as the competent Public Prosecutor is free to decide not to commence proceedings, this should be accepted by all other states, especially in the light of the principle of mutual trust governing the area of freedom, security and justice (AFSJ).

The question above cannot, of course, be answered here. To the contrary, the problem at hand constitutes the perfect illustration of how conflicts of jurisdiction in criminal matters may entail different problems, which are not typically relevant for civil litigation. Those aiming at resolving conflicts of jurisdiction of criminal law, hence, face challenges that do not exist (or, at least, are not as widespread) in the realm of civil procedure.

C. Relationship between jurisdiction and applicable law

Further differences arise when we consider the consequences of allocating jurisdiction among various state courts. In civil litigation, the circumstance that a given court has jurisdiction entails, normally,[5] no consequence on the substantive law

3 In specific areas, private litigation is regarded as an important tool of implementation and enforcement of substantive law and policies. A good example in this respect is competition law: the EU tries to facilitate private enforcement of rights arising out of this field of law, through instruments such as Directive 2014/104 on rules governing actions for damages under national law for infringements of competition law[2014] OJ L349/1, which aims at ensuring the effectiveness of arts 101 and 102 of the Treaty on the Functioning of the European Union (TFEU).

4 See section IV.D.2 below.

5 Overriding mandatory provisions and public policy constitute a rare exception to this general rule; see e.g. art 9 of Regulation (EC) No 593/2008 on the law applicable to contractual obligations (Rome I Regulation) [2008] OJ L177/6.

that will be applied to resolve the case. In particular, the problem of applicable law is resolved by another branch of private international law, which sets forth conflict rules determining which national law will apply, irrespective of which national court (if any)[6] will hear the case. As a result, it is entirely possible that the courts of a certain state will resolve a dispute by applying the substantive laws of another state.

By way of example, in the European Union, the law applicable to contracts is determined by the Rome I Regulation (Regulation No 593/2008, replacing the 1980 Rome Convention). One of the main purposes of the enactment of uniform conflict rules in the EU is exactly to avoid that the allocation of jurisdiction to a given Member State trigger the application of a substantive law that would not be applied by the courts of another Member State, hence generating an unforeseen strategic advantage for one of the parties.[7] The parties also have an important margin of autonomy: in many settings they can enter into a choice of law agreement, providing for the application of the substantive law they prefer.

In criminal matters, the allocation of jurisdiction has very different consequences, as it generally determines the substantive laws according to which criminal liability will be ascertained. This raises further questions as to the feasibility of a mechanism for the resolution of conflicts of jurisdiction in criminal law, in the absence of a preliminary (and, obviously, debatable) large-scale approximation of substantive criminal law throughout the EU.

D. The role of private autonomy

We have already mentioned private autonomy, when discussing choice-of-law agreements. In civil matters, however, the possibility for the parties to influence the exertion of jurisdiction on the part of state courts goes even further. In particular, the parties can enter into an arbitration or a jurisdiction (or choice of court) agreement.

By concluding an agreement to arbitrate, the parties submit to the jurisdiction of an arbitral tribunal and conversely waive their right to access state courts. Notably, arbitration is not governed by the Brussels I Regulation,[8] but by the national law of the state where the arbitral proceedings are seated as well as by a number of international instruments, including the 1958 New York Convention. For the purposes of this chapter it is therefore important to stress that, by entering into an arbitration

6 The parties may submit to the jurisdiction of an arbitral tribunal (see section II.D below). In that case, the law applicable to the arbitration proceedings often sets forth different conflict rules for the identification of the applicable substantive law, see UNCITRAL Model Law on International Commercial Arbitration, art 28. For an overview of such rules see Tony Cole and Pietro Ortolani, *Understanding Arbitration* (Routledge 2018 forthcoming) ch 2.

7 This rationale was already underlying the 1980 Rome Convention, as highlighted by Mario Giuliano and Paul Lagarde, 'Report on the Convention on the Law Applicable to Contractual Obligations' [1980] OJ C282/5.

8 Regulation (EU) No 1215/2012 (Brussels I bis), art 1(2)(d).

agreement, the parties have the power to displace the mechanism for the allocation of jurisdiction set forth by European procedural law. The same, of course, would not hold true for a similar mechanism in the field of criminal justice.

Even when the parties do not exclude the application of the rules for the allocation of jurisdiction in civil matters, private autonomy can have a significant impact. In particular, the parties often have the possibility to enter into a jurisdiction agreement, whereby they submit to the competence of a certain state court. This agreement, hence, has the effect of substituting the fall-back rule enshrined by the applicable regime of private international law with a different, party-created rule for the allocation of jurisdiction. Once again, such a pervasive importance of private autonomy does not seem to be transposable to the field of criminal justice.

E. The influence of fact-specificity

Finally, an important difference must be stressed with respect to the contents of the proceedings. In civil litigation, the parties do not necessarily disagree on the facts of the case: it is indeed possible that the parties agree on every relevant factual circumstance, but they litigate on the legal qualification of those facts and the legal consequences arising therefrom. For this reason, civil proceedings may reach their final conclusion (the judgment on the merits) without the need for any taking of evidence.

Criminal proceedings, by contrast, are typically more fact-specific. In order to ascertain criminal liability, the competent judicial authority must normally establish facts, before turning to the problem of their legal qualification.

This difference may affect the rationale underlying the rules allocating jurisdiction among different national courts. In particular, the need to ensure that jurisdiction is allocated to the courts of the place where the evidence is (primarily) located is likely to be perceived more strongly in criminal justice than in civil cases. Any cross-sectoral comparative analysis, therefore, must necessarily take these specificities into consideration.

III. LESSONS FROM PRIVATE INTERNATIONAL LAW IN GENERAL

A. Conflicts of jurisdiction as conflicts of sovereignty

According to a long-standing legal and political doctrine, the power to resolve disputes is one of the attributes of sovereignty. The emergence of self-contained national legal systems, characterising the Westphalian regime, has been accompanied by states' tendency to claim a monopoly over the administration of justice.[9] As a consequence, each state has developed a set of rules determining the

9 For an overview of this development see Nicola Picardi, *La giurisdizione all'alba del terzo millennio* (Giuffrè 2007).

scope of the jurisdiction of its courts, i.e. the purview of their power to perform judicial functions.

The characterisation of jurisdiction in terms of exertion of sovereign powers entails an obvious risk of conflict among states. In other words, if two or more states claim jurisdiction over a certain case, this can be seen as a clash of sovereign prerogatives. While a purely domestic case undoubtedly falls within the sovereign powers of the state where the facts took place, cross-border disputes may potentially result in a clash of sovereignties: it has been correctly highlighted that 'transnational cases place courts in the awkward position of adjudicating in the interstices of law'.[10] Private international law's aim of creating a widely accepted and shared mechanism for the coordination of national jurisdictions, then, serves the fundamental function of preventing and resolving conflicts of sovereignty. For this reason, in its basic and traditional purpose, private international law is best understood not only as a domestic branch of law governing substantive and procedural private law, but also as an international field of law, aimed at ameliorating the relations among states.[11]

There are good reasons to argue that this fundamental rationale of private international law can be transposed to the field of judicial cooperation in criminal matters. In fact, in today's world, the problem of a potential conflict of national sovereignties is probably more evident in criminal than in civil justice.

As for civil matters, the states' claim to monopoly in the administration of justice is no longer tenable, in the light of the ever-increasing importance of party autonomy. The rise of arbitration and other mechanisms of alternative dispute resolution, as well as the wide-spread use of choice of court agreements, have determined the sunset of the conception of jurisdiction as an attribute of sovereignty. In the current reality of private law, jurisdiction is perhaps better understood as a service provided by state courts in a competitive international market, blurring the public/private divide in a quest for efficiency. In criminal matters, by contrast, jurisdiction is still strongly linked to the idea of state power. The repression of criminal activities can still be seen as a state monopoly and, therefore, an epiphenomenon of sovereignty. For this reason, the same basic purpose traditionally underlying private international law is able to inspire the creation of a mechanism for the allocation of jurisdiction in criminal matters. By determining which state has competence to prosecute a crime, such a system undoubtedly has the potential of avoiding conflicts of sovereignty and bettering state-to-state relations.

10 Donald Earl Childress III, 'Comity as Conflict: Resituating International Comity as Conflict of Laws' (2011) 44 UC Davis L R 11, 14.

11 At the origins of private international law, for instance, the basic rationale justifying the application of foreign law was the *comitas gentium*: Hessel E. Yntema, 'The Comity Doctrine' (1966) 65(1) Michigan Law Review 9.

B. The importance of legal certainty and predictability in private international law

Ensuring better relations among states is not the only basic rationale prompting the development of private international law. Another mainspring of this field of law is the enhancement of legal certainty, in the interest of those who engage in cross-border relations. In a nutshell, private international law has the ambition of enabling the parties to predict which substantive law will govern their rights and which national court(s) will have jurisdiction, should a dispute arise.

The quest for certainty and predictability runs deep in the history of private international law, starting from medieval authors' aversion against the application of different laws to the same facts.[12] As long ago as in the seventeenth century, Huber stressed that ensuring predictability in cross-border cases was fundamental, in order to ensure the feasibility of 'terrestrial and maritime exchanges'.[13] Along the same lines, Savigny highlights the importance of obtaining neutral and uniform results.[14]

The transposition of the rationale at hand to the field of criminal justice leads to interesting and somewhat controversial results. Undeniably, the degree of predictability ensured by private international law does not seem to be entirely attainable in criminal cases. The main reason for this conclusion is that one of the aims of private international law is avoiding that, by allocating jurisdiction to a certain national court, this will result in the application of a different substantive law to a given set of facts. In criminal matters, the applicable substantive law will necessarily change, depending on the *forum*, and may even result in diverging qualification in terms of the legality or criminality of the relevant facts. In light of this, a system for the resolution of conflicts of jurisdiction in criminal matters cannot, realistically, ensure the same degree of uniformity and predictability as private international law does for civil cases.

A further fundamental difference between civil and criminal cases must be stressed here. Throughout the history of private international law, the pursuit of legal certainty and predictability aims at facilitating cross-border dealings and transactions. As section IV of this chapter will highlight, in the case of European private international and procedural law, this purpose is particularly important, as it is instrumental to the creation and maintenance of a single market. The same, of course, does not hold true for criminal cases: the creation of a uniform and predictable system of allocation of criminal jurisdiction cannot possibly serve the purpose of encouraging cross-border crime. In a nutshell, the existing

12 Friederich K. Juenger, 'General Course on Private International Law' (1983) 193 Recueil des Cours de l'Académie de Droit International 119, 162.

13 Ulrich Huber, 'De Jure Civitatis' quoted in Thomas Schultz and David Holloway, 'Retour sur la comity II: La comity dans l'histoire du droit international privé' (2012) 138(2) Clunet 571 n 41.

14 Juenger (n 12) 162–63.

EU rules of civil jurisdiction contribute to enforcing (and, hence, facilitating) the transactions and activities constituting the subject matter of the litigation; a prospective set of rules for the allocation of jurisdiction in criminal matters, conversely, would not be directly functional to the elimination of market frictions to the benefit of criminals.

While the observations above cannot be ignored, they should not be read as entailing that predictability and legal certainty are not desirable in the field of criminal law. To the contrary, several arguments can be put forward in order to demonstrate that the same rationale underlying private international law may be useful in this area of law too. First, predictability is in the interest of the defendant: a system for the uniform allocation of jurisdiction helps the defendant avoid having to defend him/herself in multiple *fora*, facing additional costs and personal inconveniencies.

Second, predictability ensures that like cases be treated alike. Let us consider, for instance, two defendants being accused of committing the same cross-border crime: in the case of defendant A the facts involve States X and Y, while in the case of defendant B the facts involve States Z and K. In the absence of a uniform system for the allocation of jurisdiction, States X and Y may both have jurisdiction and decide to initiate proceedings against A. By contrast, State Z may not have jurisdiction under its laws, and therefore proceedings against defendant B may be initiated solely in State K. Apart from the above-mentioned undesirability of parallel proceedings in the case of defendant A, the scenario at hand is troublesome because it entails an inequality in the treatment of two sets of circumstances (the crimes allegedly committed by A and B) which are factually identical. Ensuring that the same cross-border setting is governed by uniform jurisdictional rule (or, in other terms, that it is covered by an even *amount of jurisdiction*) seems to be particularly desirable within the AFSJ.

Third, predictability could potentially mitigate the already cited problem of prosecutorial inactivity. Namely, the problem of prosecutorial inactivity may derive from the circumstance that, when two states have jurisdiction, the national authorities of each state decide to abstain from commencing proceedings, assuming that the authorities of the other state will take care of the case. Undesirable inactivity could hence be limited if national authorities entrusted with prosecutorial tasks could rely on uniform rules for the allocation of jurisdiction. As a result, the introduction of a uniform regime for the allocation of criminal jurisdiction could improve the enforcement of criminal law in the AFSJ and ultimately contribute to the enhancement of safety in the EU, thus encouraging beneficial exchanges and interaction among Member States. In the light of the above arguments, it can be concluded that the same rationale of uniformity and predictability underlying private international law can inspire the development of shared rules on jurisdiction in criminal matters.

C. Substance-neutrality as a cornerstone of private international law

1. Introduction to the notion of substance-neutrality

While different systems of private international law may to a certain extent disagree on the content of the rules determining the scope of the jurisdiction of national courts, they all agree on the fundamental principle of substance-neutrality. According to this principle, the rules identifying the competent court should not take into account the substance of the dispute between the parties and the outcome thereof. For instance, the principle of substance-neutrality would be clearly violated by a rule providing that jurisdiction lies with the court where the plaintiff's claim has the best chances of success.[15]

Neutrality is a fundamental cornerstone of private international law. In order to understand its importance, it is necessary to consider that the purpose of private international law is not the implementation of substantive policies, but the resolution of conflicts of applicable law or jurisdiction. Furthermore, pursuant to the principle of neutrality, all legal and judicial systems are put on an equal footing, irrespective of their peculiarities and relative efficiency. In accordance with its universal aspirations, hence, private international law adheres to a relativist approach, coordinating the regulatory and judicial prerogatives of states without performing value choices.

The main exception to the general principle of substance-neutrality is public policy. In different settings, states can invoke the public policy rule to avoid conferring legal effects upon a foreign legal instrument (e.g. a law, or a judgment). The scope of public policy, however, is extremely narrow: the clause can be invoked in exceptional circumstances only, to protect fundamental values and principles of the *forum*, but it can in no way act as a general shield against the operation of the conflict rules enshrined in private international law.

2. Application of substance-neutrality to criminal justice

The question arises whether a system coordinating jurisdiction in criminal matters should also be substance-neutral. On the one hand, it could be argued that criminal and private law are fundamentally different in nature, inasmuch as the former serves the function of implementing substantive policies in the public interests, while the

15 Conversely, the principle of substance-neutrality is not violated by a jurisdiction rule, which neutrally refers to the contents of the applicable substantive law, without assessing its adequateness and potential effects on the merits of the case. By way of example, under art 7(1)(a) of the Brussels I bis Regulation, in matters relating to contract, jurisdiction is (also) conferred upon the courts for the place of performance of the obligation. While the notion of 'place of performance' must be assessed according to the applicable substantive law, the Regulation does not contain any value judgment as to whether the national law governing the notion at hand is adequate and would lead to a satisfactory decision on the merits.

latter is often a neutral infrastructure for the expression of private autonomy.[16] Following this line of reasoning, it could be argued that substance should play a role in the determination of the rules for the allocation of criminal jurisdiction. On the other hand, however, there are two fundamental reasons (described below) why the principle of substance-neutrality should be preserved in the realm of criminal justice too.

First, if a system for the allocation of jurisdiction is not substance-neutral, it necessarily becomes a tool for the implementation of certain policies. Different states, however, have adopted divergent approaches as to the appropriate degree of reaction against criminal behaviours: punishments may vary significantly from jurisdiction to jurisdiction, and the areas of criminal relevance of conducts are not coextensive across different national systems. Even limiting the scope of our analysis to the European Union, a complete harmonisation of this field of law would be impossible and, in any event, probably undesirable.

Therefore, in order for a system of jurisdiction rules to be acceptable, it must necessarily be neutral, i.e. it must operate effectively while at the same time respecting the substantive regulatory autonomy of each state participating in the system. Were jurisdiction rules to embrace substantive value choices, they would result in a creeping form of harmonisation and, thus, they would not be accepted by those states whose national legal order enshrines divergent policies.

Second, even if one were to accept the premise that jurisdiction rules in criminal matters may take into account substantive considerations, this would result in a conundrum. Whose interests should the rules favour? One could maybe be tempted to assume that jurisdiction rules should take into account the prosecution's interests, consistently with the goal of repressing criminal activities. However, this approach is not viable in practice, as the interests of the prosecution are likely to change, depending on the nature of each national criminal justice system. In some jurisdictions, for example, the main goal of the prosecution could be the ascertainment of the truth in the public interest; by contrast, in other states, the prosecution could be entrusted with the task of obtaining a conviction, in accordance with the adversarial model. Once again, given the fragmentation of national systems, neutrality seems to be the only possible solution.

The problem becomes even more complex if we enlarge the perspective and consider other stakeholders, such as the defendant (who probably has a legitimate interest to prevail on the merits and obtain an acquittal) or the victim (once again, with possible discrepancies, depending on the structure of national criminal procedure). Jurisdiction rules are not fit to determine how these different and

16 The different nature of rules conferring powers and rules imposing obligations was famously scrutinised by HLA Hart, *The Concept of Law* (3rd edn, OUP 2012, first published in 1961).

potentially conflicting interests should be balanced. The principle of substance-neutrality, hence, should be adopted in the field of criminal justice.

One final possible objection against the principle of substance-neutrality concerns prescription/statute of limitations. Were a uniform system for the allocation of jurisdiction in criminal matters to be enacted, competence to prosecute may be conferred upon the authorities of a state where prosecution is time-barred and, thus, no longer possible. This could generate potential risks of impunity. Adhering to a strict interpretation of the principle of substance-neutrality, one could argue that the contents of the applicable statute of limitation fall within the substantive regulatory autonomy of the *forum* and, therefore, they are not a problem that should be dealt with through jurisdiction rules. However, it also seems possible to adopt a more moderate approach and create a carve-out for the case at hand, while at the same time preserving the central importance of substance-neutrality.

In order to create such a carve-out, it would be necessary to investigate the nature of time-limitations in depth. While such analysis cannot be conducted in this chapter, some basic arguments can be put forward and hopefully pave the way for further research and reflections in this respect. In particular, one may wonder what inferences could be drawn from the legislative decision to qualify the prosecution of a given crime as time-barred. It could be argued that statutes of limitations do not presuppose any substantive policy choice: a time-bar, then, can be seen as an *a priori* surrender of a criminal legal and justice system, limited to a specific case. In other words, by declaring that the prosecution of a crime is time-barred, national legal systems operate a simple choice of practical convenience: they abstain from prosecuting a crime in a particular instance for reasons of opportunity, without conceding anything in terms of general substantive policy choices. Prescription, then, could be differentiated from an acquittal on the merits and rather seen as a non-substantive outcome. Were further research to confirm that this hypothesis is plausible, it would then become possible to consider statutes of limitation as a possible criterion for the (non-)allocation of jurisdiction, without breaching substance-neutrality.

In conclusion, substance-neutrality should be adopted as a general principle, as far as the allocation of jurisdiction in criminal matters is concerned. The adoption of this principle would require, at the very least, a revision of the Eurojust *Guidelines for Deciding 'Which Jurisdiction Should Prosecute?'*,[17] which contain some substance-oriented criteria. According to the Guidelines, prosecutors 'must identify each jurisdiction where a prosecution is not only possible but also where there is a realistic

17 Eurojust, *Guidelines for Deciding 'Which Jurisdiction Should Prosecute?'* Annex to the 2003 Eurojust Annual Report, 60 http://www.eurojust.europa.eu/doclibrary/corporate/eurojust%20Annual%20Reports/Annual%20Report%202003/Annual-Report-2003-EN.pdf (last accessed 12 January 2017).

prospect of successfully securing a conviction'.[18] A neutral system for the allocation of jurisdiction cannot, of course, be based on the preference for a certain outcome of the merits stage of the proceedings.

Furthermore, the Guidelines do not categorically exclude that the relative sentencing powers of courts in different jurisdictions may be taken into account as a criterion for the selection of the appropriate jurisdiction.[19] Once again, a mechanism for the allocation of jurisdiction should not express value judgments on the contents of the national law applicable to the merits of the case, which falls within the regulatory discretion of each state.

The Guidelines also state that '(p)rosecutors should . . . ensure that the potential penalties available reflect the seriousness of the criminal conduct which is subject to the prosecution'. This evaluation of adequateness, however, seems to fall within the monopoly of the national law-makers creating substantive criminal law. A system serving the purpose of allocating jurisdiction should never second-guess the policy choices underlying national substantive law.

IV. LESSONS FROM EUROPEAN CIVIL PROCEDURE IN PARTICULAR

This section of the chapter will focus on the instruments of European procedural law, with the purpose of identifying rationales and solutions that could potentially be transposed to the field of criminal justice. Examples will be drawn from different fields of civil litigation, such as civil and commercial claims and family matters.

A. Reducing overlaps in jurisdiction

Reducing overlaps in jurisdiction is the basic rationale unifying the different instruments of European civil procedure and, to a certain extent, differentiating them from the common law tradition. In a nutshell, European procedural law aims at reducing hypothetical[20] conflicts by setting forth a uniform regime for the allocation of jurisdiction in civil matters.

The rules governing jurisdiction in civil and commercial matters in the European Union are set forth in the Brussels I bis Regulation.[21] The Regulation replaced the Brussels I Regulation[22] which, in turn, substituted the 1968 Brussels Convention.

18 ibid 61.

19 ibid 65: the Guidelines only acknowledge that the relative sentencing powers 'must not be a primary factor'.

20 For a definition of hypothetical conflict of jurisdiction see section II.A above.

21 Regulation (EU) No 1215/2012 [2012] OJ L351/1.

22 Regulation (EC) No 44/2001 on jurisdiction and the recognition and enforcement of judgments in civil and commercial matters (Brussels I Regulation) [2001] OJ L12/1.

Despite this succession of different legal instruments, the basic premises and structures governing the allocation of jurisdiction have remained largely the same. For this reason, the chapter will generally refer to the 'Brussels regime', whenever a certain feature of the system has remained constant over time.

Before the entry into force of the Brussels Convention, the rules allocating jurisdiction were not harmonised across the Member States. This, of course, generated a high risk of hypothetical conflicts among national courts, but it also raised another problem: many national laws contained criteria (or 'heads') for the allocation of jurisdiction that have been labelled as 'exorbitant'. The adjective 'exorbitant' alludes to the circumstance that, although under national law the courts are entitled to exert jurisdiction, the criterion for the attribution of jurisdiction seems to be unreasonable or 'difficult to justify'.[23] The following paragraphs will offer some examples of exorbitant heads, which help elucidate the importance of shared and reasonable jurisdiction rules.

Pursuant to Article 14 of the French Civil Code, a foreigner, even if not residing in France, can be sued before French courts, if the plaintiff is French. This rule has been rightly criticised, as it confers an unjustified advantage upon French claimants and may result in disproportionate difficulties for respondents who have no connection with France. By superseding national jurisdiction rules, the Brussels regime avoids that exorbitant heads (such as the one at hand) allocate jurisdiction among Member States.[24]

Another example of an exorbitant head of jurisdiction is § 23 of the German code of civil procedure. According to this provision, a defendant who does not reside in Germany can be sued before German courts, if he/she owns assets in Germany. On the basis of a strict interpretation of this rule, a foreigner who has been present on German territory for a very short period of time could be forced to litigate before German courts, should he accidentally leave a personal item (such as an umbrella or an item of clothing) on German territory. Once again, such a head of jurisdiction is clearly undesirable, as its broadness is not justified by a defensible rationale.[25]

In order to exclude the applicability of national jurisdiction rules (and, hence, of any exorbitant rule therein), the Brussels I bis Regulation expressly provides that persons domiciled in a Member State may be sued in the courts of another Member State only by virtue of the rules set out in the Regulation itself, and not by virtue of domestic law.[26]

23 Diego P. Fernández Arroyo, 'Compétence exclusive et compétence exorbitante dans les relations privées internationales' (2006) 323 Recueil des Cours de l'Académie de Droit International 9, 26.

24 Hélène Gaudemet-Tallon, *Compétence et exécution des jugements en Europe* (5th edn, LGDJ 2015) 100.

25 It should incidentally be noted that German courts mitigated the negative effects of the provision by giving it a restrictive interpretation, requiring a reasonable connection of the defendant with Germany, Bundesgerichtshof NJW 1992, 3092 para 44.

26 Article 5(1).

The current situation of jurisdiction rules in criminal matters is characterised by wide areas of overlap, with broad criteria that can be relied upon by national judicial authorities to invoke jurisdiction. The enactment of a uniform set of jurisdiction rules, analogous to the Brussels regime, could have the beneficial effect of avoiding those cases where jurisdiction is invoked in the absence of strong links between the relevant facts and the state where the proceedings are commenced.

B. Different heads of jurisdiction in the Brussels I system

Having excluded the applicability of exorbitant heads of jurisdiction, the Brussels I system sets forth a harmonised regime by providing for three main types of criteria for the allocation of jurisdiction in civil and commercial matters:

- general jurisdiction
- specific jurisdiction
- exclusive jurisdiction.

The following paragraphs will provide a synthetic overview of some relevant features of the above-mentioned criteria.

1. General jurisdiction

The general head of jurisdiction can be generally[27] relied upon for all cases falling within the scope of application of Brussels I. In particular, pursuant to Article 4(1) of the Brussels I bis Regulation, 'persons domiciled in a Member State shall, whatever their nationality, be sued in the courts of that Member State'. This general rule of jurisdiction is in accordance with the principle *actor sequitur forum rei*, whereby the plaintiff must normally initiate proceedings in the state of the respondent.

Article 4(1) is justified by a strong rationale, which seems to be exportable to the field of criminal justice too. In particular, the position of the defendant is privileged because he/she did not choose to initiate the proceedings, but is bound by the legal consequences thereof because of the plaintiff's decision to bring a claim. Hence, in order to mitigate the defendant's costs and inconveniences associated with the need to defend him/herself, the criterion of proximity to his/her domicile is adopted. The implicit assumption behind this regulatory choice is that organising the defence and participating in the proceedings is easier, if jurisdiction is attributed to the courts of the state where the defendant is domiciled. In criminal cases there is an even stronger rationale suggesting that the defendant's ease to defend him/herself should be taken into account, especially considering the importance of the subject matter of criminal proceedings and the seriousness of their possible consequences.

27 See, however, section IV.B.6 below on the exception of exclusive jurisdiction.

Another interesting aspect of Article 4 of the Brussels I bis Regulation is its general rejection of the criterion of nationality. What matters, for the establishment of jurisdiction under the provision at hand, is exclusively the domicile, irrespective of whether the defendant is also a national of the state of domicile. Once jurisdiction under Article 4 is established, then, each Member State is left free to determine the internal rules of competence allocating jurisdictional functions to different courts within their territories. However, Article 4(2) specifies that these internal jurisdiction rules cannot differentiate between nationals and foreigners domiciled in the relevant Member State.

2. Specific jurisdiction: the case of tort

Specific heads are additional jurisdiction rules that apply exclusively to particular scenarios, rather than covering the whole scope of application of the Brussels I system. By way of example, Article 7 of the Brussels I bis Regulation contains special rules of jurisdiction, inter alia, for matters relating to a contract and to tort. Specific heads of jurisdiction do not displace the general criterion of Article 4, but rather constitute an alternative: when the claim relates to a matter covered by a specific head, the plaintiff will be able to choose between the courts of the state where the defendant is domiciled and the (potentially but not necessarily different) *forum* indicated by Article 7.

By adding specific heads of jurisdiction to the general head of Article 4, the Brussels I system allows, in certain cases, for possible overlaps of jurisdiction, potentially leading to parallel proceedings. As section IV.C will illustrate, the system resolves the problem at hand through the mechanism of *lis pendens*. Before analysing this aspect in detail, however, it is necessary to scrutinise the contents of some specific heads of jurisdiction, which could help inspire a regime of allocation of jurisdiction in criminal matters.

For the purposes of a comparison with criminal justice, the most obviously relevant specific head of jurisdiction is the one concerning torts. Albeit profoundly different in many respects, tort and criminal law are linked by some structural similarities, as implicitly suggested by the etymological root of the word 'delict', used in civil law jurisdictions to designate torts. In both tort and criminal cases, the merits of the dispute revolve around an alleged wrongful conduct on the part of the defendant. In some cases, the same behaviour could in fact be relevant from the point of view of both tort and criminal law. For this reason, the following paragraphs will offer an overview of the rules of the Brussels I system on jurisdiction in tortious matters.

In principle, the Brussels I system adheres to the principle of territoriality: pursuant to Article 7(2), 'in matters relating to tort, delict or quasi-delict', jurisdiction is conferred upon the 'courts for the place where the harmful event occurred or may occur'. Transposing this rationale to criminal justice, it would seem logical to equate the harmful event with the alleged incriminating conduct. Despite this apparent simplicity, however, two practical complications may arise in practice and must be taken into account here:

(a) the place where the harm is suffered could be different from the place where the events giving rise thereto have taken place;
(b) the event itself could be transnational in nature and, for this reason, it may be difficult or even impossible to pinpoint it to the territory of a single State.

The case law of the Court of Justice of the European Union (CJEU) offers interesting insights in both these respects. Let us briefly consider them.

3. Differentiation between place where the damage occurred and place of the harmful events

The problem of a differentiation between the place of the event and the place where the harmful consequences are suffered came to light for the first time in the case *Mines de Potasse d'Alsace*.[28] The case concerned the alleged discharge of polluting waste into the river Rhine on the part of a French company. The claimant initiated proceedings before Dutch courts, arguing that, although the discharge took place in France, its harmful effects were suffered in the Netherlands. The respondents objected to the jurisdiction of Dutch courts. In this case the Court concluded that, given the strong link between the polluting behaviour and its cross-border harmful effects, the expression 'place where the harmful event occurred' should be interpreted as covering both the place of the event and the place of the subsequent damage.

In its later case law, however, the CJEU has often differentiated *Mines de Potasse d'Alsace*, so as to avoid unnecessary hypothetical conflicts of jurisdiction. In *Kainz*, for instance, the Court concluded that if a manufacturer faces a claim of liability for a defective product, the place of the event giving rise to the damage is the place where the product in question was manufactured, and not the place where the product was commercialised by a third party.[29] Similarly, in *Marinari*[30] and *Kronhofer*,[31] the CJEU held that the plaintiff cannot invoke Article 7(2)[32]

28 Case C-21/76 *Handelskwekerij G. J. Bier BV v Mines de potasse d'Alsace SA* ECLI:EU:C:1976:166.

29 Case C-45/13 *Andreas Kainz v Pantherwerke AG* ECLI:EU:C:2014:7, para 29. However, different jurisdiction rules apply to consumer contracts, see arts 17–19.

30 Case C-364/93 *Antonio Marinari v Lloyds Bank plc e Zubaidi Trading Company* ECLI:EU:C:1995:289.

31 Case C-186/02 *Rudolf Kronhofer v Marianne Maier* ECLI:EU:C:2004:364.

32 And the corresponding Articles of Regulation (EC) 44/2001 and of the Brussels Convention.

by simply alleging that the event caused a patrimonial harm in a different jurisdiction.[33]

In sum, hence, the circumstance that the harm was suffered in a different state seems to be relevant, for the purposes of the Brussels I system, only when there is a particularly close connection between the event and its harmful consequences. By contrast, in all other cases, the difference between the place of the event and the place of the harm should not be invoked for the purposes of the allocation of jurisdiction, only the former being relevant.

4. Cross-border events

The case of harmful events that take place across national borders (and cannot thus be pinpointed to one state only) constitutes an interesting parallel for many types of cross-border crimes. As far as tort claims are concerned, a particularly relevant case is the one of events taking place in the press or on the internet.

Torts committed through the press were addressed by the CJEU in the famous *Shevill* case.[34] The case concerned a claim for defamation via the press, brought before English courts by a plaintiff residing in the United Kingdom. The claimant argued that the defendant, a French company, had caused harm by publishing a defamatory article in a newspaper. The newspaper in question was distributed not only in France, but also in a number of other states, including the United Kingdom. For this reason, the harm was allegedly caused in more than one jurisdiction. The defendant objected to the jurisdiction of English courts and the case was referred to the CJEU for a preliminary ruling.

In *Shevill*, the CJEU concluded that the notion of 'place where the harmful event occurred' should be interpreted as covering both the place where the publisher of the defamatory publication is established, and each Member State where the publication was distributed and the victim claims to have suffered injuries to his/her reputation. However, the CJEU also drew a further distinction: the courts of the state where the publisher is established have jurisdiction concerning the entire harm caused by the publication, while the courts of a different state where the publication was distributed only have jurisdiction to rule in respect of the harm caused in that particular state. For the purposes of a comparison with criminal justice, *Shevill* is

33 A different approach was adopted in Case C-375/13 *Harald Kolassa v Barclays Bank plc* ECLI:EU:C:2015:37. The outcome of this case, however, seems to be strictly linked to the particular nature of the financial transaction giving rise to the dispute: for an analysis of the jurisdictional issues connected to the circulation and holding of intermediated securities see Matteo Gargantini, 'Jurisdictional Issues in the Circulation and Holding of (Intermediated) Securities; the Advocate General's Opinion in Kolassa v. Barclays' (2014) 4 Rivista di Diritto Internazionale Privato e Processuale 109.

34 Case C-68/93 *Fiona Shevill v Presse Alliance* ECLI:EU:C:1995:61.

relevant inasmuch as it suggests that the state where a certain cross-border conduct has been organised and initiated is best placed to exert jurisdiction over the entire set of facts, including those occurring across national borders.

Further complications are entailed by torts committed through the internet. The CJEU addressed this problem in the *eDate* case,[35] which concerned alleged violations of personality rights arising out of the publication of private information on a website. The court observed that the rationale enshrined in *Shevill* cannot be entirely transposed to the case at hand, as websites (unlike newspapers) generally have an automatic worldwide reach and accessibility. The Court, thus, enlarges the interpretation of the notion of 'place where the harmful event occurred', so as to encompass the state where the centre of the plaintiff's interests is based. As a result, the plaintiff can bring a claim alternatively in the state where the publisher is established or in the state where the centre of his/her interests is based, and the jurisdiction will cover the entire harm. Furthermore, the plaintiff can sue in any other state where the online content is/was accessible, but exclusively with respect to the harm caused on the territory of that particular state.

For the purposes of a comparison with criminal law, the main lesson that can be drawn from *eDate* is the prevalence of factual criteria over purely technical ones. As subsequently repeated by the CJEU in *Wintersteiger*,[36] jurisdiction should be allocated on the basis of circumstances of fact, rather than on the basis of the place where the server is located. This principle seems to be exportable to the field of cybercrime, where reliance on technology-based criteria could entail significant complications and/or refer to jurisdictions which, in reality, have no factual links with the alleged crime.

It must also be noted that, in the case law of the CJEU, the criterion of the 'centre of interests' is mainly limited to claims relating to personality rights. By contrast, when the case concerns violations of patrimonial rights allegedly committed via the internet, the 'place where the harmful event occurred' is typically identified pursuant to the *Shevill* criteria. In *Pinckney*,[37] namely, the CJEU addressed the case of an alleged cross-border violation of intellectual property rights. The dispute concerned the unauthorised reproduction of songs by a French author, on CDs manufactured by an Austrian company and marketed by UK companies on the internet. In this case, the Court held that the courts of a Member State from where the website is/was accessible have jurisdiction, but only with reference to the damage caused in that state; conversely, the criterion of the 'centre of interests' is not mentioned. Along the same lines, in *Pez Hejduk*,[38] the CJEU concluded that the courts of a Member State

35 Joined Cases C-509/09 *eDate Advertising GmbH v X* and C-161/10 *Olivier Martinez and Robert Martinez v MGN Limited* ECLI:EU:C:2011:685.

36 Case C-523/10 *Wintersteiger AG v Products 4U Sondermaschinenbau GmbH* ECLI:EU:C:2012:220.

37 Case C-170/12 *Peter Pinckney v KDG Mediatech AG* ECLI:EU:C:2013:635.

38 Case C-441/13 *Pez Hejduk v EnergieAgentur.NRW GmbH* ECLI:EU:C:2015:28.

are competent to hear claims concerning an alleged copyright violation committed via the internet, if the website was accessible from that state.[39] By contrast, the nature of the generic top-level domain (in the case at hand, .de) was deemed irrelevant.

5. Civil claims based on an act giving rise to criminal proceedings

For the sake of completeness, it is necessary to mention another specific head of jurisdiction, which is related to criminal proceedings. Pursuant to Article 7(3) of the Brussels I bis Regulation, if a civil claim for damages or restitution is based on an act giving rise to criminal proceedings, the court seised of those proceedings has jurisdiction, to the extent that it can entertain civil proceedings under its own laws. This provision ensures coordination between the Brussels I regime and national laws conferring jurisdiction in civil matters upon a court seised of a criminal case arising out of the same facts. Albeit important for a basic understanding of the Brussels I system, however, this rule probably cannot serve as a specific source of inspiration for a mechanism of allocation of jurisdiction in criminal matters.

6. Exclusive jurisdiction

In order to understand how the Brussels I system allocates jurisdiction, it is also important to acknowledge that heads of jurisdiction are organised hierarchically. In some cases, the Brussels I bis Regulation provides for the exclusive jurisdiction of the courts of a particular Member State, thus ruling all other Member State courts out. In these cases, of course, hypothetical conflicts of jurisdiction are entirely impossible. This is the case, inter alia, with rights in rem in immovable property or tenancies of immovable properties: under Article 24(1) of the Brussels I bis Regulation, the courts of the Member State in which the property is located have exclusive jurisdiction. The *rationale* underlying the mechanism of exclusive jurisdiction is that, in certain cases, a Member State court is in a relation of particular proximity with the dispute and therefore must be preferred to all other Member State courts.

For the purposes of a comparison with criminal justice, two main lessons can be drawn from the mechanism of exclusive heads of jurisdiction. First of all, for some specific crimes, it could make sense to avoid hypothetical conflicts altogether, when it is possible to identify a particularly strong link between the case and a given state.

39 Some authors have criticised the accessibility criterion, arguing that some websites are not addressed in practice to an international audience; see, for example, the 'Geneva Internet Dispute Resolution Policies 1.0', elaborated at the University of Geneva https://geneva-internet-disputes.ch/medias/2016/11/gidrp-1-0-geneva-internet-dispute-resolution-policies-final.pdf (last accessed 19 January 2016). A different solution, acknowledging the relevance of the circumstance that the conduct was directed towards a specific Member State, has been adopted in Case C-173/11 *Football Dataco Ltd and Others v Sportradar GmbH and Sportradar AG* ECLI:EU:C:2012:642.

Second, exclusive heads of jurisdiction influence the way the Brussels I system deals with the problem of actual conflicts of jurisdiction (i.e. parallel proceedings). In order to understand this aspect, however, it is first of all necessary to introduce the *lis pendens* mechanism and its context.

C. Putting the *lis pendens* mechanism in context

The Brussels I system (and other instruments of European civil procedure)[40] resolve the problem of actual conflicts of jurisdiction through the *lis pendens* mechanism. According to Article 29 of the Brussels I bis Regulation, when proceedings involving the same cause of action and between the same parties are brought in the courts of different Member States, any court other than the court first seised must of its own motion stay the proceedings, until the court first seised establishes its jurisdiction. Pursuant to paragraph 3 of the same Article, '(w)here the jurisdiction of the court first seised is established, any court other than the court first seised shall decline jurisdiction in favour of that court'.

The *lis pendens* mechanism is, essentially, a *first-come, first-served* rule. On the one hand, its automatic nature ensures a high degree of predictability of outcomes; on the other hand, however, it does not allow for a case-by-case evaluation of appropriateness. By adopting such a solution, European civil procedure rejects the flexible common law approach of *forum non conveniens*, as expressly confirmed by the case law of the CJEU.[41]

The main rationale behind the *lis pendens* rule is to be found in the principle of mutual trust, whereby all Member State courts are put on an equal footing and deemed to be equally equipped to adjudicate cases falling within their jurisdiction according to the Regulation.[42] The reason why *lis pendens* is based on chronological priority and does not take into account any other factor is that it aims at preventing each Member State court from assessing the functioning and the efficiency of the other Member State courts. The mechanism, thus, is functional to the creation of a European judicial area governed by mutual trust.[43]

It is not desirable nor, probably, possible to export the automatic *lis pendens* rule to the field of criminal justice. The main difference, in this respect, is to be found in the fact-specificity of criminal cases. In many scenarios, the opportunity

40 See, e.g., art 19 of the Brussels II bis Regulation (Regulation (EC) No 2201/2003).

41 Case C-281/02 *Andrew Owusu v N. B. Jackson, trading as 'Villa Holidays Bal-Inn Villas' and Others* ECLI:EU:C:2005:120.

42 Case C-116/02 *Erich Gasser GmbH v MISAT Srl* ECLI:EU:C:2003:657; Case C-185/07 *Allianz SpA and Generali Assicurazioni Generali SpA v West Tankers Inc* ECLI:EU:C:2009:69.

43 On the contrary, when considering conflicts of jurisdiction between a Member State court and a non-Member State court, art 33 of the Brussels I bis Regulation introduces a discretionary mechanism, which is not in any way linked to the allocation of jurisdiction or the circulation of judgments.

to allocate jurisdiction to the courts of a given state may depend on case-specific circumstances, such as the fact that the defendant was arrested in that state. This, however, does not entail that no lessons at all can be drawn from European civil procedure: as the above analysis demonstrates, the *lis pendens* mechanism is not the only or the main device through which conflicts of jurisdiction are resolved, but rather a particular aspect of a broader legal framework. Within the AFSJ, conflicts of jurisdiction in civil and commercial matters are avoided, first and foremost, through the enactment of uniform rules for the allocation of jurisdiction, which exclude exorbitant heads and limit superfluous overlaps. This basic rationale can surely play an important role in the field of criminal justice as well. Furthermore, as the following paragraphs will illustrate, the operation of the *lis pendens* mechanism is not without limits.

As mentioned above, the Brussels I system arranges heads of jurisdiction according to a hierarchical principle. In particular, exclusive heads of jurisdiction normally trump all other criteria. Exclusive jurisdiction exists, inter alia, when the parties have concluded a choice of court agreement, submitting to the jurisdiction of the courts of a given Member State to the exclusion of all other national courts. In this case, the *first come, first served* rule does not apply: if a court upon which the parties' agreement has conferred exclusive jurisdiction is seised, all other courts must stay the proceedings, even if they were seised first.[44] Once the court designated in the agreement has established jurisdiction in accordance with the agreement, all other courts must decline jurisdiction pursuant to Article 31(3).

Furthermore, apart from the specific case of choice of court agreements, it should also be noted that the violation of the rules conferring exclusive jurisdiction upon a certain Member State court could lead to the denial of recognition and enforcement of the judgment rendered by a different national court.[45] This peculiarity has an influence on the way the *lis pendens* rule operates: as clarified by the CJEU in *Weber*,[46] if the case is covered by an exclusive head of jurisdiction, the court second seised should not immediately stay its proceedings, but must first examine whether, by reason of a failure to take into consideration the exclusive jurisdiction, the decision of the court first seised will be recognised in the other Member States.

In conclusion, the *lis pendens* mechanism is best understood when put in context. Although its automatic character cannot be exported to the field of criminal justice, the basic structure of the Brussels I system is nonetheless able to inspire solutions for conflicts of jurisdiction in criminal matters.

44 Brussels I bis Regulation art 31(1).

45 ibid art 45(1)(e)(ii).

46 Case C-438/12 *Irmengard Weber v Mechthilde Weber* ECLI:EU:C:2014:212.

D. Lessons from conflicts of jurisdiction in family and succession matters

1. Dealing with fact-specificity while safeguarding certainty

As mentioned above, the reason why an automatic *first come, first served* rule cannot be transposed to criminal justice is the higher fact-specificity of criminal cases, as compared to civil and commercial litigation. There are, however, other topics falling within the broad umbrella of private law, such as family and succession matters, which are also characterised by a significant fact-specificity. In these contexts, European private international law adopts interesting solutions, from which some useful lessons can be drawn for criminal justice. Let us scrutinise them in detail.

In family law matters, the rules governing jurisdiction must take into account a certain degree of unpredictability, arising out of factual reasons. By way of example, in cases concerning parental responsibility, Article 8(1) of the Brussels II bis Regulation generally confers jurisdiction upon the courts of the Member State where the child is habitually resident. However, it is possible that the courts of another Member State are better placed to hear the case, because the child has, on the basis of a case-specific factual analysis, a particular connection with that state. In this case, Article 15 of the Regulation makes it possible for the Member State court having jurisdiction to:

(a) stay the case and invite the parties to introduce a request before the court of that other Member State, or
(b) ask a court of the other Member State to assume jurisdiction.

By introducing this exceptional mechanism of referral to a court better placed to hear the case, the Brussels II bis Regulation allows for a certain flexibility, so as to balance the need for legal certainty and predictability with the desirability of taking into account fact-specific circumstances. This, however, should not be read as an espousal of the *forum non conveniens* doctrine, as the Regulation subjects the transfer of the proceedings to an overarching criterion: the best interests of the child. If the transfer is not in the best interests of the child, Article 15 cannot be used to confer jurisdiction upon a different Member State court.[47] Unlike *forum non conveniens*, hence, the Brussels I Regulation identifies one clear criterion in the presence of which discretion can be exerted.

47 Analogously, pursuant to art 12(1) of the Brussels II bis Regulation, the courts of a Member State exercising jurisdiction on an application for divorce, legal separation or marriage annulment also have jurisdiction in any connected matter relating to parental responsibility, if at least one spouse has parental responsibility, the jurisdiction has been accepted by the spouses and by the holders of parental responsibility, and is *in the superior interests of the child* (emphasis added). Along the same lines, art 12(3) refers (for proceedings other than those referred to in para (1) to the best interests of the child.

Another example of exceptional flexibility in European private international law is Article 6 of the Succession Regulation (Regulation No 650/2012). The Regulation sets forth a set of jurisdiction rules on succession matters, but it also takes into account the fact that a person may choose as the law to govern his/her succession the law of the state whose nationality he/she possesses at the time of making the choice or at the time of death (Article 22). Article 6, then, provides that, if the law chosen by the deceased is the law of a Member State, the courts of another Member State having jurisdiction may decline to exert it, at the request of one of the parties, if the courts of the Member State whose substantive law has been chosen are better placed to rule on the succession. This possibility to decline jurisdiction, however, is subject to an evaluation of the 'practical circumstances of the succession', including the habitual residence of the parties and the location of the assets.

For the purposes of a comparison with criminal justice, an important principle can be drawn from the rules in question: even when it is necessary to allow for flexibility so as to take into account circumstances that cannot be foreseen in general terms, it is desirable to specify ex ante, where possible, whether and to what extent those circumstances should play a role in conferring jurisdiction to the courts of a given state.

2. Ordering the criteria progressively

The rules for the allocation of jurisdiction in family and succession matters are based on the assumption that it is desirable to take into account different types of factual circumstances, but not all of them have the same importance. The criteria for the allocation of jurisdiction, therefore, are often ordered progressively. By way of example, given two factual circumstances (X and Y), jurisdiction should generally be established on the basis of X. Only if it is impossible to refer to X, circumstance Y becomes relevant and can be taken into account. Let us briefly observe how this mechanism works in practice in the Brussels II bis,[48] the Maintenance[49] and the Succession[50] Regulations.

In the Brussels II bis Regulation, cases concerning parental responsibility are generally referred, under Article 8, to the jurisdiction of the courts of the Member State where the child is habitually resident.[51] However, if the child's habitual residence

48 Regulation (EC) No 2201/2003 [2003] OJ L338/1.

49 Regulation (EC) No 4/2009 on jurisdiction, applicable law, recognition and enforcement of decisions and cooperation in matters relating to maintenance obligations (Maintenance Regulation) [2009] OJ L7/1.

50 Regulation (EU) No 650/2012 on jurisdiction, applicable law, recognition and enforcement of decisions and acceptance and enforcement of authentic instruments in matters of succession and on the creation of a European Certificate of Succession (Success Regulation) [2012] OJ L201/107.

51 If the child is lawfully moved to another Member State, the conflict of jurisdiction is resolved by art 9. The case of child abduction is addressed in art 10 (see section IV.D.3 below).

cannot be established,[52] the criterion of presence becomes relevant: the courts of the Member State where the child is present will have jurisdiction.

Article 3 of the Maintenance Regulation confers jurisdiction, alternatively, on

(a) the court for the place where the defendant is habitually resident
(b) the court for the place where the creditor is habitually resident
(c) the court competent for matters concerning the status of a person or
(d) the court competent for matters concerning parental responsibility.

If no Member State court has jurisdiction on the basis of the above criteria,[53] Article 6 of the Regulation confers jurisdiction upon the courts of the Member State of the common nationality of the parties. Finally, if even this criterion is not applicable, it exceptionally becomes possible under Article 7 to confer jurisdiction upon the courts of a Member State with which the dispute has a sufficient connection, if proceedings cannot be reasonably brought or conducted in a third state (*forum necessitatis*).

Under Article 4 of the Succession Regulation, the courts of the Member State where the deceased had his/her habitual residence at the time of death have jurisdiction to rule on the succession as a whole. If the habitual residence is not located in a Member State, Article 10 steps in and confers jurisdiction concerning the whole succession to the courts of a Member State where assets of the estate are located, if the deceased had the nationality of that Member State or had had his/her habitual residence there in the previous five years. If these criteria are not met, the courts of the Member State where assets are located have jurisdiction, but exclusively with respect to those assets. Finally, if it is impossible to establish jurisdiction according to any of the above criteria, it becomes possible to invoke the *forum necessitatis* rule of Article 11, whereby the courts of a Member State with sufficient connection may exert jurisdiction, if the case cannot be heard by the courts of a third state.

Apart from their technicalities, the provisions at hand seem to be relevant for the purposes of a comparison with criminal law, mainly because of their underlying rationale. In family and succession litigation, similarly to criminal justice, it may be desirable to ensure that no jurisdictional gaps exist within the AFSJ and that, eventually, it will always be possible to identify one competent court. However, by arranging the criteria progressively, the rules described above also acknowledge that not all criteria are equally important: some of them can only be invoked when absolutely indispensable. Since some rules confer jurisdiction only in the cases where some other rules cannot operate, the sequential order of the different heads manages to avoid not only jurisdictional gaps, but also hypothetical conflict of jurisdiction.

52 And if jurisdiction cannot be determined on the basis of art 12 (Prorogation of jurisdiction).

53 And if it is not possible to establish jurisdiction otherwise, see art 6.

By exporting the same conceptual framework to criminal cases, it could be possible to take into account fact-specificity while at the same time avoiding superfluous overlaps of jurisdiction.

3. Lawful move and child abduction: is a comparison with arrest possible?

One of the varying factual circumstances that are likely to play a role in an assessment of appropriateness, when allocating jurisdiction in criminal matters to a certain state court, is the fact that the defendant was arrested in that state. In principle, this is perfectly comprehensible, also because the arrest is normally a strong indicator of a particular link between the alleged crime and the territory of a given state. Conferring relevance upon this factor, however, could also entail the risk of abuses. Take the example of two states whose prosecutors have an interest in prosecuting the same crime: in theory, it would be possible to imagine a situation where (at least) one of the two national authorities tries to obtain an arrest not because this is necessary (pursuant to the criteria of national criminal procedure), but simply in order to establish jurisdiction. Taken in its more extreme form, this scenario could lead to cases of 'forum shopping' in criminal matters, which should absolutely be avoided.

A possible solution to the problem at hand comes from the Brussels II bis Regulation. The Regulation allocates jurisdiction, inter alia, in matters of parental responsibility, using as a criterion the habitual residence of the child (Article 8(1)). Residence, however, is a factual criterion that could change over time, if the child is moved to a different state. In extreme cases, one of the parents could even decide to relocate in order to change the allocation of jurisdiction. The Regulation resolves this problem by setting forth two provisions: Article 9 (dealing with the case of lawful move) and Article 10 (concerning child abduction). Let us consider these rules.

If a child moves lawfully to another state and acquires a new habitual residence there, the courts of the state of former habitual residence retain jurisdiction for three months, for the purpose of modifying a judgment on access rights issued in that Member State before the child moved.[54] Thanks to this provision, the courts of the state of former habitual residence can modify the previous access arrangements and ensure that the holder of access rights continues enjoying them effectively, without the need to commence proceedings in the state of new habitual residence.

The case of wrongful removal or retention of the child is even more problematic, as the change of habitual residence is triggered by unlawful behaviour. By linking jurisdiction to the criterion of habitual residence, hence, there is an implicit risk

54 The provision at hand applies if the holder of access rights continues to have his/her habitual residence in the State of the child's former habitual residence, and he/she has not accepted the jurisdiction of the courts of the state of the child's new habitual residence.

of 'legitimising' the effects of child abduction. For this reason, Article 10 sets forth a special regime, whereby the courts of the Member State where the child was habitually resident retain jurisdiction for a period of one year,[55] starting from the moment when the holder of rights of custody has had or should have had knowledge of the whereabouts of the child, and the child is settled in his/her new environment. If, in the presence of these circumstances, the person/entity having rights of custody has remained inactive,[56] the jurisdiction moves to the courts of the new state of habitual residence.

Transposing these rules to the realm of criminal justice, it would be desirable to implement a mechanism whereby the place of arrest, which may generally be one of the relevant criteria for the allocation of jurisdiction, cannot be taken into account in cases where the arrest seems to have been requested for the sole or main purpose of securing jurisdiction.

4. Exchange of information: the role of central authorities

It is finally important to stress that a system for the allocation of jurisdiction can operate in practice only if information is exchanged effectively. By way of example, actual conflicts of jurisdiction can be resolved only if the relevant mechanism is triggered: to this end, therefore, it is first of all necessary to ensure that national judicial authorities be aware of the existence of parallel proceedings pending in another Member State. The problem seems to be particularly relevant in the field of criminal justice, where the defendant may sometimes have an interest in not disclosing the existence of proceedings being conducted in a different jurisdiction.

Exchange of information could be facilitated by the institution of national central authorities, entrusted with the task of assisting with the application of the rules aimed at resolving conflicts of jurisdiction. In this respect, inspiration could be drawn from the Brussels II bis and the Maintenance Regulation, which specify the tasks of central authorities respectively in their respective Chapters IV and VII. It should, however, also be noted that, if complemented by the institution of central authorities, a mechanism for the allocation of jurisdiction in criminal matters may entail additional costs.

V. CONCLUSIONS

The main argument of this chapter has been that private international law, and European civil procedure in particular, can offer useful inspiration towards the

55 The jurisdiction of the new state of habitual residence, however, is immediately established if each person, institution, or other body having rights of custody has acquiesced in the removal or retention.

56 The conditions are laid down in detail in art 10.

establishment of a regime for the resolution of conflicts of jurisdiction in criminal matters. The first part of the chapter has set the scene by highlighting some structural differences between civil and criminal matters, which limit in some respects the feasibility of cross-sectoral legal transplants. Subsequently, the second part has drawn some lessons from private international law as a whole, namely stressing the importance of predictability and substance-neutrality. Finally, the third part has offered an overview of some relevant provisions of European procedural law, highlighting the desirability of a uniform regime of allocation aimed at minimising hypothetical conflicts of jurisdiction. Parallels between specific scenarios of civil litigation and criminal settings have also been drawn. In light of the above analysis, it can be concluded that, despite the many differences, many solutions adopted by private international law can be successfully transposed to criminal proceedings too.

8

MUTUAL RECOGNITION, CHOICE OF FORUM, AND *LIS PENDENS*

A Civil Law Threesome Transposed

AUKJE VAN HOEK

I. INTRODUCTION

The draft proposals make a bold attempt to address a pressing and controversial issue in international criminal law. The recognition of multiple grounds of jurisdiction—and the recent expansion thereof with regard to specific crimes[1]—creates a situation in which more than one country can legitimately claim jurisdiction over a specific crime or set of acts. Unlike the situation in civil procedure, there is currently no European system to coordinate criminal jurisdiction within the area of freedom of justice, and hence the international grounds of jurisdiction are also applied in full to intra-EU cases.[2] This creates ample possibilities for a positive conflict of jurisdiction in which more than one state may start investigations, prosecution, and/or criminal adjudication with regard to a similar or identical set of criminal facts. As the Working Group rightly stresses, this may lead to 'efforts and resources being wasted and potentially to arbitrary outcomes'.

The problem is exacerbated by the fact that there is no *lis pendens* rule comparable to the one developed within the field of private international law.[3] There is only a voluntary system of collaboration between authorities. This may lead to double investigation and double prosecution, with all the drawbacks this entails for the parties involved. However, as soon as one of the European Union (EU)

1 See e.g. Council of Europe Convention on Cybercrime 2001, ETS 185, art 22; Council of Europe Convention on the Prevention of Terrorism 2005, ETS 196, art 14; Council of Europe Convention against Trafficking in Human Organs 2015, ETS 216, art 10. See also Michiel Luchtman, 'Choice of Forum and the Prosecution of Cross-Border Crime in the European Union' in Michiel Luchtman (ed), *Choice of Forum in Cooperation Against EU Financial Crime* (Eleven International Publishing 2013) 5. See in the same volume: John Spencer, 'Mutual Recognition and Choice of Forum' 70 ff and Martin Böse, 'Choice of Forum and Jurisdiction' 74.

2 Some conventions contain provision on mutual consultation in case of overlapping jurisdiction—see e.g. art 14(5) of the Terrorism Convention. These will not be discussed here.

3 See e.g. arts 29 ff Brussels I bis Regulation.

Member States involved finally disposes of the case—be it by way of a decision not to prosecute, be it by a judgment finding the suspect guilty, or any other decision which ends the prosecution—all other Member States are bound by that decision through the rule of *ne bis in idem* which the Court of Justice of the European Union (CJEU) has developed in the case law building on *Gözütok and Brügge*.[4] So, double prosecution is not stopped at the very start, but at the very end of the national procedure:[5] once a decision is reached, it creates *ne bis in idem*. The *ne bis in idem* effect is granted regardless of the (trial or pre-trial) stage in which the national decision is taken and irrespective of the link of the disposing authority to the facts.[6]

In short, the area of freedom, security and justice, built on the notion of mutual recognition in criminal matters, operates a hard and fast rule of *ne bis in idem*. This rule is supported by a system of voluntary consultation in case of parallel proceedings, but this system is incomplete. There is no common binding procedure for dealing with *lis pendens* and related actions. This is all the more problematic as the recognition rule is not supported by a preliminary agreement on the distribution of jurisdiction between the Member States in intra-EU cases. The policy options described in the proposal address the latter two shortcomings.

In this contribution I will use insights from the field of private international law to comment on the current state of the law and the solutions embedded in the proposals. The Brussels I Regulation 1215/2012 (Brussels I recast or Brussels I bis) will function as the main comparator—although at some point references will be made to the wider body of private international law instruments.[7] The Brussels I bis Regulation contains rules on mutual cooperation in civil and commercial matters, a concept which includes cross-border torts. The concept of 'tort' covers the civil law response to wrongdoings which cause damage to third parties. Of all private international law categories, 'tort' has the closest link to criminal law. The regulation contains rules on jurisdiction as such, the exercise thereof in case of *lis pendens* and related actions and the mutual recognition of judgments. This contribution will discuss all these aspects and compare the solutions in private international law to the current proposal on criminal law. Each topic is self-standing and will lead to separate 'conclusions'.

4 Joined Cases C-187/01 *Gözütok and Brügge* ECLI:EU:C:2003:87.

5 This is different from the *lis pendens* rule in civil proceedings, which also operates on a first across the line basis, but takes its cue from the moment in which the case becomes 'pending'.

6 Luchtman (n 1) 38.

7 Regulation (EU) No 1215/2012 of the European Parliament and of the Council of 12 December 2012 on jurisdiction and the recognition and enforcement of judgments in civil and commercial matters [2012] OJ L351/1.

II. MUTUAL RECOGNITION AS PRINCIPLE OR GOAL

Similar to the situation in criminal law, the instruments on cooperation in civil matter are built up from the principle of mutual recognition.[8] The Brussels I bis Regulation is no exception. The original EEC Treaty of 1957 contained a provision which obliged the Member States to enter into negotiations (as far as necessary) in order to simplify the mutual recognition of court decision and arbitral awards. In the field of arbitration, such mutual recognition would shortly be ensured by the New York Convention of 1958.[9] As to the recognition of civil judgments, the then six Member States did indeed enter into negotiations—which resulted in the Brussels Convention of 1968. Hence, mutual recognition was not reached by way of court interpretation of the Treaties, but by way of common arrangement in which the Member States addressed the major obstacles to mutual recognition. The current system of the Brussels I bis Regulation is still based on the structure of the 1968 Convention. This structure was consequently used as a template for similar instruments on mutual recognition, inter alia in the field of parental responsibility (see for example Regulation Brussels IIa[10]).

III. STANDARD REQUIREMENTS FOR (MUTUAL) RECOGNITION OF CIVIL JUDGMENTS

Instruments on the recognition of civil judgments—be they national, international, or European—tend to follow a similar pattern.[11] They describe which type of decisions are covered by the instrument (requirements) and when the receiving country may refuse to give effect to a decision which, based on the requirements, would be open for recognition and enforcement (refusal grounds). Requirements may pertain to the type of judgments covered, whether the judgment should be

8 For private international law see inter alia arts 81and 82 of the TFEU and Matthias Weller, 'Mutual Trust: in Search of the Future of European Union Private International Law' (2015) 11(1) Journal of Private International Law 64, 67. For criminal law, see Luchtman (n 1) 7 and Spencer (n 1) 61 ff.

9 UN Convention on the Recognition and Enforcement of Foreign Arbitral Awards, New York 1958 http://www.newyorkconvention.org/ (last accessed 10 February 2017).

10 Council Regulation (EC) No 2201/2003 of 27 November 2003 concerning jurisdiction and the recognition and enforcement of judgments in matrimonial matters and the matters of parental responsibility, repealing Regulation (EC) No 1347/2000 [2003] OJ L338/1.

11 See for an overview of requirements based on the legal traditions of the American continents: Robert C. Casad, *Civil Judgment Recognition and the Integration of Multiple-State Associations* (University Press of Kansas 1982) 18. See for a discussion of these requirements in multilateral treaties and the law of the US and Australia, Aukje A H van Hoek, 'Erkenning van vonnissen in het privaatrecht: een studie naar de grenzen van wederzijdse erkenning' NIPR 2003-312, 337 ff. See also Weller (n 8) 69, n 6.

final and on the merits, and requirements as to enforceability etc.[12] As a rule, the instruments are restricted to judicial decisions and do not cover decisions by other officials,[13] an exception being made for decisions on costs made by court officials.[14] Settlements between the parties that are endorsed by a court decision may be covered but are often treated distinctly from judgments proper: in the Brussels I bis Regulation court settlements may be enforceable in other Member States, but do not automatically produce *res judicata* effect. Neither are they covered by the rule on irreconcilable judgments. Given these restrictions, it is interesting to note that the *ne bis in idem* rule in EU criminal law covers all (trial and) pre-trial decisions which end the proceedings. This widens the scope of the proposed instrument beyond that of the Brussels I system, which in turn has an impact on the *lis pendens* rule—as will be discussed below.

Standard refusal grounds are lack of jurisdiction of the rendering court, improper notification, violation of fair trial requirements, violation of the public policy of the receiving court, and the existence of another judgment which is irreconcilable with the one submitted for recognition and enforcement.[15] Some international conventions also mention procedural fraud as a specific refusal ground.

Most of these refusal grounds express a certain measure of distrust[16] of the foreign justice system: either as to the rules applied there or as to the application thereof by the court giving judgment. The rendering court may not have been impartial,

12 The terminology is not strictly adhered to: see for example the Hague maintenance convention 1974 (arts 4 and 5) in which the jurisdiction test is formulated as a requirement rather than a refusal ground.

13 See for instance the bilateral treaty between The Netherlands and Surinam *Tractatenblad* 1976 No 144.

14 See amongst (many) others art 2(a) Regulation Brussels I bis; art 32 Lugano Convention of 30 October 2007; art 1(2) of the Dutch–German Treaty of 1962, Treaty no 004909 http://wetten.overheid.nl/BWBV0004221/1965-09-15 (last accessed 20 April 2018); art 1(2) of the Dutch–UK Treaty *Tractatenblad* 1967-197; art 15 of The Hague Convention on the Recognition and Enforcement of Foreign Judgments in Civil and Commercial Matters 1971.

15 Notification can be an element of jurisdiction but is also closely linked to fair trial. In general, due process requirements suggest that anyone who is bound by the judgment should have had the opportunity to present their case in court. This requirement is not applied across the board, however. See inter alia Peter Hay, 'On Merger and Preclusion (Res Iudicata) in U.S. Foreign Judgments Recognition—Unresolved Doctrinal Problems' in Rolf A Schütze (ed), *Einheit und Vielfalt des Rechts, FS Geimer zum 65. Geburtstag* (Beck 2002) 335. Russell J. Weintraub, *Commentary on the Conflict of Laws* (Foundation Press 2001) 701.

16 For an interesting exposé on the differences between distrust and mistrust, see Stephen Marsh and Mark R. Dibben, 'Trust, Untrust, Distrust and Mistrust—An Exploration of the Dark(er) Side' (Conference Paper LCNS, May 2005) https://www.researchgate.net/profile/Stephen_Marsh3/publication/220852752_Trust_Untrust_Distrust_and_Mistrust_-_An_Exploration_of_the_Darker_Side/links/541832730cf2218008bf2c73.pdf (last accessed 20 April 2018) (taken from P Herrmann et al (eds), *iTrust 2005*, LNCS no 3477, 17–33 (Springer-Verlag 2005)).

the trial might have been unfair, or the outcome discriminatory or biased against the receiving state's interests. Within the EU the legislator has consistently tried to abolish the refusal grounds, calling on the principle of mutual trust.[17] This has been moderately successful. Some refusal grounds have been restricted in scope (e.g. on notification) and some checks are transferred to the country of origin (e.g. in the case of jurisdiction). In some instruments, even the public policy exception has been deleted.[18] The only refusal ground which is consistently retained is the defence of irreconcilable judgments. This is the one refusal ground which is completely neutral in that it is not based on distrust of the foreign system.

Under the current state of harmonisation in the EU, multiple courts may validly assume jurisdiction and, in doing so, may reach different outcomes. So, there is nothing wrong with the different judgments as such. Yet, if the outcomes are mutually exclusive, it is not possible to recognise both outcomes at the same time within the same legal order.[19] The problem can be mitigated by harmonisation of the rules on applicable law and/or substantive law as this increases decisional harmony—different courts reaching the same outcome. The risk can be reduced by limiting the grounds of jurisdiction and is further addressed by rules on *lis pendens* and related action. However, even these mechanisms cannot completely pre-empt the possibility of irreconcilable judgments.

In all current EU instruments dealing with patrimonial claims—a term which includes tort claims—the earlier judgment wins.[20] This priority rule seems to match the system in criminal law where the first decision which finally disposes of the issue, blocks other decisions (even identical ones). But in criminal law this is the direct effect of the *ne bis in idem* rule, which is capable of stopping any still pending procedure in its tracks, rather than a principle embedded in the rules on *lis pendens* and mutual recognition.

In short, from a structural perspective it is interesting to note that civil law and criminal law operate from opposite starting positions. In civil law rules on jurisdiction and *lis pendens* have been created in order to facilitate the mutual recognition of judgments. In criminal law, the mutual recognition of decisions is a given; the

17 See on the application of mutual trust in private international law inter alia Weller (n 8).

18 European Payment Order (Regulation (EC) No 1896/2006 creating a European order for payment procedure [2006] OJ L399/1, art 22), European Small Claims Procedure (Regulation (EC) No 861/2007 establishing a European small claims procedure [2007] OJ L199/1, art 22), European Executory Title (Regulation (EC) No 805/2004 creating a European Enforcement Order for uncontested claims [2004] OJ L143/15, art 21). See also Weller (n 8) 82 ff.

19 If conflicting legal positions exist in different legal systems, this is referred to as limping legal relationships. A well-known example is the limping marriage, which is ended by divorce in one jurisdiction, but still exists in another.

20 See the instruments mentioned in n 10. With regard to dissolution of marriages, Member States may give precedence to their own judgments, regardless of timing; see Regulation (EC) No 2201/2003 Brussel II bis, art 22(c).

current proposal only seeks to address the negative side-effects of such automatic recognition by creating rules on *lis pendens* and jurisdiction.

IV. *TRAITÉ SIMPLE, DOUBLE,* AND *MIXTE*

In the civil justice instruments on recognition and enforcement a special position is taken up by the issue of jurisdiction. However, this position has changed over time. Both in national law and under the older international instruments, jurisdiction is tested at the recognition stage. A certain measure of distrust also informs the inclusion of jurisdiction in the refusal grounds but here it takes on a specific characteristic. When a judgment from country X is submitted to a court (or other official) in country Y for recognition and/or enforcement, recognition will or may be[21] refused when the jurisdiction of the rendering court is not recognised as proper. In other words, when the rendering court should not have taken jurisdiction over the defendant and/or the case. As a rule the test of jurisdiction is not based on the assessment of whether the court of origin correctly applied its own rules on jurisdiction.[22] The fact that the rendering court assumed jurisdiction is judged against a standard of appropriateness formulated in the law of the recognising forum or the relevant international or European instrument. But the receiving court will not use the grounds for jurisdiction in its own law as the litmus test for the recognition of foreign judgments either. Rather than checking the jurisdiction of the court of origin against the jurisdictional bases that would have been available to the recognising court in the mirror situation, the latter court checks whether the competence of the court of origin is based on an *internationally* acceptable ground for jurisdiction. This check excludes any 'exorbitant' grounds for jurisdiction which might be available under national law.

Exorbitant grounds for jurisdiction in civil proceedings include the nationality or domicile of the claimant,[23] the presence within the territory of assets not related to the cause of action, and mere physical presence of the defendant within the territory at the time of notification (so-called 'tag' jurisdiction).[24] These exorbitant grounds for jurisdiction are maintained by national legislators to cater for

21 The check may be on request only or *ex officio*, depending on the system of recognition in place.

22 See, however, the system of full faith and credit under US law—described in van Hoek (n 11).

23 The domicile of the claimant can, however, be acceptable in case of weaker party protection given to consumers, employees, and maintenance creditors. See, for a list of exorbitant grounds, the draft Hague Judgment Convention Prel. Doc No 11 of August 2000, art 18 https://assets.hcch.net/docs/638883f3-0c0a-46c6-b646-7a099d9bd95e.pdf (last accessed 20 April 2018).

24 Tag jurisdiction is available in (inter alia) the UK and Ireland. See for a more extensive discussion of exorbitant grounds of jurisdiction the contribution of Ortolani, 'Conflicts of Jurisdiction in Criminal Law: Lessons from European Civil Procedure' in this volume.

situations in which the claimant cannot be expected to get an enforceable judgment in a foreign country with a closer connection to the case at hand—for instance because in absence of a treaty such judgments would not be recognised within the forum. In other words, exorbitant fora are needed as fall-back provisions to ensure access to justice and effective enforcement. As a rule, the exorbitant grounds of jurisdiction are neither needed nor acceptable in case of mutual recognition of judgments.[25] They are banned by special provision in the area of freedom, security and justice (AFSJ).[26]

Jurisdiction is a key issue in any system of recognition and enforcement. The way a mutual recognition scheme deals with the issue even determines the character of the instrument. As far as conventions on private international law are concerned a distinction is made between '*traités simples*' and '*traités doubles*'. Most conventions on recognition and enforcement are *traités simples*: they don't change the national rules on jurisdiction, but specify the link the court of origin should have with either the defendant or the dispute in order for the judgment to be open to recognition. The 1968 Brussels Convention however was a *traité double*: an international instrument which also harmonises the rules on jurisdiction of the contracting states. Within the scope of application of the convention, courts could only base their jurisdiction on the rules contained in the instrument itself. The jurisdiction of the court of origin would as a rule not be tested again at the recognition stage. Accordingly, the check for the proper exercise of jurisdiction was placed on the court of origin and removed from the system of recognition.[27] All Brussels Regulations on recognition and enforcement now follow this model, as do several of the Hague Conventions.[28] But at the time it was revolutionary as it impacted on the authority of the Member States to set their own rules on international jurisdiction.

With some exceptions the jurisdiction rules in the Brussels Convention only applied when the defendant was domiciled in the EU.[29] For non-EU defendants, the Member States were free to apply their domestic rules of jurisdiction. So, the restriction of sovereignty was limited to cases that came within the scope of application of

25 When the Netherlands created a special section on international jurisdiction in the Dutch code of civil procedure, most exorbitant grounds of jurisdiction were abolished. This matches a relatively lenient albeit unwritten rule on recognition of foreign judgments—see Supreme Court *Gazprombank*, 26 September 2014, ECLI:NL:HRL2014:2838.

26 See art 5 Brussels I bis in combination with the list published in OJ 2015 C390/10.

27 Jurisdiction can still be checked in case of exclusive jurisdiction and weaker party protection.

28 See e.g. the Convention on Jurisdiction, Applicable Law, Recognition, Enforcement and Co-Operation in Respect of Parental Responsibility and Measures for the Protection of Children 1996.

29 The convention also applied to non-EU defendants when an EU court had exclusive jurisdiction, in case of a choice of forum in favour of an EU court where one of the parties had residence within the EU. The Regulation extends its scope to some consumer, insurance and labour cases with non-EU defendants. See art 6 Brussel I bis.

the instrument. This has proven to be important for the Member States as it changes the character of the instrument. Rather than claiming or renouncing jurisdiction vis-à-vis the world at large, the instrument largely distributes jurisdiction between the Member States. When the Brussels I Regulation was being revised, the European Commission tried to lift the restriction in scope and develop rules for non-EU cases as well.[30] This largely failed as the Council would not accept the extension and jealously protected the prerogatives of the Member States in this area.

The Brussels Convention was used as a model for the Lugano Convention—which currently binds the EU and several Contracting states of EFTA. However, in the negotiations on a world-wide convention which was started within the ambit of the Hague Conference in 1992, the US rejected full harmonisation of jurisdiction and introduced the concept of a '*traité mixte*'. Such a treaty would ban exorbitant grounds for jurisdiction (black list) and explicitly allow or even prescribe certain generally accepted grounds (white list). But it would also leave some freedom to the contracting states to keep additional (non-exorbitant) grounds for jurisdiction (the grey area). Judgments based on these additional grounds would not, however, be enforceable under the convention. They would have to rely on domestic law for their extra-territorial effect.[31]

The distinction between the different models of *traité simple, double*, and *mixte* is based exclusively on the way in which the check for jurisdiction is integrated in the instruments. Out of the three proposals put forward by the Working Group only Model 3 (the allocation model) contains rules on jurisdiction. When comparing this model with the concepts described in the previous paragraphs, the difference between them stands out first. None of the European Law Institute (ELI) proposals is dealing with recognition as such—mutual recognition is based on the Treaty (as interpreted by the CJEU) and hence outside the scope of the proposals. So, the *traité simple* model is irrelevant in this context. Nevertheless, the distinction between the *traité double* and the *traité mixte* may be of interest for a better understanding of Model 3.

Model 3 does not formulate the rules on jurisdiction as part of the refusal grounds for recognition. It merely states in Article 4 that: 'Within the Area of Freedom, Security and Justice, each Member State shall only exercise jurisdiction in respect of offences committed in its own territory as determined by national law'. The explanatory note adds that: 'Territoriality is the general rule for the allocation of exercise of jurisdiction in the Area of Freedom, Security and Justice. Extraterritoriality is therefore excluded. The definition of *locus delicti* is left to national law. The same applies

30 COM(2010) 748 final 8, art 4.

31 See the letter of the US to the Secretary General of the Hague Conference https://www.state.gov/documents/organization/65973.pdf and the response of the Secretary General https://assets.hcch.net/docs/bd6dcaab-b2a4-4255-84ec-eca3b7233588.pdf (both last accessed 20 April 2018).

for the rules of the location of the conduct of accomplices, instigators and of other participants'. Although the wording of Article 4 suggests that we are dealing with direct rules on jurisdiction (as one would expect in a *traité double*) the technique used borrows some important characteristics from the *traité mixte*.[32]

Model 3 contains a direct prohibition on the exercise of extra-territorial jurisdiction—which is deemed exorbitant in intra-EU relations. Accordingly, the personality principle (both active and passive), the protection principle, and the principle of universal jurisdiction are put on the black list. This is the harmonising element of the proposal in which it can be compared to the Brussels I bis Regulation. However, in stark contrast to Brussels I bis—which is based on autonomous interpretation of the concepts used to establish jurisdiction—Model 3 does not harmonise the positive grounds for jurisdiction. It merely stipulates that all national rules based on the territoriality principle may be maintained. The concept of territoriality itself is not defined or further circumscribed. This creates a grey area of jurisdictional bases which may not be present in all Member States but are still allowed under the instrument. A full transition to a *traité double* would require autonomous interpretation of the concept of the *locus delicti*—something that is deliberately not foreseen in the current instrument. In a separate paragraph I will discuss the interpretation of that concept in the case law on tortious liability under Brussels I. Suffice to say here, that even Model 3 stops short of harmonising jurisdiction in criminal matters. It merely does away with the use of exorbitant grounds for jurisdiction over crimes committed within the AFSJ. For extra-EU offences, these jurisdictional bases are maintained—which further (in parallel to the Brussels I regime) limits the impact on the sovereignty of the Member States.[33]

In short, as a result of the limitation in scope Model 3 does not attribute jurisdiction to EU criminal courts, but rather distributes it among the Member States. And even the distribution is not absolute, as the instrument merely rules out the use of certain 'exorbitant' grounds of jurisdiction in intra-EU cases. The ensuing restriction of sovereignty is limited compared to private international law instruments.

V. THE *LOCUS DELICTI* IN CIVIL JUSTICE CASE LAW

Under the Brussels I bis Regulation persons domiciled in a Member State shall, whatever their nationality, be sued in the court of that Member State. However, in certain disputes, the Regulation offers an alternative forum. For the purpose of this

32 However, as is explained in the text, under the *traité mixte* model proposed by the US in 1992, jurisdictional bases in the grey area did not lead to a right to recognition under the treaty. This is different in criminal matters in the EU, as proper jurisdiction is not a prerequisite for creating *ne bis in idem*.

33 See art 2 for the scope of application.

comparison, the most interesting alternative is Article 7(2), which stipulates that in matters relating to tort, delict, or quasi-delict, a person domiciled in a Member State may also be sued in the courts for the place where the harmful event occurred or may occur. This ground for jurisdiction is commonly referred to as the *locus delicti.* There is a sizeable body of case law on the interpretation of this concept. In 1976, the Court decided that in case the damage is felt in a different location than that in which the act is committed, both the *locus actus* and the *locus damni* qualify as *locus delicti.*[34] This is true for both physical damage (pollution of the river Rhine) and non-tangible damage caused by the publication of defamatory statements.[35] This matches the use of the territoriality principle in criminal law and is sometimes referred to in literature as the ubiquity principle.[36] However, there is no complete parallel between the use of the latter concept in civil law and in criminal law.[37] This is evident when we take a closer look at the further interpretation of terms and the application of the principle to compound torts.

Both the *locus actus* and the *locus damni* are legal concepts which require further interpretation. The CJEU was consulted with regard to such diverse torts as defamation and invasion of privacy on the internet, product liability, participation in a cartel, infringement of IP rights, and directors' liability etc. A striking feature of this case law is that the court seems to interpret the concepts in close relation to the type of delict at stake.[38] The rule for infringement of personality rights does not apply to cases of infringement of IP rights, the damage arising from a misleading prospectus is situated differently from the damage caused by a mistake in a legal opinion. This is supported in the case law and literature by pointing out that each tort has its specific fact pattern, which determines the relevant loci.[39] Again, a parallel can be found here as regards the territoriality principle in criminal law. But whereas the

34 Case C-21/76 *Bier v Mines de Potasse d'Alsace* ECLI:EU:C:1976:166.

35 Case C-68/93 *Shevill* ECLI:EU:C:1995:61 and Case C-509/09 *eDate* ECLI:EU:C:2011:685.

36 Ulrich Magnus and Peter Mankowksi (eds), *European Commentaries on Private International Law, Brussels I Regulation* (2nd edn, Sellier 2012) art 5 para 203 ff; Ulrich Magnus and Peter Mankowksi (eds), *European Commentaries on Private International Law, Brussels I bis Regulation* (Sellier 2016) art 7 para 251 ff.

37 Admittedly, there is no universal interpretation of the concept in criminal law either. See for the Netherlands H D Wolswijk, *Locus delicti en rechtsmacht* (Gouda Quint and Willem Pompe Instituut voor Strafrechtswetenschappen 1998) 91 and 108 ff.

38 Magnus and Mankowski, *European Commentaries on Private International Law, Brussels I Regulation* (n 36) art 5 para 222 and para 233. Magnus and Mankowski, *European Commentaries on Private International Law, Brussels I bis Regulation* (n 36) art 7 para 295.

39 In the *Kolassa* Case (C-375/13, ECLI: ECLI:EU:C:2015:37, para 47) the CJEU refers to 'the elements that constitute liability'. Magnus and Mankowski link the location of the tort to the interest protected under law. However, Andrew Dickinson (*The Rome II Regulation* (OUP 2008) 310, para 4.29) emphasises that 'damage' under Brussels I is an autonomous concept and hence cannot be linked to the interests protected under national law.

constituent elements of the crime play an important role in the localisation thereof, the specific elements of each tort do not seem to play a similar role in localising the delict.

The basic requirements of tortious liability consist of a tortious act, damage and causation. Causation as such is not used as a connecting factor for establishing jurisdiction, but the act and the damage are. The *locus actus* or *Handlungsort* refers to the place where the alleged perpetrator of the tortious act engaged in the activity (or lack thereof), which is claimed to be a relevant cause of the damage sustained.[40] The concept is less ambiguous than the place of the damage (see below), but does nevertheless raise some questions.[41] One question is whether torts have a single *locus actus* or may have multiple relevant *loci*. Mankowski maintains that all contributory acts are relevant acts for the assessment of the *locus actus*. However, in the case law of the CJEU in most cases the court identifies one relevant *locus* for the tort in question—often by selecting the relevant act first. For example, in case of product liability the relevant *locus actus* of the manufacturer is the place of production of the defective goods and not the place where these are put on the market.[42] For directors' liability towards third parties the relevant *locus* is the place where the company that has not been administered properly is established and economically active rather than the place from which the directors actually operate.[43] For unlawful publications and advertising on the internet, the relevant place is the place where the publication was conceived, rather than the place of uploading or the targeted audience.[44] Cartels are 'committed' in the place (or places) were the competitors enter into the illegal agreement rather than on the market they distort.[45] When several constitutive or contributory acts are performed by different people, however, the courts will have to distinguish between the several defendants: the *locus actus* of one perpetrator

40 Compare the difference between the physical act and the violation of the protected good (*rechtsgoedschending*) in criminal law: see Wolswijk (n 37) 99. article 7(2) also applies to potential future torts. This aspect of the rule will not be discussed here.

41 In 2012, Mankowski (n 36) writes that the concept 'has not generated judgments dealing with complicated matters or even stirred a major discussion in legal writing' (para 214). This sentence has been omitted from the 2016 edition (para 263). There are several instances of liability—especially in complex corporate settings, in which the court will have to identify the relevant act or acts before being able to decide on its location. See e.g. Case C-147/12 *ÖFAB* ECLI:EU:C:2013:490, para 53.

42 Case C-45/13 *Kainz v Pantherwerke* ECLI:EU:C:2014:7.

43 Case C-147/12 *ÖFAB* ECLI:EU:C:2013:490—the court is not entirely clear whether this place constitutes the *locus actus* or the *locus damni*.

44 It is further assumed that an infringing publication is conceived in the place of establishment of the user/publisher: Case C-68/93 *Shevill* ECLI:EU:C:1995:61 para 24; Case C-509/09 *e-Date* ECLI:EU:C:2011:685; Case C-523/10 *Wintersteiger* ECLI:EU:C:2012:220, paras 34 and 37; Opinion AG Jääskinen in Case C-170/12 *Pinckney* ECLI:EU:C:2013:400, para 57.

45 Case C-352/1 *CDC Hydrogen Peroxide* ECLI:EU:C:2015:335.

does not create jurisdiction over co-perpetrators or accomplices who have not acted within the same forum.[46]

The place of the damage (*locus damni* or *Erfolgsort*) refers to the place where the direct damage is sustained by the direct victim.[47] The fact that a French mother company-owner of a German subsidiary sustains financial losses when a German bank wrongfully cancels a bank loan which is crucial to the financial viability of the German subsidiary does not create a *locus damni* at the domicile of the mother company. The primary damage was sustained by the subsidiary and is located in Germany. Similarly, a fatal accident in Italy does not cause direct damage to the bereaved family in Romania, even if the bereaved in question have an independent claim against the tortfeasor under national law. All primary damage was sustained in Italy.[48] Accordingly, not all damages suffered as a result of a tortious act qualify for creating a *locus damni*.

A heated debate is currently raging as to the relevance and location of pure financial loss for jurisdictional purposes. In the 2015 *Kolassa* case, the CJEU located the loss resulting from prospectus liability with regard to financial products in the bank account which the victim held in his home state. In the earlier *Kronhofer* case, however, the bank account from which the investor initially transferred money to a foreign investment account was not relevant for jurisdiction purposes—the loss incurred in a call-options transaction was deemed to have fallen at the foreign account. In the 2015 *CDC* peroxide cartel case, the relevant damage caused by a cartel was deemed to be the surcharge paid by the customers (or any customers further down the chain). This damage is consequently located in the place of establishment of the client companies. In contrast, in the *Universal Music* case, which

46 See Case C-228/11 *Melzer* ECLI:EU:C:2013:305 (fraudulent investment/embezzlement, intermediary in Germany, investment vehicle in England); Case C-387/12 *Hi Hotel* ECLI:EU:C:2014:215 (breach of copyright in Germany resulting from unauthorised handing over of copyrighted materials in France); Case C-360/12 *Coty* ECLI:EU:C:2014:1318 (sale and resale of counterfeit perfumes) '*wechselseitige Handlungsortzurechnung*'. Contrary to Magnus and Mankowski, *European Commentaries on Private International Law, Brussels I Regulation* (n 36) art 5 para 221 and Magnus and Mankowski, *European Commentaries on Private International Law, Brussels I bis Regulation* (n 36) art 7 para 282. It should be noted, however, that the court stipulates that in the cases before it a single claim has been filed against a perpetrator who has not acted within the forum. In case of multiple defendants, the claimant may sue all 'co-perpetrators' in the domicile of one of them. Moreover, when the *locus damni* of all those actions does coincide, this creates another option for the joinder of claims—see *Hi Hotel*, para 33ff, *Coty*, para 52ff. Accordingly, the regulation does allow for concentration of proceedings, albeit not in the dispersed places in which the defendants acted. For criminal law jurisdiction over multiple perpetrators, see Wolswijk (n 37) 193 ff, in particular 199 and 203–05.

47 Case C-220/88 *Dumez* ECLI:EU:C:1990:8; Case C-364/93 *Marinari* ECLI:EU:C:1995:289; Case C-168/02 *Kronhofer* ECLI:EU:C:2004:364.

48 Case C-350/14 *Lazar* ECLI:EU:C:2015:802 (judgment given in the context of the Rome I Regulation on applicable law).

concerned a mistake with regard to a price calculation in the context of contract negotiations, the place of establishment of the legal entity suffering the damage was deemed to be irrelevant for jurisdiction purposes. The CJEU located the damage in the country where the loss caused by the wrong price calculation became irreversible, rather than the location of the account from which the price was eventually paid. The court explicitly stated that financial loss was in itself insufficient to create jurisdiction in the circumstance of the particular case.

The *Kolassa* and *CDC* cases suggest that the place of establishment of the victim might be a relevant factor for determining the location of pure financial loss, at least for certain market-related torts. Interestingly enough, in both these cases the market affected by the tortious acts was not relevant for jurisdiction purposes: it was neither *locus actus* nor *locus damni*. This stands in stark contrast with public law, where effects on the market are the main justification for assuming jurisdiction over market behaviour. Moreover, by using a largely financial concept of 'damage' the CJEU seems to ignore the impact on the legal order of the torts concerned as a relevant connecting factor.[49]

A single act may result in widespread damage, e.g. in the case of defamation or copyright infringements through the internet. In case damage is done by one person to one other person in multiple jurisdictions, each court where damage is sustained may assume jurisdiction over the tort, but this jurisdiction covers local damage only—this is referred to as the mosaic principle.[50] If there are multiple victims, as in the *CDC* cartel damage case, the place of the damage has to be assessed for each victim individually.

This very succinct overview of the case law on the *locus delicti* demonstrates that, although the term *locus delicti* suggests a close similarity to concepts of criminal law, the jurisdictional base operating under that term in the Brussels I bis Regulation is not an adequate starting point for autonomous interpretation of the related concept in criminal law. Admittedly, both distinguish according to the characteristics of the tort or crime concerned and both apply the ubiquity principle. Also, the problems encountered in further defining the *locus delicti* show a remarkable overlap. But this is where the parallel ends. Upon closer scrutiny, ubiquity is interpreted much more

49 For a principled critique of the *Kolassa* judgment see *inter alia* Matthias Lehmann, 'Prospectus Liability and Private International Law: Assessing the Landscape after the CJEU's Kolassa Ruling (Case C-375/13)' [2016] Journal of Private International Law 318 ff. See for a more market oriented approach to the *locus delicti* Case C-167/00 *VKI v Henkel* ECLI:EU:C:2002:555, para 42, in which the tort was deemed to consist of the 'undermining of legal stability by the use of unfair terms'. See also Case C-191/15 *VKI v Amazon* ECLI:EU:C:2016:612.

50 Case C-68/93 *Shevill*; a slight variation of this rule is applied in online defamation cases; see Joined Cases C-509/09 *e-Date* and C-161/10 *Martinez*.

narrowly in civil law than it is in criminal law.[51] In other aspects too the jurisdiction given to the *locus delicti* is more narrowly construed.

The narrow interpretation given to the *locus delicti* concept in civil law fits well into the larger framework of the Brussels I Regulations. Jurisdiction under Article 7 Brussels I bis constitutes a deviation from the main rule of Article 4, which grants general jurisdiction to the country of domicile of the defendant. Accordingly, the provisions of Article 7 have to be interpreted restrictively and should not be stretched beyond their purpose. This is in radical opposition to criminal law, in which territorial jurisdiction is the most basic—and under Model 3 the only remaining—ground of jurisdiction. All in all, this leads to the conclusion that the body of case law on the *locus delicti* in civil law is not a good starting point for the interpretation of the same concept in criminal law.

Moreover, the long road to clarity travelled there might be a warning sign for those who would favour the use of an autonomous concept in Model 3. Jurisdiction at the *locus delicti* was introduced in the Brussels Convention of 1968. In 2012 the authors of the commentary on Brussels I edited by Magnus and Mankowski took positions on its interpretation which were based on an extensive review of literature and both European and national case law. Yet on several points their interpretation of the provision has since then been falsified by the case law of the CJEU.[52] Differences concern such diverse issues as the localisation of the act of deception, the place of damage in case of pure financial loss, and the relevance of the localisation of contributing acts for determining the *locus delicti*. This means that it can take many years and many referrals to the CJEU before the concepts achieve a modicum of clarity. Especially in criminal law, where predictability has a constitutional character,[53] this seems to pose a contra-indication to autonomous interpretation of the concept of territoriality Unless, of course, the concept is already far more developed in the text of the instrument itself.

In short, the case law on the *locus delicti* in private international law demonstrates the difficulty of reaching a common understanding of the concept at the European level. Given the different role of the concept in civil procedure—as an alternative only—the interpretation thereof in private international law cannot be transposed to the area of criminal law. The long road to clarity seems a contraindication for autonomous interpretation, unless the concept is far better specified at EU level.

51 For the criminal law term, see Kai Ambos, *Treatise on International Criminal Law, Volume III: International Criminal Procedure* (OUP 2016) 213 ff and Wolswijk (n 37) 90 ff and 'Locus Delicti and Criminal Jurisdiction' [1999] Netherlands International Law Review 361 ff.

52 Compare the 2012 revised edition on Brussels I with the 2016 edition on Brussels I bis and, in particular, 2012 para 221 versus 2016 para 282; 2012 227a versus 2016 paras 308–09.

53 See on choice of forum as an element of legality Luchtman (n 1) 21 ff and Böse (n 1) 79–80.

VI. *LIS PENDENS* AND RELATED ACTIONS—DEALING WITH PARALLEL PROCEEDINGS UNDER BRUSSELS I BIS

The core of the ELI proposal is its attempt to deal with situations in which authorities in more than one Member State are investigating and prosecuting the same or a related set of facts. This is referred to as 'parallel proceedings'. The simultaneous character of these proceedings brings to mind the private international law concept of '*lis pendens* and related action'. The rules on *lis pendens* and related actions are currently laid down in Articles 29 ff of the Brussels I bis Regulation. Interestingly enough, the current rules cover *lis pendens* and related actions in intra-EU cases as well as cases involving both a court of an EU Member State and a court of a third state, where it is expected that the court of the third state will give a judgment capable of recognition and enforcement in the EU Member State. The provisions for extra-EU cases were introduced at the time of the recast and demonstrate the close link between mutual recognition and *lis pendens* (preamble 23).

The rules on *lis pendens* and related actions in the Brussels I Regulations serve a double function. They mainly aim to prevent irreconcilable judgments but can also—to some extent—be used to further the proper administration of justice.

The *lis pendens* provisions (Articles 29 and 33) apply when proceedings involving the same cause of action and between the same parties are brought in the courts of different Member States. The rule for intra-EU cases is a hard and fast one: when *lis pendens* is established, the court last seised must stay the proceedings and decline jurisdiction as soon as the jurisdiction of the court first seised is established. There is no discretion for the judge, the order of preference being based on timing only. The advantages of this rule are ease of use and legal certainty. The major drawback is its rigidity: it does not allow the courts to take the proper administration of justice into account and transfer the case to the court best suited to deal with it. It also induces a race to the court: parties accused of committing a tort may start proceedings in the court best suited to their strategies[54] and demand a declaration of non-liability, thereby blocking the aggrieved party from effectively filing suit elsewhere. This kind of pre-emptive strikes are known as 'torpedo actions' and may severely harm the interests of tort victims. The fear of a race to court may also frustrate mediation attempts and other consensual manners of dispute resolution. And lastly, the first across the line rule could until recently also frustrate a choice of forum made by the parties themselves. Even when the parties to a contract had given exclusive jurisdiction to the courts of country X, a torpedo action in the courts in country Y could still be effective as the chosen court would have to wait for the court first seised

54 Some courts are chosen simply for being slow in rendering judgment. Even when the court seised is blatantly not competent to deal with the case, the rule will still operate.

to decline jurisdiction.[55] This latter rule was reversed in the recast of the Brussels I Regulation: the current rules give precedence to a court designated by the parties over another court seised in contravention thereof, regardless of timing.

The provision on related actions of Article 30 can be used whenever related actions are pending in different Member States. The rule on related actions states that any other courts than the court first seised may stay the proceedings and, when both proceedings are pending in first instance, even refer the case to the first court.[56] Actions are deemed to be related where they are so closely connected that it is expedient to hear and determine them together to avoid the risk of irreconcilable judgments. This 'definition' combines *ne bis in idem* arguments with the search for the proper administration of justice.

The provision does not specify when or why the other courts should or should not stay proceedings. It does make clear, however, that the court first seised may not decline jurisdiction and/or transfer the case.

As mentioned above, the existence of irreconcilable judgments may hamper mutual recognition. In the rules pertaining to recognition of judgments, the order is largely determined by the date of the judgment.[57] For the rules on *lis pendens* and related actions, the crucial date is the date on which a case is 'pending'. Member States have different national traditions with regard to this concept (is discovery part of the trial or rather a pre-trial action; is the relevant element the notification to the defendant or the registration at the court?). This decreased the predictability and clarity of the rule under the convention and the original regulation. The recast addresses the issue by giving some specifications in Article 32, which seeks to combine the different ways of starting civil proceedings that prevail in the Member States.

The new rules on identical and related actions pending in non-EU courts are more flexible than the ones for intra-EU cases. The focus is on the proper administration of justice. When deciding on whether or not to stay or terminate proceedings before them, the EU courts should take account of all the circumstances of the case. This check includes an appraisal of the connections between the facts of the case and the parties and the third state concerned. Special weight is given to claims of exclusivity of the third state's jurisdiction—at least in cases in which EU courts would have exclusive jurisdiction in the reverse situation.[58] Other elements to be taken into consideration are the stage of the proceedings and the likelihood of the foreign court giving judgment within a reasonable time.

55 Case C-116/02 *Gasser* ECLI:EU:C:2003:657.

56 Only if that court also has jurisdiction over the case to be referred. Referral as such does not create jurisdiction.

57 In Brussels I bis, the decisions of the forum state prevail over foreign judgments.

58 Preamble 23 and 24.

In all cases, the decision to stay the proceedings or even decline jurisdiction is taken unilaterally by the court declining jurisdiction. There is no duty to consult or cooperate in any of the provisions of Brussels I bis. The Commission proposal included such a duty in the specific circumstance of a case being pending on the merits in one Member State, while a provisional measure was being requested in another. However, this provision did not make it into the adopted text.[59] Another proposal which was not included in the final text was the introduction of a time limit in which the court first seised should decide on its jurisdiction.[60] This effort to counter torpedo actions has lost part of its relevance, but not all, through the rule which gives precedence to the court chosen by the parties.

VII. PARALLEL PROCEEDINGS IN CIVIL AND CRIMINAL LAW—SIMILARITIES AND DIFFERENCES

Any rule on *lis pendens* brings about the need for a definition of both the identity of the case and the moment it is deemed to be pending. The project rightfully dedicates ample attention to this issue in its provisions. It uses the term 'parallel proceedings' for what in private law would amount to *lis pendens*, whereas the term 'multiple proceedings' is used to designate related actions. It is interesting to note that the concept of multiple proceedings is wider than the private law concept of related actions. Whereas the latter still refers to the need to avoid irreconcilable judgments, the rule on multiple proceedings explicitly applies in cases in which *ne bis in idem* cannot arise, but concentration is nevertheless advisable for reasons of the proper administration of justice or the interest of the accused.

An important decision in any rule on *lis pendens* is to define the moment in which cases become pending for the application of the rule. In civil law, this is the moment the case is brought before a court. This moment is further specified in Article 32 of the Brussel I bis Regulation. As mentioned above, this restriction to the trial stage of a dispute (in combination with the priority rule based on timing) has the disadvantage of creating disincentives for extra-judicial conflict resolution. For criminal law purposes, such a restriction would not do justice to the fact that, even in the investigation stage, *ne bis in idem* may be created. Accordingly, a broader definition is needed there. The legislative proposal includes 'proceedings about to be conducted' in the definition of both parallel and multiple proceedings. This term also covers the investigation stage. However, the proposal largely wants to avoid parallel prosecutions, stipulating that parallel investigations may be useful and needed. This still leads to a lack of clarity as to the exact duties of the authorities in case of ongoing investigations.

59 COM(2010) 748, art 31.

60 ibid art 29(2).

Once a situation of *lis pendens* (or related actions) is established, the rule should specify the effect on the jurisdiction of the courts or authorities involved. Under Brussels I bis, there is an obligation to dismiss in cases of *lis pendens* in the EU and an option to desist in cases of related actions or *lis pendens* involving third states. The possibility of declining jurisdiction is an important effect in civil cases as civil courts—as a rule—may not refuse to exercise the international jurisdiction granted to them under the regulation. In criminal law, however, prosecutors may have discretion to prosecute or not. In that case, the dominant effect of a binding *lis pendens* rule would be the duty to abstain from (further) acts of prosecution and/or acts creating *ne bis in idem*. This result, however, is only firmly prescribed where consensus or some other type of binding decision is reached on the exercise of jurisdiction. The explanatory note to Article 8 of model 1 stipulates that:

> in case of parallel proceedings, and where appropriate, in case of multiple proceedings, the consensus should be achieved before any of the authorities takes the case to court or takes other measures with the effect of finally disposing of the case. It is, however, not prohibited for both national authorities to go ahead with parallel proceedings even though this may eventually trigger and produce the ne bis in idem principle.

This means that the authorities may still finally dispose of the case before the end of the consultation phase. This shifts the focus of the instrument from the prevention of improper *ne bis in idem* to the prevention of parallel prosecution.

Finally, a *lis pendens* rule needs an order of priority. In the original Brussels Convention, priority was based on timing only. This rigid rule led to type of abuse referred to as torpedo actions and induced a race to the courts. The current text of the Brussels I Regulation deviates from this rule in two situations. First, in intra-EU cases, priority is given to the court designated in a choice of forum agreement. This is a strict priority rule, favouring one ground of jurisdiction over all others. The second deviation is to be found in the rules on *lis pendens* and related actions involving third country courts. In the latter case, the provisions contain a set of considerations to be taken into account in the decision to defer or not—the main arguments being related to the prevention of conflicting judgments, the proper administration of justice, and the right to trial within a reasonable time. The ELI proposal largely uses this third model of establishing priority. This avoids the pitfalls of the Brussels I model, but increases the need to consult both the other authorities and the parties involved.

In all cases covered by the Brussels I bis Regulation, the decision to suspend or terminate the procedure is taken unilaterally by the court involved: there is no previous consultation of the court given priority. As the contribution of Ortolani explains, another EU Regulation (Brussels II bis) does contain a consultation mechanism in which a court seised of an action may refer the case to another court which is better placed to deal with the issue. This *forum non conveniens* rule is not restricted to cases of *lis pendens* and can only be used if one of the parties either requests or consents to the referral. The two courts involved are supposed to work in cooperation to effectuate the transfer. This latter mechanism of coordination and cooperation seems to be the current state of the art in criminal law—a main difference being that in criminal law no consent of the parties is needed. It should be noted, however, that the model used in private international law is less complicated than the one used in criminal law, as the parties involved in the conflict would already be aware of the cases pending.[61] So, no information duty has to be introduced here, and any objections to the decision of the court to transfer the case would be a judgment under the relevant rules of appeal.

In short, there are good reasons for not adopting the Brussels I model of *lis pendens*. The Brussel I model is rigid and open to abuse through so-called torpedo actions started with the purpose of frustrating litigation elsewhere. Its rigidity may lead to a race to court, thereby frustrating attempts to reach a consensual solution. And the court being granted priority might not be the court best placed to deal with the case.[62] The *ne bis in idem* principle as it is currently applied by the CJEU copies much of the drawbacks of the Brussels I system of *lis pendens*. Although the situation in criminal law is different from the situation in civil law, inter alia because the decision to open a prosecution is often the prerogative of the state, the current proposal is wisely trying to reverse this situation. Interestingly, the model used in criminal law is more akin to the Brussels I rules on parallel proceedings involving third states than to the *lis pendens* rules for intra-EU cases. The discretion afforded to the authorities in these latter models offer the benefit of justice in the individual case, and the drawback of legal uncertainty for the individuals and authorities concerned.

61 Save in cases on imperfect notification.

62 In the recast the general rule was maintained, but an exception was made for *lis pendens* in the presence of a choice of forum by the parties: in that case the chosen forum is prioritised, independent of the time factor.

9

CHOICE OF FORUM, EUROPEAN CITIZENSHIP, AND FUNDAMENTAL RIGHTS

The Position of the Defendant

MICHIEL LUCHTMAN

I. INTRODUCTION

The Court of Justice has stated that 'the founding treaties of the EU, unlike ordinary international treaties, established a new legal order, possessing its own institutions, for the benefit of which the Member States thereof have limited their sovereign rights, in ever wider fields, and the subjects of which comprise not only those States but also their nationals'.[1] The wording highlights the differences between the European legal order (the European Union (EU) and its Member States) and the international legal order. Whereas international law is regarded as a matter between states, the Court's characterisation of the European Union expressly makes room for individuals, EU citizens to be more precise. In line with this, Article 3(2) of the Treaty on European Union (TEU) states that the EU shall offer its citizens an area of freedom, security and justice without internal frontiers, in which the free movement of persons is ensured in conjunction with appropriate measures with respect to external border controls, asylum, immigration, and the prevention and combating of crime.

It is in light of this that the question arises to which extent the concept of EU citizenship has added value in relation to conflicts of jurisdiction. Does an integrated (EU) legal order with citizens' rights make a difference ('from conflicts of jurisdiction to choice of forum')? What is the role, and what are the rights, of the defendant, taking into account the European Convention on Human Rights (ECHR) and the European Union Charter of Fundamental Rights (EUCFR)? Is

1 Court of Justice EU, Opinion 2/13 of 18 December 2014 on the Accession of the European Union to the European Convention for the Protection of Human Rights and Fundamental Freedoms, para 157.

there a need for judicial review or 'justiciability'? This contribution aims to address these issues.[2]

In the following, I will explore the relationship between EU citizenship, fundamental rights, and forum choices. The goal is to identify what requirements follow from the Charter (and the ECHR) in relation to such choices. To date, there is little to work with. With the exception of Articles 45 CFR (free movement) and 50 CFR (*ne bis in idem*), none of the articles and principles of the Charter has an explicit transnational scope. In the following sections, I will first discuss conflicts of jurisdiction and choice of forum in relation to the framework for transnational cooperation in criminal matters (section II). After that, I will explore the concept of citizenship in relation to choice of forum (section III) and try to establish the link between citizenship, choice of forum, and fundamental rights (section IV). I will conclude with some observations (section V). Throughout the chapter, I aim to link my analysis to the findings and models of the entire research group of this project and will define choices of forum as the decision of the competent authorities on which EU state investigates, prosecutes, and tries alleged offences. The stage of the execution is not the focus of this contribution, although some references are made to it.

Before I start, a caveat is appropriate. In line with the overall design of the research group, this chapter seeks to explore if and to what extent the concept of EU citizenship can offer a vehicle for extending the protection of these rights beyond the state borders. Although the position of EU citizens is therefore this chapter's focus, warranted particularly in light of the Treaties and the above-mentioned position of the Court of Justice, a citizenship approach is likely to raise (at least) one point of criticism. The fundamental rights that are addressed in this contribution are—at least in the setting of national criminal justice—human rights, not citizenship rights.[3] It is one of the great achievements of the ECHR that it has extended the scope of human rights protection in the area of criminal justice beyond (national) citizenship to anyone present on the territory of a state party to the Convention.[4]

2 Many of the ideas advanced here have already been published in earlier work (and are now updated), most notably Michiel Luchtman, 'Choice of Forum in an Area of Freedom, Security and Justice' (2011) 7(1) *Utrecht Law Review* 74; Michiel Luchtman (ed), *Choice of Forum in Cooperation Against EU Financial Crime—Freedom, Security and Justice and the Protection of Specific EU-interests* (Boom/Lemma 2013); Michiel Luchtman, 'Towards a Transnational Application of the Equality Principle in the EU's Area of Freedom, Security and Justice?' (2013) 9(4) *Utrecht Law Review* 11; Michiel Luchtman, 'Principles of European Criminal Law: Jurisdiction, Choice of Forum, and the Legality Principle in the Area of Freedom, Security and Justice' [2012] *European Review of Private Law* 347–80.

3 On the differences between human rights, citizenship rights, and fundamental rights, see Ernst Hirsch Ballin, *Citizens' Rights and the Right to Be a Citizen* (Brill Nijhoff 2014) 6 ff, 74–76.

4 That being said, the European Court of Human Rights (ECtHR) uses the concept of the citizen and the individual interchangeably, for instance in its definition of the concept of law; cf. *Sunday Times v United Kingdom* App no 6538/74 (ECtHR, 26 April 1979) para 49: 'a norm cannot be

If EU citizenship is thus understood in its legal-technical meaning, an approach that strictly connects fundamental rights protection to the status of EU citizenship can be perceived as excluding third-country nationals from such protection.[5] But why would we introduce such a distinction between different categories of individuals in transnational criminal justice? That is why I propose to take the concept of EU citizenship not too literally, that is, not in its technical legal sense. I propose a wider interpretation of the narrative of European or transnational citizenship,[6] that is, one not connected to the narrow, legal concept of EU citizenship as it stands now, but to the transnational free movement of persons, the 'transnational emancipation' of individuals resulting from it and the way in which the EU has facilitated these processes.[7]

II. CHOICE OF FORUM AND EU COOPERATION IN CRIMINAL MATTERS

The agenda of the European Union in relation to conflicts of jurisdiction or, as a more encompassing concept, choice of forum does not appear to be particularly innovative.[8] With the important exceptions of Eurojust and the framework on the transnational *ne bis in idem* rules, the EU has followed a more or less traditional approach, the roots of which are firmly established in the law on international cooperation in criminal matters. The focus has been mainly on improving cooperation,[9] and on expanding and harmonising claims of jurisdiction for certain types of crime.[10] The response of the EU and its states may therefore be termed rather cautious (if one is friendly) or reluctant (if one is less friendly), relying mostly on the

regarded as a 'law' unless it is formulated with sufficient precision to enable the citizen to regulate his conduct'.

5 On this, see Hanneke van Eijken, *European Citizenship & the Constitutionalisation of the European Union* (Europa Law Publishing 2014).

6 Cf. Peter Kivisto and Thomas Faist, *Citizenship: Discourse, Theory and Transnational Prospects* (Blackwell 2007).

7 Some support for this is found in the wording of art 3(2) TEU and, particularly, the Court's case law on art 54 CISA, in which it connects its innovative, transnational interpretation of the *ne bis in idem* principle to free movement of persons; therefore, by implication, not only to EU citizens; see Joined Cases C-187/01 and C-385/01 *Gözütok and Brügge* [2003] ECR I-1345, paras 36, 38.

8 I consider the latter to be the broader concept as it implies that there may be other reasons for dealing with decisions on in which state(s) to start investigations, prosecutions, the trial stage, or the execution of sanctions than only (positive or negative) conflicts between prosecutors. Obviously, those reasons may include the interests of EU citizens.

9 Obviously, the concept of mutual recognition as such is innovating, but not the way in which mutual recognition instruments deal with conflicts of jurisdiction.

10 See, inter alia, Andé Klip, *European Criminal Law—An Integrative Approach* (Intersentia 2016), for an overview.

authorities 'on the ground' and on how they deal with the discretion they have. I will illustrate this point below by a brief examination of the relevant instruments. My main goal will be to illustrate how these discretionary margins have come to exist in the current framework, after which I will address the issue of how these margins could harm the interests of EU citizens, also where no conflicts between prosecutors exist (sections III and IV).

Before I do so, I wish to make another observation. Particularly in the 1970s, the framework of the Council of Europe has been innovative in shifting the focus from the law on transnational cooperation as a matter between states to transnational cooperation as a matter in which the defendant (much less the victim) plays an important role as well. New instruments, such as the transfer of the execution of sanctions, as well as the transfer of proceedings, were introduced in the first place because of the adverse consequences of an ever-increasing amount of conflicts of jurisdiction to which the laws of jurisdiction, extradition, and mutual legal assistance (MLA) offered no satisfying answers. But they had a second goal as well. The new option of transferring the responsibility for the criminal trial from one state to another was also warranted by a stronger focus on the re-integration of offenders in their home state,[11] or—in more general terms—the proper administration of justice in transnational cases. The European Court of Human Rights has often pointed to this in its case law on the relevant instruments, stressing that particularly these newer instruments promote 'the current trend towards strengthening international cooperation in the administration of justice, a trend which is in principle in the interests of the persons concerned'.[12] This second rationale of the new instruments is best illustrated by the 1983 Convention on the Transfer of Sentenced Persons,[13] which makes transfer of the execution of sanctions dependent, as a rule, on the consent of the sentenced person. Swart has argued that a similar approach might also serve as a solution in cases of transfers of proceedings.[14] One of his main arguments for that was that the requirement of consent gives *standing* to the accused in international criminal law cooperation and ensures that the proper administration of justice is not only in the hands of the prosecutors. The latter would be at odds with such concepts as the *gesetzlicher Richter* or *giudice naturale*.

11 Albertus H. J. Swart, 'De overdracht van strafvervolgingen' [1982] *Nederlands Juristenblad* 209; C. F. Rüter and Albertus H. J. Swart, 'De toepasselijkheid van de Nederlandse strafwet; van locus delicti naar goede rechtsbedeling' in Jeppe P. Balkema et al (eds), *Gedenkboek honderd jaar Wetboek van Strafrecht* (Gouda Quint 1983); Albertus H. J. Swart, *Goede rechtsbedeling en internationale rechtshulp in strafzaken* (Kluwer 1983) (all in Dutch).

12 *Drozd & Janousek v France and Spain* App no 12747/87 (ECtHR, 26 June 1992) para 110.

13 ETS 112.

14 Swart, *Goede rechtsbedeling en internationale rechtshulp in strafzaken* (n 11).

Recent instruments in the EU, however, clearly deviate from that evolution. FD 2008/909/JHA on the application of the principle of mutual recognition to custodial sanctions has significantly reduced the scope of the requirement of consent.[15] It is also a telling sign that a specific instrument on the transfer of proceedings was never enacted into law.[16] The proposed instrument more or less followed the approach of the 1972 European Convention on the Transfer of Proceedings in Criminal Matters,[17] but particularly the concept of secondary jurisdiction, that is, jurisdiction based on a combination of the rules in the proposed framework decision and primary jurisdiction rules of other Member States, proved untenable for a number of Member States.

Therefore, requiring the consent of the accused in forum choices has clearly not been an option for the EU legislator. But how are the interests of the defendant then taken into account in the EU framework for forum choices? Keeping the foregoing observations in mind, the EU framework on choice of forum is best described by focusing on the harmonisation of the rules of jurisdiction, the grounds for refusal in cooperation schemes and the specific rules on conflicts of jurisdiction in the relevant instruments.

A. Jurisdiction

There is an increasing number of EU instruments, based on Article 82(2) and (3) TFEU, in which Member States are obliged to define the territorial reach of their criminal laws beyond national boundaries. Those instruments typically not only introduce the territoriality principle as a jurisdictional principle, but also the active personality principle. Other instruments have moreover introduced variations on the principle of *aut dedere, aut judicare*, and the protection principle, whereas more recent directives also make way for the, in light of foreseeability of the law, controversial principle of passive personality.[18]

This seemingly ever-increasing expansion of the reach of national criminal laws has been a deliberate choice, for good reasons. It was motivated primarily by the ambition to prevent criminals from escaping justice. To that extent, overlapping claims of jurisdiction are created deliberately by the EU legislator to create a network of criminal justice systems (*Netzgedanke*). Overlapping competences may facilitate

15 See art 6(2) of that Framework decision.

16 Draft Council Framework decision on the transfer of proceedings in criminal matters, Council Document 11119/09 of 30 June 2009, which has been altered substantively during later negotiations; see Council documents 13504/09 COPEN 173 of 21 September 2009; 14133/09 COPEN 191 of 7 October 2009; and 16437/1/09 Rev 1 COPEN 231 of 26 November 2009. For the Explanatory Report, see Council Document 11119/09 Copen 115 Add 1.

17 ETS 073.

18 Cf. art 10(2) Directive 2011/36/EU on preventing and combating trafficking in human beings and protecting its victims [2011] OJ L101/1.

transnational cooperation, and on occasion allow certain Member States to correct incompetence or inactivity by authorities of other states. Networks of national authorities, certainly once facilitated by such institutions as Eurojust, inevitably also play a role in mutual convergence and in the development of a truly transnational legal area. Yet, from a citizens' perspective, there are also clear disadvantages. Those are related to the foreseeability of the applicable law (including contradictory national criminal policies and/or to the multiplication of the burden of criminal proceedings). I will come back to that later.

B. Refusal grounds in cooperation instruments

Overlapping jurisdictional reach inherently increases the risk of conflicts of jurisdiction. In turn, this may harm transnational cooperation. Cooperation instruments increasingly include refusal grounds to protect national interests in cases of conflicts. Compared to the situation in international criminal law, many instruments of mutual recognition (quite paradoxically) even contain more refusal grounds than their predecessors of the Council of Europe. This is because they are modelled after previous instruments of mutual recognition (particularly the Framework Decision on the European arrest warrant (FD EAW)). Refusal grounds of extradition law are now also introduced in other areas of cooperation, where they previously did not exist. In my opinion, the majority of these refusal grounds either serve the goal of inter-state confidence-building, or the interests of *nation* states, *national* citizens, and/or *national* territory. I do not think this is a coincidence. Ultimately, the existence of public authority over a certain population on a certain territory is what defines a sovereign state under public international law. It does, however, leave us with the question of how the interests of citizens, as defendants, are integrated into the framework.

The requirement of double criminality is the most well-known example of how the interests of state *authority* are protected within the mutual recognition framework. Clearly, this requirement is at odds with the concept of mutual recognition as such. Not surprisingly, the Commission originally proposed to reduce significantly the scope of this pillar of extradition law,[19] but those attempts failed, as a result of which the so-called list offences were introduced, even in areas where they previously did not exist. The requirement of double criminality even made a surprising comeback in the instruments that were adopted shortly before the Treaty of Lisbon entered into force.[20] Other good examples are, of course, those refusal grounds that

19 See COM(2001) 522, 16, 37: 'The principle of double criminal liability is abolished.'

20 FD 2008/909/JHA allows Member States to reintroduce the condition of double criminality. The Netherlands, for instance, have made use of this possibility.

allow national authorities to refuse (or postpone) the execution of foreign judicial warrants, because national investigations are also ongoing.[21]

Similar observations can be made with respect to the *individual* who may be subjected to all sorts of investigative measures. In my opinion, there is clear tendency in a number of framework decisions, particularly those that imply the use of custodial measures, to allow Member States to differentiate between national citizens and citizens of other Member States (or third country nationals). Historically, this connection is perfectly understandable, particularly for those countries which have established strong links between the active personality principle and the prohibition on extraditing nationals, such as Germany. From the perspective of EU law, however, the non-discrimination principle clearly comes into play. In its original proposal on the European arrest warrant (EAW), the European Commission made innovative proposals taking the principle of reintegration (which is closely aligned to the residence of the claimed person), rather than nationality, as an exception to the strict principle of mutual recognition.[22] As is evident from the wording of the FD EAW, this proposal failed. One might say that Member States are still reluctant to assume responsibility for individuals other than their own nationals, also when they are EU citizens.

Finally, the protection of national *territory* has clearly been an interest for Member States in the negotiations on mutual recognition instruments. The so-called territoriality exception allows Member States to protect their criminal policies where conduct is said to have taken place on their territory and does not constitute a criminal offence there. However, this cannot be termed a 'forum rule' as it only blocks cooperation, but does not stop the proceedings in the issuing state.

It is apparent from this brief analysis of the refusal grounds in the mutual recognition instruments that the principle of mutual recognition is limited in many ways. These grounds for refusal often relate to the protection of national interest-driven visions of which state is best placed to protect certain (nationally defined) interests; to that extent, they are expressions of the desire to retain national sovereignty as much as possible. Not only is this a significant barrier to transnational cooperation in the area of freedom, security and justice (AFSJ), but it also allows Member States a tremendous amount of (unilateral) discretion to determine where prosecution is best to take place, *if at all*. The Commission was right to state in 2000 that

> [i]n the absence of a ranking of competent jurisdictions, all one could do would be to foresee a derogation from mutual recognition in cases where the

21 Cf. art 4(2) FD EAW. The EIO has a different, more balanced approach: *postponement* of execution is possible (only) where execution of the EIO would *prejudice* an ongoing investigation; see art 15.

22 COM(2001) 522, 18–19, 39.

> recognising Member State has jurisdiction and does prosecute or had jurisdiction but decided not to take proceedings. This, however, appears like a serious undermining of the principle of mutual recognition.[23]

It turns out this is indeed what happened.

C. Existing mechanisms for dealing with conflicts of jurisdiction

Existing instruments in transnational criminal law cooperation take account of conflicts of jurisdiction in three ways. First, it is to a large extent due to the case law on Articles 54 ff CISA that the issue of conflicts became a prominent issue on the agenda. That case law gave an important impetus to the adoption of FD 2009/948/JHA on prevention and settlement of conflicts of exercise of jurisdiction in criminal proceedings. To many, this framework decision came as a disappointment,[24] now that it essentially only forces national authorities to consult each other in cases of a possible 'bis in idem-situations'. (Only) in those instances, Member States are urged to find 'effective solutions'. The definition of 'effectiveness' is left open. Although it does not exclude a broader definition of the concept, the preamble suggests that the term refers mainly to considerations of cost-efficiency.[25] In any event, the framework decision contains no reference whatsoever to the interests of citizens, nor does it provide them with remedies. Member States cannot be obliged on the basis of this framework decision to start or stall parallel proceedings in the interests of the citizen.

Second, another approach is taken in the Framework decision on combating terrorism and its successor, the new Directive on combating terrorism.[26] Those instruments introduce a number of *jurisdictional criteria* in cases of overlapping competences for the same offences. Article 19 of the new directive reads:

> When an offence falls within the jurisdiction of more than one Member State and when any of the Member States concerned can validly prosecute on the basis of the same facts, the Member States concerned shall cooperate in order to decide which of them will prosecute the offenders with the aim, if possible, of centralising proceedings in a single Member State. To this end, the Member

23 COM(2000) 495, 18.

24 See, for instance, Klip (n 10) 450–55, 533; Jannemieke Ouwerkerk, *Quid Pro Quo—A Comparative Law Perspective on the Mutual Recognition of Judicial Decisions in Criminal Matters* (Intersentia 2011) 275–77; Luchtman, *Choice of Forum in an Area of Freedom, Security and Justice* (n 1) 74–101.

25 Recital 4.

26 Directive (EU) 2017/541 of the European Parliament and of the Council of 15 March 2017 on combating terrorism and replacing Council FD 2002/475/JHA and amending Council Decision 2005/671/JHA [2017] OJ L88/6.

> States may have recourse to Eurojust in order to facilitate cooperation between their judicial authorities and the coordination of their action. Account shall be taken of the following factors: (a) the Member State shall be that in the territory of which the offence was committed; (b) the Member State shall be that of which the offender is a national or resident; (c) the Member State shall be the country of origin of the victims; (d) the Member State shall be that in the territory of which the offender was found.[27]

Finally, there are examples that deal with *cooperation*. They hamper the transfer of suspects or evidence, but do not stop criminal proceedings. It is also important to note that these mechanisms are not motivated (or only implicitly) by the interests of the accused. Article 16 of the FD on the EAW for instance deals with competing EAWs, a situation which occurs not infrequently in judicial practice.[28] That article holds that the executing authority (who is most likely not informed on the merits of the case) must decide which of the European arrest warrants shall be executed 'with due consideration of all the circumstances and especially the relative seriousness and place of the offences, the respective dates of the European arrest warrants and whether the warrant has been issued for the purposes of prosecution or for execution of a custodial sentence or detention order'. And, as I already noted, the exception of territoriality essentially boils down to a quasi-forum rule, to the extent that it allows Member States to refuse cooperation where the conduct took place on their territory and is not a criminal offence there.

We must conclude for now, first of all, that we are left with a complicated picture, in which the interests of the accused do not seem to hold a prominent place on the legislative agenda. The picture is moreover fragmented. Different instruments touch upon the issue in different manners and, consequently, it is difficult to discover an integrated EU approach that consistently ties criminal jurisdiction to mutual recognition and instruments for forum choices. My third conclusion is that, somewhat surprisingly (at least if seen from the perspective of the common goals of the AFSJ), the existing framework leaves national authorities with tremendous discretion to protect national interests, even when this comes at the expense of EU citizens. At this point in time, EU citizens and others are only protected against a second consecutive prosecution for the same offence by the *ne bis in idem*-principle. However important this may be, it cannot be seen as an encompassing answer to the problems individuals may face once confronted (as

27 The factors are the same in both instruments, but whereas art 9(2) of the FD provided that 'sequential' account shall be taken of them, art. 9 of the new Directive drops the 'sequential' and accords equal importance to all specified factors. Other examples are found in Klip (n 10) 454–55.

28 Based on my own experience as a substitute judge in the District Court of Amsterdam, the Netherlands.

defendants) with the possibility of conflicts of jurisdiction, as I will try to demonstrate in the next section.

III. CHOICE OF FORUM AND EUROPEAN CITIZENSHIP

The problems for individuals in relation to conflicts of jurisdiction and forum choices essentially relate to three issues. Current instruments for cooperation, jurisdiction and choice of forum mainly protect the interests of nation states. As a result, first of all, there is a lack of *standing* and fragmented judicial control for the individual. In the second place, a fragmented framework causes problems of the *foreseeability* of the applicable law. Particularly this problem, in my opinion, expands the importance of dealing with conflicts of jurisdiction beyond those conflicts that do actually occur. The mere possibility of conflicts of jurisdiction also creates problems for the individual, in that it may hamper him to regulate his conduct on the basis of a clear legal framework. Finally, a third problem is related to the *double or multiple burdens* of criminal proceedings that will be caused by parallel or consecutive proceedings in multiple states.

These problems are not typical for EU law. They also occur in the context of international law.[29] Why, then, is the situation different in the EU? One answer, which is the focus of this chapter, lies in the goals of the European Union, particularly in Article 3(2) TEU, and in the concept of European citizenship. Citizenship, after all, is originally concerned with the relation between the individual and the polity, creating a status which links the citizen, constitutionally, to that polity.[30] In the words of Marshall, citizenship is a 'status bestowed on those who are full members of a community. All who possess the status are equal with respect to the rights and duties with which the status is endowed'.[31] In the context of criminal justice, citizenship implies that individuals have engaged in a mutual commitment to organise their polity, including through the criminal law but, on the other hand are also protected by that same criminal law, particularly against arbitrary interferences with their fundamental rights.

29 See André Klip, 'The Decrease of Protection under Human Rights Treaties in International Criminal Law' (1997) 68 *Inter'l Rev Penal* 291–310; and most notably Albin Eser, Otto Lagodny, and Christopher L. Blakesley (eds), *The Individual as Subject of International Cooperation in Criminal Matters* (Nomos 2002).

30 Hanneke van Eijken, Jessy Emaus, Michiel Luchtman, and Rob Widdershoven, 'The European Citizen as Bearer of Fundamental Rights in a Multi-Layered Legal Order' in Ton van den Brink, Michiel Luchtman, and Mira Scholten (eds), *Sovereignty in the Shared Legal Order of the EU—Core Values of Regulation and Enforcement* (Intersentia 2015) 249–98; Hirsch Ballin (n 3) 8, 74.

31 Thomas H. Marshall, *Citizenship and Social Class* (CUP 1950 [reprinted 1992]) 18.

The question is how this basic model of criminal justice in relation to fundamental rights and citizenship works out for the transnational setting of the AFSJ. It is true, after all, that nowadays the fundamental rights that are associated closely with criminal justice are regarded as human rights; they apply to all individuals present on the territory of European states that are party to the ECHR.[32] Interferences with their privacy, property, and liberty therefore need a decent legal basis. Criminal offences must also be clearly defined (*nullum crimen, nulla poena sine lege*). And individuals are entitled to a trial by a court, established by law (*nullum judicium sine lege*).[33] The law thus enables individuals to regulate their conduct and to exert control. To that extent, the relationship between those safeguards and the ability of citizens to help shape their polity has been loosened. Hirsch Ballin has noted in this regard that the best way of specifying what citizenship is, is to determine what rights are fundamental but not human rights.[34] He regards the right of every citizen to be protected by his sovereign—including the access to the territory of his or her state—among such citizens' rights.[35] An equivalent to that is found in Article 45 CFR stipulating that every citizen of the Union has the right to move and reside freely within the territory of the Member States. Its corollary is the protection of citizens against the forceful removal from that territory, for instance through extradition.

It is interesting that the Court of Justice recently applied a similar reasoning in the setting of extradition proceedings to Russia with respect to an Estonian national, residing in Latvia. Whereas Latvian nationals would have been protected against extradition because of their nationality (and the corresponding jurisdiction of Latvian authorities on the basis of *aut dedere aut judicare* would have applied to prevent impunity), the Estonian citizen would not receive such protection, although he exercised his rights of free movement as an EU citizen. After having established the applicability of Articles 18 and 21 TEU, the Court noticed a difference in treatment between nationals and other EU citizens and held that the difference in treatment affects the freedom of those citizens to move within the European Union.[36] Although the prevention of impunity is a legitimate justification for that, the Court instructed the authorities to assess whether less intrusive

32 Cf. Alec Stone Sweet, 'A Cosmopolitan Legal Order: Constitutional Pluralism and Rights Adjudication in Europe' [2012] *Journal of Global Constitutionalism* 53–90.

33 Cf. Willem Pompe Instituut, *Gedachten van Willem Pompe over de mens in het strafrecht* (Boom 2008) 13 ff.

34 Hirsch Ballin (n 3) 74.

35 ibid 75–76.

36 Case C-182/15 *Aleksei Petruhhin* ECLI:EU:C:2016:630, para 32.

interferences (in the exercise of the rights of Article 21 TFEU) were available. It held that:

> [i]n the absence of rules of EU law governing extradition between the Member States and a third State, it is necessary, in order to safeguard EU nationals from measures liable to deprive them of the rights of free movement and residence provided for in Article 21 TFEU, while combatting impunity in respect of criminal offences, to apply all the cooperation and mutual assistance mechanisms provided for in the criminal field under EU law. Consequently, . . . the exchange of information with the Member State of which the person concerned is a national must be given priority in order to afford the authorities of that Member State, in so far as they have jurisdiction, pursuant to their national law, to prosecute that person for offences committed outside national territory, the opportunity to issue a European arrest warrant for the purposes of prosecution. Article 1(1) and (2) of FD 2002/584 does not preclude, in such a case, the possibility for the Member State of which the alleged offender is a national of issuing a European arrest warrant with a view to the surrender of that person for the purposes of prosecution.[37]

The case indicates that EU citizens should not be deprived de facto of their rights as EU citizens (particularly free movement) when less intrusive means to avoid impunity are available. Differences in treatment of EU citizens should not unduly deprive them of their free movement rights. Once again, therefore, it has been the principle of non-discrimination in combination with the right to free movement that has removed national obstacles for European citizens (in the technical-legal definition of EU citizenship). But clearly the development of EU citizenship cannot depend only on taking away national obstacles? Specific EU legislation, however, still lacks behind, meaning that EU law is often not in play (and, therefore, neither is the Charter). What is needed then in EU legislation, to protect the interests of citizens? What are these interests? And how can EU legislation—including, particularly, common rules on the choice of forum—protect European citizens against interferences with their rights to free movement within the AFSJ?

In order to realise the potential of European citizenship fully, it is conceivable to interpret the above-mentioned human rights related to criminal justice in light of their transnational setting. Indeed, in one of the few examples where EU legislation is related to choices of forum (Article 54 CISA), the Court of Justice has stressed precisely this. It indicated that Article 54 CISA must be interpreted in light of both

37 ibid paras 47–48.

Article 50 CFR, as well as Article 3(2) TEU. This means, according to the Court, that Article 54

> is intended, on the one hand, to ensure, in the area of freedom, security and justice, that a person [note that the Court does not refer to EU citizenship, ML] whose trial has been finally disposed of is not prosecuted in several Contracting States for the same acts on account of his having exercised his right to freedom of movement, the aim being to ensure legal certainty—in the absence of harmonisation or approximation of the criminal laws of the Member States—through respect for decisions of public bodies which have become final. . . . On the other hand, however, whilst Article 54 of the CISA aims to ensure that a person, once he has been found guilty and served his sentence, or, as the case may be, been acquitted by a final judgment in a Contracting State, may travel within the Schengen area without fear of being prosecuted in another Contracting State for the same acts, it is not intended to protect a suspect from having to submit to investigations that may be undertaken successively, in respect of the same acts, in several Contracting States.[38]

Unlike in the international legal order,[39] Article 3(2) TFEU explicitly connects the *ne bis in idem*-principle to the establishment of a transnational area of freedom, security and justice.[40] EU Citizens are offered a legal area wherein individuals enjoy rights of free movement, that is, the autonomy to decide where they wish to go and reside and, therefore, to which legal regime they wish to subject themselves. The EU legal order thus recognises individuals as autonomous subjects in a transnational setting.

Obviously, with this status as a transnational area of law also come the responsibilities, for those individuals, the Member States and the EU itself. The creation of the AFSJ necessarily also entails measures to prevent and fight transnational crime. This, of course, is where a cornerstone of criminal justice—the principle of legal certainty—comes into play. There is no doubt that criminal trials may interfere with this autonomous position.[41] As indicated above, the Court of Justice has

38 Case C-486/14 *Piotr Kossowski* ECLI:EU:C:2016:483, paras 44–46. See also Luchtman (ed), *Choice of Forum in Cooperation Against EU Financial Crime—Freedom, Security and Justice and the Protection of Specific EU-Interests* (n 1).

39 In (public) international law, the interests of individuals are generally presumed to be represented by their state of nationality. A right of free movement does exist with respect to nation states (cf. art 2 of the fourth Protocol to the ECHR), but not in a transnational setting.

40 Cf. also the Opinion 2/13 of 18 December 2014 on the Accession of the European Union to the European Convention for the Protection of Human Rights and Fundamental Freedoms, para 157.

41 One only needs to think of the forced surrender on the basis of the FD EAW from one state to another.

explicitly recognised this with respect to extradition proceedings to third countries, at least to the extent that the facts of the case come within the scope of EU law (Articles 18 and 21 TFEU).[42] From a citizenship perspective, a problem also arises in situations where the exercise of prosecutorial discretion (as to where in the AFSJ to concentrate investigations and prosecutions) cannot be reasonably foreseen or controlled, and leads to interferences with the rights of citizens. In these instances, we must ask ourselves how the concept of European citizenship influences the requirement that interferences with such rights meet the requirements of accessibility and foreseeability.[43] Unlike in the many cases that have been answered by the European Court of Human Rights (ECtHR) on the above-mentioned fundamental rights this far, the problem with respect to choices of forum in the AFSJ is not (primarily) that individual national laws are absent, vague, or disregarded, but that there is a multitude of diverging national laws, that may even produce contradictory approaches to the same set of facts that can come within the sphere of free movement rights. A cognisable link to the criminal law of a particular legal order may even be absent.

In these cases, the concept of European citizenship and one of its core elements (personal autonomy through rights of free movement) are easily frustrated. There is a paradox in encouraging, on the one hand, individuals to cross borders, while simultaneously abstaining from a framework that allows them to foresee the consequences of their free movement, or the free movement of others in a common area of criminal justice. My proposal therefore is that—with free movement as a core element of European citizenship—the laws of the *state of stay* are, *as a general rule*, decisive for offering individuals guidance on what they are allowed to do, and what not. The individual's presence in that particular state is, after all, the outcome of the deliberations that he made, and was allowed to make autonomously. Yet an orientation on that particular legal order will not necessarily show him the *additional* consequences his actions may have, particularly through extraterritorial claims of jurisdiction by the legal orders of other EU Member States. Those claims will, almost by definition, interfere with free movement rights. Therefore, those additional consequences, in particular, need to be laid down in accessible and foreseeable laws, at any rate where fundamental rights are involved.

42 Case C-182/15 *Aleksei Petruhhin* ECLI:EU:C:2016:630. The question is whether a similar decision would have been given, had the EU citizen not (yet) made use of its rights to free movement; cf. Case C-34/09 *Ruiz Zambrano* ECLI:EU:C:2011:124, paras 41 and 42.

43 Cf. conclusion 5 of the Tampere conclusions: 'Judgements [*sic*] and decisions should be respected and enforced throughout the Union, while safeguarding the basic legal certainty of people and economic operators. Better compatibility and more convergence between the legal systems of Member States must be achieved'.

To conclude, European citizenship in my opinion implies that individuals are now introduced as full, autonomous actors in the AFSJ. This, in turn, means that they are entitled to laws that enable them to regulate their conduct, also in transnational constellations. As the goal of the EU is to promote free movement of citizens and other individuals, I see no reason to differentiate between national and transnational cases, nor between (conflicts of jurisdiction caused by) their own free movement, or the movement of others (and resulting prosecutions on the basis of passive nationality). I derive from this that any source of public power, exercised within the AFSJ that interferes with the fundamental rights of citizens needs to be accessible and foreseeable. Unless there is a clear legal basis that provides otherwise, the concept of free movement then logically implies that the primary point of reference for individuals is their state of stay. Interferences by other legal orders are not prohibited, but need a decent legal basis. The promotion of free movement of persons (cf. Article 3(2) TEU) in this reading therefore brings along a redefined notion of such concepts as the accessibility and foreseeability of the law. It challenges the existing state-centred cooperation structures and to protect the autonomy of the individual vis-à-vis the joint European Member States, also in transnational situations.

IV. CHOICE OF FORUM, EUROPEAN CITIZENSHIP, AND FUNDAMENTAL RIGHTS

The finding that Charter guarantees need to be interpreted in light of Article 3(2) TEU does not in itself answer the question of whether conflicts of jurisdiction are actually covered by those guarantees. Certainly, choices of forum, and conflicts of jurisdiction in particular, may cause problems of foreseeability and accessibility, but are these problems a concern in terms of the legality principle? Do they for instance interfere with the right to privacy, liberty, property, or a fair trial? In particular, we need to explore to what extent these conflicts: (a) relate to a state's jurisdiction to prescribe norms and, possibly, to the substantive legality principle of Articles 7 ECHR and 49 CFR; (b) its jurisdiction to adjudicate those offences (Articles 47 CFR and 6 ECHR: 'a tribunal (previously) established by law'); as well as (c) what could be learned from this for the EU.

The ECtHR has consistently held that the concept and meaning of 'law' under both (and other) Articles of the Convention is the same. With respect to Article 7, for instance, it 'alludes to the very same concept [of "law"] as that to which the Convention refers elsewhere when using that term, a concept which comprises statute law as well as case-law and implies qualitative requirements, including those of accessibility and foreseeability'. The goal is that 'the citizen must be able to have an indication that is adequate in the circumstances of the legal rules applicable to a given case'. In addition, 'a norm cannot be regarded as a "law" unless it is formulated with sufficient precision to enable the citizen to regulate his conduct'.[44]

A. Lex certa

The question of the relevance of the substantive legality principle in relation to conflicts of jurisdiction will be discussed in relation to two different issues. The first is related to the problem of multiple national claims for the same offences (the problem of the double burden); the other relates to the issue of (extraterritorial) jurisdiction. These issues overlap.

The first point is best illustrated with reference to *Camilleri v Malta*, where the ECtHR was asked the question of whether the Maltese system of criminal justice was compatible with Article 6 ECHR, now that it allowed the public prosecutor a degree of discretion to decide in which court the accused would be tried (for the same offence, but under different minimum and maximum penalties).[45] Under Maltese law, the Court of Magistrates is allowed to impose custodial sanctions of six months to ten years, whereas the Criminal Court may impose four years to life imprisonment. Camilleri was prosecuted before the Criminal Court and sentenced to fifteen years' imprisonment. The ECtHR rephrased the complaint of a violation of Article 6 ECHR into a complaint under Article 7, and then observed that

> while it is clear that the punishment imposed was established by law and did not exceed the [statutory] limits . . . it remains to be determined whether the Ordinance's qualitative requirements, particularly that of foreseeability, were satisfied, regard being had to the manner of choice of jurisdiction, as this reflected on the penalty that the offence in question carried.[46]

The Court found that '[i]t would therefore appear that the applicant would not have been able to know the punishment applicable to him even if he had obtained legal advice on the matter, as the decision was solely dependent on the prosecutor's discretion to determine the trial court'.[47] In the absence of cognisable criteria for making this choice and a lack of procedural safeguards, fixing different minimum sanctions posed an 'insoluble problem', according to the ECtHR, as it gave the competent Attorney General 'unfettered discretion to decide which minimum penalty would be applicable with respect to the same offence'.[48]

44 Cf. *Sunday Times v United Kingdom* App no 6538/74 (ECtHR, 26 April 1979), para 49.

45 *Camilleri v Malta* App no 42931/10 (ECtHR, 22 January 2013).

46 ibid para 40.

47 ibid para 42.

48 ibid para 43.

The case illustrates that, even where the underlying offences are identical and the sanctions are defined by law, there may still be an issue of foreseeability (of offences and sanctions) where the 'system as a whole' leaves it to the executive to determine which specific procedure is to be followed (and, hence, which minimum sanction may be imposed). It is clear that similar problems may arise with the prosecutorial decision of forum choice in the EU, even in areas with harmonised offences. It is, however, unclear—even unlikely—that the ECtHR would apply the same reasoning to the transnational setting. This has to do with the second point, mentioned above. The question is to which extent the legality principle, as defined in Article 7 ECHR read in conjunction with Article 1 ECHR, also sets limits to the territorial reach of the criminal laws of states, or to the simultaneous applicability of diverging or even contrasting national laws and policies.

In other words, do the rules of jurisdiction also fall under the scope of Article 7 ECHR/49 CFR? This is a highly controversial issue. First of all, the question is to which extent the rules on jurisdiction are part of the *offence* and *sanctions*, as these are the concepts that are referred to in the above-mentioned articles. In the second place, the question is to what extent it follows from these articles, even assuming their applicability, that the applicability of the criminal law of a *particular* state must also be accessible and foreseeable. There is no consensus on this. An oft-cited position, at least on the Continent, is, however, that there is a certain nexus between the guarantees of Articles 7 ECHR and 49 CFR and the rules on jurisdiction.[49] These guarantees do not apply directly, but without a clear and accessible link to a criminal law system, one does not have a chance to become acquainted with its offences and penalties either.[50] This means that the requirements of accessibility and foreseeability are also of relevance for rules of jurisdiction. However, most authors are satisfied that the thresholds of these requirements are met, once the individual could have known that his actions are *criminal* (somewhere), for instance through the application of the requirement of double criminality. They therefore deny their relevance with respect to the issue of *which particular state* ultimately prosecutes the offender.[51]

In light of my findings in the previous section, I wonder if this conclusion is also worth following in the specific context of the AFSJ. After all, any orientation on the legal order of the state of stay (for instance, the state of residence) will teach an individual nothing as to the *additional* consequences his actions may have under the

49 See also Council of Europe, European Committee on Crime Problems, *Extraterritorial Criminal Jurisdiction* (Council of Europe 1990) 22–25.

50 Most notably by Gerardus A. M. Strijards, *Internationaal strafrecht, strafrechtsmacht—Algemeen deel* (Gouda Quint 1984) 43–47; see also Kai Ambos, *Internationales Strafrecht* (C.H. Beck 2006) 5–6; Hirsch Ballin (n 3) 98–99.

51 Minority positions are taken by Strijards (n 50), and Dietrich Oehler, *Internationales Strafrecht: Geltungsbereich des Strafrechts, internationales Rechtshilferecht, Recht der Gemeinschaften, Völkerstrafrecht* (Heymanns 1983).

criminal laws of other Member States. Yet it is precisely this double burden which complicates the legal position of the European citizen and interferes with the goal of free movement. Particularly where these specific consequences cannot reasonably be foreseen at the time of action, they will catch that citizen by surprise. That citizen is then confronted with the consequences brought forward by the laws of a legal order which he did not choose, possibly does not know and could not in any event foresee. To that extent, it is an interference with the autonomy of citizens to move freely within the AFSJ. He or she may be confronted with diverging or even contradictory national rules on offences and sanctions, and with the possibility of multiple prosecutions (cf. the *Camilleri* case). It may also occur that his actions are perfectly legal in the state of *locus*, but criminal conduct in another state. From a European citizen's perspective an element of arbitrariness may thus creep into the system, which is closely connected to the guarantees of Articles 7 ECHR and 49 CFR.

In light of this finding, three observations need to be made with respect to the current EU approach, as well as its alternatives:

1. Fragmented harmonisation of criminal law jurisdiction: divergent criminal law systems

The efforts of the European Union are currently geared towards the extension of the jurisdictional bases beyond the national territory for serious, cross-border crimes. They are limited to the scope of Articles 83 and 325 TFEU. Other areas of criminal law remain in the hands of the nation states. The current situation certainly does not fully prevent citizens from being confronted with a double burden, the scope of which they could not have predicted at the time of their actions. This may happen, either because they themselves crossed the internal borders, or because they were confronted with the actions of others. Particularly in the latter case, as long as EU law is silent on this matter, there is not always a clear link with the EU legal order or the Charter (cf. Article 51(1) CFR), even though the EU promotes free movement. This also means that it will not be possible to interpret Article 49 CFR in a 'transnational fashion', that is, in light of Article 3(2) TEU, as the court has done with Articles 54 CISA and 50 CFR.

One problem that is particularly urgent is the problem of the 'true' or 'actual' conflicts of jurisdiction, that is, those types of conflict where a certain type of behaviour is not a criminal offence in the state of stay, but does constitute an offence in another state claiming extraterritorial jurisdiction over it. In those cases, the Member State where the actions took place is at most excused from its duty to provide cooperation. Obviously, these situations interfere with free movement as it is defined here.

2. The foreseeability of the double burden

In those cases where European laws do interfere with national law, my analysis reveals other problems. The network approach of the European Union—wide jurisdictional bases and enhanced cooperation—aims to prevent impunity, yet is not concerned with double burdens and related problems of foreseeability and accessibility. The directive on human trafficking, for instance, seems to encourage the use of the passive personality principle, rather than to discourage it.[52] To that extent, the European legislator clearly goes in another direction than that advocated here. As soon as the *criminality* of behaviour is foreseeable (which will be so in cases of (minimum) harmonisation),[53] the double burden (the question of which *particular* Member State has jurisdiction) is apparently not regarded as a problem in terms of substantive legality.

The cogency of this approach depends, in my view, on the perspective one takes. If one agrees that the European Union does indeed offer its citizens the right for persons to subject themselves to the legal order of their choice and that limitations to this (caused by extraterritorial jurisdiction) must meet certain standards, then that legal order will principally determine the consequences of their actions. This is the expression of the autonomous position of the European citizen vis-à-vis the Member States. Although this rule is not absolute, it does influence the concept of foreseeability. At the least, the full potential of the consequences of one's actions, brought forward by the criminal laws of the joint Member States, should be foreseeable at the time of action, and not only those of his state of stay. If this turns out to be unachievable, those consequences should be mitigated. At present, only Articles 54–58 CISA offer some degree of protection, in cases of consecutive proceedings. Yet there are certainly other examples of how to do this, for instance by applying the *lex mitior*, by enhancing the procedural position of the defendant (cf. the proposals in the horizontal and vertical models of the Working Group) or by a ranking of jurisdictional principles, thus reducing the potential for conflict (cf. the third model of the Working Group). These solutions are not explored, however, let alone enacted into law to date. This means that the legal position of the defendant is currently flawed.

3. The quest for viable alternatives

Assuming that the guarantees of Article 49 CFR indeed cast their shadow on the laws of jurisdiction and that certain jurisdictional criteria—for instance the passive personality principle, the principle of subsidiary jurisdiction, or, sometimes, even the territoriality principle—are problematic in terms of their capacity to show the citizen the full range of the possible consequences of his actions, what should be the consequence of this? Should the laws of that particular state remain inapplicable?

52 See arts 9 and 10 of Directive 2011/36/EU [2011] OJ L101/1; Luchtman (ed), *Choice of Forum in Cooperation Against EU Financial Crime—Freedom, Security and Justice and the Protection of Specific EU-Interests* (n 1) 3–4.

53 Assuming, of course, that all Member States correctly transpose European *norms* into national *offences*.

Some have argued that these types of problems could lead to a successful plea of *error iuris/error facti*.[54] That might be a reasonable solution. Yet it also has a few drawbacks. One might expect that the more the legal orders of the European Member States become intertwined and the more the European Union continues to promote the establishment of extraterritorial jurisdiction, the more this leads to a need for these types of exceptions.

Ultimately, I think, the situation calls for a more substantial solution. Successful pleas with respect to *error iuris* or *error facti* must remain a means of last resort, as they could harm the legitimate interests of victims, other Member States or the European Union. This applies in particular where the state of the *locus delicti*, although competent, does not take further action.[55] The question therefore arises as to what the European Union and its Member States should do to prevent problems like these. Once again, with EU law being silent, these issues are currently left to the national level and seem to be ignored there, leaving the European citizen in a complicated position.

B. Tribunal established by law

The principle *nullum judicium sine lege* is dealt with, in particular, by the requirements of Article 6 ECHR that tribunals be independent, impartial, and 'established by law'. The latter requirement (or: *previously* established by law, in Article 47 CFR) aims to ensure that 'the judicial organization in a democratic society [does] not depend on the discretion of the executive, but that it [is] regulated by law emanating from Parliament'.[56] This reasoning is not as circular as it seems. By stressing the requirement of a *parliamentary* law, the Court uses a different, more limited concept of law than with other Convention rights. The rationale of this lies in the separation of powers, as well as in the rule of law.[57] The requirement of a tribunal established by law envisages 'the whole organizational set-up of the courts',[58] including the overall

54 On this, see also Hans-Joseph Scholten, *Das Erfordernis der Tatortstrafbarkeit in § 7 StGB* (Max-Planck-Institut für ausländ. und int. Strafrecht 1995) 97ff; Strijards (n 50) 47–49; Ambos (n 50) 4; Martin Böse, 'Die Stellung des sog. Internationalen Strafrechts im Deliktsaufbau und ihre Konsequenzen für den Tatbestandsirrtum' in René Bloy, Martin Böse, Thomas Hillenkamp, Carsten Momsen, and Peter Rackow (eds), *Gerechte Strafe und legitimes Strafrecht—Festschrift für Manfred Maiwald zum 75. Geburtstag* (Duncker & Humblot 2009).

55 This is why Martin Böse and Frank Meyer, 'Die Beschränkung nationaler Strafgewalten als Möglichkeit zur Vermeidung von Jurisdiktionskonflikten in der Europäischen Union' [2011] *ZIS* 336, suggest, with reference to the principle of non-discrimination, that the latter state should protect those interests. See also Martin Böse, Frank Meyer, and Anne Schneider, *Conflicts of Jurisdiction in Criminal Matters in the European Union—Volume II: Rights, Principles and Model Rules* (Nomos 2014).

56 Cf. *Jorgic v Germany* App no 74613/01 (ECtHR, 12 July 2007), para 64; *Coëme et al. v Belgium* App nos 32492/96, 32547/96, 32548/96, 33209/96 and 33210/96 (ECtHR, 22 June 2000), para 98.

57 Cf. *Jorgic v Germany* App no 74613/01 (ECtHR, 12 July 2007), para 64.

58 Cf. *Sokurenko and Strygun v Ukraine* App nos 29458/04 and 29465/04 (ECtHR, 20 July 2006), para 24.

organisation of the judiciary, the establishment of the various courts, and their territorial and material jurisdiction.[59] This does not mean that executive discretion is completely outlawed; a certain degree may be necessary, in order to serve the interests of justice. The exercise of such discretion may however never be 'arbitrary',[60] or, to put it in a positive perspective, it must be 'reasonable'.

In relation to choice of forum, we must keep in mind that prosecutorial authorities are usually not part of the judiciary. This begs the question of how their activities relate to the requirement of a '*tribunal* established by law'.[61] In my opinion, it would be unjust to exclude forum choice by the executive from court organisation. Particularly in criminal justice, where the prosecution service is an integral part of the criminal justice system and in essence holds the key to it, a certain degree of control on which entrance it takes to that system is necessary.[62] This seems to be confirmed in the scarce case law available on the matter of the European Court and Commission of Human Rights.[63]

With regard to forum choice in the European Union, the challenges and problems do not so much lie in the court organisations of the Member States per se, but in the interplay between these systems, which may result in negative or positive conflicts of jurisdiction. Interpreting the requirement of a 'tribunal established by law' in light of the goals of Article 3(2) TEU draws our attention to three issues of particular interest.[64]

1. The quest for reasonableness

Unlike the guarantees of Articles 49 CFR and 7 ECHR, a 'tribunal established by law' does not require utmost certainty as to which court will try the case at the time

59 Martin Kuijer, *The Blindfold of Lady Justice—Judicial Independence and Impartiality in Light of the Requirements of Article 6 ECHR* (Wolf 2004) 184–85.

60 ibid 185, with reference to the *Crociani* case.

61 Incidentally, Panzavolta has rightfully pointed out that art 5 ECHR is also concerned with the concept of the 'lawful judge'.

62 Within the context of Dutch criminal justice, Corstens has argued that the more room there is for prosecutorial discretion in choosing the forum, the greater the need for a guarantee like the Dutch *ius de non evocando*; see Geert J.M. Corstens, *De verhouding rechter—openbaar ministerie. Een lat-relatie in het strafrecht* (Gouda Quint 1983) 30; see also Geert J. M. Corstens, 'Naar een geïnternationaliseerd strafrecht? Enkele inleidende opmerkingen' in Jan Fiselier (ed), *Internationalisering van het strafrecht* (Ars Aequi Libri 1986) 10 (international context); Erwin Beyeler, *Das Recht auf den verfassungsmässigen Richter als Problem der Gesetzgebung* (Juris-Verlag 1978) 15; Dietrich Oehler, 'Der gesetzliche Richter und die Zuständigkeit in Strafsachen' [1952] *ZStW* 292.

63 See Luchtman, *Choice of Forum in an Area of Freedom, Security and Justice* (n 1) 87–89, with further references.

64 See also Michele Panzavolta, 'Choice of Forum and the Lawful Judge Concept' in Luchtman (ed), *Choice of Forum in Cooperation Against EU Financial Crime—Freedom, Security and Justice and the Protection of Specific EU-Interests* (n 1) 143–66.

of the commission of the offence. There is also no such thing as a right for the defendant to choose his own court, or to have proceedings against him combined.[65] Rather, the requirement demands that all courts have a decent legal basis and that forum choices are 'reasonable' and stay within the legislative framework. It is geared towards warding off extraneous factors from influencing the fairness of the trial, including the proper administration of justice. However, factors that are decisive for forum choices may very well come into focus only *after* the offence was committed and still be very legitimate factors for court competences and forum choices.

In the transnational setting of the European Union, the problems experienced are different from the cases on Article 6 ECHR we have seen thus far. The problem in the EU—comprising well over twenty different national systems—is not so much the absence or impreciseness of national court competences. Rather, even assuming all national systems are in line with Article 6 ECHR, the problem is that prosecutorial authorities have a choice between (theoretically) all of those divergent national systems.[66] They are able to choose the court and procedural framework that is most to their liking, possibly to the detriment of other parties to the proceedings (defendants, victims).

In light of European citizenship, this wide discretionary margin has a twofold connotation. From a negative angle, it easily produces arbitrary results for citizens. Arbitrary, not because citizens are not able to predict ex ante where the trial will take place, or that they may be tried in another state than the state of stay (their 'natural judge'), or that they are not allowed to choose their forum (cf. the proposal by Swart, mentioned earlier), but because the content and scope of the procedural framework under which they are tried—their procedural rights and duties—is de facto chosen by their direct adversaries in the same proceedings. In my opinion, such a system is not capable of warding off extraneous factors to the administration of justice. I believe the requirement of a tribunal established by law is directly related to the principles of adversarial proceedings and equality of arms. It should not be up to a party to the proceedings to choose unilaterally which rules apply to the proceedings.

From a positive angle, the main concern is that citizens' interests are not integrated at all into the existing framework. In addition, we face the dilemma that, on the one hand, mutual differences in legal systems may themselves become a relevant factor in forum choice, which could be perceived as a challenge to the integrity of those systems instead of their guaranteeing justice (forum shopping) and therefore also

65 Cf. *G. v Switzerland* App no 16875/90 (EComHR, 10 October 1990) (competence *ratione loci*); *Kübli v Switzerland* App no 17495/90 (EComHR, 2 December 1992) (competence *ratione materiae*).

66 Particularly on the basis of the principle of subsidiary jurisdiction; cf. the mechanisms of the 1972 Convention on the Transfer of Proceedings.

a danger to the proper operation of the principle of mutual recognition, whereas, on the other hand, the element of arbitrariness that thus creeps into the system is difficult to pinpoint because the yardstick to assess these choices remains vague and open to many interpretations. The absence of a framework for dealing with forum choices thus leads to the situation where forum decisions may very well be 'lawful' (because of the competence of the courts under national law), but their reasonableness is, at times, questionable and depends entirely on the integrity of the person who operates the system.

Therefore, the requirement of a 'tribunal established by law' defines as the overarching challenge for the European Union the design of a statutory system that supports a workable concept of 'reasonableness', in which citizens' interests are included.[67] That system should reduce the double burden on European citizens as far as possible, protect the common interest, and avoid arbitrariness in the way forum choices are made, forum shopping in particular.

2. The need to break open national law

My second point concerns the need to 'break open' national criminal law systems. It is not that difficult to identify factors which currently lead to a certain degree of legal protectionism or to preferential treatment for national citizens or national perspectives above the interests of those of other European Member States, citizens, or the EU itself. We see traces of this, for instance, in the limited powers of Eurojust members who are not always given the power to operate without consulting their superiors at home;[68] in the fact that Member States sometimes exclude cooperation, *ipso iure*, in cases where national interests are involved; in their preference to exert jurisdictional control over their nationals (instead of their residents) when they travel abroad; or in their reluctance to assume responsibility for citizens from other states, for instance at the stage of the execution of sanctions (section II).

Clearly, this attitude is not only explained by the desire simply to retain as much power at the national level as possible. The German Constitutional Court,

67 Cf. Tom Vander Beken and Gert Vermeulen, *Finding the Best Place for Prosecution—European Study on Jurisdiction Criteria* (Maklu 2002); Tom Vander Beken, Gert Vermeulen, and Otto Lagodny, 'Kriterien für die jeweils "beste" Strafgewalt in Europa' [2002] *NStZ* 624; and Otto Lagodny, *Emphielt es sich, eine europäische Gerichtskompetenz für Strafgewaltskonflikte vorzusehen? Gutachten im Auftrag des Bundesministeriums der Justiz* (Bundesministerium der Justiz 2001), who refers to a *Qualitätsprinzip*.

68 I must admit that this statement may be challenged. It depends on the view one takes on Eurojust's tasks. Those who submit that Eurojust (unlike the EPPO for instance) is there to assist national investigations will object to this statement. Yet those who are of the opinion that the coordination of criminal proceedings is something more than that, also in light of preventing negative conflicts, will find this statement presumably less difficult to accept.

for instance, has consistently linked it to considerations of *national* democracy.[69] Sovereignty protects such essential rule of law benchmarks.[70] At the same time, however, such a position seems to take it for granted that non-nationals, or nationals crossing the internal borders, are a lesser concern and that the interests of national criminal justice take precedence over other interests *qualitate qua*.[71] In light of the concept of European citizenship, I find this difficult to accept.[72] What is particularly problematic is that national laws sometimes even block the application of a test of reasonableness in a transnational AFSJ. Nonetheless, although this is clearly not in the interest of a proper administration of justice, seen from an EU perspective, we may doubt whether the requirement of a 'tribunal established by law' prohibits this. The term 'law' refers to statutory legislation, not to constitutional law.[73] This means, in my opinion that the final word remains with the national legislators, unless the European legislator intervenes.

3. The need to coordinate national legal systems

Even where national law does not openly protect national interests, interests other than national interests may not always be accounted for, also where the actors involved are fully aware of the European dimension of their tasks and cases. Conflicts of jurisdiction are by their very definition a problem that is caused by the interplay between multiple legal orders. However, there is no overarching framework for forum choice at present. My third point is that even where national systems do not pose statutory impediments to European coordination, 'reasonableness' as such will remain an empty phrase without intervention at the European level. The EU and its Member States must not only undertake action to break open national

69 Cf. Bundesverfassungsgericht, 2 BvR 2236/04 (*Darkanzanli*). See also Mark Bovens, Deirdre Curtin, and Paul 't Hart (eds), *The Real World of EU Accountability—What Deficit?* (OUP 2010) 188–91, and J. Komárek, 'European Constitutionalism and the European Arrest Warrant: In Search of the Limits of "Contrapunctual Principles"' (2007) 44(1) CMLR 9 with respect to that court's rulings.

70 Cf. Neil Walker, 'Late Sovereignty in the European Union' in Neil Walker (ed), *Sovereignty in Transition* (Hart Publishing 2003).

71 The German Constitutional Court's *Darkanzanli* ruling of 18 July 2005, 2 BvR 2236/04, is a good example of this; see in particular paras 85 and 86, where a difference is made between acts with *maßgeblicher Inlandsbezug* and acts with *maßgeblicher Auslandsbezug*. A similar reasoning can be found in Bernd Schünemann (ed), *Ein Gesamtkonzept für die europäische Strafrechtspflege—A Programme for European Criminal Justice* (Heymanns 2006) 95 ff.

72 Cf. Bovens, Curtin, and 't Hart (eds) (n 69) 190: 'The point the *Bundesverfassungsgericht* missed, it simply cannot reach any of what happens at the collective supranational level, and nor can any of the national parliaments. In effect, this kind of purely intergovernmentalist attitude is the equivalent of the ostrich with its head in the sand, choosing to ignore the realities around it that it does not wish to see or engage with'.

73 Stefan Trechsel, *Human Rights in Criminal Proceedings* (OUP 2005) 50–51.

systems, but they must simultaneously unfold a general perspective on 'reasonableness'. Without providing guidance on the substantive criteria, on the procedures, and on the organisational framework, including supervision, national authorities will continue to have insufficient materials to work with.[74]

Of course, it is one thing to emphasise the need for substantive criteria, but quite another to define criteria which are precise enough to offer clarity to the authorities and the possibility of control for others. The original ambitions of the 2009 Framework Decision on conflicts of jurisdiction were mitigated precisely as a result of this.[75] On another occasion,[76] I have argued that the Swiss system of inter-cantonal case allocation is interesting in this respect, because it 'reverses' the approach: instead of enumerating a non-exhaustive list of (positive or negative) factors for forum choice, as in the Eurojust Guidelines of 2003,[77] it combines a system of statutory case allocation, with room for deviations from that system, provided that a series of goals is achieved, at all times.[78] Forum choices must in any case take account of the interests of the place where most of the damaging effects of criminal conduct were felt; those of the suspect (and his counsel) to defend himself effectively; those of the courts, which must be put in the position to obtain, as far as possible, a complete overview of both the person of the accused and his actions; and those of the speedy and efficient administration of justice.[79] These criteria, which partially deviate from those advanced in the joint project group's models or those in the latest version of the EPPO proposal,[80] put the burden on the authorities, to the

74 Cf. Maartje de Visser, *Network-Based Governance in EC Law—The Example of EC Competition and EC Communications Law* (Hart Publishing 2009) 293–94.

75 Cf. Hans-Holger Herrnfeld, 'Mechanisms for Settling Conflicts of Jurisdiction' in Luchtman (ed), *Choice of Forum in Cooperation Against EU Financial Crime—Freedom, Security and Justice and the Protection of Specific EU-Interests* (n 1) 189–90. Compare also the original proposal for a Council Framework Decision on prevention and settlement of conflicts of jurisdiction in criminal proceedings, Council Document 5208/09 of 20 January 2009, with the final text, published in [2009] OJ L328/42.

76 Luchtman, *Choice of Forum in an Area of Freedom, Security and Justice* (n 1) 74–101.

77 See also the horizontal and vertical models developed by the research group on the basis of a revised version of the Guidelines, as well as the criteria in the allocation model (art 9).

78 On that system, see Patrick Guidon and Felix Bänziger, 'Die aktuelle Rechtsprechung des Bundesstrafgerichts zum interkantonalen Gerichtsstand in Strafsachen' [2007] *Jusletter* (21 May); Erhard Schweri and Felix Bänziger, *Interkantonale Gerichtsstandsbestimmung in Strafsachen* (2nd edn, Stämpfli Verlag 2004); Max Waiblinger, 'Die Bestimmung des Gerichtsstandes bei Mehrheit von strafbaren Handlungen oder von Beteiligten' [1943] *ZStr* 81 ff.

79 Cf. Bundesstrafgericht, 21 October 2004, no. BK_G 127/04.

80 See Annex A to the horizontal and vertical models of the project group, art 9 of the group's proposal on allocating the exercise of jurisdiction, art 22 of the Proposal for a Regulation on the establishment of the European Public Prosecutor's Office—Draft Regulation of 31 January 2017, Council Document 5766/17, Interinstitutional File 2013/0255 (APP).

extent that they—when asked by a relevant 'accountability forum'—have to show how these criteria have been met.[81] On the other hand, these criteria also show that these forums should not 'second guess' the forum choice: their task is to test the reasonableness of these decisions.

A final remark on the procedural aspects: substantive criteria need to be backed by procedures for two reasons.[82] In the first place, procedures are necessary to guarantee that all interests are indeed taken into consideration *before* the decision is taken. In that regard, we may notice that the position of the defendant,[83] as well as that of the European institutions, is virtually non-existent at present. In the second place, forum choices—although perhaps not causing any *direct* changes in legal position—certainly determine the future scope of rights and duties of all actors involved. They determine the applicable legal regime, as well as the scope of the double burden. These consequences are often irrevocable. This is why, as a matter of procedural fairness,[84] forum choices need to be accounted for by the decision-makers to a 'forum' (political or legal) with the power (a) to extract information from them, (b) to engage in a debate with them regarding their performance, and, possibly, (c) to create non-trivial consequences.[85]

At present, there is no such forum; or rather: there is no coordination between the many forums available. On the one hand, it is doubtful if forum choices will become a real issue before national courts. The task of those courts is after all to establish their own competence, not the reasonableness of the outcome of the deliberations between the prosecution services. On the other hand, technically speaking, forum choice is in many aspects not a matter for European law. The European framework is fragmented. That implies, once again, that our primary point of reference for assessing legality—the CFR—is only applicable where there is secondary EU legislation in place that needs implementation or—possibly—where

81 Cf. the proposals by Vander Beken, Vermeulen, and Lagodny (n 67) 626; and particularly Lagodny (n 67) 106 ff.

82 Cf. Vander Beken and Vermeulen (n 67) 16–17; Albertus H. J. Swart, *Een ware Europese rechtsruimte: wederzijdse erkenning van strafrechtelijke beslissingen in de Europese Unie* (Kluwer 2001) 16.

83 Cf. the contributions by Stijn Franken, 'The Perspective of the Defence Lawyer: Choice of Forum and the Proper Administration of Justice' 109–13, and Jan M. Sjöcrona, 'The Perspective of the Criminal Defence Lawyer: Choice of Forum, a Legal Vacuum in the EU' 113–22 in Luchtman (ed), *Choice of Forum in Cooperation Against EU Financial Crime—Freedom, Security and Justice and the Protection of Specific EU-Interests* (n 1). In some instances, there is a duty to inform the defendant at most; see for instance art 17 of the 1972 Convention on the Transfer of Proceedings.

84 I therefore oppose the idea that 'the allocation of cases is hence not a question of transferring competence but merely one of dividing work'; see de Visser (n 74) 298. A similar line of reasoning is found in recital 4 of the preamble to the 2009 Framework Decision.

85 Cf. Bovens, Curtin, and 't Hart (eds) (n 69) 176; Mark Bovens, *The Quest for Responsibility—Accountability and Citizenship in Complex Organisations* (CUP 1998).

national law interferes with the Treaty freedoms (cf. Article 51(1) CFR). Moreover, even in those rare instances where European laws do provide for rules on choice of forum, the question is who is in the position to steer and supervise the complex interplay of legal orders. At present, the competences of Eurojust, as well as the Court of Justice, are limited.[86] Eurojust itself does not take decisions on choice of forum; these decisions are ultimately taken by national authorities. The Court's competences under Article 263 TFEU are therefore not in range.[87] Simultaneously, that Court has no competences over the 'operational' activities of the authorities of the Member States (Article 276 TFEU).

All of these factors easily lead to the situation that no one is really responsible for the problems faced by European citizens at the interface of multiple European criminal justice systems or for the negative conflicts that hamper the EU's financial interests. To that extent, practice in choice of forum shows a clear accountability gap: the powers of national authorities are limited, and the same goes for those of the European institutions: where many are competent, no one is accountable, particularly not for those interests that supersede or compete with the national perspective.[88]

C. *Ne bis in idem*

At this moment, the guarantee of Article 50 CFR is without doubt the most effective safeguard against double burdens. It ensures that once a first set of proceedings is concluded, *consecutive* prosecutions or punishment for the same acts are, in principle, prohibited. Particularly the integration of the *Schengen-acquis*, including Articles 54–58 CISA, into the framework of the former third pillar by the 2nd Protocol to the Amsterdam Treaty [1997] OJ C340/93 led to the further development of a *ne bis in idem*-principle beyond the internal legal orders of the Member States, in order to enable 'the European Union to develop more rapidly into an area of freedom, security and justice'.[89] Article 50 CFR has, in theory at least, expanded the territorial scope of

86 Incidentally, there are arrangements for the accountability of Eurojust, but these concern the overall functioning of the agency, not its operational activities; see Elena M. Busuioc, *The Accountability of European Agencies—Legal Provisions and Ongoing Practices* (Eburon 2010); Martijn Groenleer, *The Autonomy of European Union Agencies* (Eburon 2009) 309–42.

87 Cf. art 263(2) TFEU (annulment action by a Member State, which is problematic in light of art 276 TFEU) and art 263(4) TFEU (annulment by an individual). In the latter case, we would have to ask ourselves whether these types of decisions bring about changes in the legal position of the individual.

88 Cf. Groenleer (n 86) 103–04; Busuioc (n 86) 8; Bovens, Curtin, and 't Hart (eds) (n 69) 44–46, 192–93; Carol Harlow and Richard Rawlings, 'Promoting Accountability in Multilevel Governance: A Network Approach' (2007) 13 *European Law Journal* 542; Yannis Papadopoulos, 'Problems of Democratic Accountability in Network and Multilevel Governance' (2007) 42 *European Law Journal* 473; Bovens (n 85) 45–52.

89 Cf. Council Decision of 20 May 1999 determining the legal basis for each of the provisions or decisions which constitute the Schengen acquis (1999/436/EG) [1999] OJ L176/17.

the guarantee further.[90] According to that article, *ne bis in idem* comprises the whole EU. In *Mantello*, the Court of Justice explicitly confirmed its 'Auslegungshoheit' and applied the concept of the 'same acts', which it developed under Article 54 CISA, outside the Schengen-framework.[91] There is, in other words, ample evidence of the genealogy of a principle of European criminal law that originates from, but now develops beyond the full range of control of the Member States.

In its case law on Article 54 CISA, the Court of Justice stressed from the outset the link between the internationalised *ne bis in idem*-rules and their transnational context, that is, the free movement of persons.[92] Obviously, this reference to free movement is not directly concerned with any of the five Treaty freedoms; it refers to the goal of (what is now) Article 3(2) TEU.[93] This explains why the Court in *Brügge and Gözütok*, despite the absence of a clear link to a specific free movement right in that particular case,[94] nevertheless found that

> Article 54 of the CISA, the objective of which is to ensure that no one is prosecuted on the same facts in several Member States on account of his having exercised his right to freedom of movement, cannot play a useful role in bringing about the full attainment of that objective unless it also applies to [out-of-court settlements].[95]

In *Gasparini*, the Court added to this that '[Article 54 CISA] ensures that persons who, when prosecuted, have their cases finally disposed of are left undisturbed. They must be able to move freely without having to fear a fresh prosecution for the same acts in another Contracting State'.[96] The message is clear: once the first set of criminal proceedings is concluded, the individual is free to go where he wishes; he is not to be prosecuted again for the same set of facts anywhere in the Schengen area.[97]

90 This is confirmed by the Explanations to the Charter [2007] OJ C303/31: 'the "non bis in idem" rule applies not only within the jurisdiction of one State but also between the jurisdictions of several Member States'. It is not entirely clear how this provision relates to Protocol (19) to the Treaty of Lisbon (13 December 2007) on the Schengen Acquis integrated into the framework of the European Union, which confirms the special position of a few Member States in relation to Schengen.

91 Case C-261/09 *Gaetano Mantello* ECLI:EU:C:2010:683, paras 38–40. Surprisingly, the ECJ does not refer at all to art 50 CFR in that case.

92 Article 54 CISA and art 3(2) FWD EAW share the same objective; Case C-261/09 *Gaetano Mantello* ECLI:EU:C:2010:683, para 40.

93 Seen 40 above.

94 Cf. Luchtman, *Principles of European criminal law: Jurisdiction, choice of forum, and the legality principle in the Area of Freedom, Security, and Justice* (n 1) 363–67; Robin Lööf, '54 CISA and the Principles of *ne bis in idem*' (2007) 15 *European Journal of Crime, Criminal Law and Criminal Justice* 309, 324–25.

95 Joined Cases C-187/01 and C-385/01 *Gözütok and Brügge* [2003] ECR I-1345, para 38.

96 Case C-467/04 *Gasparini and Others* [2006] ECR I-9199, para 27.

97 Lööf (n 94) 325, refers to the AFSJ as a 'single contractual unit'.

The *effect* of the Court's case law is that state authorities, in principle, only get one chance to prosecute the offender for his acts/offences. In a multi-level setting like that of the AFSJ, that is a risky step.[98] The Court tackles this argument by pointing to the fact that the scope of Article 54 CISA has not been made dependent on accompanying harmonising measures by the Member States.[99] It considers that the Member States, by introducing Article 54 CISA and integrating it into the former third pillar, have expressed a significant amount of mutual trust in each other, not only in the mutual quality of their legal systems, but apparently also in their mutual willingness to coordinate their efforts. The latter is relevant, because even the highest possible degree of mutual trust in the quality of each other's systems will not always prevent that several Member States think that they are best placed to prosecute.[100]

Combined with the ratio of free movement, the Court, in my opinion, has effectively introduced, as far as Article 54 CISA is concerned, the individual as a full actor at transnational level very much in the way it was advocated in the above (section3): those Member States that come second and feel that their interests have not been taken into account by the first set of proceedings, are nevertheless prohibited from starting a second set. It is up to the Member States to decide whether they can live with this de facto conflict rule of 'first come, first served' and the adverse consequences it may have. This way, the principle has organisational consequences, indeed,[101] and is closely related to the principle of legality. The stricter the limits set by *ne bis in idem*, the more likely the legislator will have to intervene in order to tackle the potential adverse consequences of this indiscriminate conflict rule, in particular forum shopping, either by defendants or authorities.

V. CONCLUSIONS

The preceding sections have analysed choice of forum in light of the key questions related to the legality principle, under its substantive, as well as its procedural law heading. The position of the defendant is complicated. Official documents often

98 Cf. Valsamis Mitsilegas, *EU Criminal Law* (Hart Publishing 2009) 147–53.

99 Joined Cases C-187/01 and C-385/01 *Gözütok and Brügge* [2003] ECR I-1345, paras 31–33.

100 Cf. Joachim Vogel, 'Internationales und europäisches ne bis in idem' in Andreas Hoyer, Henning Müller, Michael Pawlik, and Jürgen Wolter (eds), *Festschrift für Friedrich-Christian Schroeder zum 70. Geburtstag* (C. F. Müller 2006) 882, who notes: 'Kein Souverän [soll] einem anderen das Recht nehmen können, souverän über den Schutz der in dessen Sicht strafschützigen Interessen entscheiden zu dürfen'.

101 Cf. Michiel Luchtman, 'Transnational Law Enforcement in the European Union and the ne bis in idem Principle' (2011) 4(2) *Realaw* 7. I understand this is also what Marco Mansdörfer, *Das Prinzip des ne bis in idem im europäischen Strafrecht* (Duncker & Humblot 2004) 32–40, means, where he refers to *ne bis in idem* as a 'Förderung systemorganisierter Freiheit'. Yet where Mansdörfer defines this *Förderung* as a goal of *ne bis in idem*, I am inclined to qualify it as a result of the principle.

state that criminals should 'not escape justice', 'should not profit from the abolishment of the internal borders', or 'from differences between legal systems', *et cetera*. The reasoning seems to be that the legality principle is not to facilitate all kinds of abuses of free movement and forum shopping by individuals.

As I hope to have demonstrated, this type of 'framing' is only one side of the story. There is enough evidence in legal sources that European citizens are perceived by the Treaties not only as instruments promoting European integration, but also as *citoyens* (or *Union citizens*).[102] The status of citizenship implies membership of a political entity which grants the individual political rights of representation and rights of free movement.[103] The central claim of this article is that this not only implies that such rights cannot without due cause be taken away from him (for instance by extradition to a third country), but that it also requires interpreting the Charter rights in this new, transnational setting. Arbitrary interferences with such an autonomous position of citizens in such a setting must be prevented. The law not only influences the behaviour of citizens; it also guarantees them the rule of law and legal protection.

One of the recurring phrases of the Strasbourg Court, dealing with the legality principle, is that the law must enable citizens to regulate their conduct. There is no reason to deviate from it in the case of transnational law enforcement, now that this concept of law and citizenship are so closely related. We do have to keep in mind, however, that it is not a requirement of the Convention, nor the Charter, that all possible consequences of one's conduct must be foreseeable and accessible by law. In order words, the law only offers a framework for interests that are considered *legitimate*. What interests are legitimate is defined largely by the fundamental rights at stake.

The right to a fair trial, for instance, does not require that at the time of the commission of the offence, citizens must already be put in the position to know what courts will be competent to try their case. That kind of regulation of conduct is not required by Article 6 ECHR/47 CFR. The point is rather that the principle of fair trial—including adversarialism and equality of arms—precludes the possibility that one party to the proceedings unilaterally chooses the set of applicable procedural rules and courts under which the case is prosecuted and tried, to the detriment of the interests of other parties. In this light, it is problematic that in the EU situation the absence of a clear regulatory framework leaves forum choices between more than twenty different systems in essence with the executive, not the legislator.

102 On the various positions an individual may have in the European policy areas, see Christopher McCrudden, 'The Future of the EU Charter of Fundamental Rights' [2001] NYU School of Law, Jean Monnet Working Paper Series No 10/01, 20 ff and the opinion of AG Sharpston in Case C-34/09 *Ruiz Zambrano* ECLI:EU:C2010:560, para 3.

103 Cf. n 31 above.

'Regulation of conduct' therefore refers primarily to the applicable set of procedural rules (in light of inter alia the possibility of preparing a defence strategy), and to the ability to exert a certain amount of control over forum choices.[104]

The picture changes once we assess the conduct of individuals in light of Article 7 ECHR/49 CFR. Here, I do think it is essential that individuals need to be able to understand what consequences their actions will have, if these actions constitute criminal offences. In a transnational setting, these consequences are the result of the simultaneous applicability of multiple legal systems. Therefore, the fact that certain behaviour is criminal in one particular state will offer that individual only limited guidance on how to regulate his conduct, and more specifically on how to exercise his free movement rights. 'Regulation of conduct' is to be understood in this specific setting.

To conclude, it is useful to summarise my main findings. These are the anchor points for any model for dealing with conflicts of jurisdiction and choice of forum. Many, although not all, are addressed in the models of the joint research group:

1. Forum choices do interfere with fundamental rights of citizens. The law should therefore offer citizens an adequate indication of how to regulate their conduct, also in transnational cases.
2. When speaking of 'law', this does not necessarily have to be statutory law (except for the requirement of a tribunal previously established by law).[105] This implies that forum choices may also be dealt with via prosecutorial policies, if a decent basis in statutory law is provided for.
3. From the principle of substantive legality, the fact that multiple legal systems may be applicable to the same conduct is as such acceptable, as long as the full consequences of one's conduct (under multiple applicable criminal laws) are foreseeable at the time of conduct. Ideally, systems for dealing with forum choices should allow citizens—if needed with legal advice—to assess (a) if one's actions are criminal in the state of stay, (b) the scope of the double burden (multiple trials for the same conduct), and (c) the rules on how the trial state is determined (cf. *Camilleri*).[106] The three models (the horizontal, vertical, and allocation model) tackle these in different ways, via mechanisms of procedural law or via an a priori determination of jurisdiction in the AFSJ.

104 Cf. the explanatory note of the project group to the three models.

105 For the reasons, see section IV.B above.

106 By comparison, the explanation to the models of the research group reads on p 17: 'A coherent solution for conflicts of jurisdiction within the AFSJ should at least: a) avoid that ne bis in idem remains the only rule to resolve jurisdictional conflicts; b) ensure a non-arbitrary choice of jurisdiction; c) avoid parallel prosecutions; and aim at d) ensuring the choice of the best forum'.

4. From the principle of substantive legality, I consider contradictory (with respect to offences or sanctions) criminal laws as a particular problematic issue. If European citizenship indeed means that citizens themselves are free to subject themselves to the legal order of any EU Member State (free movement), then that legal order will provide the primary point of reference for their conduct. By consequence—and it is fair to note explicitly that this finding has not been taken over in the models—citizens should not be prosecuted for conduct that is not a criminal offence in that state on the basis of extra-territorial jurisdiction (except perhaps for cases of evident abuse of free movement rights, or on the basis of a clear legal basis in an EU regulation or the national law of the state of stay).
5. From the perspective of substantive legality, I see no reason to differentiate between conflicts of jurisdiction that have actually occurred, or conflicts that *may* occur (actual/abstract conflicts). The legal framework should offer guidance to citizens at the time of action. This is different from the perspective of Articles 6 ECHR and 47 CFR. From the latter perspective, I consider hypothetical conflicts to be less problematic (although not completely without problems).
6. From the perspective of Article 6 ECHR/47 CFR, it is essential that forum choices are integrated into a framework of law, in order to prevent that any party to criminal proceedings may unilaterally choose the rules under which a case is prosecuted and tried, to the detriment of others. In my view, this is directly related to the principle of equality of arms and adversarialism.

10

WHAT ROLE FOR CRIME VICTIMS IN THE FORUM CHOICE?

MICHELE SIMONATO

I. INTRODUCTION

The consequences of globalisation are perceived by victims of crime, too. It is not difficult to imagine a situation in which a person is harmed by criminal conduct that, in principle, could be legitimately investigated and adjudicated in several jurisdictions. As observed by Letschert and Groenhuijsen:

[c]ross-border victimization can impose difficulties in many ways; either the victim becomes victimized in another country than his country of residence, or the victim is victim of a crime committed in another jurisdiction than his own but the effects of the victimization take place in his country of residence (for example cybercrimes); a further complication is that such crimes are often committed by a network or group of (foreign) criminals residing in different countries'.[1]

Owing to the multitude of grounds for establishing criminal jurisdiction, it may happen that more than one country actually exercises jurisdiction in relation to the same facts. The resolution of such conflicts, however, 'is still seen as a matter of international relations rather than as a part of the criminal process'.[2] Some international instruments provide for consultation between national authorities;[3] nonetheless, the persons involved in the proceedings are not expressly considered in the choice of the adjudicating jurisdiction, if any choice is ever made.

Victims may have interests in influencing such a choice of forum.[4] However, there are no binding international instruments in force saying whether and how their

1 Rianne Letschert and Marc Groenhuijsen, 'Global Governance and Global Crime: Do Victims Fall in Between?' in Rianne Letschert and Jan van Dijk (eds), *The New Faces of Victimhood* (Springer 2011) 16.

2 Martin Böse, Frank Meyer, and Anne Schneider, 'Comparative Analysis' in Martin Böse, Frank Meyer, and Anne Schneider (eds), *Conflicts of Jurisdiction in Criminal Matters in the European Union, Vol. I: National Reports and Comparative Analysis* (Nomos 2013) 460.

3 Council FD 2009/948/JHA of 30 November 2009 on prevention and settlement of conflicts of exercise of jurisdiction in criminal proceedings [2009] OJ L328/42; European Convention on the Transfer of Proceedings in Criminal Matters [1972] *European Treaty Series* 073.

4 See, among others, M. Cherif Bassiouni, 'International Recognition of Victims' Rights' (2006) 6(2) Human Rights Law Review 203; Jonathan Doak, *Victims' Rights, Human Rights and Criminal*

interest should be considered in the identification of the most appropriate place for prosecution. At the European Union (EU) level, only the Eurojust guidelines provide, among the various criteria, that '[p]rosecutors must take into account the interests of victims and whether they would be prejudiced if any prosecution were to take place in one jurisdiction rather than another'. Victims (in particular their residence) are also considered for the choice of jurisdiction by the Proposal on the establishment of the European Public Prosecutor's Office (EPPO).[5]

In the academic debate, it is generally agreed that any future instrument should take into consideration not only the perspective of the prosecution, but also that of the individuals involved, namely the defendant and the victim. Neglecting such interests might even run counter to the global trend of enhancing the position of victims in criminal procedure. Other research projects have tried to include, to a different extent, the victim's perspective in the proposed instrument: in some cases by focusing on the jurisdictional grounds, in other cases by according them a procedural role in the settlement of the conflict.

The concept of victims' 'interests', however, remains vague. This is owing due to the fact that it is very difficult to identify its content. As emerged from the field research at Eurojust,[6] it is often interpreted by prosecutors as the interest in having the trial in their country of residence. Nevertheless, this might be only a partial vision, or an assumption that may be rebutted if ever victims were given the possibility of expressing their preference on the forum. The objective of this contribution, therefore, is to address the questions: in the choice of forum, what victims' interests should be taken into consideration? And how should they be taken into consideration?

The first version of this chapter was prepared before the finalisation of the proposed instruments. The arguments presented during the project meeting contributed to the definition of those instruments and were meant to apply to every scenario. They potentially apply both to 'positive' and 'negative' conflicts, whenever a decision in order to allocate the jurisdiction is necessary, whether because two or more Member States want to exercise jurisdiction or because all of them decline to exercise jurisdiction, thereby depriving victims of adequate protection.

Justice (Hart Publishing 2008); Luca Lupària (ed), *Victims and Criminal Justice. European Standards and National Good Practices* (Wolters Kluwer 2015); Tyrone Kirchengast, *Victims and the Criminal Trial* (Springer 2016); Thorsten Bonacker and Christoph Safferling, 'Introduction' in Thorsten Bonacker and Christoph Safferling (eds), *Victims of International Crimes: an Interdisciplinary Discourse* (Springer 2013) 1.

5 Article 27(4)(d) of the Proposal for a Regulation on the establishment of the European Public Prosecutor's Office (COM/2013/0534 final) identified as last criterion the 'place where direct victims have their habitual residence'. The text has been changing within the Council, and now it provides for 'the place where the direct victim has its seat'.

6 See Angelo Marletta, 'Report on the Field Research at Eurojust' in this volume.

II. A PRELIMINARY ISSUE: WHO IS A VICTIM?

The first question to be addressed is: what category of victims should we take into consideration? The problem emerges because there is no uniform legal definition of 'victim' in the EU territory; and in some Member States there is no definition at all. From a lawyer's perspective, Directive 2012/29/EU[7] adopts a vague definition,[8] which might appear at the same time too broad or too narrow. 'Broad' because not only is the person owning the legal interest protected by law included, but also any person who 'suffered harm'[9] as a direct consequence of crime[10] including also family members of deceased victims. 'Narrow' because legal persons do not fall within the scope of the Directive;[11] nevertheless, they could still be considered victims in some Member States.

As a result, in the current scenario it might happen that a person is recognised as a victim in one Member State, and not granted this status in another. Consequently, any attempt to create a new instrument should consider whether to rely on the Directive's definition or develop a new legal definition for the purpose of the forum choice, in the same way as the proposal for the establishment of the EPPO did. A new definition—considering, for example, only direct victims—is certainly more ambitious and would ensure more certainty in the application of the instrument. On the other hand, it might have a difficult impact on national legal systems, which would need to recognise a different concept of victims imposed by an instrument of cooperation that does not have the purpose of harmonising national approaches to victims' rights.

It seems more realistic, therefore, not to deal with the definition of victim and assume that 'victim' is a criminological concept much more variable than 'suspect'

7 Directive 2012/29/EU of 25 October 2012 establishing minimum standards on the rights, support and protection of victims of crime, and replacing Council Framework Decision 2001/220/JHA [2012] OJ L315/57.

8 According to art 2 of Directive 2012/29/EU victim means '(i) a natural person who has suffered harm, including physical, mental or emotional harm or economic loss which was directly caused by a criminal offence; (ii) family members of a person whose death was directly caused by a criminal offence and who have suffered harm as a result of that person's death'.

9 See art 2 of Directive 2012/29/EU. Therefore, as a minimum standard, victims are natural persons who have physical, mental, emotional, or financial damage as a result of a violation of national criminal law. See Maria Mousmouti et al, 'Protecting Victims' Rights in the EU: the Theory and Practice of Diversity of Treatment During the Criminal Trial, Comparative Report and Policy Recommendations' (Athens, Centre for European Constitutional Law and the Institute for Advanced Legal Studies, 2014) 64.

10 Without, however, defining what a 'direct consequence' is.

11 This aspect was clarified in several occasions by the CJEU with regards to the previous FD 2001/220/JHA. See in particular Case C-467/05 *Dell'Orto* [2007] ECLI:EU:C:2007:395; Case C-205/09 *Eredics* [2010] ECLI:EU:C:2010:623.

or 'defendant'. This is attributable also to the absence of a solid anchorage to determine who should play that role: contrary to the defendant, a victim is not only whom law enforcement authorities identify as such, but also anyone who seeks reparation for the wrongdoing.[12] In other words, victims are those who claim to be victims, and some rights provided by Directive 2012/29/EU (e.g. information and support; see section III below) need to be protected even before law enforcement authorities exercise jurisdiction and determine who can actually play the role of victims in criminal proceedings. This can also lead to a proliferation of (alleged) victims with different interests.

III. THE SCOPE OF VICTIMS' RIGHTS IN THE EU

When dealing with victims' rights, it is necessary to be aware of their multi-level dimension. The EU has been active for some fifteen years with the objective of ensuring a uniform treatment of victims of crime in the whole continent, especially in order to improve the situation of those who fall victim in a country other than their country of residence ('cross-border victims'). The most recent instrument (Directive 2012/29/EU) aims to be a sort of comprehensive charter of (minimum) rights that victims should enjoy everywhere in the EU, and aims to remedy the shortcomings that led to an unsatisfactory implementation of the previous legal framework, namely the Framework Decision 2001/220/JHA.[13] The EU instruments, however, have to be integrated in the national systems, which may have very different approaches to victims' rights in criminal procedure. Spurred on by EU and international instruments, most countries are increasingly adopting some provisions aiming to strengthen the protection of victims; nevertheless, in most cases it is difficult to identify a coherent policy.[14] The result is still a patchwork that, due also to the heterogeneity of victims' rights, makes it difficult to compare two systems and decide which one offers a better treatment.

Directive 2012/29/EU establishes minimum standards concerning (a) information to be provided to victims, (b) support by victim support services, (c) participation in criminal proceedings, (d) protection (both from 'secondary' and 'repeated' victimisation), and (d) reparation. It is important to stress that the ambition of the EU is not necessarily to guarantee an equal treatment of victims everywhere, but

12 See André Klip, *European Criminal Law* (3rd edn, Intersentia 2016) 331.

13 Council Framework Decision 2001/220/JHA on the standing of victims in criminal proceedings [2001] OJ L82/1. See, in Italian, Silvia Allegrezza, Hervé Belluta, Mitja Gialuz, and Luca Lupària, *Lo scudo e la spada. Esigenze di protezione e poteri delle vittime nel processo penale tra Europa e Italia* (Giappichelli 2012); Michele Simonato, *Deposizione della vittima e giustizia penale. Una lettura del sistema italiano alla luce del quadro europeo* (Wolters Kluwer 2014) 65.

14 'Protecting Victims' Rights in the EU' (n 9) 61–62.

to ensure a uniform approach to some issues that should be particularly beneficial to cross-border victims. The expected level of harmonisation (not yet officially assessed by the Commission) is different in relation to the different rights: for example, one might expect a higher convergence as regards the support services, and more differences as regards participation in criminal proceedings.[15]

In this regard, indeed, one may observe that the Directive is not very far-reaching as regards the active role of victims. The minimum level to be ensured in every Member State consists essentially of: (a) the right to be heard at some point in the proceedings;[16] (b) the right to ask for a review of the decision not to prosecute;[17] (c) the right to obtain a decision on the compensation by the offender, unless national law provides that such a decision is made in other legal proceedings; and (d) some 'ancillary' rights, such as the right to legal aid, to the reimbursement of expenses and the return of seized property. These rights are not further specified by the Directive (and are therefore entirely determined by national law) and, more importantly, there is no real indication as to which powers victims should be granted in every system. In other words, there is no obligation whatsoever to recognise victims as proper *parties* in criminal procedure.[18] In some legal systems, however, victims have the possibility of triggering the jurisdiction to adjudicate: the problem, in this regard, is to understand whether victims' position in a national criminal procedure has an impact on the allocation of the case in that jurisdiction (see section IV below).

As mentioned above, Directive 2012/29/EU pays specific attention to cross-border victims: it contains provisions on the interpretation and translation of information to be given to victims,[19] and provisions specifically aiming to 'minimise the difficulties faced where the victim is a resident of a Member State other than that where the criminal offence was committed'. In particular, the Directive envisages the possibility ~~of~~ for victims to make~~ing~~ a complaint from their Member State of residence, with recourse to video-conferencing in order to ensure their testimony during the proceedings without travelling to another country.

In this regard, it is worth observing that the Directive seems to suggest that a certain level of cooperation between Member States is necessary in order to take

15 The deadline for the transposition in national law was on 16 November 2015. The Commission was supposed to publish the implementation report by November 2017.

16 Article 10 of Directive 2012/29/EU.

17 Article 11 of Directive 2012/29/EU. Its second paragraph specifies that in the Member States in which the role of victims 'will be established only after a decision to prosecute the offender has been taken, Member States shall ensure that at least the victims of serious crimes have the right to a review of a decision not to prosecute'.

18 See recital 20 of Directive 2012/29/EU, and recital 9 of FD 2001/220/JHA.

19 Article 7 of Directive 2012/29/EU.

care of these special victims, in particular making sure that they can make a complaint in their country of residence and that such a complaint is transmitted to the competent authorities in another Member State. Nevertheless, such a duty of co-operation seems to cease when there is a conflict of jurisdiction: Article 17(3) states that Member States shall transmit the complaint only 'if the competence to institute the proceedings has not been exercised by the Member State in which the complaint was made'. This seems to imply that victims do not have any role in the choice of forum: the duty of cooperation between national authorities is necessary to ensure that an investigation is started somewhere in the EU territory, but not in order to give victims the choice between several *fora*.

A role of victims as regards the exercise of jurisdiction was recognised by the Advocate General of the Court of Justice of the European Union (CJEU) in *Kossowski*, the most recent chapter in the development of transnational *ne bis in idem* in the EU.[20] The case concerned a Polish citizen who, after allegedly having committed a crime in Germany, drove back to Poland, where he was arrested for other reasons. At the same time, the Polish authorities, having legitimate jurisdiction, opened an investigation of the facts regarding the crime committed in Germany. In order to proceed with the investigation, the Polish prosecutor contacted the German authorities, who transmitted a copy of their file on Mr Kossowski. The Polish authorities, however, decided to drop the case and not to prosecute him on the basis of insufficient available information, in particular because it had not been possible to hear witnesses residing in Germany, including the victim. Some years later, a prosecutor in Hamburg intended to prosecute Kossowski in Germany for the same facts already considered in Poland, inter alia because the Polish authorities did not really assess the merits of the facts, since they dropped the case owing to the insufficiency of evidence and—most importantly—without conducting detailed investigations.

The Advocate General too believed that the Polish authorities did not examine the merits of the case, and therefore the EU *ne bis in idem* would not be triggered. One of his arguments for the possibility of prosecuting Kossowski again in Germany was based on victims' rights, namely the right to compensation, which would be jeopardised by the application of *ne bis in idem*.[21] The Court of Justice followed most of the Advocate General's reasoning by concluding that the Polish final decision did not enter into the merits of the case; however, in its judgment the Court did not use the argument based on the protection of victims' rights, probably deeming it too far-reaching or not entirely convincing.[22] The EU legal framework, indeed, aims to ensure that certain victims' rights are recognised and respected in every

20 Opinion of Advocate General Bot in *Kossowski*, Case C-486/14, ECLI:EU:C:2015:812.

21 ibid paras 80–83.

22 Case C-486/14 *Kossowski* ECLI:EU:C:2016:483.

country, but it does not suggest that, if such rights are not correctly protected in one country, new criminal proceedings can be initiated in other Member States in order to ensure such protection. A fortiori, it does not provide that in cases of concurrent jurisdiction criminal proceedings should be brought in one Member State rather than another, exactly because a homogeneous level of protection should be ensured everywhere in Europe.

In conclusion, the ambition of the EU is to create a uniform area where victims are able to exercise their rights anywhere without major obstacles. The tangible reality, however, is different, and the treatment of victims may differ from one jurisdiction to another. In this regard, the supranational dimension of their rights does not give indications on the relation between national levels of protection when there is a conflict between legitimate exercises of jurisdiction.

IV. MULTIPLE LEGITIMATE JURISDICTIONS: WHAT IS THE PROBLEM (FOR VICTIMS)?

Victims' needs and expectations are so variegated that it is difficult to analyse all the possible scenarios: some victims seek compensation, others broader reparation, or public recognition, or exemplary sentences, or simply some privacy. In particular, one may observe different types of interaction between victims and criminal justice systems. A crime victim can participate actively (e.g. as a *partie civile*) or unwillingly (e.g. as a witness) in the proceedings against the perpetrator. Particularly in the first case, one may imagine that she welcomes the conflicts of jurisdiction (i.e. that more than one country is exercising its jurisdiction on the same facts). Multiple investigations are more likely to satisfy her 'right' to truth and ultimately to avoid the impunity of perpetrators. In the international context there are many examples of multiplication of jurisdictions that are beneficial from the perspective of 'collective' victims, especially where the prosecution has encountered major obstacles in some countries.[23] Also looking at the EU context one may affirm that the proliferation of *fora* does not represent a real threat for victims, but rather a resource. Although such considerations should be backed by empirical evidence, victims may not have any real interests in avoiding the conflicts by limiting the number of jurisdictions.[24]

On the contrary, provided that a Member State is competent, victims in some Member States have some possibilities to activate the jurisdiction (e.g. private

23 For example, one may think of the recent investigations conducted in Argentina on the crimes committed by the Francoist regime in Spain. See Ofelia Ferrán and Lisa Hilbink, 'Introduction' in Ofelia Ferrán and Lisa Hilbink (eds), *Legacy of Violence in Contemporary Spain: Exhuming the Past, Understanding the Present* (Routledge 2016) 1.

24 This view was also presented by Eurojust representatives during the project's meetings.

prosecution)[25] or to exercise a control on the non-exercise of jurisdiction (e.g. review of the decision not to prosecute). The private prosecutions recognised in some Member States entail that victims have more possibilities than the defendant to exercise a sort of 'forum shopping', given the regulatory function of the EU *ne bis in idem* working as a 'first come, first served' rule. In other words, through private prosecutions victims may help one Member State run faster in the 'race to prosecution' (i.e. in order to be the first getting a final decision and thereby triggering the EU *ne bis in idem*). To some extent this may contribute to the 'problem', in the sense that even if private prosecutions do not necessarily create a conflict (if other jurisdictions are not informed or not willing to exercise the jurisdiction), at least they increase the possibility that the forum is chosen unilaterally by victims. Furthermore, they may create a conflict (increasing the jurisdictions interested in a case), if the private prosecution were brought before a (competent) Member State that otherwise would not have exercised its jurisdiction.[26]

If it is true that, unlike the defendant, victims do not seem to be endangered by the fact that one or more Member States are competent on the same facts and willing to start parallel investigations, one may wonder what happens in the following phase, when different national authorities intend to bring the suspect to trial in their own jurisdiction. In this case, the same reasoning might apply: several prosecutions on the same facts do not represent necessarily a problem, but a chance to get a conviction or reparation somewhere. In the composite rationale of *ne bis in idem* there does not seem to be room for the protection of any victims' right: on the contrary, such a principle might be seen from the victims' perspective as an obstacle in their quest for truth and justice.

However, in at least two situations victims might be affected by the multiple exercise of jurisdiction. The first case is represented by the victim who is an unwilling participant in the proceedings: one may think, for example, of minors and other vulnerable victims. Contrary to a person who is interested in participating and able to activate the preferred competent jurisdiction, a subject who only wants to forget the wrongdoing may be nonetheless summoned as a witness in several jurisdictions. This might create excessive burden, and further harm, that might be only partially overcome by the cooperation between Member States (e.g. through the use of video-conferencing). The rationale of their protection—explicitly embraced by EU Directive 2012/29/EU, for example when stating that 'the number of interviews of victims is kept to a minimum and interviews are carried out only where strictly

25 The EU legal framework does not provide for a right to private prosecution. See Case C-507/10 *Criminal proceedings against X* ECLI:EU:C:2011:873.

26 See the example of the crash of the Air France airbus off the coast of Brazil, mentioned by Martin Böse, Frank Meyer, and Anne Schneider, 'Comparative Analysis' in Böse, Meyer, and Schneider (eds), *Conflicts of Jurisdiction in Criminal Matters in the European Union, Vol. I* (n 2) 445.

necessary for the purposes of investigation'[27]—should apply even more when authorities from different Member States are investigating and conducting the interviews.

The second problematic scenario concerns also the actively participating victim, and it is helpful to understand that victims may want to have a say in the moment in which a choice of forum must be made. If the exercise of multiple jurisdictions is not a threat as such, indeed, the problem arises when a choice needs to be made for other reasons, such as the protection of the defendant's rights or the efficient use of resources. Like defendants, victims may prefer one forum to another; and that forum may not necessarily be the one favoured by the prosecutor. Indeed, there are still manifest complications in exercising victims' rights abroad; the EU 'ambition' mentioned above, namely the attention to cross-border victims, is a clear demonstration in this regard. As has been argued, '[a] major challenge for the future is that national criminal justice systems not only exchange evidence and transfer offenders across borders but also cooperate regarding the involvement of victims residing outside national territories in the administration of justice'.[28]

V. THE INTERESTS OF VICTIMS IN THE CHOICE OF ONE FORUM

A. How are victims' interests currently considered?

It has been explained above that, like defendants, currently victims do not have a clear position in the resolution of conflicts of jurisdiction in the EU. In the present scenario: (a) the choice of forum, if any, is made by prosecutors; (b) the Eurojust guidelines refer to a vague concept of 'interests of victims' without defining it; (c) there is no hierarchy between the different criteria provided by the Eurojust guidelines; (d) victims do not express their views during the choice of forum. Therefore, one may expect that prosecutors define and consider victims' interests on a case-by-case basis.

The interviews conducted at Eurojust in the framework of the project had the objective to explore the practice as regards the forum choice, including the consideration of victims' interests.[29] The results of the research confirm the uncertain definition of the nature of victims' interests at stake (and their weight in the decision on the forum). If there have been some national desks admitting that victims'

27 Article 20(b).

28 Letschert and Groenhuijsen (n 1) 37.

29 See Angelo Marletta, 'Report on the Field Research at Eurojust' in this volume, particularly question no 7 of the questionnaire: 'How would you define the "interests of victims"? And which consideration should be given to them? Can you describe a case where those interests have been expressly evaluated?'.

interests are not normally considered (e.g. Ireland) or that at least they are not a decisive factor (e.g. Czech Republic, Sweden, Germany, Denmark), other interviewees reported a relevant impact of those interests in the forum choice (e.g. Italy, France), in particular in cases of cross-border trafficking of human beings (e.g. Spain, United Kingdom). Where taken into consideration, victims' interests seem to be interpreted as the possibility to have the trial in the Member State in which the victim has her residence (e.g. Italy, France, Denmark, United Kingdom) or in which most of the victims reside (e.g. Belgium).

In this regard, one may have the impression that taking into consideration victims' residence (without hearing victims' opinions) means to consider victims mainly in their capacity as witnesses, or at least to consider victims' interests as long as they coincide with the interests of prosecution (of having the victims in the adjudicating jurisdictions). One may imagine, however, that victims' interests do not necessarily coincide with the prosecution's interests, and that they do not necessarily consist of having the trial in their country of residence. In other words, in the current scenario prosecutors (at most) assume that victims want to have the trial in their country of residence, whereas they might find elsewhere a better recognition, procedural role, or compensation.[30] In this regard, further empirical research could better clarify what victims' interests actually consist of.

Considering such a scenario, one may therefore wonder whether the current approach is sufficient to ensure that victims' perspective is taken into account as a 'third view' different from those of the prosecution and the defendant. On the other hand, one may wonder whether this approach is correct, in the sense that concerns may arise, for example, as regards the low foreseeability of the decision (owing to the lack of definition of 'victims' interests'); or as regards an excessive practical relevance of the victims' residence criterion over defendants' interests (owing to the lack of hierarchy between the criteria).

B. Towards a new instrument: what type of victims' interests?

In order to include victims' perspectives in the new instrument, therefore, the first question to be addressed is: what victims' interests should be taken into consideration? Such a question, however, is strictly intertwined with other fundamental questions related to the objective of an instrument on conflicts of jurisdiction. Should the new instrument ensure that a neutral choice is made (i.e. that the decision on the jurisdiction is not used to advance any specific policy)? Or should it be admitted that a neutral choice is not possible[31] and that it suffices to ensure the 'foreseeability' of the adjudicating jurisdiction?

30 Spain has reported cases in which victims' protection needs were considered.

31 Nathalie I. Thorhauer, 'Conflicts of Jurisdiction in Cross-Border Criminal Cases in the Area of Freedom, Security and Justice' (2015) 6(1) *New Journal of European Criminal Law* 84.

Furthermore, the choice on the victims' interests deserving consideration depends also on the 'procedural design' of the instrument. Should victims participate in the decision (i.e. should victims sit at the same table with prosecutors and suspects)? Or should victims' interests continue to be interpreted and considered only by prosecutors? It is evident that a flexible instrument, allowing victims to participate in the choice but not necessarily aiming to ensure a neutral choice, would leave some margin to consider the 'subjective' preference of victims as regards the forum. This might regard, for example, legal systems recognising a stronger victims' participation in criminal proceedings than others, or systems providing for higher penalties for a specific crime. It is worth observing that the participation of victims in the deliberation on the forum would be important in order to bring a third viewpoint, which is different not only from the defendant's but also from the prosecutors' interests. Such an inclusion would therefore contribute to limiting the hegemony of the prosecution in the forum choice; on the other hand, however, it is not self-evident that the interests of victims correspond to 'legitimate' expectations on the adjudicating jurisdiction.

Several reasons—including those linked to the foreseeability of the choice—suggest looking for criteria which are as 'objective' as possible, that is, not linked to a mere preference for one forum (for example, because of the best chance of obtaining a high sentence). Similarly to the resolution of conflicts of jurisdiction in international private law,[32] the 'qualities' of a particular system should not have much weight in the choice. The rationale of mutual trust—especially given the harmonising objectives of the EU in the field of victims' rights—rules out the possibility of comparing different systems on the basis of the supposed chances accorded to victims, as well as to assess which one is better than others, also in terms of efficiency.[33]

Especially if victims do not directly participate in the forum choice, the identification of objective criteria (i.e. applicable regardless of victims' subjective will) is important in order to limit the arbitrariness of the decision. Nevertheless, it is not an easy task, since there is the risk to rely on variable factors that render such criteria unforeseeable for the suspect; furthermore, such criteria might not correspond to the real interests of the victim(s) in that specific case. The proposed instruments have, therefore, provided for the possibility for victims to submit written observations during the procedure for the forum choice. The horizontal and vertical mechanisms have also tried to identify what interests could be considered, namely the possibility to avoid secondary victimisation and to resort to protective measures, especially in

32 Pietro Ortolani in this volume.

33 The expected duration of the proceedings cannot be a relevant criterion for the forum choice in international private law; see Case C-116/02 *Gasser* ECLI:EU:C:2003:657, para 72.

the case of vulnerable victims or violent crimes, and the possibility of obtaining adequate compensation.

On the other hand, it was decided not to mention other factors, such as the damage suffered by the victim, the number of victims, or the costs they have to bear. Each of them, indeed, presents a number of pitfalls. For example, considering the place in which the event of the crime occurred could be useful to identify territoriality in case of transnational crimes, provided that such a consequence is foreseeable by the defendant; however, it is more dangerous to compare the level of damage suffered in different countries:[34] it would still depend on the initial claim of the alleged victims, thereby increasing the risk of privatisation of forum choice. The number of victims seems to be more objective: if the same conduct harmed more people resident in one Member State than in others, it might appear appropriate to hold the trial in that jurisdiction. Nevertheless, there is the risk that many victims are not recognised yet at the initial stage, but are identified during the course of the proceedings. The costs of the proceedings ('procedural economy') are mentioned in the Eurojust guidelines[35] and play a more relevant role in the context of international private law;[36] even in this case, however, it depends on many factors, such as the number of participating subjects, or on the number of pieces of evidence requested by the prosecution, defendants, and victims.[37] Finally, it is worth mentioning that the residence of victims may raise some concerns in light of EU citizenship (see section V.d above), and could be used at most as a subsidiary criterion if the others do not lead to a solution.

C. A hierarchy between different interests?

One of the most debated issues is whether the forum choice should be based on a hierarchical list of criteria, or should consist of a case-by-case decision that balances equivalent criteria. This depends also on the ultimate objective of the instrument: if a certain hierarchy would better guarantee the certainty (or foreseeability) of the forum, a 'basket' of equally-important criteria would at least ensure the transparency of the choice: in this context, the list of criteria would indeed be useful to provide a legal basis for the deliberation, especially in view of judicial review.[38]

34 As in Switzerland: see Michiel Luchtman in this volume.

35 Eurojust guidelines mention the 'costs of prosecuting' as a factor, which is only to be considered when all the other factors are equally balanced.

36 Namely in the *forum non conveniens* doctrine, see Aukje van Hoek in this volume.

37 Look at the example of the ICC, where there is one legal representative.

38 See Tom Vander Beken, Gert Vermeulen, Soetekin Steverlynck, and Stefan Thomaes, *Finding the Best Place for Prosecution: European Study on Jurisdiction Criteria* (Maklu 2002) 21.

Also in the case of non-hierarchical criteria the decision needs to be properly reasoned, and all the criteria 'have to be weighed up against each other'.[39] It is always necessary, therefore, to compare the perspectives of defendants and victims. Looking at the nature of the opposite interests may be a starting point to reflect whether we are dealing with equal interests, and whether there is a sort of implicit hierarchy between two opposing claims. An affirmative answer would require thorough reasoning when according priority to 'lower' criteria. The first question to ask is therefore: do victims have fundamental rights at stake in the forum choice?[40]

Luchtman has explained that some fundamental rights of the defendant might be endangered by an arbitrary choice of forum.[41] Concerns arise in particular with regard to the legality principle, that is, to the foreseeable law applicable,[42] and to the tribunal (previously) established by law, that is, a judicial organisation not depending on the discretion of the executive.[43] As to victims, the question becomes whether they have a legitimate expectation of being considered in the choice of the adjudicating jurisdiction.[44] In order to answer it, it is worth briefly exploring the scope of some fundamental rights enshrined in the ECHR.[45]

According the European Court of Human Rights (ECtHR), which has developed an extensive body of case law on 'positive obligations', some victims' rights directly derive from certain fundamental rights enshrined in the ECHR, namely Article 2 (right to life), Article 3 (prohibition of torture), Article 4 (prohibition of slavery and forced labour), and Article 8 (right to respect for private and family life).[46] According

39 Anke Biehler, Roland Kniebühler, Juliette Lelieur-Fischer, and Sybil Stein (eds), *Freiburg Proposal on Concurrent Jurisdictions and the Prohibition of Multiple Prosecutions in the European Union* (Max Planck Institute for Foreign and International Criminal Law 2003) 16.

40 It is worth observing that the traditional distinction between rights and interests, based on the enforceability of a certain claim, is probably less clear in practice than in theory. It has been argued, for example, that the CJEU adopts the same standard for review in cases concerning fundamental rights and cases concerning other interests, i.e. a proportionality test, whose intensity may vary in the two types of cases—see for example Janneke H. Gerards, 'Fundamental Rights and Other Interests: Should It Really Make a Difference?' in Eva Brems (ed), *Conflicts between Fundamental Rights* (Intersentia 2008) 655, 681. Furthermore, the ECtHR has significantly stretched the scope of some traditional fundamental rights—going beyond the literal interpretation of the Convention and producing a sort of 'proliferation' of fundamental rights—by using the concepts of 'positive obligations' and 'living instrument'.

41 See Michiel Luchtman in this volume.

42 Article 7 ECHR, art 49 CFREU.

43 Article 6 ECHR, art 47 CFREU.

44 Not even the defendant has such a right, as stressed by Michiel Luchtman in this volume.

45 The approach of the ECHR will also serve as a benchmark to assess the scope of the rights enshrined in the CFREU, according to its art 52(3).

46 Andrew Ashworth, *Positive Obligations in Criminal Law* (Hart Publishing 2013) 211, observes that there may be some scope for the development of positive obligations in relation to art 9 (freedom of thought and religion), art 10 (freedom of expression), and art 11 (freedom of assembly

to such an approach, when one of these fundamental rights is violated, even if there is no immediate evidence that the violation is a direct result of an action of the public authority, Member States should not only criminalise the conduct violating such rights (substantive obligations), but also undertake effective and independent investigations in order to identify and punish those responsible for such a violation (procedural obligations). Although not fully defining them, on several occasions the ECtHR has clarified some features that such investigations must have.[47] Among them, for our purposes it is worth stressing that: (a) the investigations should ensure some form of participation of victims, at least in the sense that they should accord them (or their next of kin) the possibility to be heard; (b) Member States also have a duty of cooperation, that is, an obligation to seek the cooperation of foreign authorities (using all the cooperation instruments) when it is necessary to gather relevant information abroad.

In the context of international cooperation in the investigation on the violation of rights deserving a 'positive' protection, 'the corollary of the obligation on an investigating State to secure evidence located in other jurisdictions is a duty on the State where evidence is located to render any assistance within its competence and means sought under a legal assistance request'.[48] The case law of the ECtHR is strongly based on the idea of territoriality, in the sense that national investigations must cover (at least) events occurring in their national territory.[49] This is understandable, because the ECtHR judges the behaviour of single nation states. Nevertheless, in the case of transnational crimes—namely trafficking of human beings—the Court has suggested a certain vision of 'collective responsibility' (still based on territoriality: country A investigates in its territory and seeks cooperation, country B investigates in its territory and offers cooperation) endorsing the idea of concurrent jurisdiction and parallel investigations:

. . . [t]he Court reiterates that trafficking is a problem which is often not confined to the domestic arena. When a person is trafficked from one State to another, trafficking offences may occur in the State of origin, any State of transit and the State of destination. Relevant evidence and witnesses may be located in all States . . . the Anti-Trafficking Convention explicitly requires each member State to

and association), 'although at this stage one cannot be sure what form they would take'. See also Liora Lazarus, 'Positive Obligations and Criminal Justice: Duties to Protect or Coerce?' in Lucia Zedner and Julian V. Roberts (eds), *Principles and Values in Criminal Law and Criminal Justice* (Hart Publishing 2012) 135.

47 See *Söderman v Sweden* App no 5786/08 (ECtHR, 12 November 2013).

48 *Rantsev v Cyprus and Russia* App no 25965/04 (ECtHR, 7 January 2010) para 245.

49 ibid paras 243 and 308, where the Court observed that: 'The recruitment having occurred on Russian territory, the Russian authorities were best placed to conduct an effective investigation into Ms Rantseva's recruitment'.

establish jurisdiction over any trafficking offence committed in its territory . . . Such an approach is, in the Court's view, only logical in light of the general obligation, outlined above, incumbent on all States under Article 4 of the Convention to investigate alleged trafficking offences. In addition to the obligation to conduct a domestic investigation into events occurring on their own territories, member States are also subject to a duty in cross-border trafficking cases to cooperate effectively with the relevant authorities of other States concerned in the investigation of events which occurred outside their territories. Such a duty is in keeping with the objectives of the member States, as expressed in the preamble to the Palermo Protocol (12 December 2000), to adopt a comprehensive international approach to trafficking in the countries of origin, transit and destination . . . It is also consistent with international agreements on mutual legal assistance in which the respondent States participate in the present case . . .[50]

As regards transnational proceedings, however, the Court focuses on the investigative phase and—differently from domestic situations[51]—does not go as far as to exercise a scrutiny on the decision whether to prosecute and punish the offender or not. To our knowledge, the ECtHR has never said that in transnational cases every Member State is obliged to prosecute the perpetrators for the (part of the) conduct committed in their own territory. In other words, in order to protect victims, Member States have the obligation to establish and activate their jurisdiction, to conduct effective investigations, and not to create obstacles to the prosecution and punishment of the offenders. On the other hand, the ECHR does not provide for the right to a 'private revenge',[52] that is, for a victim's right to have the perpetrator prosecuted or punished in a specific jurisdiction. For this reason, it is difficult to imagine that a country that has conducted effective investigations and transferred the proceedings to another country could be condemned on the basis of the positive obligation doctrine.

The right to activate a jurisdiction, but not necessarily a trial, may better be grasped by looking at the question of whether victims have a right to a fair trial (i.e. whether Article 6 ECHR applies to victims). The answer is not straightforward, and the approach of the ECtHR can be summarised as follows. First, the victim enjoys the right provided by Article 6(1) as regards its civil limb (i.e. the general right to a fair trial, in the sense that she has the right of access to justice, but that justice could consist also of civil proceedings).[53] However, there is no

50 ibid para 289.

51 See, among others, Françoise Tulkens, 'The Paradoxical Relationship between Criminal Law and Human Rights' (2011) 9 *Journal of International Criminal Justice* 579, 584.

52 See, among others, *Giuliani and Gaggio v Italy* App no 23458/02 (ECtHR, 24 March 2011) para 306.

53 Including the possibility to bring civil proceedings against the accused after he has been acquitted, if based of different criteria independent of any criminal responsibility. *Ringvold v*

right to a private criminal prosecution.[54] In this regard, the decision *Mihova v Italy* is relevant. The case concerned a victim who had not been consulted within a mechanism of 'negotiated justice' (a soft sentence in exchange for the avoidance of the trial) between prosecutor and suspect in the course of the investigation. She had, however, the possibility to sue the alleged perpetrator before a civil tribunal to obtain compensation, but she complained that if she had had the opportunity to participate in the 'negotiation' on the sentence and to challenge the prosecutor-suspect agreement, the final outcome would have been different and the sentence higher. The ECtHR considered the application inadmissible, because the right to have a private 'revenge' in a criminal forum—provided that the possibility to obtain compensation is however ensured—is not provided by the Convention.[55]

Second, the victim enjoys also the right to a fair criminal trial as long as a role in criminal proceeding is provided in that specific legal system. In other words, the ECHR does not provide for a fundamental right to have an active role in criminal proceedings, but if the victim is allowed to play such a role (e.g. as *partie civile*) then the proceedings must be fair also for her, insomuch as 'the civil component remains closely connected with the criminal component', and insofar as 'the criminal proceedings affect the civil component'.[56]

Furthermore, in the concept of fair trial (for the defendant) the Court has often observed that victims' needs (e.g. of protection from secondary victimisation) should be taken into consideration, whatever the role she is playing during the trial.[57] In other words, in the concept of fair trial there is room to accommodate the safeguard of victims' interests; however, this does not mean that victims enjoy the same rights expressly provided only for the accused, in the sense that victims

Norway App no 34964/97 (ECtHR, 11 February 2003) paras 37 and 38; see also Rusen Ergec and Jacques Velu, *Convention européenne des droits de l'homme* (2nd edn, Bruylant 2014) 481.

54 *Ernst and Others v Belgium* App no 33400/96 (ECtHR, 15 July 2003) para 47. With regard to the EU framework, see also *Criminal proceedings against X* (n 25).

55 '[L]a requérante souhaitait, pour l'essentiel, exercer dans le procès pénal une action à but répressif ou bien le droit à la 'vengeance privée', qui n'est pas, en tant que tel, garanti par la Convention' (*Mihova v Italy (dec.)* App no 25000/07 (ECtHR, 30 March 2010)).

56 *Perez v France* App no 47287/99 (ECtHR, 12 February 2004) para 67; see also *Pieniazek v Poland* App no 62179/00 (ECtHR, 28 September 2004) para 20.

57 'It is true that Article 6 does not explicitly require the interests of witnesses in general, and those of victims called upon to testify in particular, to be taken into consideration. However, their life, liberty or security of person may be at stake, as may interests coming generally within the ambit of Article of the Convention . . . Against this background, principles of fair trial also require that in appropriate cases the interests of the defence are balanced against those of witnesses or victims called upon to testify' (*Doorson v Netherlands* App no 20524/92 (ECtHR, 26 March 1996) para 70).

could not apply to the ECtHR because they have not had the same procedural rights as are afforded to the defendant.

One may wonder whether and to what extent the concept of lawful judge enshrined in Article 6 ECHR applies also to victims. The principle of a tribunal (previously)[58] established by law precludes that one party chooses alone the court for the trial, that is, the rules of the game to the detriment of the other parties.[59] In this regard, one might argue that Article 6 ECHR could come into play for the victims when they are parties in the proceedings. Nevertheless, the ECtHR has never applied it to victims as regards criminal tribunals, since the rationale of the (criminal) tribunal previously established by law primarily consists of the protection of the accused against arbitrary choices of the executive, requiring an act of Parliament establishing the tribunal.[60] Article 47 of the Charter of Fundamental Rights of the European Union (CFREU) does not give different indications in the sense of applying the requirement of a lawful (criminal) judge also to victims.

As stated above, the EU legal framework accords some other rights to crime victims (assistance, information, participation, reparation, etc). The objective of harmonisation typical of such instruments implies that the essence of these rights should be respected in every Member State. Therefore, every Member State taking over a criminal proceeding should ensure that EU victims' rights are not violated. Provided that these rights are respected, one may imagine that victims have interests in choosing one jurisdiction rather than another on the basis of practical aspects (language, travelling, costs, etc) and on their assessment of the 'best forum' (highest penalties, possibilities of participation, highest efficiency, etc). For example, victims may be interested in having the proceedings in one country because in another one there are negotiated justice mechanisms that exclude victims from the criminal trial contest. As clarified by the ECtHR, such claims do not reflect rights protected by the ECHR: victims must be able to launch a civil action, but they are not necessarily entitled to ask for the punishment of the offender. So far the CJEU has not ruled differently on this point, according to victims a sort of right to a specific criminal jurisdiction.

In conclusion, there seems to be a major difference between the interest of the defendant and the interest of the victim in a multi-jurisdictional setting: the defendant

58 Compared with art 6 ECHR, art 47 CFREU adds the word 'previously' to the requirement of the judge established by law. See Michele Panzavolta, *Choice of Forum and the Lawful Judge Concept* in Michiel Luchtman (ed), *Choice of Forum in Cooperation Against EU Financial Crime* (Eleven International Publishing 2013) 161.

59 Michiel Luchtman in this volume.

60 Furthermore, it is worth recalling that in many countries the victims cannot become a party at all in criminal proceedings, and also in Member States providing for the *partie civile* it is clear that they are ancillary—and not essential—actors in the trial, which would be held also in their absence.

has some fundamental rights endangered by the choice of one jurisdiction rather than another, while it is more difficult to define the nature of victims' interests in having the trial in one specific jurisdiction. In this regard, one could observe that there are many cases in which the defendants' fundamental rights are respected by the forum choice, for example when he is aware of acting in several jurisdictions and the forum choice is foreseeable. One may argue that in these cases the defendant does not have any legitimate expectation to be tried in one jurisdiction, and that his interests are not more relevant than those of the victim. Nevertheless, even in that case a sort of implicit hierarchy could derive from the risks linked to the forum choice, since only the defendant may be subject to punishment at the outcome of criminal proceedings.

D. What is the impact of EU citizenship?

The concept of EU citizenship might add something to the reflection, primarily because of the EU goal to offer its citizens an Area of Freedom, Security and Justice (AFSJ).[61] One may wonder, indeed, whether victims can derive further rights from that principle.

Among the various citizens' rights enshrined also in Title V of the CFREU (e.g. the right to vote, to diplomatic protection, to petition, etc) the main aspects of EU citizenship are linked to the non-discrimination principle, that is, the equal treatment of individuals regardless of nationality,[62] and the freedom of movement, even when someone is not conducting any economic activity.[63] In this regard, the CJEU has clarified that: (a) Member States must comply with EU law even when exercising powers related to their sole competence (i.e. criminal law and procedure cannot be discriminatory for EU citizens);[64] (b) EU citizenship is a fundamental status of the Union for every citizen, even when they do not actually move across borders (i.e. whenever the ability to move is made 'less attractive');[65] therefore, EU citizenship 'precludes national measures which have the effect of depriving citizens of the Union of the genuine enjoyment of the substance of the rights conferred by virtue of their status as citizens of the Union',[66] such as

61 Article 3 TEU. See Katalin Ligeti and Angelo Marletta, 'EU Criminal Justice Actors. Accountability and Judicial Review vis-à-vis the EU Citizen' (2016) 7(2) *New Journal of European Criminal Law* 175.

62 Article 18 TFEU.

63 Article 21 TFEU, art 45 CFREU.

64 For example, see Case C-186/87 *Cowan v Trésor public* ECLI:EU:C:1989:47, where the CJEU clearly stated that an EU citizen may not be excluded from a victim compensation scheme on the sole ground of his/her nationality.

65 Case C-34/09 *Ruiz Zambrano* ECLI:EU:C:2011:124; see also the opinion of Advocate General Sharpston in this case, ECLI:EU:C:2010:560, para 72; and the opinion of Advocate General Kokott in Case C-192/05 *Tas-Hagen* ECLI:EU:C:2006:223, para 50. See Elspeth Guild, 'Free Movement of EU Citizens and their Family Members' (2016) 7(2) *New Journal of European Criminal Law* 231.

66 Case C-34/09 *Ruiz Zambrano* (n 65) para 42.

the right to decide where to 'produce, work, love, marry, live, travel, consume, and cook'.[67]

Although the dimension of EU citizenship has influenced the EU policies on victims' rights, consequently strengthening their protection and their position within criminal justice systems, being an EU citizen does not seem to give a victim further possibilities to be considered in the choice of the competent jurisdiction (to adjudicate). On the contrary, if compared with the defendants' position, if the EU citizenship has an impact on the solution of conflicts of jurisdiction, this is in the sense of limiting the influence of the victim *vis-à-vis* the suspect.

It has been observed that EU citizenship entails a new approach of the individuals to the states, that is, a 'recalibrated notion of personal autonomy which now goes beyond the context of the nation state, and also encompasses the position of the individual *vis-à-vis* the joint EU Member States'.[68] If—owing to the complexity of the citizens' approach to EU identity[69]—it still sounds utopian to affirm that 'the interest of the victim should be satisfied by the mere fact that the offender is prosecuted, irrespective of the question by which Member State',[70] from the perspective of EU citizenship one may at least argue in favour of the abolition of passive nationality jurisdiction. Many authors, indeed, convincingly argue that any future instrument should focus only on territoriality, limiting—or excluding—jurisdictional grounds based on (active or) passive personality,[71] which is seen as 'an anachronism, because there is no need for additional protection by the criminal law of the victim's home country'.[72]

If a defendant's freedom of movement may be hampered because of the risk of being subject (in an unforeseeable manner) to the *ius puniendi* of another Member

67 Rephrasing Ulrich Beck and Edgar Grande, *Cosmopolitan Europe* (Polity Press 2007) 36, quoted by Michiel Luchtman in this volume. See also Elise Muir and Anne P. van der Mei, 'The "EU Citizenship Dimension" of the Area of Freedom, Security and Justice' in Luchtman (n 58) 123.

68 Michiel Luchtman, 'Choice of Forum and the Prosecution of Cross-Border Crime in the European Union: What Role for the Legality Principle?' in Luchtman (n 58) 25.

69 See, among others, Joseph H. Weiler, 'To be a European citizen: Eros and Civilization' (1997) 4(4) *Journal of European Public Policy* 495.

70 Thorhauer (n 31) 99.

71 Martin Böse, 'Chapter 2: Fundamental Freedoms of the Union' in Martin Böse, Frank Meyer, and Anne Schneider (eds), *Conflicts of Jurisdiction in Criminal Matters in the European Union, Vol. II* (Nomos 2014) 45; Anne-Sophie Massa, 'Jurisdiction in England and Wales and in the Netherlands: a Comparative Appraisal with a European Touch' in André Klip (ed), *Substantive Criminal Law of the EU* (Maklu 2011) 103; Pedro Caeiro, 'Jurisdiction in Criminal Matters in the EU: Negative and Positive Conflicts, and Beyond' (2010) 93(4) *Kritische Vierteljahresschrift für Gesetzgebung und Rechtswissenschaft* 366, 374; Regula Echle, 'The Passive Personality Principle and the General Principle of *ne bis in idem*' (2013) 9(4) *Utrecht Law Review* 56.

72 Martin Böse and Frank Meyer, 'Introduction' in Böse, Meyer, and Schneider (eds), *Conflicts of Jurisdiction in Criminal Matters in the European Union, Vol. I* (n 2) 11.

State, individuals may be less keen to move across borders if they risk becoming a victim of crime and being treated differently in another Member State. In many cases, however, the hurdles to the victims' freedom of movement are not necessarily linked with the exercise of jurisdiction in one specific country, but can be removed either in the non-prosecuting Member State or through cooperation between Member States. For example, the assistance by victim support services and the protection from 'repeat' victimisation could be obtained also in the Member State which is not conducting any criminal proceedings against the perpetrator; whereas the right to information (from another country), participation (in another country), and protection from 'secondary' victimisation could be ensured by various mechanisms of cooperation between national authorities (as stated earlier, this is nothing other than the main objective of the EU action on victims' rights).

Provided that the protection of victims can be recognised regardless of the exercise of jurisdiction in a specific Member State, the victim may still prefer a different forum, for example because of greater possibilities to participate and to be recognised as an autonomous subject within criminal justice systems. This is of course a legitimate interest; nevertheless, it does not seem to receive an increased protection in the light of EU citizenship. The obstacles to moving within the EU because of the risk of not obtaining something (e.g. compensation, recognition, truth, etc) seem to be less compelling than the obstacles to moving because of the risk of being subject to unforeseen jurisdictions. In other words, the consequences of EU citizenship seem to be more relevant for EU defendants than for EU victims.

Nonetheless, if no further rights should be granted to victims in the choice of forum because of their EU citizenship, such a dimension can have at least one minor implication. In the Freiburg proposal,[73] for example, the reference to a victim's nationality does not seem to be in line with the rationale of EU citizenship. A reference to residence, thereby 'codifying' the practice of Eurojust, would already be an improvement, provided that it is only in the form of a presumption as to the preferable forum.

VI. CONCLUSIONS

Fully understanding what victims' interests should be taken into consideration in the forum choice would probably require further empirical research to clarify the vast array of victims' expectations. Given the lack of literature on that aspect, interviews with defence lawyers and victim support services would be useful in order to better understand when the problem of multiple jurisdictions actually arises for victims, and what the exact interest(s) in having the proceedings take place in one Member State rather than another may be.

73 Biehler, Kniebühler, Lelieur-Fischer, and Stein (n 39).

Even in the absence of such an empirical background, however, the legal analysis conducted in this chapter has tried to identify some conditions in order to include the victims' perspective in any future EU instrument aiming at the prevention and settlement of conflicts of jurisdiction. It is argued that a vague reference to victims' 'interest' should be replaced by the indication of criteria that are as objective as possible, in order to avoid the risk, for example, that a jurisdiction is chosen only because it provides for higher sanctions, or that such a choice is completely unforeseeable for the defendants. In this regard, some criteria related to victims could be useful in the identification of the territory in case of multiple jurisdictions based on territoriality (e.g. the Member State in which the result of the conduct occurred). Furthermore, this chapter has tried to indicate what should not be considered as a valid criterion. A reference to victims' nationality, for example, would be inconsistent with the concept of EU citizenship. Also, passive personality as a jurisdictional ground should not apply in the EU context which is necessarily characterised by mutual trust between sovereign states.

Other research projects on conflicts of jurisdiction have reached similar conclusions, too. Vander Beken and others, for example, clearly suggest limiting the ubiquity theory by affirming that 'the concept of territoriality shall not be interpreted in the sense that facts that only produce an effect on the territory are considered to be committed on the territory'.[74] Sinn and others identify some criteria related to victims, such as the Member State where most harm has been inflicted, the degree of upset of the local population, and the 'significant' interests of victims. According to that proposal, in the determination of the territoriality of a cross-border offence, the priority should be given to the location of criminal conduct, while the location of the result is a subsidiary criterion in case the conduct takes place in several Member States.[75] Böse and others envisage a clear abolition of the passive personality principle. Furthermore, their proposal identifies the location of the result of crime as a secondary criterion (compared with the location of the criminal conduct) for the identification of the territoriality.[76] According to their proposal, victims should be entitled to apply for the transfer of proceedings;[77] their interests are considered in complex cases involving multiple offenders charged in several jurisdictions[78] and in case of crimes committed outside the EU; moreover, victims have some possibilities

74 Vander Beken, Vermeulen, Steverlynck, and Thomaes (n 38).

75 Arndt Sinn (ed), *Jurisdiktionskonflikte bei grenzüberschreitender Kriminalität; Ein Rechtsvergleich zum Internationalen Strafrecht. Conflicts of Jurisdiction in Cross-Border Crime Situations* (Universitätsverlag Osnabrück at V&R Unipress 2012).

76 Martin Böse, Frank Meyer, and Anne Schneider (eds), *Conflicts of Jurisdiction in Criminal Matters in the European Union, Vol. II* (Nomos 2014).

77 Articles 8 and 12.

78 Article 11.

to participate in the procedure provided for the forum choice,[79] in order to 'make representations if it appears to be necessary for safeguarding his/her rights to effectively participate in the proceedings and if it does not improperly delay the course of proceedings or jeopardise the investigation'.

The procedural rules for the victims' participation in the determination of the forum have not been specifically addressed in this chapter, but were discussed with the Working Group members during the elaboration of the horizontal and the vertical instrument. One of the most debated issues concerned the standing of victims in such a mechanism, that is, whether they should be granted the same possibilities as defendants. This issue is closely related to the question of whether there should be a hierarchy between different criteria. In this regard, this chapter argues that the interests at stake in the forum choice are very different depending on whether they concern victims or defendants, and victims' expectations seem to be secondary if balanced against the defendants' rights that might be endangered by an arbitrary forum choice. For this reason, it does not seem even necessary to provide for the possibility for victims to seek a judicial review of the decision on the choice of forum.[80]

In conclusion, including the perspective of victims in the prevention and settlement of conflicts of jurisdiction would improve, at least in principle, the quality of the administration of justice in the AFSJ. However, this should be a prudent and balanced inclusion, since the primary objective of such instruments is to prevent the risk of parallel proceedings and/or unforeseeable choices on the forum from the suspects' perspective. Victims' possibility to be heard and not to be forgotten—especially in case of negative conflicts[81]—should not perpetuate the risk of unfair and arbitrary choices.

79 Article 12.

80 The proposal elaborated by Sinn and others did not provide for that possibility for the victim either; see Sinn (n 75) 606.

81 See Hans-Holger Herrnfeld, 'Mechanisms for Settling Conflicts of Jurisdictions' in Luchtman (n 58) 198.

11

CHOICE OF FORUM AND CASE ALLOCATION IN THE EPPO REGULATION

HANS-HOLGER HERRNFELD*

I. INTRODUCTION

The subject matter of 'conflicts of criminal jurisdiction' has already required attention of the EU legislator in the negotiations on the regulation on the establishment of the European Public Prosecutor's Office (EPPO). The purpose of this contribution is to present issues that have arisen in this respect and the solutions that have been found in the course of the negotiations on the EPPO Regulation. As will be shown further below, the outcome of the negotiations on the EPPO Regulation may to a limited extent serve as inspiration also in view of possible models to be developed for a resolution of conflicts of criminal jurisdiction between Member States.

The European Commission had presented a proposal for the EPPO Regulation on 13 July 2013[1] on the basis of Article 86 of the Treaty on the Functioning of the European Union (TFEU), according to which the Council, acting unanimously and after obtaining the consent of the European Parliament, may establish a European Public Prosecutor's Office in order to combat crimes affecting the financial interests of the Union. Negotiations in the Council on the regulation concluded in June 2017.[2] As the Council could not reach the unanimity required under Article 86(1) TFEU, a 'general approach' was established by the Council on 8 June 2017 in the framework of the specific procedures set out in sub-paragraphs 2 and 3 of Article 86(1) TFEU allowing for an adoption of the EPPO Regulation by way of enhanced cooperation. Following the European Parliament's consent given on the draft regulation, the formal adoption of the EPPO Regulation by a group of twenty Member States took place at the October 2017 Council meeting and the Regulation (EU) 2017/1939[3]

* The contribution reflects the author's personal views and not those of the German Federal Ministry of Justice and Consumer Protection. It has been updated to reflect the text of the EPPO Regulation following its formal adoption.

1 Proposal for a Council Regulation on the establishment of the European Public Prosecutor's Office, COM(2013) 534 final.

2 Council document ST 9545/2/17 Rev2 of 2 June 2017.

3 Council Regulation (EU) 2017/1939 of 12 October 2017 implementing enhanced cooperation on the establishment of the European Public Prosecutor's Office (the EPPO) OJ 2017 L283/1.

entered into force on 20 November 2017. The EPPO will have its seat in Luxembourg and is expected to take up its operational work by 2021.

This contribution will focus on conflicts of jurisdiction and case allocation within the EPPO and the EPPO territory. It will also address conflicts of competence between the EPPO and the national prosecution authorities of the participating Member States as well as possible conflicts of jurisdiction between the EPPO and non-participating Member States.[4]

To start out with, however, it will be necessary to look at some of the basic elements of the conceived EPPO in terms of its structure and the law applicable to investigations and prosecutions to be carried out by the EPPO. As will be seen, the EPPO will not operate in a 'single legal area' and the heavy reliance of the EPPO Regulation on the national law applicable in a specific case will make the 'playing field' not as 'level' as it could be. This is one of the reasons why case allocation within the EPPO and choice of forum by the EPPO will not be a merely 'technical matter' of allocation of resources, but will have an impact on the applicable national law and thus—potentially—on the rights and interests of the suspects.

II. BACKGROUND—SOME BASIC ELEMENTS OF THE EPPO REGULATION

A. Structure of the EPPO

The European Public Prosecutor's Office will be established as a 'body' of the European Union with own legal personality (Article 3). The EPPO will be independent and the Member States and the Union institutions, bodies, offices, and agencies are expected to respect the independence of the Office and not to seek influence over the exercise of its tasks (Article 6). In terms of internal structure, the EPPO is supposed to consist of a Central Office, which will include the European Chief Prosecutor and two Deputies (Article 11), as well as one so-called 'European Prosecutor' for each of the participating Member States (Article 12), who will form the 'College' of the EPPO (Article 9) and carry out certain functions within the 'Permanent Chambers' of the EPPO (Article 10). In addition, the EPPO will also have a 'decentralised level' (Article 8(2)), consisting of so-called 'European Delegated Prosecutors' ('EDPs') in the Member States.

4 The EPPO Regulation uses the term 'Member State(s)' to refer to those Member States which participate in the enhanced cooperation on the establishment of the EPPO and 'Member States of the European Union' when referring to all Member States (cf. art 2(1) of the EPPO Regulation). For the purpose of clarity, this contribution uses instead the phrase 'participating Member State(s)' when referring to the Member States that participate in the enhanced cooperation. The term 'non-participating Member States' is used here for those EU Member States that will not participate in the adoption of the EPPO Regulation.

While the European Chief Prosecutor and the European Prosecutors will be engaged as 'temporary agents' in accordance with the Staff Regulations of the European Union (Article 96(1)), the EDPs will not be temporary agents of the Union. Instead, they will remain to be active members of the public prosecution service or the judiciary of their Member State (Article 17(2)), wearing a 'double hat' as EDP under the EPPO Regulation.

Even though there will be one European Prosecutor from each Member State, they are certainly not supposed to be acting as 'representative' of their Member State of origin in the College. However, bringing in the necessary knowledge of the national language(s) and legal expertise from the Member State of origin, their role will be to supervise the investigations carried out by and on behalf of the EPPO in 'their' Member State and act as liaison between the Permanent Chambers and 'their' European Delegated Prosecutors.

While the European Prosecutors will primarily have a supervisory role at the central level, the responsibility for the EPPO investigations will rest with the EDPs, who, save for certain exceptional circumstances (Article 28(4)), will be responsible for all investigations and prosecutions which they have initiated, which have been allocated to them or which they have taken over from national authorities, using the EPPO's right of evocation (Article 13(1)). The European Delegated Prosecutors may, 'in accordance with this Regulation and with national law', either undertake the investigation measures and other measures themselves or instruct the competent authorities in their Member State to do so. These authorities shall, 'in accordance with national law', ensure that all instructions are followed and undertake the measures assigned to them (Article 28(1)).

B. Legal regime applicable to EPPO investigations and prosecutions

The EPPO Regulation contains some procedural law provisions on the competence of the EPPO, the opening of an investigation, on case allocation within the EPPO, on investigative measures and procedural rights, as well as on decisions to prosecute or to dismiss a case, and on judicial review of procedural acts of the EPPO. However, these provisions do not build a fully-fledged, stand-alone 'EPPO code of criminal procedure'.

1. Subsidiary application of the national law of the Member State where the investigation is conducted

The general provision in Article 5(3) shows that the EPPO Regulation is not expected to provide final answers to all questions of criminal procedure law when it states that 'national law shall apply to the extent that a matter is not regulated by this Regulation'. Moreover, many procedural law provisions of the EPPO Regulation specifically refer to applicable national law in view of conditions or procedures for their application.

The original Commission proposal, in principle, had already used the same approach of referring to applicable national law in a number of provisions. However, it did not really clarify, in situations where more than one Member State is involved in a case, which Member State's law applies in addition to or in the absence of relevant provisions of the Regulation. According to Article 11(3) of the original Commission proposal, this was supposed to be 'the law of the Member State where the investigation or prosecution is conducted'. But what if investigative measures in the course of a particular investigation are carried out in several Member States? Which of the Member State's laws applies in such a case to matters not regulated by the Regulation? Furthermore: according to the original Commission proposal it was possible for the European Chief Prosecutor to conduct the investigations himself/herself and in 'cross-border cases' to 'associate several European Delegated Prosecutors with the investigation'. Which Member State would in such a case be considered to be 'the Member State where the investigation . . . is conducted'—thus determining the Member State whose law becomes applicable?

In the course of negotiations in the Council, the provision of Article 5(3) now clarifies that—in principle—this is the law of the Member State whose European Delegated Prosecutor is handling the case in accordance with Article 13(1). Apart from this general rule, the Regulation now contains numerous specific provisions clarifying which Member State's national law applies to the issue at hand.[5]

2. Application of national law on investigative measures

This is true inter alia for the provisions on investigative measures. Contrary to some expectations, the EPPO Regulation does not contain a set of own rules on investigative measures available to the EPPO such as for example those of the 'European Model Rules for the Procedure of the future European Public Prosecutor's Office'.[6] Instead, the Regulation largely refers to the applicable national law—as did the original Commission proposal. Thus, EDPs shall 'be entitled to request or to order any measures in their Member State which are available to prosecutors under national law in similar national cases' (Article 30(4)). The EPPO Regulation itself formulates two overall conditions for taking any investigative measures: that 'there are reasonable grounds to believe that the specific measure in question might provide information or evidence useful to the investigation', and that 'there is no less intrusive measure available which could achieve the same objective'. Furthermore, it states that 'the procedures and the modalities for taking the measures shall be governed by the applicable national law' (Article 30(5)).

5 Cf. e.g. arts 26(1), 28(1), (2), and (4), 30, 31, 32, 33, 38, 39(1), 40, 41(2) and (3), 42(1), 43, 45(2), 46, 47(3), 49(6), 80(1), and 104(5), (6), and (7).

6 Available at http://www.eppo-project.eu/index.php/EU-model-rules/english (last accessed 12 April 2018).

In addition, the EPPO Regulation does, however, contain a 'minimum catalogue' of measures, which the Member States must make available (also) to the EDPs when investigating a case on behalf of the EPPO (Article 30(1)). The list includes: search and seizure, obtaining the production of relevant objects and of computer data, including banking account data and (communications) traffic data, freezing of instrumentalities, and proceeds of crime, as well as the interception of telecommunications. The only additional overall condition provided for in Article 30(1) is that the offence is punishable by 'a maximum sanction of at least four years of imprisonment'.

After some intense negotiations, Article 30(2) and (3) were added, which allow the Member States to subject the measures listed in Article 30(1) to additional conditions under national law where 'national law contains specific restrictions that apply with regard to certain categories of persons or professionals legally bound by an obligation of confidentiality' (Article 30(2)). In respect of particularly intrusive measures listed in points (c), (e), and (f) of Article 30(1), the newly inserted paragraph 3 now allows Member States to make the 'availability' of these measures 'subject to further conditions, including limitations, provided for in the applicable national law'. In respect of the interception of electronic communications and technical measures to 'track and trace' (points (e) and (f) of paragraph 1), Member States may limit the ordering of these measures to 'specific serious offences'. Paragraph 3 thus allows Member States to continue to apply certain conditions and limitations under national law, which are considered to be necessary, for example in order to take due account of the principle of proportionality already on the level of the legislator, rather than foreseeing this to be merely a principle to be observed by the EDP or the judge when ordering an investigative measure in a particular case.

While these references to national law in Article 30 are, indeed, inevitable as long as the EU legislator refrains from establishing own rules for the EPPO on the conditions and limitations for investigative measures, the Regulation will thus lead to differences in the measures available, as well as procedural rights in respect of these measures, depending on the Member State in question, where the investigation measure is carried out.

3. Application of national law in cross-border investigations

This was one of the reasons, why in particular the provisions of Article 31 on cross-border investigations led to strong controversies in the negotiations in the Council Working Groups. The result—in my view—is still one of the weaker points of the Regulation.

The EPPO is considered to be a 'single office' (Article 8(1)). However, the EPPO Regulation does not overcome the territoriality of application of national law and of judicial (court) decisions. If—in the absence of an own 'EPPO Code of Criminal

Procedure'—the Regulation refers to national law in respect of the substantive conditions for ordering of investigative measures, the Regulation also has to determine, which law shall apply in case of a cross-border investigation. The same is true for any requirements and procedures for judicial (i.e. court) decisions on coercive measures (such as telephone interceptions) as well as for the modalities for the enforcement of measures ordered by an EDP or a court. Instead of using the legal concepts of mutual recognition as enshrined in the EIO Directive,[7] the majority of Member States favoured a different approach. The outcome now is a complicated set of rules that differentiate depending on whether a judicial (court) authorisation is required under the law of the Member State where the investigation as such takes place (law of the 'handling EDP' Member State) and/or under the law of the Member State where the specific investigative measure is to be carried out ('assisting EDP' Member State).

In terms of applicable national law, in any event, the decision to adopt an investigative measure as well as its justification shall be done in accordance with the law of the handling EDP's Member State (Article 31(2)). However, the national law of the Member State, where the measure was supposed to be carried out, may give reason to refrain from doing so (Article 31(5), (6), and (7)).

In addition to the 'adoption' of the measure by the handling EDP, a judicial authorisation or court order may have to be obtained, depending on the situation, either in the assisting EDP's Member State (Article 31(3), first sub-paragraph) or in the handling EDP's Member State (Article 31(3), third sub-paragraph)—in both cases the applicable law will be the law of the Member State whose courts are in charge of giving such judicial authorisation/order. Thus, here again, applicable procedural law on the adoption of an investigative measures by an EDP depends on the Member State, where the handling EDP is located. Additionally, however, where that measure requires a judicial authorisation (or court order) under the law of the Member State where a particular investigative measure will be carried out, that Member State's law will apply as well.

4. Substantive national law

Not only will the procedural law applicable to an investigation or a specific investigative measure thus differ depending on which EDP is handling the case and/or where a specific investigative measure is to be carried out, but national law will also apply in terms of the relevant substantive criminal law applicable in case of EPPO investigations and prosecutions.

7 Directive 2014/41/EU of the European Parliament and of the Council regarding the European Investigation Order in criminal matters [2014] OJ L130/1; cf. in this context also the considerations by the EP in the resolution of 5 October 2016 on the EPPO and Eurojust, P8_TA(2016)0376.

According to Article 22(1) of the EPPO Regulation, the EPPO 'shall be competent in respect of the criminal offences affecting the financial interests of the Union that are provided for in Directive (EU) 2017/1371, as implemented by national law'. Thus, while reference is made here to the 'Directive on the fight against fraud to the Union's financial interests by means of criminal law' (so-called 'PIF Directive'),[8] the applicable substantive criminal law will depend on the implementation of that Directive in the Member State where the investigation/prosecution is taking place.

When the EPPO has to decide on the opening of an investigation, it will have to determine, whether 'in accordance with the applicable national law, there are reasonable grounds to believe that an offence within the competence of the European Public Prosecutor's Office is being or has been committed' (Article 26(1)). The 'applicable national law' in this case will be the law of the Member State, whose EDP takes that decision, or to whom a Permanent Chamber allocates the case (Article 26(3)). Similarly, the decision whether to prosecute (Article 36) or to dismiss (Article 39) a case will need to be made in light of the applicable substantive criminal law of the Member State, whose EDP is handling the case. While the PIF Directive will provide for a certain degree of harmonisation of substantive criminal law in the Member States, differences between the relevant national laws will remain. That does not only apply to the definition of the offences but also to the applicable sanctions and prescription periods.

5. Competences of the EPPO

As stated above, Article 22(1) of the EPPO Regulation provides that the EPPO competence will be determined by the PIF Directive 'as implemented by national law'. In principle, this does seem appropriate because the investigation and prosecution of a particular case in a particular Member State needs to take into account the specific criminal law provisions of that Member State. However, this intertwining of PIF Directive and domestic criminal law may cause difficulties in practice when it comes to determining whether the EPPO has competence for a particular case or not. First of all, it will be necessary to know whether a particular offence under national law is considered to be an implementation of the PIF Directive. Second, uncertainties may arise where a domestic provision that is considered to implement the Directive actually—in terms of criminalising certain conduct—goes beyond the specific obligations stemming from the corresponding provision of the PIF Directive.

It may therefore be that a certain conduct considered within the jurisdiction of one Member State as an offence within the competence of the EPPO would not be considered as such if it had been committed within the jurisdiction of another Member State. This

8 OJ L198, 28 July 2017, 29.

may also be true in situations where a national of one Member State commits a certain offence within the territory of another Member State. Thus, the question of whether the EPPO can exercise a competence could, for example, depend on whether the EPPO considers to initiate an investigation in the Member State of territoriality or in the Member State, whose national has committed the offence. Such differences may in particular arise where the EPPO intends to exercise a competence also in respect of 'inextricably linked offences' in accordance with Article 22(2) and (3) and Article 25(3) and (4), for which the EPPO may have a competence in one Member State but not in the other.

Finally, also the rules on the application of the personality principle by the EPPO build on an intertwining of EPPO Regulation and applicable national law: Whereas the EPPO would always be competent for offences committed within the territory of a Member State that is participating in the establishment of the EPPO, the exercising of a competence in respect of extraterritorial offences committed by (own) nationals or by EU officials depends on whether the particular Member State in accordance with its domestic law has jurisdiction for such offences (cf. Article 23: 'personal competence').

III. CONFLICTS OF JURISDICTION AND CASE ALLOCATION WITHIN THE EPPO AND THE EPPO TERRITORY

A. Choice of jurisdiction in a 'single office'

Article 25(1) of the original Commission proposal for the EPPO Regulation stated: 'For the purpose of investigations and prosecutions conducted by the European Public Prosecutor's Office, the territory of the Union's Member States shall be considered a single legal area in which the European Public Prosecutor's Office may exercise its competence'. The idea of a 'single legal area' has also been used in the course of the negotiations as a political principle which several delegations wanted to see preserved by the draft Regulation. However, even the original Commission proposal actually did not quite live up to that principle. While it is true that references to 'applicable national law' have been added to a number of provisions in the course of negotiations, already the original proposal did not do without such references. Apart from the fact that the original proposal certainly was not an all-encompassing 'EPPO code of criminal procedure' but had to rely on a subsidiary application of national law,[9] in particular the provisions on competence, investigative measures, and procedural rights made reference to the applicable national law.[10] And for the purpose of judicial review, the EPPO was supposed to be 'considered as a national authority',[11] thus making the possibility to request judicial review of procedural acts

9 Cf. specifically art 11(3) of the original Commission proposal (n 2).

10 Articles 12, 26, and 32 to 35 of the original Commission proposal.

11 Article 36 of the original Commission proposal.

of the EPPO fully dependent on whatever procedures, conditions, and modalities the different national laws may provide for this.

In the course of negotiations in the COPEN Working Group, the idea of a 'single legal area' was eventually replaced by the notion of the EPPO being a 'single office'.[12] In spite of the decentralised nature of the network of EDPs, each operating only within the territory of its own Member State, this does, indeed, more properly describe the concept. The EPPO thus will be a 'single office', operating on the basis of the EPPO Regulation, however, in an environment consisting of a patchwork of national laws which will need to be taken into account by the EPPO in its operative work.

Thus, the applicable legal framework will differ depending on which Member State will be the one where the EDP handling the case is located and, in respect of specific investigative measures, (also) where the measure is supposed to be carried out. In situations where two or more Member States may have jurisdiction for a particular case, such as an offence committed over the territory of two or more Member States or an offence committed by a national citizen of one Member State on the territory of another, a decision will have to be made as to which EDP should be competent to investigate and eventually prosecute the case.

In terms of such a horizontal division of competence—between the EDPs of different Member States—the original Commission proposal seems to have considered this as a largely technical matter where cases could be allocated to EDPs irrespective of territory and/or jurisdiction of the respective Member State. Only at the end of the investigation phase, the EPPO was to determine the Member State where it wants to see the case to be heard by a court. In this respect, the Commission proposal had foreseen a rather flexible list of criteria which the EPPO would take into account in making the decision on the choice of forum.[13]

This approach would have neglected the fact that the opening of a case by an EDP of a certain Member State may already have had an impact on the rights and interests of the suspect (cf. sections II.B.2, 3, and 4 above). To the extent that national law on criminal procedure applies whenever the EPPO Regulation does not regulate a certain aspect of the investigations, the decision on which Member State's EDP opens and carries out the investigations will have an effect on the question of the applicable national law. The same applies for the applicable substantive criminal law (even when harmonised to an extent by the PIF Directive). Also, it may make a great deal of difference for the suspect whether the investigations are carried out in the Member State where he/she lives or whether the EPPO—for whatever reason—chooses a different Member State for this purpose and requires the person to be

12 Cf. art 8(1): 'an indivisible Union body operating as one single office'.

13 Article 27(4) of the original Commission proposal.

surrendered to that Member State. The issue is not whether to grant the suspect the right to choose the Member State where investigations take place, but the decision must not be arbitrary and should take due account of his/her rights and interests. Furthermore, situations should, whenever possible, be avoided where an investigation of a case is started and carried on by an EDP of one Member State and then the EPPO only in the final stages takes the decision on the choice of forum for the prosecution in the courts of a particular Member State. Such late decisions would not only negatively impact the efficiency of the investigation and prosecution but could also seriously impact the position of the defence.

B. Decision-making process and criteria foreseen in the EPPO Regulation

It thus was an important achievement that the Council has agreed to make major changes to the original approach: the Regulation now foresees an early decision on which EDP should be handling the case, based on a specific list of criteria. First of all, the Regulation now clarifies, that an investigation can only be opened by an EDP from a Member State that has, in accordance with its domestic law, jurisdiction over the offence (Article 26(1)). Also where a Permanent Chamber instructs an EDP to open an investigation, it can do so only if the respective has jurisdiction for the case in question (Article 26(3)).

Therefore, the question of 'choice of jurisdiction' in respect of which EDP should be handling the case, can only arise where two or more Member States have jurisdiction, such as for example where a national of one Member State commits a PIF crime on the territory of another Member State. Here, Article 26(4) now clearly states that 'as a rule', investigations shall be initiated and handled by a European Delegated Prosecutor from the Member State 'where the focus of the criminal activity' is. The principle of territoriality here applies to the location of the criminal activity and not the place where the damage occurs. The Regulation allows for certain deviations from that rule, but only on duly justified grounds, 'taking into account the following criteria, in order of priority': the place where the suspect or accused person has his/her habitual residence, the nationality of the suspect or accused person, and the place where the main financial damage has occurred. The reason why it had been proposed to include the latter criterion as the last in the list, was to ensure that only where none of the other criteria apply—such as for example where a non-EU-citizen commits a PIF crime in a country outside the EU, the EDP of the Member State 'where the main financial damage occurred' could investigate and prosecute the case provided that this Member State has jurisdiction for such extra-territorial offences.

These rules apply in all situations where an investigation in respect of a particular case is first opened by the EPPO in accordance with Article 26. The Regulation, however, also addresses the situation where a Member State's judicial or law enforcement authority had already opened an investigation in respect of the same set of facts and the EPPO is informed thereof (Article 24(2)) with a view to a possible use of its right of evocation (Article 27(2) and (3)). If the EPPO decides to exercise this right, the national authorities will be required to transfer the file and refrain from carrying out further acts of investigation in respect of the same offence (Article 27(5)). In these cases, the internal competence to exercise the right of evocation is limited to the EDP(s) of the Member State (or possibly those Member States), whose competent authorities have initiated that investigation in this case (Article 27(6)). At least in situations where the authorities of only one Member State had already opened an investigation, this provision thus ensures that the decision to exercise the right of evocation does not automatically also lead to a cross-border reallocation of the case.

After an investigation has been initiated or taken over by way of evocation, a subsequent reallocation of the case is possible, but only 'in the general interest of justice' and in accordance with the criteria mentioned above (Article 26(5)). Furthermore, the Regulation now no longer offers the EPPO to simply 'choose' the Member State where the case shall be prosecuted[14] once the investigation is deemed to be completed. As a principle, the Regulation now foresees that the EDP, who has been handling the case, will bring the case to court in his/her own Member State. The Permanent Chamber may decide to bring the case to court in a different Member State, if it considers that there are 'sufficiently justified grounds to do so, taking into account the criteria set out in Article 26 paragraphs 4 and 5' (Article 36(3)). If the Chamber decides to do so, the case will be reallocated to an EDP of that Member State for purposes of prosecution and will thus no longer be handled by the EDP who had been leading the investigations. Depending on circumstances, the Chamber may also decide to join several cases, where investigations have been conducted by different EDPs against the same person(s) with a view to prosecution of these cases at the court of one Member State, provided that this Member State, in accordance with its law, has jurisdiction for each of these cases (Article 36(4)).[15]

C. Judicial review of EPPO decisions on case allocation and forum choices

The original Commission proposal had been based on the idea that in general judicial review against decisions of the EPPO should be sought at the proper courts of the Member States rather than the Court of Justice of the European Union (CJEU).

14 Article 27(4) of the original Commission proposal in this respect contained only a rather 'flexible' list of criteria to be taken into account.

15 A similar possibility to merge or split cases during the investigation phase is foreseen in art 26(5). Here again, such decisions may be taken 'when in the general interests of justice' and taking into account of the criteria set out in art 26(4).

To this end, the proposal worked with a 'legal fiction' according to which the EPPO 'shall be considered as a national authority for the purpose of judicial review'.[16]

After much discussion, the text of Article 42 now has been subjected to a complete overhaul. However, the underlying principle still is that the national courts should be competent for judicial review of procedurals acts of the EPPO 'which are intended to produce legal effects vis-à-vis third parties' (Article 42(1)). The latter phrase has been worded along the lines of Article 263(1) TFEU. The intention was to give the national courts not only a competence, but to clarify that the procedural acts of the EPPO, which could otherwise be challenged before the CJEU in accordance with Article 263(1) TFEU, 'shall' be subject to review by national courts. While Article 42(1) also states that such review shall be possible 'in accordance with the requirements and procedures laid down by national law', recital 88 of the EPPO Regulation clearly points in this respect to Article 19(1) of the Treaty on European Union (TEU), as well as the jurisprudence of the Court of Justice on the principles of equivalence and effectiveness.[17]

The Regulation foresees only one exception to the principle set out in Article 42(1): according to Article 42(3), the national courts will not be competent for judicial review in respect of decisions of the EPPO to dismiss a case (i.e. decisions under Article 39), in so far as they are contested directly on the basis of Union law; such decisions shall be subject to review only before the CJEU in accordance with Article 263 TFEU.

While the majority of Member States clearly favoured—in principle—this approach over the possible alternative to have the CJEU review all procedural acts of the EPPO in proceedings in accordance with Article 263 TFEU, there was quite a bit of discussion, whether this could also apply in respect of the judicial review of EPPO decisions on the internal allocation of cases and the final decision on the Member State where the EPPO intends to prosecute the case. Three different stages in the course of an investigation were discussed: the initiation of an investigation (Article 26 (1) and (4)), a possible reallocation of a case to an EDP of another Member State in the course of the investigations, including where that takes place in conjunction with a decision to merge or split cases (Article 26(5)) and the decision on the choice of forum for prosecution (Article 36(3) and (4)).

As described above, an investigation may be initiated by an EDP of a Member State that, in accordance with its law, has jurisdiction for the case. Where there are

16 Article 36 of the original COM proposals (cf. n 2).

17 Recital (88)(1): '[N]ational procedural rules governing actions for the protection of individual rights granted by Union law must be no less favorable than those governing similar domestic actions (principle of equivalence) and must not render practically impossible or excessively difficult the exercise of rights conferred by Union law (principle of effectiveness)'. On these notions, cf. Case C-583/11 *Inuit* ECLI: EU:C:2013:625, para 102.

two or more Member States that have jurisdiction, the EPPO Regulation foresees certain criteria to be taken into account in the decision, in which of these Member States the investigation should be opened by an EDP. In such a situation the decision of a particular EDP to open an investigation will thus at the same time be a decision on the internal case allocation. And, unless the competent Permanent Chamber subsequently decides to reallocate the case to a different EDP, this decision will already determine the choice of forum for a possible prosecution (Article 36(3)). Nevertheless, a majority of Member States did not consider this initial decision to be a 'procedural act' that should—as such—be subject to judicial review before the CJEU. It has been argued during the negotiations in the COPEN Working Group, that this decision on internal case allocation would—in light of the jurisprudence of the CJEU—be considered to have a merely preparatory character and not to be a 'measure the legal effects of which are binding on, and capable of affecting the interests of, the applicant by bringing about a distinct change in his legal position'.[18] Also, it was argued, that it would, in many cases, not even be possible or appropriate to immediately inform the suspect of the decision to open an investigation and thus on the internal allocation of the case.

It could be considered that the situation is different where the Permanent Chamber decides in the course of the investigations on a reallocation of the case to an EDP of another Member State (Article 26(4) or (5)) or, perhaps, where the Chamber fails to do so, even though the criteria set out in these provisions would call for such a reallocation. And it had, indeed, been proposed in the course of negotiations to amend Article 42(3) and specifically foresee a competence for the CJEU to ensure judicial review against such decisions taken by the Permanent Chamber in accordance with Article 263 TFEU. However, the majority of delegations did not consider this to be appropriate either. In particular, it was argued that the situation here would not be much different than in the first scenario and that a competence of the CJEU to review such decisions in proceedings in accordance with Article 263 TFEU would unnecessarily prolong the investigations.

Finally, when it comes to the decision of the Permanent Chamber on the forum for prosecution (Article 36(3)), there was a general understanding amongst delegations that judicial review should be possible; the competence, however, should be left to the national courts. First of all, an EPPO decision to bring the case to court in a particular Member State does, of course, not prevent the national court from determining whether or not it actually has jurisdiction in accordance with the domestic law of that Member State. A different question is whether the court will be in a position to consider whether the EPPO also has taken due account of the

18 Case 60/81 *IBM v Commission* ECLI: EU:C:1981:264, para 9; along the same lines: Case T-193/04 *Tillack v Commission* ECLI:EU:T:2006:292, para 67.

above-mentioned criteria of the EPPO Regulation (Article 26(4)) when deciding on the choice of the Member State where the case shall be brought to court.

In the course of negotiations, it has been argued that it would not be appropriate to expect a court of a Member State to decide not only whether it has jurisdiction in accordance with domestic law but also whether amongst several possible Member States' jurisdictions the EPPO has chosen the right one.

On the other hand, considering that the Regulation now does contain a list of criteria on the choice of forum including a clear order of priority, it would appear to be possible to leave judicial review of adherence to these criteria also to the national courts. And, indeed, following further discussions under Slovak EU Presidency, this interpretation has made its way into the recitals of the Regulation, which now clearly state that 'procedural acts that relate to the choice of the Member State whose courts will be competent to hear the prosecution, which is to be determined on the basis of the criteria laid down in this Regulation, are intended to produce legal effects vis-à-vis third parties and should therefore be subject to judicial review before national courts at the latest at the trial stage'.[19] This wording clarifies that Member States will need to ensure that—at least—their trial courts will be positioned to exercise judicial review on the EPPO's decision on the choice of forum. It also leaves room for the application of any national procedural law that may allow for such review by national courts even prior to the trial phase.

Existing mechanisms for requesting a preliminary ruling by the CJEU then will allow—or even oblige—national courts to request from the CJEU a ruling on the interpretation of the respective provision of the EPPO Regulation (cf. Article 42(2)(b)) in order to ensure that these criteria are applied in the same way throughout the EPPO territory.

IV. CONFLICTS OF COMPETENCE BETWEEN THE EPPO AND NATIONAL AUTHORITIES

The character of the EPPO as a 'single office' thus leads to specific rules on internal case allocation and on decisions of the EPPO on the choice of forum for prosecution. Issues of 'conflicts of competence' will further arise in terms of delineation of competence between the EPPO and national authorities of the Member States participating in the establishment of the EPPO. And in this respect the situation will be quite different in relation to national authorities of Member States, not participating in the EPPO.

19 Cf. recital (87)(2).

A. Possible conflicts in case of participating Member States

In principle, the competence to investigate and prosecute PIF offences will be shared between the EPPO and the national authorities. An exception will apply for minor offences as described in Article 25(2), that is, where a criminal offence falling within the scope of Article 22 caused or is likely to cause damage to the Union's financial interests of less than €10,000, the EPPO shall in principle refrain from exercising its competence and thus leave the case to the national authorities. However, there are certain exceptions to this exception, set out in sub-paragraphs (a) and (b) of Article 25(2). Also, in case of offences that caused damage not only to the Union's financial interests but also to another victim (e.g. a Member State in case of tobacco smuggling which involves evasion not only of customs duties but also of national tobacco tax and VAT), the Regulation excludes an EPPO competence where the damage caused to the Union does not exceed the damage caused to the other victim (Article 25(3)(b)). Again, there are certain exceptions to the exception: irrespective of the relative level of damage, the EPPO will have a competence in case of offences referred to in Article 3(2)(a), (b), and (d) of the PIF Directive. And even where these criteria are not met, the EPPO may, with the consent of the competent national authorities, exercise a competence 'if it appears that the EPPO is better placed to investigate or prosecute' (Article 25(4)).

Further complex rules on the delineation of competences between the EPPO and the national authorities of the participating Member States apply where a PIF offence as defined in Article 22(1) is 'inextricably linked' to another type of offence under national law (Article 22(3)). Here, the EPPO may only exercise its competence for the PIF offence and the inextricably linked other offence where the PIF offence is considered to be preponderant in terms of the seriousness of the offence or the mere ancillary ('instrumental') nature of the linked non-PIF offence (Article 25(3)(a) or if the PIF offence has been committed in the framework of a criminal organisation provided that the focus of the criminal activity of such a criminal organisation is to commit PIF offences (Article 22(2)).

These provisions of the EPPO Regulation on the delineation of competences will normally not have an impact on the cross-border choice of forum for prosecution. They are intended to determine only whether the case will be investigated and prosecuted by the EPPO or the competent national investigation and prosecution authorities. However, in a cross-border situation, the question of whether a case investigated by the EPPO or by a national authority may also have an impact on the question, in which Member State the investigation/prosecution takes place. Thus, there could for example be a conflict of jurisdiction between the EDP of the Member State of territoriality and the national prosecutor of another Member State investigating the case based on the active personality principle, perhaps because the person is suspected of having committed several similar fraud offences in different Member States.

While the competences shared between the EPPO and the national authorities may raise issues of 'conflicts of competence', the EPPO's competence will become an exclusive one, preventing national prosecution authorities from exercising an own competence (cf. Article 25(1)) as soon as the EPPO has decided to open its own investigation (Article 26) or has decided to take over an investigation which had already been opened by a national authority (the so-called 'right of evocation'—Article 27). The mechanism for 'conflict resolution' thus in principle is a vertical one: it will be the EPPO itself which decides—by exercising its competence—that the national investigation/prosecution authorities must refrain from exercising their own ('shared') competences.

However, this vertical mechanism, giving the EPPO a 'priority competence' for PIF offences,[20] will only apply in cases where there is no dispute between the EPPO and the national prosecution service over the question of whether the conduct under investigation falls within the scope of Article 22(2) or (3) and/or Article 25(2) or (3). In such a case, 'the national authorities competent to decide on the attribution of competences concerning prosecution at national level' shall decide who is to be competent for the investigation of the case (Article 25(6)). Thus, where there is disagreement for example on the question of whether the conduct in question constitutes two or more 'inextricably linked offences' (Article 22(3)), and, if so, whether the PIF offence is 'preponderant' (Article 25(3)(a)), the EPPO cannot simply exercise its right of evocation in order to draw a case into its own hands. The same applies where there is dispute between the EPPO and the national prosecution service over the question of whether the offence is of a minor nature (Article 25(2)) or whether the damage on the part of the Union exceeds the damage caused to other victims (Article 25(3)(b)).

In these situations, the idea, however, is not that the national prosecutor, who is in disagreement with the EPPO, takes a final decision. Instead, the decision is to be made by 'the national authorities competent to decide on the attribution of competences concerning prosecution at national level'. Recital (62) further clarifies that the term 'national authorities' is to be understood as referring to 'judicial authorities' competent for taking such decisions under national law. And Article 42(2)(c) further clarifies the role of the CJEU to give any preliminary rulings on the interpretation of Articles 22 and 25 'in relation to any conflict of competence between the European Public Prosecutor's Office and the competent national authorities'. The decisions making competence given to national authorities in Article 25(6) has been considered by a number of delegations in the negotiation phase as an important element in order to 'counterbalance' the priority competence of the EPPO in accordance with Article 25(1).

20 Cf. recital (58).

Where the competent national authority has decided in accordance with Article 25(6), that the conditions for exercising an EPPO competence are not met, the EPPO would consequently not be in a position to initiate an investigation or to exercise its right of evocation. Where the EPPO had already opened an investigation before such decision in accordance with Article 25(6) is taken, the EPPO would be obliged to transfer the file to the competent national authority and close the case (Article 34(7)).

B. Possible conflicts of jurisdiction in relationship between the EPPO and non-participating Member States

The EPPO Regulation does not contain any provisions on conflicts of jurisdiction or choice of forum in relationship with Member States that are not participating in establishing the EPPO. As the EPPO Regulation will not be binding on those Member States (Article 20(4) TEU), the EPPO Regulation could not singlehandedly establish any conflict resolution mechanism in this respect.

Such conflicts of jurisdiction will, however, arise. As the EPPO will have a competence for extraterritorial offences committed by nationals of the participating Member States or by EU officials and staff members (Article 23, points (b) and (c)), provided that a participating Member State, in accordance with its law, has jurisdiction for such extraterritorial offences,[21] this will also apply where offences have been committed on the territory of a non-participating Member State. Equally so, conflicts of jurisdiction may arise where a national of a non-participating Member State has committed an offence on 'EPPO territory'. Similarly, conflicts may arise in case of multi-territorial offences where the constituting acts have been partially committed within the territory of a non-participating Member States and partially within the territory of a participating Member State.

Given the fact that the EPPO Regulation does not and could not attempt to provide a proper solution in this respect, it should be considered to establish proper criteria and mechanisms for such conflicts of jurisdiction in a separate legal instrument that would be binding upon the EPPO as well as the non-participating Member States. Such rules could be part of the same separate legal instrument that will in any case be needed in order to properly provide for mechanisms of judicial cooperation between the EPPO and the non-participating Member States.[22] In the absence of such a legal instrument, existing horizontal mechanisms for providing information on any parallel investigations[23] or seeking a non-binding opinion from Eurojust,[24] may,

21 Cf. section II.B.5 above.

22 Cf. recital (110).

23 Framework Decision 2009/948/JHA [2009] OJ L328/42.

24 Cf. art 7(2) of the Eurojust decision (Council Decision 2002/187/JHA as further amended).

perhaps, be utilised—in spite of the fact that these instruments don't specifically apply to the EPPO.

V. CONCLUSION

The EPPO Regulation will be the first EU criminal law instrument that does provide for certain criteria for decisions on case allocation and choice of forum as well as relevant mechanism for decision-making. But are there any 'lessons to be learned' for the ELI Project on Prevention and Resolution of Conflicts of Jurisdiction in Criminal Matters?

Well, to a limited extent, yes. The consideration that went into the formulation of criteria for the (internal) allocation of cases between EDPs of different Member States (Article 26(4)), could be utilised for the present project when it comes to developing a possible list of criteria to decide on 'the best-placed jurisdiction' in a cross-border situation. In principle that could be true for either of the three models presented in this publication. The same applies to the approach of the EPPO Regulation, which does not attempt to change in any way the jurisdictional rules of the Member States that also apply where an EDP intends to open an EPPO investigation. A similar approach is used not only in the 'horizontal' and 'vertical' models presented here but also in the third model. The mechanism of case allocation in the EPPO Regulation merely sets out to determine in case of a cross-border 'conflict of jurisdiction' which EDP—and thus eventually which Member State's courts—shall be competent to exercise the jurisdiction established in accordance with national law. Thus, in spite of possibly two or more Member States' courts, in accordance with their domestic law, having jurisdiction for a particular offence, the EPPO Regulation will bring about a system of shared responsibilities—not only in terms of the internal allocation of cases between EDPs of different Member States in the 'single office' but also in terms of resolving—to a certain extent—existing conflicts of jurisdiction between the involved Member States. The third model proposed in this publication follows a similar approach of shared responsibilities for investigation and prosecution in cases that could affect the jurisdiction of two or more Member States.

On the other hand, the decision-making processes for case reallocation between EDPs of different Member States (Article 26(5)) as well for deciding on the Member States where the case shall be brought to prosecution (Article 36(3)) are clearly designed for the EPPO operating as a 'single office' and cannot be considered as a model for solving horizontal conflicts of jurisdiction between Member States' authorities outside of the EPPO context. The same would apply to the procedures and mechanisms foreseen in the EPPO Regulation in terms of conflicts of competence that may arise in relationship between the EPPO and the national prosecution services of the Member States which would not provide for a proper solution along the lines of either the 'horizontal' or the 'vertical' models described in this publication.

INDEX

Index

The manufacturer's authorised representative in the EU for product safety is Oxford University Press España S.A. of el Parque Empresarial San Fernando de Henares, Avenida de Castilla, 2 – 28830 Madrid (www.oup.es/en or product.safety@oup.com). OUP España S.A. also acts as importer into Spain of products made by the manufacturer.

www.ingramcontent.com/pod-product-compliance
Ingram Content Group UK Ltd.
Pitfield, Milton Keynes, MK11 3LW, UK
UKHW020849150926
475595UK00003B/93

* 9 7 8 0 1 9 8 8 2 9 1 1 9 *